Jack London
AND HIS TIMES

JACK LONDON

Jack London
AND HIS TIMES

AN UNCONVENTIONAL BIOGRAPHY

By JOAN LONDON

WITH A NEW INTRODUCTION BY THE AUTHOR

UNIVERSITY OF WASHINGTON PRESS
Seattle and London

Copyright © 1939, 1968 by Joan London
Reprinted by the University of Washington Press in 1968,
with a new introduction by the author, as Volume 9
of the Americana Library series, Robert E. Burke, editor
Second printing, 1974
Washington Paperback edition, 1974
Library of Congress Catalog Card Number 39-33408
ISBN (cloth) 0-295-73861-8
ISBN (paper) 0-295-95355-1
Printed in the United States of America

"*The pity of it is that the writer-folk are writing for bread first and glory after; and that their standard of living goes up as fast as their capacity for winning bread increases,—so that they never get around to glory,—the ephemeral flourishes, and the great stories remain unwritten.*" JACK LONDON

PREFACE

To THE MACMILLAN COMPANY for permission to quote from *The Call of the Wild;* to the Librairie Hachette for permission to use a portion of the introduction written by Anatole France for a French translation of *The Iron Heel;* to the D. Appleton-Century Company, W. J. Ghent, Charmian London, Waldo Frank, Ernest Untermann, Austin Lewis, Leon Trotsky and others, my thanks for their co-operation.

After some deliberation I have reluctantly decided to omit a bibliography for this book. In order that there may be no misunderstanding on the part of anyone I hasten to explain that this is not due to ingratitude for the many valuable sources I have used, nor for the generous co-operation which has been given me, but because most of the principal sources—books, manuscripts, letters and recollections of Jack London's friends—are to be found in the text. As for the others, especially those consulted in gathering material for the historical background, none, with the exception of the private papers, personal documents and opinions of participants in the events of the times, will long elude anyone desirous of prying deeper into the subject. Why, then, lengthen the book with needless appendages?

It is my hope that this staring down of a convention will not be taken amiss. And I repeat: to all who have aided me directly and indirectly I am and shall always be profoundly grateful.

JOAN LONDON

Berkeley
May, 1939

CONTENTS

Introduction	xi
Chapter 1	1
Chapter 2	15
Chapter 3	26
Chapter 4	36
Chapter 5	54
Chapter 6	65
Chapter 7	82
Chapter 8	92
Chapter 9	106
Chapter 10	125
Chapter 11	139
Chapter 12	151
Chapter 13	165
Chapter 14	179
Chapter 15	192
Chapter 16	206
Chapter 17	222

x

Contents

Chapter 18   239

Chapter 19   251

Chapter 20   264

Chapter 21   281

Chapter 22   297

Chapter 23   316

Chapter 24   338

Chapter 25   354

Index   383

INTRODUCTION

MORE than half a century has passed since Jack London's death in November, 1916. After such a lapse of time, it would seem that his life and works should be of purely historical interest, and that readers would seek him out today for that reason alone. By 1919 his era had been labeled "prewar" to distinguish it from the new postwar times; twenty-odd years later it would sink further into the past when it became necessary to relabel it "pre-World War I."

Sweeping changes have, indeed, taken place in the United States and the world during the past fifty years, but in certain ways, fundamental to an appraisal of Jack London as man and author, there has been little change. Problems that concerned him remain of concern to those who search for the solutions he failed to find. The use of war (far more frightful than in London's day), instead of peaceful means to settle disputes between nations and peoples; poverty, malnutrition, starvation itself, and the ravages that follow in their train; limited, often totally lacking educational opportunities and inevitable illiteracy; denial of civil rights; chronic unemployment; child labor—these still prevail, not only throughout the world, but in London's own land, the most advanced, the most affluent of all the countries.

His anguished protests against these evils, his ardent hope for a future in which the brotherhood of man would be realized, kindle the hearts and minds of today's practical idealists, as they have in all the years since first he voiced them. But this is only a part of the reason why, as America's most widely translated author, he is still read and studied and admired by people all over the world.

Sharp and clear against the varied backgrounds of most of his novels and stories stands his repeated assertion that desired goals are only seemingly unreachable. And blazing throughout his writings is his joyous acceptance of the challenges of nature, society, and life itself, to the realization of man's hopes and dreams. For nearly seven decades these vigorous affirmations have evoked an eager response from his readers, overriding language and cultural barriers and the passing of the years.

Recognition of Jack London in the United States and Europe followed closely upon the start of his writing career; and the continued appeal of his stories, as well as of his colorful life, nourished a rapid growth of reader interest. Nevertheless, the far wider acceptance, affection, and serious consideration he enjoys today, notably in foreign lands, were long in the making.

For a time after his death, new editions and translations of his works showed a substantial increase. By the end of the 1920's the surge had spent itself. In America the depression began; in Europe developments moved inexorably toward World War II. Publication of London's writings and of books and articles about him diminished until, with the start of the war, they almost ceased. At no time, however, did he suffer an eclipse or fall into obscurity, as Melville had done in the United States, to be tardily rescued by critics and scholars.

Actually, until quite recently American critics, with some exceptions, have done little to enhance his reputation. From the beginning they seemed unable or unwilling to decide whether London, admittedly an internationally famous writer, was also a great writer. Thus, they have shied away from attempting to "place" him in literary history. Pigeonholing him as a "realist" or a "naturalist" or a combination of both solved nothing. Some ignored him, and still do; some dismissed him as a "hack" who wrote only for money, or scorned him as a "bestseller" (which, except for *The Call of the Wild* in 1903 and *The Sea Wolf* the following year, he never was). On the one hand, he was assailed for his Socialist beliefs, and on the other, for his racial prejudice and glorification of the Anglo-Saxon "blond beast." The uneven quality of his work, the hasty writing, his confusion and contradictions, were among faults cited to prove him unworthy of serious consideration. A good deal of such criticism was, of course, merited, but the problem remained.

Fred Lewis Pattee had warned that it was "easy to criticize him, easy to deplore him, impossible to avoid him"; and C. Hartley Grattan had prophesied in 1929 that Jack London would "remain to puzzle the historians of American literature for years to come." Ever and again the viability of this prophecy was demonstrated. In 1942 Alfred Kazin asked: "Was London the almost great writer some have felt in him?"; ten years later Edward Wagenknecht wondered what place in literature would finally be assigned to him; both admitted that it was "hard to say." Even as late as 1965 a scholar reported that London had continued to be "an enigma." After a while a few American critics openly doubted that London's fame would last: "Much of his work is fading," they said. "*The Call of the Wild* is becoming a boy's book." With regret, one commented that he seemed to be "slipping away even as a boy's hero."

By 1946, with war hostilities at an end, London's last-written works were thirty years old; earlier and better-known novels and stories were older by ten or fifteen years. Was it possible that he had anything meaningful to say to people anywhere in the postwar world? That he did is evident, for what might be described as a world-wide explosion of interest in his writings began in the late 1940's and continues to this day.

It is only since the publication of *Jack London: A Bibliography** in the autumn of 1966 that a comprehensive view of the extent of Jack London's readership in foreign countries has become available. As one turns the pages of this bibliography, noting the familiar and the unfamiliar languages in which he has been read since the early years of this century, some astonishing facts appear. Of Jack London's fifty-one titles, all but four have been translated into at least one and usually many of fifty-eight different languages, including Esperanto. In addition, nearly four hundred anthologies and collections, often in many-volumed sets, may be found in thirty-six of these languages. Publications in Russian are by far the most numerous. Outstanding among other languages are Finnish, Polish, German, Swedish, Bulgarian, French, Dutch, Italian, Danish, Hungarian, Norwegian, and Spanish. The most widely translated title is *The Call of the Wild,* followed by *White*

* Compiled by Hensley C. Woodbridge, John London, and George H. Tweney (Georgetown, Calif.: The Talisman Press, 1966).

Fang, Martin Eden, The Sea Wolf, The Iron Heel, Smoke Bellew, Before Adam, Burning Daylight, and *John Barleycorn.*

Before death ended his brief writing career, London was already well-known abroad. The compilers of the bibliography found serialization of *The Sea Wolf* in Spanish within a year of its publication in the United States in 1904; 1907 and 1908 saw translations in the Scandinavian languages, as well as in Finnish, German, French, and Russian; the first Dutch version appeared in 1910, followed in 1912 and 1913 by those in Icelandic, Latvian, Estonian, and Czechoslovakian; in 1916 he was being read in Japanese.

With his world outlook and awareness of the complexities of life in far-off countries which he would perhaps never see, London was immensely gratified by this early and spreading recognition. Knowing no language but his own, he was deeply moved by the realization that his words were being read by people with whom he could never converse directly. How amazed he would be by some of the languages into which, especially during the past ten or fifteen years, his books have found their way: Irish and Catalan; Greek, Macedonian, Turkish, Hebrew, and Persian; and, in Asia, Chinese, Japanese, Korean, Bengali, Indonesian, and Vietnamese. Even the blind now have some access to his writings: in the United States and England many titles are in Braille, and at least one Braille book has been done in Russia; several titles are listed among the "talking books." Although a few motion pictures based on his works were made during his lifetime, that list now totals more than forty. Many of these have been exhibited abroad, while a small number have been produced in Soviet Russia, Czechoslovakia, and one or two other countries.

Among the reasons suggested for Jack London's enduring appeal have been the love of out-of-doors shared by most peoples, and the widespread rapport with the social undercurrent of his writings. Both were true from the start in his immediate acceptance, for example, by the Scandinavians, the Finns, and the Russians, who took him to their hearts and made him so much their own that, like a national heritage, he has been passed on from parents to children. Not surprisingly, and for the same reasons, the number of Jack London titles that have been published and the number of his readers have greatly increased in Latin America during the past twenty years.

The urbanization of Europe has grown apace; in America, the

frontier disappeared long ago. Today, our country is locked in battle to preserve the remaining wilderness areas within its boundaries, yet the lure of the wild abides. "Jack London's world will never live again," Eugene Burdick wrote a few years ago, adding that his stature as a writer has grown because he makes that "lost and savage world" live again. And at no time has an audience responsive to the "social undercurrent" in his works been lacking in the United States or elsewhere.

In demonstrating its boundless enthusiasm for Jack London, the Soviet Union, more than any other nation, has publicized the facts and figures of his popularity, as well as the reasons for it. Because of that country's vast size and huge, largely literate population, the figures are staggering, but the reasons are no doubt essentially the same among other peoples who read and admire him.

Vil Bykov, Jack London authority at the USSR Academy of Sciences in Moscow, has estimated that some twenty-seven million copies of London's books have been sold in the Soviet Union. As early as 1911, publication of what was to be a complete edition of his works was undertaken; it ended short of its goal on the eve of the Revolution. Between 1928 and 1929 appeared a second set in twenty-four volumes, followed in 1956 by an eight-volume edition, and another in fourteen volumes in 1961. The 1956 edition was especially planned to commemorate the eightieth anniversary of his birth and the fortieth of his death; reportedly, its six hundred thousand sets were subscribed for within five hours. Over the years innumerable separate titles have been published in magazines, brochures, and books, along with scores of articles and critiques.

In listing the most popular books—the Alaskan short stories, *Martin Eden, The Call of the Wild, The Sea Wolf, White Fang,* and many of the South Sea tales—Bykov has corrected a widely held misapprehension that London's popularity in Soviet Russia has been based primarily on his Socialist beliefs. The attraction in all of London's writings, Bykov says, is their virility, their "life-asserting spirit" and "life-sustaining force." The irresistible appeal of London's unshakeable belief in man's ability to rise to incredible heights of courage and in the will to win against overwhelming odds, his compassion for the poor and hatred of everything that deforms the human spirit, his faith in man's future—these are inseparable from the sheer beauty and excitement of his novels and stories. Indicating the affection with which both man and author is regarded, and borrowing London's own words, Bykov concludes, "In the eyes of millions, he was a man!"

The renewal of interest in Jack London which followed World War II was evident throughout the world. His books reappeared in languages in which they had not been published since the 1930's or even earlier, and in more than a dozen other languages for the first time. Books and articles about him were published throughout Europe and in Latin America.

In a similar way, interest in London was reawakened in the United States and Great Britain. Although a complete set of his works in English does not yet exist, and some have been long out of print, a large number of his titles, as well as numerous anthologies, are now available. This has resulted from several factors, in addition to perennial and growing reader interest: the tremendous increase in paperbacks and their popularity among book buyers; the yearly expiration of more of his copyrights; and to a limited extent, to the new appraisal of London that has appeared in the last decade, largely the result of younger critics and scholars, and new readers.

Essentially, it is a rediscovery of Jack London that is taking place, and out of this, fresh opinions and evaluations are emerging. London's faults and weaknesses are not ignored. Instead, with a knowledgeable perspective of the era which shaped and necessarily limited him, and an awareness of the temper and problems of our own time, the new critics and scholars emphasize the qualities and themes in his writings which have appealed and will continue to appeal to peoples everywhere.

At the same time, light is being shone on a number of dark places. For example, in *Martin Eden,* one of the most misunderstood of London's novels, the author's true intent is recognized. During his lifetime, London reiterated in vain that this was not a story of success, but of the inevitable failure of individualism. The questioning of his oft-stated belief in the superiority of certain "races" suggests a basic conflict within London himself. Readers are reminded that in *The Sea Wolf,* long regarded as a celebration of the Nordic superman, Wolf Larsen does not triumph; that on viewing the disease-ridden valley once so glowingly described in Melville's *Typee,* London had said bitterly, "The Anglo-Saxon corrupts everything he touches."

His place in American literature, the question of whether he was a great or almost-great writer, are of less importance to the younger critics than his kinship with those identified with the progressive and humanitarian traditions of our country. In a larger sense, his confusions and contradictions are seen as poignant proof of his active engagement in the age-long battle between "good" and "evil."

When this biography was written nearly thirty years ago, Jack London's position at home and abroad was still secure, but the future was uncertain. Even his most devoted readers felt that his reputation would dwindle as the years passed and history enclosed his name and his works. The resurgence of his fame was not foreseen.

Now a new generation of readers has found him, a generation that is informed, seeking realistic answers to the challenging issues of the day, basically optimistic. In writings long ago completed, Jack London's passionate affirmation of life, his love for his fellows, his faith in the ultimate perfectibility, through struggle, of man and society, speak clearly today to them and to the world.

JOAN LONDON

Pleasant Hill, California
June, 1967

Jack London
AND HIS TIMES

CHAPTER

1

DURING the second half of the nineteenth century America was constantly swept by epidemics of movements which ebbed and flowed, merged and split apart, as men and women earnestly sought the most effective means to reform society. The intellectual ferment of the times, at work in a new, rapidly expanding country that was culturally isolated to a great extent from the rest of the world, expressed itself in curious ways. Any cause whose appeal was either humanitarian, pseudoscientific or religious, or which promised freedom from old beliefs and restraints, found enthusiastic followers.

In the 'forties and 'fifties impulses long suppressed by Puritanism had burst forth in revivalistic sects, free love in theory and practice and spiritualism; various utopian-socialist doctrines were put into practice in innumerable colonies; the woman's suffrage movement was launched. The Doctrine of the Second Advent flourished and waxed prosperous until the Fox sisters gave modern spiritualism to the world, and Americans turned to table-tipping, spirit raps, and the firm belief that this was a newer and better revelation.

A little later rumors of developments in science began to seep out of the few centers of learning. These were promptly exploited by hordes of self-appointed enlighteners, who sold the new knowledge, diluted, perverted and highly colored, to the common people. "Professors" of phrenology, astrology, astrophysiology and the like, flanked by itinerant apostles of the Second Advent and spiritualism, roamed the country, lecturing, publishing magazines and pamphlets, and making their living out of the eager credulity of the American public.

Meantime Marx's First International gained a foothold in the country—a small and precarious foothold, however, since it was at the mercy of all to whom a cause was an end in itself, and better if other causes were added to it. Thus Section Twelve of the International Workingmen's Association was dominated for a time by Victoria Woodhull and Tennessee Claflin, who stood for free love, astrology and spiritualism, as well as woman's suffrage, organized labor, revolution if necessary, and the rights of man however and whenever they were violated.

Not all of what Daniel De Leon was later to characterize as the "lunatic fringe" of any movement which sought to break with the past were as broad minded as Victoria and Tennessee. Spiritualists and astrologers might endorse free love and yet deny the vote to women; labor unionists who laughed at spooks, table-tipping, and the cabalistic wisdom of the stars, might support woman's suffrage as determinedly as they rejected sexual freedom; and suffragettes who made labor's cause their own might accept spiritualism but decry free love. On the other hand, there were many who, like Victoria, lacked the courage of their convictions and recanted when affirmation of their principles was inconvenient or unprofitable. With dismal frequency the popular isms of the day broke under the strain when they came into conflict with traditional beliefs and standards of behavior, and tragedy frequently resulted.

One of these occurred in San Francisco in the early summer of 1875. The principals, William Henry Chaney, an astrologer, and Flora Wellman, a spiritualist, might have lived through their long lives unnoticed except by a few of their contemporaries, and died to be forgotten by all, save that from their brief union came a child who was destined to be famous at home and abroad.

Little is known of Flora Wellman before she came to San Francisco. All her life she was a closemouthed woman, with few intimates who might recall certain things she desired to be forgotten. Of her childhood and early youth, however, she later spoke often to her grandchildren, remembering the big, elegant home in Massillon, Ohio, where she had been born, the youngest of five, on August 17, 1843; her father, Marshall Wellman, canal builder and pioneer in the Ohio country, and one of the wealthiest citizens of the town—"a just man," she used to say; her stepmother who, she constantly reiterated, was very good to her, but whom she had resented and defied; her indulgent older sisters; and, finally, all the details of a life that even a half a century later glowed warmly in the memory of an old woman who had not known a like pride and security again until it was too late to matter.

Marshall's first wife, Eleanor Garrett Jones, daughter of a Welsh circuit rider known as "Priest" Jones, had died when Flora was a baby. Father, older sisters, relatives and nursemaids promptly spoiled the motherless child. When her stepmother entered the scene, Flora was four years old, willful, stubborn, hot tempered. Stormy years followed, although they were years in which every luxury, frocks and toys from New York, tutors, piano and elocution lessons, were showered on the little girl. Flora did as she pleased, received what she demanded. Sentiment was ranged on her side; the stepmother was helpless. And when, some years later, Flora fell desperately ill with the long fever which was to stunt her growth and ruin forever her eyesight and beauty, all efforts to curb her will and soften her sharp individuality were abandoned. She ran away from home when she was sixteen, went to stay with first one, then another married sister. And from this time until she was thirty-one and earning her living by giving piano lessons in San Francisco, nothing definite is known about her.

Once she told her granddaughters about having gone to balls and parties during the Civil War, recalling pridefully that she had been a "good dancer," and that everyone had admired her tiny hands and feet. They were tiny, beyond a doubt. When she was a very old lady she wore a number twelve child's shoe, and had delicate ankles and pretty calves. Hands and feet were in perfect proportion to her height; she was a very small woman, well under five feet. Her granddaughters wondered if she minded being so small. She used to speak of her father and uncles, all of them "fine, upstanding men, over six feet tall," and sometimes she seemed to regret her size, and sometimes was proud of it. At any rate, by that time she had long since learned to accept things as they were. In her difficult life, being small in a world of tall people was comparatively innocuous; there had been many, much harder things to accept.

After the Civil War, the Far West began to glow in men's minds as an escape from unsatisfactory conditions in the more settled portions of the country. The lure of gold and silver in the mountains and tales of fertile farming land had long been drawing a steady stream of prospectors and farmers to California. But the teeming center of all activity in the West—"The City" they called it even then—was an irresistible magnet to emigrants of a different sort. Ill prepared, San Francisco had become a metropolis, her needs constantly outstripping the frantic pace of her building. Yesterday a barren waste of hills that rose from an empty bay to dunes that dropped slowly to the Pacific, today a quarter of a million people overflowed her dwellings, jammed her streets and found her public buildings and business facilities far from adequate.

Workers with bitter knowledge of unemployment in the East, and confident of steady jobs in San Francisco, had been coming by the thousands. On their heels, and in larger numbers when the completion of the transcontinental railroad rendered travel easier, were shopkeepers, professional men, financiers and promoters, soldiers of fortune of both sexes, rebels from older communities whose more rigid way of life had grown distasteful, those with messages and those with axes to grind, all converging on a city which promised easy fulfillment of their desires and ambitions.

No city in the Union at the time was more cosmopolitan, and yet few were more American. Successive waves of emigration had deposited a heterogeneous population from all over the world on the sand hills, where it scrambled for homes and jobs and quickly became part of the city's life. Out of the maelstrom of widely differing manners, customs and ideas, and far from the steadying influences of the older East, was emerging a society that was flexible yet independent, scorned hidebound beliefs and principles, and welcomed anything that was new.

The only reason Flora ever gave for coming to San Francisco was that she had accompanied a lady as a traveling companion. From what one knows of her, it is easy to see how life in stodgy Ohio towns must have palled on her. Certainly she must have bitterly resented the restrictions imposed on a young, unmarried woman of good family. The balls and parties of the Civil War years were over. Visualizing the narrow, deadly circle of her days, one can appreciate the enthusiasm with which she had embraced spiritualism.

She had been a little girl of eight when the Abby Warner case, one of the most famous in the history of spiritualism, occurred right in her own town of Massillon. The rappings of Abby's spirits had rendered the congregation of St Timothy's Episcopal Church so indignant on Christmas Eve of 1851 that suit was brought against the young woman for having "willfully and in malice prepense disturbed a Christian assembly in the solemn act of worship." Nothing could be proved against Abby, but the publicity attendant on the trial, of which the spiritualists quickly took advantage, spread the practices far and wide. Flora must have heard of spiritualism from her childhood, and although Chaney undoubtedly did his best to convert her to astrology, she remained faithful to her earlier belief.

However the opportunity came to leave Ohio, she must have snatched at it eagerly, packed her trunk, informed her family of her decision, and departed without one backward glance of regret. In San Francisco she found a city that did not look askance at young unmarried women, no matter what they did. She made a few acquaintances and friends, among them the Slocums—Mrs Amanda, who was superintendent of the Woman's Publishing Company, a thriving book and job-printing establishment on Montgomery Street, and Charles and William, who were journalists, and Miss Eva, who was learning to be a compositor, and all of whom lived in a large, comfortable house at Third and Bryant streets. And without much trouble she found a sufficient number of piano pupils to meet her modest living expenses.

The characteristics of the San Francisco that was to be destroyed in 1906 were already present. Gone were the ramshackle, hastily built structures of the gold-rush era, their places taken by buildings whose jumbled architectural styles became typical of the city where each one built to suit himself and strove to duplicate what he had liked best elsewhere. The bay-window craze had been given full rein. Gingerbread scrollwork, ostentatious trimmings, ornate cornices (which fell off during earthquakes), mansard roofs, and iron-grilled, stained-glassed front doors were on hotels, houses and public buildings.

Horsecars ran along Market Street, which marched, as now, straight from the bay toward Twin Peaks. It had been paved with blocks of basalt laid directly on the sand and was never either level or clean. Handbills of every description littered the crowded sidewalks, and each season brought forth its crop of banners, advertisements and political signs which fluttered from lines stretched across the street from building to building. It was a great

city for parades and spectacles of all sorts. Bands headed funeral
corteges, torchlight processions always drew crowds, and mer-
chants were sure of getting customers if they sent wagons through
the streets, ringing bells and loudly announcing their bargains.

San Francisco was tolerant and even proud of the "public characters" who roamed her streets. Emperor Norton was in his heyday; at Lotta's Fountain Father Elphick preached his gospel of
socialism and "air, water and sun"; Li Po Tai, the Chinese herb
doctor, announced that the liver was the source of all human ills;
"Crisis" predicted the end of the world and did a brisk trade in
tracts; and Krause, the poet of the sidewalks, chanted and hawked
his ballads. Elsewhere in the city spiritualists, astrologers and fortune tellers held forth, solving both mundane and spiritual problems for all who sought their advice.

Rumors of new bonanzas on the Comstock Lode filled San
Francisco throughout the spring and summer of '74, and gambling
on the Stock Exchange, in which rich and poor alike took part,
was constant and frenzied. The "nabobs" were building their
palaces on Nob Hill. Ambrose Bierce had gone to London. Dennis
Kearney, destined in a few years to become the firebrand of the
sand-lot agitation, was peacefully occupied with his draying business. And William Chapman Ralston, lord of the Comstock and
financial dictator of the West coast for nearly two decades, was
entering the last and greatest year of his life.

Flora had never imagined that there could be such a place as
San Francisco. Something was happening or about to happen at
every moment, at every street corner. Something might even happen for her at last! Massillon and the barren years were behind
her now. Surely, if Flora Wellman ever tasted happiness or knew
a lifting of the heart at sight of unbounded horizons, it was during
this short, thrilling period which followed her arrival in San Francisco.

Compared with the meager details of Flora Wellman's early
life, a great deal is known about William Chaney, thanks to his
strong autobiographical bent and the survival of a handful of his
writings. Earnest crusader in the cause of astrology, he wrote
among other things a *Primer of Astrology and Urania*. How better to illustrate his theories than by relating how the planets had
influenced his own life? He was forty-five years old when he met
Dr Luke Broughton, preacher of astrology on the Atlantic coast,

and, after a lifetime's espousal of causes that he considered new and progressive, became an ardent convert to one of the oldest beliefs in the world. Before this time his life had been difficult and unsatisfying; now he had a purpose.

Circumstances had early made him a rebel, but his indignation with what he recognized as injustice never blazed up clearly after he was nineteen and gave up his intention to become a pirate. Instead it simmered down through the years, with occasional flare-ups, until it came to express itself in mere contentiousness. He was always difficult to get along with and he never mellowed, although he was in his eighties when he died.

Offspring of old New England families, the Chaneys and the Linscutts, William Henry was born in a log cabin in a Maine forest on January 13, 1821. His father's death as a result of an accident changed the course of his life when he was nine years old. There was no one left to farm the Chaneys' fifteen hundred acres, and so it was disposed of, his mother and four sisters going their separate ways, while he was bound out to a neighboring farmer. Books and studies had meant much to him, and even at that early age he had determined to go to college. Resentment of the farm work which deprived him of the opportunity to continue his education was instantaneous and permanent; all his life he loathed manual labor. This and the probable harshness of his master shortly became unendurable and he ran away, and he continued to run away from six subsequent masters until he was sixteen and free to set out on his own.

He claimed that his family considered him a black sheep because of his violent antipathy to farm work, but to Chaney the world was ever full of enemies who misunderstood and persecuted him. Nevertheless, no member of the family came forward now to help him obtain the education he so desired, and he had to fall back on the manual labor he abhorred. He worked for a while in a sawmill and as a carpenter, his youthful despair turning to bitterness and hatred of all mankind. In this mood he made up his mind to get revenge by joining the pirates who still harried the Mississippi and the Gulf.

Very practically he went about preparing himself for his profession. A backwoods farm boy turned pirate must know something of the sea and ships, so for two years he sailed on fishing schooners, then joined the navy to polish off his knowledge. But this was a fatal mistake. Either the tardy realization of the amount of time it would involve, or his inability to adapt himself to a disciplined regime, prompted him to desert nine months later.

Fearful of being apprehended, he made for the Gulf, sleeping in the daytime and traveling at night, but when he reached the Ohio he fell ill, and his flight was at first temporarily, then finally abandoned. Touched by the kindness of the farming people who took him in and nursed him back to health, love for his fellow men welled up in his heart. Thenceforth, although sooner or later he quarreled with everyone he met, he considered himself a humanitarian, and insofar as it was possible for a man of his temperament, guided his life accordingly.

Everything he learned convinced him that humanity was in a very bad way indeed and urgently needed reforming. Any belief or course of action that would help to bring this about he followed enthusiastically, but twenty-five years were to pass before he was to discover astrology and recognize in it the weapon he had sought so long.

These were years of restless wandering from place to place. Politics and journalism interested him greatly; he seems to have been an excellent speaker and to have written stories and novels, long since lost, as well as edited newspapers. Self-taught, he became an attorney, a profession he disliked and at which he was never successful for long. Always outspoken and with stern concepts of justice, his diatribes against the dishonesty of the courts and his fellow lawyers constantly made enemies and lost clients. Time and again he found himself bankrupt, but ever he moved on and started in again.

During these years occurred the first two of his six marriages, none of which, with the possible exception of the last, brought any degree of happiness to either partner. His first wife died; his second left him after six years. There is little doubt that few of his many marriages were legal. Certain remarks in his various writings indicate that he was not uncordial to Victoria Woodhull's free-love doctrine, and later he was to be publicly accused of this in San Francisco.

There is no clue whatsoever as to his whereabouts during the Civil War, but in the autumn of 1866 his path crossed that of Dr Broughton in New York, and within a month he had accepted astrology. It was not sufficient, however, for Chaney merely to accept this doctrine; he must put it into practice, convert others, propagandize. With characteristic energy he flung himself into study, and in a few months was delivering lectures and writing articles for *Broughton's Monthly*.

The next year was turbulent. The New York daily papers were relentless in their attacks on astrology and astrologers, and the authorities looked the other way when hoodlums broke up their meetings, stole their signs and otherwise persecuted them. When Chaney, outraged, finally had one of their tormentors arrested the culprit was merely reprimanded, while Chaney found himself jailed on a charge of having brought about a false arrest. For twenty-eight weeks he languished in Ludlow Street prison, without a trial, before he was honorably released. His time there was well spent, however. Among his fellow prisoners was a woman whom he first converted to astrology, then wooed and won. Despite the objections of her brother, and the even more important warnings of astrology, the marriage took place in December 1867.

For a year he continued his work in New York, then his old restlessness returned. It must have always been difficult for Chaney to remain long in one place. Through decades of old city directories runs the zigzag trail of his wanderings from coast to coast. Within a few weeks after the completion of the transcontinental railroad he had bade his wife good-by and was on his way to bring astrology to the Pacific coast. He did not intend to stay long, but this plan miscarried, and it was not until October 1873, after four years spent principally in the Northwest, that he made ready to return. But as chance would have it, his pocket was picked before he bought his ticket, and he was stranded, penniless, in San Francisco.

He had lived by his wits too long to be dismayed by his immediate financial problem. As a matter of fact he solved it rather easily, making arrangements with a "gentleman" to advance him sufficient money to hire Dashaway Hall and advertise a series of eight lectures on "Astrotheology" in exchange for one half of the profits. Perhaps the sum realized was not sufficient to pay for the journey home, perhaps the stars directed him to linger a while longer in the West, perhaps business prospects were good—at any rate he spent the winter in the little town of San Jose at the southern end of San Francisco Bay, quiet months of lecturing, teaching and practicing astrology, enlivened only by an eight-day debate with Elder Miles Grant, a well-known Second Adventist from Boston.

If Chaney were to be judged solely by his own account of himself, his sincerity and passionate devotion to his beliefs would seem unassailable, and no charge of charlatanism could be laid against him. But knowledge of certain facts which he omitted alter the picture he has left of himself. His conduct in San Francisco clearly indicates that he was derelict in accepting responsibilities that were germane to his theoretical scheme of things, and challenges the basic integrity of the man himself.

Spring found him in San Francisco, ready once again to return to New York, but, to quote his nonchalant words: ". . . just before starting, (I) received an anonymous letter from my wife . . . stating that she was divorced and could marry again, but if I ever married again she would have me imprisoned.

"This roused my ire and on June 11th, 1874 . . . three weeks later . . . I took another wife. We lived together till June 3d, 1875 . . . almost a year . . . then separated."

From the badly reproduced likeness which heads the *Primer*, published sixteen years later, it is difficult to judge Chaney's appearance, but he amply revealed himself in many ways with every biographical detail. Out of these emerges a short, stocky, vigorous man of positive opinions and emphatic speech, an egotist of the first water. He considered accurate and always remembered a phrenologist's reading of his head when he was thirty-four years old: "Here is a strange man with a strange disposition. He can be as tender as a child, or as brutal as a savage, according to his environments. He remembers a kindness like an Indian; he holds a grudge like an Indian; he will seek revenge like an Indian and in short, he looks like an Indian."

This was the man who, at fifty-three, and to spite his wife, made Flora Wellman the fourth Mrs Chaney. Flora left no autobiographical notes, and it is said that she aged rapidly in the years that followed, but it is not impossible to visualize her then—small, trim, quick stepping, with scanty, short fair hair and light blue eyes, a spirited, independent young woman with a flashing temper when her will was crossed, and a determination to get on which was to take years of failure to crush.

A combination home and office was arranged at 314 Bush Street. A little later they moved to 122 First Avenue, between Mission and Valencia streets, where Chaney practiced his profession and Flora kept house and dutifully studied astrology, although in her heart she preferred the more tangible inspiration of spiritualism. At Chaney's lectures she took charge of the astrological pamphlets and magazines, the sale of which added to their income. The activity of astrologers, fortune tellers and clairvoyants was at flood tide in San Francisco, and even Chaney could scarcely fail to benefit therefrom. The next year outraged and respectable citizens would force their Board of Supervisors to order a licensing fee of fifty dollars per quarter for these "professions," but by that time Chaney would be gone.

Neither Flora nor Chaney were easy-going people, but the union was apparently satisfactory to both parties. Chaney's advertisements, which first read: "The Professor has located temporarily in San Francisco," were soon changed to: "The Professor has located permanently in San Francisco." The two were part of a group of people quite as enthusiastic in their devotion to causes and nearly as broad minded as Victoria Woodhull and her sister. Chaney's meetings were well attended and reported by a sympathetic press.

Inspired by the success of *Woodhull and Claflin's Weekly*, a number of similar periodicals sprang up throughout the country. In the spring of 1874 *Common Sense, a Journal of Live Ideas*, made its appearance in San Francisco with William Slocum as editor and Mrs Amanda as business manager and assistant editor. It was pro-labor, -Negro, -Grange, -free love and all free thinking, and strongly antirevivalist. The phrase, "the emancipation of labor from the chains of capital," glittered on many pages, flanked by articles on spiritualism, social reform, woman's suffrage and astrology. During his stay in San Francisco, Chaney was one of its most valued contributors.

Although Chaney was not above taking advantage of favorable circumstances to make a living out of astrology he would have indignantly rejected any dismissal of his science as quackery. He studied constantly both the mechanics and theory of his subject, and earnestly believed that astrology could be a most powerful factor for bettering the world by ensuring the breeding and raising of superior human beings. He frequently lost patience with the stupidity of people who rejected the simple solution offered by astrology for all the ills of mankind.

To proper astrological mating, easily ascertained by the comparison of the natal charts of the prospective parents, add a carefully forecast birth month and day, and, permitting nature to do its share, a potentially superior being is produced. Then—and

Chaney was very insistent on this point and carried on polemics about it for years with the English astrologers—remembering that the stars incline but do not compel, intelligent, astrologically guided parents can bring their infant to a marvelous maturity as scientifically and as certain of the result as a chemist achieves a successful experiment in a laboratory.

This phase of astrology was the one which, from the beginning, had most deeply appealed to Chaney, answering his long quest for an effective means to reform the world. And yet when Flora told him, when their year together was almost over, that they were to have a child he seems to have brushed away every vestige of his beliefs and principles. He rejected fatherhood, harshly demanded that she rid herself of the child, and when she refused, after one can only guess what scenes, he left her.

Flora fought to the last to keep the man she loved. Then in despair she sought death. Friends reached her before she could inflict fatal injury upon herself, but all her life she carried the scar of a pistol wound on her forehead. It was Mrs Amanda who came to Flora at this time, stanchly defending her heartbroken friend and heaping such scornful diatribes on Chaney that up in Portland, Oregon, Mrs Abigail Scott Duniway, early suffragette and editor of the *The New Northwest,* promptly launched a scathing attack upon him in the columns of her paper.

William Chaney never saw or communicated with Flora again. His precipitate flight took him back to the Northwest where he married a fifth time, and then, seventeen years after he had left New York, he turned east again. For a long time he lived in Chicago and other towns in the Middle West, practicing astrology, writing books and articles, finding perhaps a little happiness with Daisy, the sixth and final Mrs Chaney, quarreling with his fellow astrologers here and abroad, and dying at last in poverty and obscurity almost at the moment when his son, whom he never acknowledged, was receiving world-wide acclaim as the author of *The Call of the Wild.*

As soon as Flora could be moved from the hospital Mrs Amanda brought her to the big house at Third and Bryant streets, and there, on January 12, 1876, her son was born.

The birth was difficult for Flora, and her strength and desire to live returned very slowly. Capable Mrs Amanda saw to everything, and was probably the one who first realized that the child was not doing well on his mother's milk and consulted with the doctor as to the advisability of procuring a wet nurse. Inquiries were made, and the doctor found Mrs Prentiss, a Negro woman a few years older than Flora, who had just lost a baby and whom he recommended unreservedly. The child was taken to the Prentisses' clean little house, and Flora, sharply aware for the first time of the need to support herself and her son as quickly as possible, fought her way back to health. She gathered together her scattered music pupils and wearily began to build her life anew.

Jennie Prentiss, who lived long enough to hold in her arms the grandson of her foster child, had been born a slave in Virginia and separated from her mother by the auction block so young that she could not remember her. Virginia she called herself after her state, but as Mammy Jennie she was known for the greater part of her life. She would accept little money for caring for the baby—so fair in contrast with the ebony skin of herself and her two children, Will and Annie. Her warm heart had gone out at once to both mother and child. Besides, her white husband earned a good living as a carpenter, and Jennie's thrift had accumulated a comfortable savings account.

In her girlhood Flora had been taught to sew beautifully, and now, to express her gratitude to Jennie, she undertook to make shirts for Mr Prentiss. It was through these shirts that she met John London, who had recently come to California from the Middle West with his two motherless little girls, and was the contractor for whom Prentiss was working at the time. He admired the shirts, asked Prentiss where similar ones could be obtained, and Prentiss obliged, seeing an opportunity for Flora to add a little to her slender income.

The acquaintance between Flora Chaney and John London quickly ripened into friendship. Both were lonely, both hungered for affection, companionship and a home. The little girls were in the Protestant Orphan Asylum, Flora's son was still with Jennie. Faltering ambition and confidence in their abilities to be successful reawakened as they made plans for the future. On September 7, 1876, they were married in San Francisco by Justice of the Peace James C. Pennie.

Flora found in John London a man strikingly different from Chaney, less vital, with no brilliant personality or bludgeoning mind or dictatorial ways, but with much kindness and loyalty and consideration. He gave Flora's son his name and raised him as his own, and although he died before the boy's struggle to become a writer began, his faith in him never wavered.

The bright future John and Flora had visioned glowed always on the farthest horizon, no matter how conscientiously they plodded toward it. John was past fifty and his health had been permanently shattered by the Civil War. Misfortune dogged them, but it was years before they gave up the unequal struggle. John London's life had been spent largely in the open as farmer, railroad worker, carpenter, contractor and builder, and his experiences had not fitted him to prosper in the city, even if hard times had not broken him. It was not long before he ceased to be a contractor. The year after the marriage found him a canvasser for the Victor Sewing Machine Company, but thereafter, until they left San Francisco, he worked as a carpenter. His ambition to escape permanently from the city and return to the land was never to be realized, and thus it was as part of the city proletariat that his stepson grew to manhood.

CHAPTER

2

THE Londons' modest plans for the future could hardly have
been made at a more inauspicious time. The land was full of ferment and dissatisfaction, and not only in California but throughout the nation powerful social forces were at work which would
doom their efforts and those of countless others to failure.
The railroads had destroyed the splendid isolation of the West,
linking it for better or worse with the rest of the country. As a
matter of fact its very newness and plasticity made it extremely
sensitive to the currents of national life. The pendulums of depressions and recoveries now swung from coast to coast. Agrarian
protests and industrial strikes in the East and Middle West found
instant response west of the Rockies. And in the decades to come
California would not only participate in but contribute to the
various movements of the common people whose growing discontent flamed into rebellion from time to time.
It was the period when industrialization was beginning to make
itself both seen and felt. Out of the confluence in various places
throughout the country of mills, factories, railroads, workers,
businessmen and shopkeepers, banks, credit institutions and vast
accumulations of capital, was rising the city, as typical of the new
order as the Southern cotton plantation and Northern small farm
had been of its predecessor.
For the first time large numbers of Americans, far from the
stultifying isolation of the farm and plantation, were getting
acquainted with each other, sharing ideas, opinions and experiences, voicing common aims and grievances; and some of them

were getting acquainted with the rest of the world as well, thanks to the daily newspapers and the presence in their midst of immigrants from older European cities. In another generation many of these Americans would be known as the working class, for class lines emerged quickly in the city where a worker, unlike a farmer, was under no illusion of being his own boss. Labor unions were forming and growing; strikes were looming; later socialism would gain a foothold.

But neither the quickening tempo of American life nor the voicing of grievances was confined to the city. By the end of the 'seventies conditions in agriculture were such that the farmers, convinced that they were surrounded by enemies determined to ruin them, had begun the free-silver, cheap-money agitation that was to be a turbulent force in American politics until the turn of the century.

More than in any other country in the world, American agriculture has been commercial capitalist in character. After the Civil War its erratic ups and downs were clearly dictated by the spasmodic extension of the needs of the national and international markets. America was not only supplying the food for the tremendous expansion of British imperialism, but with her agricultural products was buying the foreign goods and services she needed for her own development. During these years the amount of land under cultivation and its value kept increasing, but in the meantime vast grasslands elsewhere in the world were being plowed and seeded, and a day of reckoning was inevitable.

High prices during the Civil War had drawn thousands of small farmers into the Middle West and West. The slump after the war began the crippling process which later events would continue. Mortgage was piled on mortgage as bad years followed good in bewildering succession, and the farmers paid their debts by lumping them together and borrowing more money from the obliging banks.

No matter how low prices went, however, interest rates remained stationary; money was scarce; banks would not loan money on crops, but only on land and improvements; the railroads refused to lower their rates and brazenly discriminated against the little fellows; manufacturers used the tariff to protect their high prices; and the government, whom the farmers praised or blamed for everything, continued to tax land rather than incomes.

Vaguely the farmers sensed the outlines of their predicament, and at one time or another demanded the various reforms which they were sure would lighten their burdens and give them a chance to get on. But from the beginning one issue was paramount: cheap money. If they could obtain this they fondly believed that they would then be in a position to fight against the remaining obstacles that impeded their progress.

They characterized as the "crime of 1873" the Congressional bill which had in effect demonetized silver by omitting the silver dollar from the list of coins. Actually this had been merely a tardy recognition of the fact that silver had been out of commercial use in the United States for nearly twenty years, but it happened to coincide with the discovery of the great silver mines in Nevada, Colorado, and a little later in Utah. As the hard-pressed farmers saw it, here was plenty of silver, and yet they had to pay their debts in gold. Small wonder that they recognized in this, and the fact that many European countries had also recently adopted the single gold standard, a gigantic international conspiracy, engineered by high finance and directed against them and everyone else who owed money.

From all parts of the countryside rose the silver orators, endlessly agitating for free silver and greenbacks. Beginning in the late 'seventies and lasting through the 'nineties, a bill calling for the unlimited coinage of silver was bitterly fought over in almost every Congress. And in the interims the embattled farmers vented their rage against the railroads, the trusts, the banks and the rest of their enemies.

The whole struggle, including the activity of their political parties, Greenback, Populist and others, represented essentially the revolt of small property owners against the inexorable workings of swiftly developing capitalism, which during these years was mercilessly carving out class divisions in the United States. On and off, however, large sections of the working class were drawn into these movements, because they also had their grievances against the farmers' enemies. This was especially true in the Far West where class differences crystallized more slowly.

The West had become part of the United States rather late, and its rapid growth was the result of a sort of hothouse forcing. Almost before it knew what had happened it was up to its neck in debt. Great masses of capital had poured in from the East and

from England by way of the Eastern banks to develop its agriculture, mines and infant industries. Like the Middle-Western
farmers, the Westerners had to pay their debts in gold or its
equivalent which was scarce and dear. So, as elsewhere, "Down
with gold!" became their slogan, their obsession and their dream.

But this alone would not have ensured popular support in the
West, even briefly, if they had not coupled with their demands
for financial governmental intervention, others for municipal and
governmental ownership of public utilities, thus striking a blow
at the secondary tyrants—the railroads, and the irrigation, power,
light and heat companies which, operating under government
charters, cheated and oppressed them.

The crash of Ralston's empire in the autumn of 1875 was felt
in financial centers in America and abroad, but the West was
hardest and most immediately hit. Staggering under this as well as
the increasing strangle hold of the 1873 depression, which was
culminating on the West coast, California saw not only the failure of its crops in 1876, but the disillusionment of its belief that
the completion of the transcontinental railroad would open up
vast new markets for its products. The reverse occurred, and the
state was flooded with manufactured goods produced in the older
industrial sections more cheaply than they could be in the West.
At the first contact with the brutal competition its young industries collapsed pathetically. Failures, sharp retrenchment and resultant unemployment were the order of the day.

In the late autumn and winter the ranks of the unemployed in
the city were swelled by the usual influx of agricultural workers
from all over the state. The mechanization of agriculture was pro-
ceeding rapidly, and the predecessors of the twentieth-century
factory-farms were already in existence. Large gangs of men were
needed at certain seasons and then turned loose to shift for themselves in the interims. Later, as agriculture developed, the intervals between employment were to grow shorter, until the dilapi-
dated automobile caravans of agricultural workers and their
families would become a familiar sight on the highways, following the crops from the South to the North and back again. But
then, as now, the wages of these workers were scanty, and their
need for jobs in the winter was desperate. It was not uncommon
during these years, especially as growing industry produced more
and more disemployment, for numbers of them to band together

in gangs of one or two hundred and ride on freights throughout
the West in search of work.

During the winter of 1876 there was no work for these men,
nor could they look forward to much from the hard-hit farmers
in the coming spring and summer. So they stayed in San Francisco, their discontent adding fuel to that of the city's unemployed. Hatred of the Southern Pacific, whose monopoly in California was greater than that of any of the railroads anywhere,
and the Chinese question dwarfed all other issues, but there were
plenty of minor grievances. Criticism of politics and politicians
could draw a street-corner crowd at any time. Bitter experience
had taught the people that they could place no confidence in
either the courts of law or the governing bodies of the state. The
corporations owned the legislatures body and soul, and each was
worse than its predecessor. "The legislature of a thousand drinks,"
"The legislature of a thousand steals,"—such were the scornful
epithets bestowed upon them.

County government was little better, and city government was
even worse. The daily papers were full of accusations of jobbery
and bossism, and, pointing to the dangerous and unsanitary
planked streets and sidewalks, they exhorted the taxpayers to demand to know how their money was being spent. Later, in the
sand lots, the unemployed remembered this and sometimes added
the cry for better streets and sidewalks to "Let bullets replace
ballots!" and "The Chinese must go!"

In the early summer of 1877 the great railroad strike in Pittsburgh occurred. Sympathy of the Western workers was intensified by the fact that the Southern Pacific had just announced
similar wage reductions. A mass meeting, called to express unity
and solidarity with the Eastern strikers, coincided with the news
of the rioting in Pittsburgh, but although feeling ran high nothing untoward occurred. Nevertheless the newspapers played it
up sensationally, recalling the Vigilance Committee of 1856, and
panicky citizens hastily formed the "Pick Handle Brigade" to
maintain law and order.

During the early days of what became known as the July riots
Dennis Kearney, the drayman, was a member of the Pick Handle
Brigade, but as the bitterness increased, Kearney dropped his
pick handle and turned up in the midst of the unemployed—the
demagogue whom the time, now more than ripe, was calling for.

A great showman, an opportunist with a strong sense of organization, a fairly successful politician, Kearney remains to a great extent a controversial and questionable figure. His presence in the Pick Handle Brigade was neither forgiven nor forgotten, but his fame is based, nevertheless, on his spectacular leadership of the unemployed and, to a lesser degree, of the organized workers in California.

His showmanship was worthy of Barnum's, but although he has been accused of never missing an opportunity to feather his own nest, he consistently used his talents for social and political purposes. He agitated the unemployed to petition for relief and organized them into parades that bristled with banners, riding at their head on horseback and pausing at strategic points to deliver his famous dithyrambic harangues.

Shortly after the July riots he applied for admission to the Workingmen's party of the United States, which had been organized the preceding year, and was affiliated to the Marxian First International. Because of his known contempt for the workers and the record of his carrying the pick handle for the employers, he was refused. Nothing daunted, he promptly formed his own, the Workingmen's party of California, which, for a brief time, was a political force in the West.

Everything was grist to his mill, with the result that the party's aims were a conglomeration of social reform and chauvinism. In addition to unemployment and low wages, he capitalized on the strong anti-Chinese sentiment of the time. This had been a basic issue in the labor movement in California since the early 'sixties, when Stanford, Crocker and others began to import Chinese coolie labor. Even before the completion of the transcontinental railroad in 1871, which threw an enormous number of both Chinese and whites out of work and posed the issues sharply, anti-Chinese sentiment in California had reached a high peak when the Burlingame Treaty between the United States and China was signed in 1868. Throughout the country Socialist opinion favored free immigration, but the California workers would have none of it.

The basis for the prejudice was obviously economic. Of the total Chinese population in the United States of one hundred and fifty-one thousand, a hundred and sixteen thousand were in California. In numbers Chinese workers practically equaled the whites, and competition between them was bitter. At first the anti-Chinese feeling was confined to the workers, but when the growing competition of the Chinese middleman ·and small manufacturer made itself felt, the middle class lined up also. This chauvinism became traditional in the California labor movement, penetrating even its radical section, and in later years was expressed in similar fashion against the Japanese and Filipinos.

For some years Kearney's Workingmen's party was very successful in political elections throughout the state, capturing the offices of mayor in Oakland, San Francisco and other cities, as well as returning many state senators. Through these great days Kearney rode high and handsome. He allegedly made and lost a great deal of money and was involved in scandals pertaining to bribery and the misappropriation of funds. And with him, although always in the background, was Carl Browne, editor of his papers, sometimes his "private secretary"; but Carl Browne's real role was to be played later.

The Workingmen's party of California even attracted national attention for a brief time. A little later Kearney deflected what he could of his following into the blind alley of the Greenback Labor party. The destiny of the first national group he had sought to join was far different, however, for at its second meeting in December 1877 the Workingmen's party of the United States became the Socialist Labor party.

The passage of the Federal Exclusion Act of 1882, which forbade the further entry of Chinese laborers into the country, knocked the props out from under what remained of the California Workingmen's party by removing the one sure rabble-rousing issue its leaders had always been able to count on. Its one tangible accomplishment—the procapitalist, antilabor constitution of the state of California—was a tragic denial of its early aims. Once Kearney had captured the masses and organized their revolt, he himself was captured and his party used as a tail to many kites, all of which were skillfully manipulated by capitalists and landowners to put over a constitution that was in no sense of the word a workingman's.

It entrenched vested rights, especially in land, more thoroughly than before, and interposed barriers to future radicalism by a provision in regard to amendments, which Henry George—a young man in San Francisco at the time, reading gas meters and writing *Progress and Poverty* in his spare time—claimed would require almost a revolution to break through. It is not extraordinary that California eventually became one of the several states in the Union which not only passed a criminal-syndicalist law but has militantly enforced it.

It was this same Henry George who, writing a few years after the events, summed up the proposals of Kearney and his party as merely: "elect honest men to office, and have them cut down taxation; a remedy which belongs to the same category as the recipe for catching a little bird by sprinkling salt on its tail."

Hard times, the increasing scarcity of work, and a diphtheria epidemic in San Francisco were responsible for the Londons leaving the city to try their luck across the bay with the first of a series of small farms. Until Flora's son, now named John Griffith London and called Johnny, was ten years old they wandered from place to place, working hard, hoping much, bewildered by failure, and only at the end permitting their dream for the future to collapse.

These years left their ineradicable imprint on the growing child. The endless moving (Flora was in her sixties before she finally resigned herself to living in the same house for any length of time) brought first a terrifying feeling of insecurity, and finally indifference to home and home ties. One of his most poignant memories dated from those early years. He was about three and had been left alone briefly in a house from which they were in the midst of moving. The quietness of the dismantled room, the grotesque piles of furniture and boxes of household goods oppressed him with a sense of desolation that quickly turned to fear. In the yard next door a woman was beating carpets. To the frightened child the monotonous whacking was the only familiar thing in the suddenly alien world. He clung to it, listening with all his ears, but after a while the noise ceased and silence closed in about him completely. It seemed more dreadful to try to escape than to remain, but summoning all his courage, he clenched his fists and fled.

Out of his awareness from babyhood of the constant struggle, not to get along so much as to get ahead, developed his firm but erroneous conviction that he had grown up in the midst of privation and want. They lived frugally, it is true, but the necessities and many of the comforts of life were never lacking. Flora was saving money with a definite purpose in mind. She had flung her not inconsiderable energy into their undertakings, and whenever it was possible, as in the early years in Oakland when John was raising vegetables, first near the bay in Emeryville and later on increased acreage in Alameda, she gave music lessons and even conducted a private kindergarten. For a while, despite various misfortunes and setbacks, success seemed within their grasp. Flora visioned broad, fertile acres in the near future, acres they would own, not lease, and the end of the back-bending toil which she was accepting with as good grace as possible only because she was sure it was temporary. John did well in Alameda, and for a little time there was some continuity to their life. Johnny started to school, and though John and Flora often left the children alone at night when they went visiting or attended séances with spiritualist friends, Mammy Jennie lived near by and kept an eye on her foster child, and Eliza, the elder of John's little girls, was a devoted companion.

John would have been content to remain in Alameda, but Flora's eyes were fixed on bigger things. Again the home was uprooted, and John leased a larger parcel of land to grow potatoes on the peninsula south of San Francisco. In a relatively short time this was abandoned, and they made their last stand on the soil on sixty-nine acres in the Livermore Valley, where John became a vinegrower.

Johnny's clearest impressions of these years were of the hardships endured by all about him, the solitude and loneliness of country life, the absence of either playmates or books, the clearly enunciated precepts of his mother that they were the only "Americans" in the vicinity and therefore superior to their immigrant Irish and Italian neighbors, and vivid memories of being twice intoxicated. He found beauty neither in the peninsula ranch, often smothered in fog or swept by winds, nor in the valley where the sun beat mercilessly during the long hot summer, but where, also, the alchemy of the changing seasons clothed the softly rolling hills in green or gold, thrust the green spears of grain through the fertile soil, and ripened the grapes in the spreading vineyards. Instead he carried away with him a hatred of country life which took years to overcome.

Solitude fostered contemplation, made him conscious of self at a precocious age, and, at the expense of the normal development of his gregarious impulses, sharpened his appetite for reading and other hobbies to be pursued and enjoyed by himself. He would grow into a man of few close friendships, acquainted with many but known to few, and concealing his uneasiness with strangers under a boisterous bonhomie.

His education, continued in schools typical of those in rural districts throughout the country, neither attracted nor repelled him, but he did learn to read, and this was the door through which he escaped from the persistent drudgery of his surroundings. Of the few books which passed through his hands at this time, he remembered four: a life of Garfield, Paul du Chaillu's African travels, Washington Irving's *The Alhambra* and Ouida's *Signa*. The glitter and glory of old Spain fired his imagination, but *Signa*, despite the fact that the last forty pages of his copy were missing, caught at his heart. Signa was his own age and, like himself, trapped in the hardship and toil of farm life. Identification of his lot with that of the young Italian peasant was inevitable, and that another boy, in circumstances similar to his own, had broken through all obstacles and finally won to success awakened ambition in him to do likewise.

Reading and rereading, he absorbed unknowingly much of Ouida's faintly rebellious philosophy, her conviction that in society as it now exists there is no place for genius and goodness and high-mindedness, her passionate espousal of democratic ideals, and the curious mingling of extravagant romance and bleak realism which characterizes everything she wrote. His frequent mention of this story later, both in conversation and in his books, testifies to the deep impression it made upon him. For a vital youngster with a lively mind and imagination, growing up in an environment which could not nourish him, the stimulation of *Signa* cannot be underestimated. When he came to live in the city his appetite for reading was voracious, and throughout his life his confidence in the speed and accuracy with which knowledge could be gained from books never wavered.

The Londons' wandering years drew swiftly to a close. The times, John's years and failing health, and Flora's and his naïveté in financial matters (how often the spirits directed their expenditures, or money needed for the ranch went for lottery tickets and other Wallingford schemes) dictated their failure to establish themselves on a farm and drove them back to Oakland. Here, unable to understand their misfortunes and aging rapidly, they were to spend the remainder of their lives.

Their fragile belief in a rosy future did not long survive the realities of the past nor the immediate sharp struggle to make a living in the city, but for a little while they refused to recognize defeat. The Oakland City directory for 1886 lists John London as a farmer, residing on Seventeenth Street, East Oakland. This was a large house to which they had moved from the Livermore ranch, and was the scene of the last of Flora's plans to make money.

Drafting the services of everyone in the family, including Eliza who had married and lived near by, she opened a boarding house, meantime scrimping and saving to accumulate sufficient capital to build a rooming house on the lot next door and provide tasteful apartments for the women workers in the near-by California cotton mills. When this ambition came to nothing both surrendered. Thereafter the directory lists John London as a deputy constable, special officer or watchman, and the addresses of their dwellings move quickly toward West Oakland.

CHAPTER

3

WHILE San Francisco moved swiftly toward cityhood in the years that followed the gold rush, Oakland, her metropolitan ambitions frustrated by the strangle hold obtained on her water front by the Southern Pacific and other private interests, remained a small town. The pressure of industrial development throughout the country could not be withstood indefinitely, however, and in the early part of the 'eighties, water transportation facilities or no, factories began to appear in the East Bay. By 1888 the population had jumped to sixty-five thousand. Civic pride had awakened and a great to-do was being made over the newly macadamized and gas-lit streets. About twenty public electric lights had been installed, and the citizens were beginning to agitate for "cable roads" to take the place of the "ambling streetcars," and for stone curbings and crosswalks to put an end to the mud and dust that constantly plagued them.

That part of the city west from Broadway to the edge of the bay and from Twelfth Street to the estuary was the oldest residential section. As the town expanded and the early settlers grew more affluent their ugly, hastily built frame cottages were abandoned to the less fortunate. Small business concerns, livery stables, factories and warehouses began to shoulder aside the shabby houses and the few mansions whose one-time grandeur was rapidly fading. Dingy, angular, the old houses faced wide, unpaved streets, rutted and dusty in summer and deep in mud when it rained. For a long time West Oakland was a neighborhood of people who had not got on, but when the industrial boom began it became the city's working-class district.

Low rents undoubtedly drew the Londons there after a brief excursion to the northern outskirts of the town. John's earnings were small, and Flora was always susceptible to the lure of Chinese lottery tickets. Many people whom she knew won a little, but Flora was unlucky. Since five- or six-room houses in the better residential areas could be rented then for fifteen or twenty dollars a month it is not improbable that, with a family soon reduced to three by the marriage of John's younger daughter, they were able to be fairly comfortable in various small cottages whose rent rarely exceeded ten dollars monthly. The late 'eighties saw them living on Pine Street, two blocks from where the railroad tracks that parallel the bay swing out on the "Point" toward the Southern Pacific mole, and not far from the estuary.

Free at last from the frustrations of ranch life, Jack (the Johnny had been gladly dropped soon after his arrival in Oakland) was almost content. Access to the public library was satisfying his hunger for books, companionship with other boys was his if he desired it, proximity to the bay and estuary where ships from all over the world lay at anchor made his dreams of travel and adventure more tangible, and the very fact of his parents' poverty was giving him independence and self-confidence, for his small earnings from delivering papers and doing odd jobs had become an indispensable part of the family income.

His life was of necessity ordered and disciplined. Daily, basic demands on his time had to be met: so many hours in school, so many for his paper route and other jobs, so many for eating and sleeping. But there remained sufficient time at his own disposal, if he cared to make use of it, to keep the routine supple. He did care tremendously, and although by the time he was eleven he was certainly more serious than many boys his age, he nevertheless was managing to do a great many things he thoroughly enjoyed.

He had found his way to the public library soon after his arrival in Oakland. Cards were procured for every member of the family, and he had gorged himself on books until health and nerves rebelled. Then he made a second discovery. Dramas and operas played intermittently at Dietz's Opera House and the Tivoli. Except on rare occasions, gallery seats cost from fifteen to twenty-five cents. Flora allowed him ten cents weekly out of his earnings, and this he sometimes augmented by selling various items to the rags-bottles-sacks men. These sums he carefully hoarded, and on as many Saturdays as possible he climbed the steep gallery stairs to lose himself in *East Lynne*, *The Mikado*, *Erminie* or *True Devotion* as completely as he did in a book.

His lively curiosity, starved so long on the ranches, drove him to take full advantage of everything he encountered. With his first paper route his eyes were opened to places and people and types of existence such as he had never seen before. Sometimes he accompanied John as he made his deputy constable's rounds through the tenderloin district. Sweeping out saloons, setting up pins in a bowling alley, helping an iceman on Saturdays, cutting lawns and trimming hedges—these and other odd jobs added to his store of knowledge.

Especially did he like to listen to the talk along the water front where seafaring men loitered on the wharves or in the saloons, swapping yarns, drinking, arguing and fighting. Frequently he explored the estuary on Sundays with John and Shep, his dog, in a small rented boat, fishing, digging for clams and asking excited questions about the ships tied up on either side of the narrow waterway. Because he knew he would soon return to the busy streets, he liked the quietness of the lonely marshes where the clean, sharp wind bent down the reeds, and where the flight of wild ducks and gulls was the only movement in the empty sky.

The small figure of Flora London, thickening and stooping as she neared her fifties, dominates these years. While poverty tarnished and even destroyed in part the middle-class standards she had known as a girl and clung to as best she might during the years of hardship, no others came to take their place. Whenever she could afford to she raised her tattered banner of "respectability" and a "decent" way of life. But when the lash of necessity was upon her she would abandon it without remorse, her lips tighter than usual, her eyes colder and more stubborn. Thus she had suggested to Jack that he get a paper route, because, he always remembered her saying, "he needed the exercise." When the opportunity came to take a second as well she recommended it heartily. "You have lots of stamina, son," she assured him. She pocketed his contributions without comment, and as occasion required, did not hesitate to ask him for more, no matter what precious object the boy might be saving up for.

Sometimes it was no easy matter to make both ends meet. She

worked very hard herself, and because, as she saw it, life had dealt with her harshly, she was harsh with others. From the time of Chaney's desertion nothing had gone as she desired. She did not actually blame anyone for this, but if she suffered those about her suffered as well. As she aged her earlier defiance sank under a morose silence, as much to be feared in its way as her temper, which still flared up uncontrollably from time to time.

With her marriage to John London, far too negative and gentle a person to cope with her, she became undisputed mistress of her household. Jack grew out of babyhood regarding her as all-powerful and all-wise, but his opinion of her altered as time went on. Warmth and affection no longer came easily to Flora, even in motherhood. Melancholy, withdrawn, she made no effort to help the boy to understand her. No matter how much he criticized her, however, he did not lose his respect for her. She was the one positive individual in his childhood and adolescence, and no one replaced her until he came to rely fully upon himself in all matters.

Years later he told his friend, Henry Mead Bland, of his first disillusionment with Flora. One day, tired and harassed no doubt, she had punished him unjustly. Whether he was more sensitive than other children, most of whom have similar experiences and forget them, or whether his incorrigible urge to dramatize the facts of his life was responsible for retaining this infantile memory of injustice, there is no knowing, but when he told the story to Mr Bland he was certain that from that time on he had decided the right and wrong of things for himself.

One more factor contributed to the boy's independence, and that was Flora's belief in spiritualism which became more fervent as her fortunes fell. Spiritualistic practices provided a thrilling escape from the drabness of her everyday life. She was considered something of a medium by her friends and acquaintances, and from all reports the séances she conducted were not only convincing but exhilarating.

For a long time mediums had been reporting the presence of Indian spirits in their circles, sometimes poor, ignorant souls of a low, inactive order whom the spiritualists worked to reform, but more often haughty and intelligent braves who had once been leaders of their people. "Black Hawk," "Osceola," "King Philip," "Red Jacket," and "Logan" brought comforting messages, predictions and advice to many little groups of earnest people in darkened rooms throughout the country. Flora followed this tradition, her favorite control being "Plume," an Indian chieftain. He usually announced his arrival with a terrifying whoop, and his otherwise sober discourse was frequently punctuated with unexpected yells and gibberish.

Jack had heard talk of spiritualism from babyhood and more than once had witnessed Flora in one of her "trances." His scornful rejection of the whole business long before he was twelve as claptrap fit only for weak-minded people undoubtedly rose from childish fear of the unlovely performance. If this were religion he would have none of it. When he died he knew that he would be dead, as dead as dogs struck by the Seventh Street trains, or fish the tide threw upon the beach, and he would never return to bulge the eyes and contort the mouth of anyone. Learning to be acutely aware of the first approach of what he called his mother's "fits," he would hastily leave the house until they had run their course.

There is no indication that he rebelled against his environment at this time. Knowing no other, save from the somewhat incredible descriptions of the life of the wealthy gleaned from the penny-dreadfuls he had devoured for a while (and even these generally made heroes of boys as poor as himself who overcame all obstacles and won to success), comparisons were impossible. The rhythm of his days was comforting, satisfying an innate love of order, and his disappointments did not differ from those of most of his schoolmates, the majority of whom came from working-class families like his own. In common with all youth that is not feeble minded, his acquisition of knowledge of self, and of self in relation to others was painful. As he entered adolescence he was alternately stung by the half-perceived beauty and promise of life, and sorrowfully oppressed by premonitions of inadequacy and failure. Sometimes, escaping his torment by way of books, he dreamed great dreams of manhood or, momentarily freed from the compulsion of growing up, he flung himself wholeheartedly into boyish activity out of doors.

It was during his last few years in grammar school that the one friendship of Jack's boyhood was formed. Early solitude had accentuated his natural shyness and developed interests unlikely to be shared by boys whose playgrounds had been the streets and empty lots of a working-class neighborhood. Experience of shared activity was almost entirely lacking. With a limited time at his disposal, his choice between joining the games of his schoolmates and reading had been quickly made; he preferred to read. But this decision was not always easy to abide by.

During these years coupons were being given away with certain brands of cigarettes and smoking tobacco. These were exchanged for various premiums, the most popular with the boys being picture cards of actors and actresses, prize fighters, race horses, birds and flags of all nations. To make complete collections, the boys traded and swapped duplicates. Jack was an enthusiastic collector, but this hobby brought him into but brief contact with his schoolfellows. Often lonely, he longed for a chum to rejoice with him over his small triumphs and share his interests.

Frank Atherton was a newcomer to the Cole school in West Oakland. A quiet lad from the country, his acquaintance with the boisterous city boys grew slowly. Jack, his nose buried in a book throughout most of the recesses and noon hours, roused his curiosity. As soon as school was out Jack disappeared in evident haste. His lack of popularity was obvious. The boys not only scorned him as a bookworm, but resented his apparent indifference toward them. On the other hand, they had learned to respect his ready fists in defense of his right to do as he pleased in the schoolyard, and his ability to take care of himself in similar encounters elsewhere.

A chance meeting while Jack was delivering papers and a mutual interest in picture cards finally brought the boys together. The friendship that grew quickly between them was compounded of the desire of each for a companion and the interests both had outside the scope of the neighborhood gangs, but it endured because of Frank's ability to adapt himself to Jack's needs and demands and his genuine admiration for his strange new friend. Jack's schedule remained unaltered, but many of the hours formerly spent alone or with John were now shared with Frank.

Often Frank came home with Jack for supper, the boys crowding into the bare, well-scrubbed kitchen after Jack's paper route had been served to talk or listen to John's stories, while Flora bustled about preparing the meal. The menu seldom varied: thick, juicy beefsteaks, potatoes, bread and butter, and coffee. Frank used to marvel that such obviously poor people managed to eat so well, but Flora, with only a small sum at her disposal for food, had long since solved the problem (and simplified her work) by omitting dessert and what she regarded as similar nonsense and concentrating on what was essential. She was justly famous for her steaks, possessing the rare secret of dry-skillet frying, although she herself denied her art and gave all credit to the particular skillet she used. John and Jack might laugh at her all they wished, she refused to part with that skillet, even when a household accident broke a great piece out of its side.

They always ate in the kitchen at a table spread with newspapers. Once Jack teased Flora about the newspapers, telling Frank that they were too poor to use anything else. Flora indignantly denied this, but Jack would not desist. She rose abruptly and left the room, returning in a moment with a pile of snowy tablecloths. "Do you think Frank wants to associate with a family of paupers!" exclaimed Flora Wellman, the rich man's daughter from Massillon, Ohio, her eyes flashing. And when they burst into laughter she would not join in their merriment.

Companionship inevitably created new interests, and the boys were soon deep in grandiose schemes which neither would have thought of alone. But because between them and the absorbing, imaginative games one usually associates with boyhood was the poverty of which both were aware, it was not unnatural that much of their activity should have been colored by the desire to make money.

The slingshots that were popular with all the boys at school, and John's Sunday expeditions on the estuary were responsible for an enterprise which not only absorbed them for months, but in the end nearly terminated their friendship. Not content with the small slings which at best could merely terrify a Chinese laundryman's horse or agitate a schoolteacher past endurance, they made heavier ones, and in the leather pocket between the wide leather bands placed "bullets" which they molded themselves from old lead. When they tried out the weapons in Jack's yard they discovered with amazement and delight that the bullets nearly penetrated the inch-thick boards in the back fence. The possibilities that opened up before them were staggering; their immediate thought was of next Sunday's fishing trip with John. The marshes and estuary were filled with ducks!

Disappointment awaited them. It was impossible to achieve any accuracy of aim with the slings, but failure merely increased their determination. During the week they spent their spare hours collecting lead and making more bullets and practicing with smaller targets than the back fence. But it seemed hopeless. Always the ducks rose unharmed from the water, always the mud hens floated indifferently. They grew to hate the stupid females, not only because they did not fly away, but because even when they tried they could not hit them.

The day their luck finally changed saw the metamorphosis of their hope of catching ducks merely to bring home into a business venture. A furious barrage into a flock netted two of the despised hens, good for nothing except Shep's supper. A little later, "firing" simultaneously, they brought down a real duck and fell to quarreling over whose bullet had been the lucky one. As they argued the wind carried the floating bird into deep water. Too late they bent their efforts to recover it, but the wind won the uneven contest.

As they trailed dejectedly homeward with the mud hens, chewing the bitter end of their argument, a Chinese hailed them from the door of his laundry. To their astonishment he bought both hens for forty cents, and Jack's great idea was born. They would catch more hens and ducks and sell them to the Chinese! Better yet, they would catch wildcats, prized as food by the Chinese during tong wars because of their strength and ferocity. The hills back of Lake Merritt must be full of wildcats, and perhaps even a few grizzly bears!

Preparations for the great wildcat hunt were immediately under way. They made a list of what they would need: two slingshots apiece, ten pounds of bullets, two sharp butcher knives (to be borrowed from their respective kitchens), two bundles of extra heavy cord (for stringing dead wildcats together) and ten yards of cloth (to conceal dead wildcats from curious eyes). Looking ahead, they planned to enlarge the scope of their activity to include the fomenting of tong wars to keep up the demand for wildcats. This would make school attendance impossible, but that was a small matter for they would be earning so much money that they could easily afford private teachers.

The great scheme was a dismal failure. From start to finish of a long summer's day they failed to see a single wildcat. Discouraged, they fell back on the ducks. But if only they had rifles! Then the unexpected happened: Frank acquired a secondhand pistol. Together the two boys collected and sold enough junk to buy a similar weapon for Jack and ammunition for both.

Brimming with confidence, they rented a boat and rowed into San Leandro Bay where great flocks of ducks nested in the marshes that fringed the water. That day they found no ducks, only mud hens and when, lacking other targets, they began to shoot at the despised birds, they had no better luck than with the slingshots. The bullets made a brave splattering in the water, but the mud hens merely blinked and paddled around with their usual unconcern.

Something went wrong with Jack's gun. The bullets emerged reluctantly and struck the water just a few feet beyond the boat. Finally the barrel was completely clogged. He pounded it impatiently on the edge of the boat. Nothing happened. Angrily he brought the pistol down against the gunwale with such force that it slipped from his grasp and sank swiftly into the muddy water.

Frank dared not speak, Jack could not. There was a long silence. The gently rocking boat drifted slowly, the mud hens swam their monotonous circles.

Jack looked up, anger wiped from his face, confidence in his smile. Frank knew how to swim, didn't he? . . . Sure, but the water in the creek up in the mountains wasn't very deep. . . . But if Frank could swim he could swim, and so he certainly could find Jack's pistol. Jack would do it himself, but he didn't know how to swim. Frank pointed out that wind and tide had guided the drifting boat, and even if they knew the exact spot where the gun had fallen it was probably deeply embedded in the mud at the bottom. But Frank could at least try, argued Jack. And get himself drowned, retorted Frank, thoroughly frightened at the prospect, and for what? For a lousy old pistol. . . . It wasn't an old pistol, it was just shopworn! Frank had heard the man say so himself. . . . Anyway, Frank insisted, it wasn't as good as his. His worked, and he had paid only half as much for it.

Eyes blazing, Jack seized the oars. It was an old pistol, and a lousy one, was it? Well, he'd make Frank swim whether he wanted to or not! He flung both oars as far as he could into the water and glared triumphantly at his friend. Again there was silence, broken only by the lapping of the water and the shrill cries of the sea gulls. The oars drifted apart, further and further from the boat. The late afternoon sun was beginning to lose its warmth, and the breeze was sharper.

Frank moved uneasily, cleared his throat. Jack could have his pistol if he wanted it. Jack shook his head. What an idiot he had been to lose his temper like that! The loss of the pistol didn't matter any more. The real problem now was how to get back to the boathouse.

Again they were comrades. Frank discovered a fairly long fish-line at the bottom of the boat; Jack cut the thong that held one of the oarlocks and weighted one end of the line. Paddling with their hands, they managed to get close enough to one of the oars so that Frank could lasso it and pull it within reach. Jack sculled over to the other oar and brought the boat to shore while Frank tried vainly to bail the boat with cupped hands. Soaked to the skin, the boys hurried home through the gathering darkness.

This was their last attempt to make their fortunes by hunting wild game, for in a short time the brief period of companionship came to an end. In the spring the Athertons left Oakland for a ranch in the northern part of the state. During the summer Jack spent the only real vacation of his boyhood with Frank. The boys explored the countryside, stole peaches and were chased by irate farmers, and Jack learned how to swim. But when it was time to return to Oakland Jack went not unwillingly back to the solitary routine to which he had been accustomed. The next year he graduated from grammar school, and an altogether different life began.

CHAPTER

4

COMPLETION of the eighth grade shattered the schedule by which Jack had lived for so long. No longer would he spend the greater part of his day in a classroom. The question of his going on to high school was not even considered. Whatever tradition of higher education may have been in Flora's family had not survived the years of poverty and struggle for a bare living, and no such tradition existed in John London's past. Nor, despite his interest in reading, was Jack especially concerned at that time with more schooling. This was to happen later when education had become a means to an all-important end. Meantime one thing was certain: he must go to work.

For some time he had been aware of how important his small earnings were to the family income. Now he knew he must contribute more. He did not question this. All about him in his own neighborhood boys and girls got jobs as soon as they finished grammar school. It was what kind of work he was to do that was not clear.

John had no trade for the boy to follow. Even if it had occurred to him that the youngster might be apprenticed out and so learn to make a living at some skilled or semiskilled work, the problem of supporting the family unaided while the boy was being trained would have been too much for the aging man to face. It is unlikely that either he or Flora openly discussed the situation with Jack. John did not want to rush him to work, while Flora, as long as no financial crisis presented itself, kept silent. Nevertheless, while the boy floundered toward a solution of his problem, he was hampered and harassed in one way or another by the two elderly people, by turns anxious and apathetic and far more helpless and bewildered than he.

For many months after graduation he continued selling papers and doing odd jobs, turning his earnings over to his mother as always. He read a great deal, but home saw him seldom. Long since it had become merely a place in which to eat and sleep. The lives and interests of his parents were completely alien to him now. Living more and more in the past, they had nothing that might hold him, who was young, vital, with his eyes fixed on today, tomorrow and all the years of tomorrows. He had acquired a small skiff, and in this he spent days on end, sailing, fishing and exploring the furthest reaches of the estuary and San Leandro Bay. Often he lost himself in the books from the public library which he usually brought with him, and as he planned adventures for himself as exciting as any in the books, he forgot the gloomy home, the problem of earning a living and all that his youth rejected.

Perhaps the household unexpectedly needed more money, perhaps the factories, in the incessant clamor for workers which marked this period, were offering higher wages than usual and special inducements—at any rate shortly after he was fifteen his days of freedom came to an end and he went to work in Hickmott's cannery on Myrtle Street in West Oakland. His memories of these months were bitter and resentful. From seven in the morning until noon and from one until six in the afternoon, he stood at a machine, endlessly repeating the same operations. This ten-hour day was the minimum he worked. Pressed by the family's need for money, he usually worked overtime, often, he wrote later, as much as eighteen and twenty hours at a stretch, and once for thirty-six consecutive hours. Sometimes he earned fifty dollars a month, a staggering sum for a fifteen-year-old boy, considering the basic rate of pay—ten cents an hour and very little more for overtime.

Overnight the complexion of his life changed entirely. The vagabond days, the sense of being able to order his life as he pleased, to accept and reject at will, the fresh winds and clean air, the space and quietness of the estuary and bay—these were gone. He came home from work at midnight, numb with fatigue and scarcely able to keep his eyes open while he ate his supper. Flora awakened him for a hasty breakfast long before he had his fill of sleep, for the whistle at the plant blew inexorably at seven. Hatred of the cannery work was immediate. He felt trapped, rendered a slave to a machine which devoured his vitality and left him at the end of each week sapped and apathetic. Rebellion against this way of life grew swiftly, but he was slow to act upon it. He must earn his living—he understood this at an early age. Unquestioning acceptance of his parents' dependence upon him as well as ignorance of other, pleasanter ways in which he might make a living tied him to the machine for long months.

At first all his energies went into merely keeping up with the new schedule and adjusting himself to the sudden curtailment of sleep. Companionship he did not miss; no one had taken Frank's place. For a long time his recreations had been solitary—reading and sailing alone in his boat. Now he was too tired to read, and for a time he rarely even thought of his boat. But as his loathing of the job grew, the boat came to be his only escape from a situation fast growing intolerable. He had known the estuary for years but now, in the brief respites from the cannery, he looked at it with new eyes, hungry, appreciative and finally calculating.

These were the last great years of sail on the Pacific coast, and ships of every size, shape and description tied up in the Oakland estuary between voyages—trading schooners, the United States revenue cutter, the Coast survey schooner, and a host of smaller craft which rarely ventured outside the Heads but whose activity, if the tales were true, equaled in excitement anything the deep-water ships did. Every winter the northern whaling fleet lay up near the marshes, great graceful boats with towering masts, their sides scarred from years of battle with the elements. And at all times of the year the saloons that lined the estuary were filled with seafaring men, sailors, harpooners, and boat pullers from all over the world, bay sailors, bargemen and oyster pirates, all with their yarns of adventure and escapades.

As the weeks passed Jack's thoughts began shaping themselves toward a definite end. He knew that he had reached the limit of his endurance of machine toil. During his boyhood and until he had finished school the horizon of his life had been vague but unobstructed; now there was no horizon, no end or aim. With his usual practical bent, he calculated the peak of his earnings if he continued to work in canneries and factories and saw himself tied to machines and removed forever from the realization of his boyhood's objectives. His curiosity about life and the world, his vitality and untried strength clamored for escape from the narrow confines of the cannery, for opportunities to know more and be more. As he groped toward a solution the situation posed itself thus: on the one hand, there was the cannery and its long hours of stupid, underpaid work, and "home," which meant a bed and two meals a day; and on the other hand, there was the water front where there were no machines or deadening toil, and where the winds and waters of all the world beckoned in the tall ships and in the sailors' taller tales.

Alone in his small boat, he was master, not slave. He could go where he wished, past the lonely marshes in the upper reaches of the estuary, or down near the mouth where expert sailing was necessary to avoid collisions with other boats. Or, sail furled, he could lie back, daydreaming, drawing on his scanty lore of sky and wind to speculate upon the weather, watching the wild ducks flying against the sunset-stained sky. But most often he was drawn to the saloons. Here, unobserved, he drank in the sailors' stories and water-front gossip while he watched and learned the names of the best-known characters—Scratch Nelson and Young Scratch, "the greatest oyster pirate of them all," French Frank, Spider Heeley and others.

He knew what he would like to do, and that was to spend all of his time, not one day a week, on the water. But what of this matter of earning a living? How could the two be reconciled? Driven by his determination to be quit of the cannery and by the imperiousness of his desire to sail, eyes and ears open to the tales of water-front exploits and the money to be made there, his solution is not surprising. Before he was sixteen Jack had become an oyster pirate.

Conditions peculiar to the oyster industry in the San Francisco Bay had given rise to piracy some years before. Because the early settlers had believed that the small native oysters were inedible, the market had been supplied from Willapa Bay, Washington, via the coastwise schooners. These oysters were widely known as "California," and considered vastly inferior to "Eastern."

As soon as the transcontinental railroad was completed the first experiment was made in transplanting seed and yearling oysters from the Atlantic seaboard. Mud flats were created by leveling stretches of tidelands, and here the spats were bedded to fatten and become marketable. As the beds were exposed at low tide it was possible to protect the young oysters from their traditional enemy, the sting ray, by setting stakes closely together in the shallow water. Eastern oysters were still superior, but the experiment was regarded as successful and the industry grew rapidly.

Monopoly marked its development from the beginning. The extensive flats at the lower end of the bay made the best beds, but the railroads, who had long before grabbed these tidelands, sold them at prices prohibitive to any but large entrepreneurs. The few minor firms were soon absorbed by the larger, and before long one or two companies controlled the entire industry on the coast.

Monopoly set high prices, and high prices brought the oyster pirates. Ownership of the beds they blithely ignored, aware only that there was money to be made in oysters, and that, despite watchmen, the beds could be profitably raided by fearless men in swift boats. They were of many races, French, Italian, Irish, Greek, Scandinavian, British from all parts of the Empire, and they were of all ages. French Frank was in his fifties, Whisky Bob was sixteen, Young Scratch Nelson and Spider Heeley were twenty. Lawbreaking was not the casual thing it was to become years later during the era of Prohibition, and the risks and hazards of life, as well as the money to be gained, attracted men who were daring and unscrupulous.

Their sloops bore large mainsails and were built for speed. Many of the pirates were excellent sailors and handled their boats skillfully. Ashore, they spent their time drinking and boasting of their exploits. Their life was exciting enough. They fought the treacherous currents and tide rips, the winds and storms and fogs of the bay; they fought armed watchmen on the oyster beds and outraged Chinese fishermen, whose catches they took and whose nets they often wantonly destroyed; they fought the Fish Patrol; and they fought among themselves.

When Jack heard that French Frank's sloop, the Razzle Dazzle, was for sale his decision to throw up his cannery job was instantly made. For some weeks he had been gathering information about oyster pirating, and having ascertained how much it was possible to make out of the average raid, he hastened to the only person he knew who could lend him the necessary three hundred dollars—Mammy Jennie. Unhesitatingly she gave him the sum, glad to help him get on in the world.

The sale was quickly arranged aboard the Razzle Dazzle, and Jack, dazed by the sudden turn of affairs, accepted French Frank's invitation to join him and his guests over a jug of wine. Sitting on the deck, glass in hand, listening to the gay talk and laughter around him, he could scarcely believe his good fortune. The transition had been too swift for immediate realization. Yesterday a machine slave, today he was drinking with a notorious bay pirate on a boat that would be his on the morrow. Across from him was a girl whose name was woven into many of the water-front stories. She was known as the Queen of the Oyster Pirates, and for the moment she was French Frank's girl. She made love to Jack that afternoon, and French Frank was furiously jealous, but the boy was not aware of it. The sun glittered on the water, the west wind brought odors of sea and marsh to his nostrils, other sloops and racing yachts passed up and down the estuary; he was almost sixteen and life was very good.

When, uninvited, the Queen joined him on the sloop a few days later he was at first more astonished than anything else. Ownership of the boat, freedom of choice to sail it where and when he wished—he had not thought that one could wish for more. But when the water front began to hum with the gossip and to speculate upon French Frank's revenge he woke to the fact that he, not quite sixteen, had actually won a girl from a man three times his age, with an established reputation for daring and a well-known way with women. Jack's self-confidence grew enormously, but he was careful. He may have stepped into boots as yet too large for him, but no one would know it.

The Queen had found the lad attractive. Never very tall, and in those days quite slender, he nevertheless appeared larger and older than he was. Although she did not stay with him long her choice was probably responsible in part for the title he cherished in later years—the Prince of the Oyster Pirates. She may have been near his own age or she may have been older, but there can be no doubt that she was mature and wise in the ways of the world as he was not, and he learned from her, as he learned from everyone who entered his life.

The long, dark days in the cannery vanished in the sunlit freedom of his new life. Lack of opportunity and the smallness of his skiff had limited his roving on the bay. Now he began to explore it with zest.

Twenty-five miles south of San Francisco the bay comes to

an end in shallow water that gives way finally to sprawling mud flats and slough-threaded marshes. There the pirates took their oysters, but profit and adventure lay in the other direction as well. Eleven miles north and east of the Golden Gate, Points Pablo and Pedro mark the entrance to San Pablo Bay, ten miles long and about as wide, and often whipped to a fury by winds that scarcely roughen its less sheltered neighbor. On its eastern side it narrows suddenly into the Carquinez Straits whose eight miles form one of the most treacherous pieces of water in the world to navigate. Beyond is Suisun Bay, and at its end, sixteen miles from the straits, two great rivers flow together: the San Joaquin, which rises in the Sierra Nevadas and flows north through the valley that bears its name, and the Sacramento, which flows south from its source near perpetually snow-covered Mount Shasta and through divers passages meets the San Joaquin and the tidewaters of the bay.

The geographical features of these linked waterways—seventy miles from the mud flats at the southern tip to the juncture of the two rivers—had favored the development of the fishing industry. In the beginning the Greeks introduced the Mediterranean feluccas with their pointed ends and three-cornered lateen sails, the Chinese their junks. Later sloops came to be commonly used. Shrimps, oysters, shad, sturgeon, salmon and trout were the outstanding catches which filled the markets of the coast and were shipped from San Francisco to many ports. It was a lucrative business for the big fish companies, and some of the leaders of the various colonies of fishermen made good money, but in general the fishermen worked hard for their gains. Taken by and large, they were sober and industrious, knew their boats and their business, and broke the law no oftener than they could help.

The oyster pirates were a different element, cynical of law and careless of life. They raided the privately owned oyster beds and the catches of other fishermen as well, and they never hesitated to use any and all illegal methods of fishing. They knew no loyalties, not even to each other. Their activity began at night, and under the cover of darkness, amidst storms and fogs, private feuds were frequently settled.

Jack's crew on the Razzle Dazzle consisted of one man, who did the cooking and assisted in general, while he sailed the boat and made all decisions. Until he joined Nelson he had no partner in his ventures. Later he used to chuckle over how he had exploited his hired labor even as he himself had been exploited in the cannery. Despite the fact that he and his crew equally risked their lives and liberty he, as captain and owner, kept two thirds of the profits.

The pirates, singly or in groups, anchored at night off the beds and waited for low tide. Then, in flat-bottomed skiffs, they rowed up the shallow channels between the shoals of oysters to the picking grounds. The oysters were put into sacks and carried back to the boats which the turning tide soon floated clear. Sometimes they were undisturbed and could get full loads; at other times the watchmen's guns would force them to leave before they had finished. But dawn found their boats moored to the city wharf in the estuary. The oysters were arranged in three piles according to size. A little later the peddlers arrived and the bargaining began. It was a noisy business, for the pirates were determined to make as much as possible from each trip. A load that sold for two hundred dollars usually took two men three or four dangerous nights to get.

Twenty-five dollars a day and more must have seemed extraordinary pay to the boy who had worked inhumanly long hours at the machine in the cannery for at most fifty dollars a month. The risks involved, the chance shots that might find their mark in the dark, the constant threat of wind and weather, the penitentiary sentence if he were caught red handed by the watchful fish patrol—these factors he would not consider. He had hungered long for excitement, adventure, independence. For such benefices a dollar a day would have seemed good pay, for now he was shaping the pattern of his life as he willed, was no longer a machine tender, catching brief glimpses of life, but a participant.

With the amazing sums he obtained from doing what he wanted to do he repaid his debt to Mammy Jennie and contributed generously to his family's support. What was left over was his to do with as he wished. Later perhaps he would save some of this money in order to realize other dreams for the future, but now it must be spent for more immediate and urgent needs. He was the youngest of all the oyster pirates but he would not be found wanting, for he was fearless, owned as fine a boat as any and could sail it better than most, and in addition had youth, vitality, and what for years he loved to call a cast-iron stomach.

Jack soon made a name for himself in this life. His reputation, refreshed by his autobiographical writings, lingered on the water front long after he had left it. His accounts of these days in *John Barleycorn, Tales of the Fish Patrol,* and scattered stories and essays are vividly descriptive, but it must be borne in mind that the details of *John Barleycorn* were in large measure subservient to its theme, and that the narrative is colored by looking backward across the years. Also, it is wise to remember that one of Jack London's gifts as a storyteller was his ability to absorb and make his own the actual or rumored experiences of others. The lines that accompany an autographed copy of *Tales of the Fish Patrol* are significant: "Find here, sometimes hinted, sometimes told, and sometimes made different, the days of my boyhood when I, too, was on the Fish Patrol."

Always, ashore, there was drinking; Jack, disliking the taste of liquor, distrustful of its effects, but determined to be a man among men, drank with them. Out of the exaggeration and bombast of *John Barleycorn* emerges a clear picture of a boy not unlike the numerous youngsters who grew up during the era of America's Prohibition, when to drink excessively was more or less compulsory for the preservation of social standing. Pride and a sound stomach saved Jack much of the humiliation attendant upon youthful drinking, but they likewise led him into drinking orgies whose far-reaching effects were lamentable.

Step by step, over whiskies and beers, his education progressed. Discovery of the custom of treating and realization of all that it signified in fellowship, and credit at Johnny Heinhold's bar signaled the break with his boyhood. He asked his mother to dispose of his picture card and other collections, now become distastefully juvenile to one whose days and nights were spent with men of the water front. On the bay as ashore he watched his new acquaintances in order to become like them as quickly as possible, and listened avidly whenever any of them began to talk.

He went home rarely. Frank Atherton recalls that Jack came in one day while he was there, changed his clothes and was off again immediately, leaving his friend from the country feeling very youthful and inexperienced. Jack's new activity did not please Flora. It was scarcely "respectable," and she worried constantly about his health and the accidents that might befall him. Both she and John seem to have been impressed, however, with the boy's determination and ability to live as he pleased, and did little to deter him. Long afterward Flora admitted how relieved she was when what she scornfully called Jack's "goose-chasing" days were over.

One afternoon Jack drank long with Young Nelson's father, "Old Scratch," who was then owner and master of a scow-schooner, but who, in his younger days had crossed and recrossed the seas of the world in sailing ships. Although Jack had not yet wrung everything he might from his experiences on the San Francisco Bay he knew that this was not to be the end and aim of his life. There was more, much more, to see and to do. Strange, foreign places beckoned and called as he listened to old Nelson, but confident, secure in the knowledge of his youth and strength, he knew that they would wait for him. The present was good, a dream fulfilled, and tomorrow's dreams would likewise be fulfilled.

Thus several months passed. Then Scotty, his "crew," carelessly set fire one night to the Razzle Dazzle's mainsail. Before Jack could cast about for the ways and means to provide a new sail, the money for which he did not have, occurred a night of drinking and fighting on the sand pits opposite the Oakland water front. At dawn he and Nelson considered their separate situations. Jack and Scotty had quarreled and fought and Scotty had left. Nelson's hand had been wounded, and he, too, was without a crew. Circumstances and inclination made them partners on Nelson's Reindeer. The deserted Razzle Dazzle was later raided by other pirates and set adrift; when Jack finally recovered the hulk he sold it for twenty dollars.

He always recalled this period as one of high adventure. Young Scratch, the "wildest, maddest of them all," sailed magnificently, was utterly without fear, delighted in taking chances, and when ashore drank and brawled lustily. Their operations took them from one end of the bay to the other, and Jack became familiar with the water fronts of scores of towns and villages on the shores.

Then slowly the glamour of the life began to tarnish. At first it had seemed extraordinary; now it was familiar and more and more narrowly circumscribed. He grew bored, disgusted, but the way out was no longer as simple as it had been when he had escaped from the cannery. Nothing in his life with the pirates had matured and crystallized his ambitions, and the original problem —to earn a living—remained unsolved, because doing this either at a machine in a factory or as an oyster pirate on the bay had become equally distasteful. Unable to make a decision, he drifted aimlessly with the days.

Nelson grew homesick for the Oakland water front and decided to return. The estuary held nothing for Jack that he did not already know, and although he no longer owned a boat he decided to remain in the upper bays. He was completely at loose ends. With acquaintances at Benicia he sometimes went salmon fishing, sometimes merely loafed and drank. There was still no incentive to leave the bay for wider fields, and the matter of a livelihood was acute. When he was offered an opportunity to become a deputy fish patrolman, which would not only solve his economic problem but also permit him to spend much of his time on the water, he promptly accepted. No moral revulsion against the pirate life prompted his decision, nor any desire to array himself with the forces of law and order. He was sixteen, and in many ways still more boy than man. To earn a living and to maintain his independence of time clocks and long hours at a machine, to know still more of the life on the San Francisco Bay, to satisfy his delight in sailing—these were the factors involved.

The fish patrol had begun functioning in 1883 when a marked decrease in salmon and other fish forced the state authorities to realize that the fishing industry was facing a serious situation if steps to control it were not immediately taken. Various laws were drawn up, specifying legal types of nets, condemning the small-meshed shad nets, the so-called "Chinese" sturgeon lines and bag nets for catching shrimp, regulating salmon fishing during the open season, and the fish patrol was created to enforce them.

Patrolmen were appointed by the board and received a salary, but the deputies who served under them were not appointed and their earnings depended upon a percentage of the fines paid by the violators in whose apprehension they had assisted, and on rewards offered by private persons and firms for the conviction of certain outstanding offenders. While the service maintained a patrol boat, privately owned sloops and yachts were frequently borrowed, rented or commandeered.

Jack's stories and even the humdrum reports of the Fish Commission are colored by the strong anti-Chinese feeling then prevalent in California. The Commission reported in 1886 that between fifteen hundred and two thousand Chinese were active on and around the bay in catching and preparing fish for the market, not including those directly engaged in San Francisco itself. Shrimp and sturgeon seem to have been their favorite catches. They congregated in villages, some on the western side of the lower end of the bay where they fastened their shrimp nets to stakes along the tidewater and as far out as the main channel, and others at Points Pedro and Pablo. Whether they had invented the illegal sturgeon line and shrimp net cannot be proved, but they were given full credit for these ingenious devices and were watched more closely by patrolmen and informers than the fishermen of other races. Throughout Jack's stories of these days they are the blackest of all the offenders.

For a short time Jack found this life satisfying enough. It had its share of excitement. The fishermen, ignorant and resentful of the fish laws, did their best to outwit the patrolmen; the offenders had to be caught in the act with the fish and the illegal hooks and nets, which was not always easy; and throughout his life defying the elements in a small sailing boat was to be ever a source of pleasure. He was earning a living doing what he liked; he was still his own master. Nevertheless, a deep, inner dissatisfaction was growing.

He was drinking more heavily when ashore, and his drunken decision to commit suicide one night when he stumbled into deep water is significant of the extent of his disorientation. He was drunk, but he was young and healthy and strong, his curiosity about the world still fresh and ungratified, and he could look back on his boyish exploits and achievements with nothing but pride. Nevertheless, swimming easily close to shore, he determined to go out with the tide. The events of the last years, his horror of factory work, his abrupt acquaintance with the brutally realistic water front, and the swift disillusionment of whatever ideals he had absorbed from his school years and library reading—all this was unassimilated. He knew neither what to do nor what he wanted to do, and weariness, born of alcohol, bewilderment and frustration, turned his face toward death. When it was almost too late cold water and sobriety made him change his mind, and he fought desperately for life until he was rescued by a chance fisherman.

The fish patrol could not hold him. He drifted back to Oakland where he worked at odd jobs on the water front and loafed between times in saloons. One day, having nothing else to do and needing the ten dollars the trip would bring, he and a water-front comrade went up to Port Costa on Suisun Bay to bring a stolen boat back to its owner. Lacking both an authorization from the owner and the promised twenty-five-dollar reward, they made off with the boat under the very nose of the constable who had recovered it. Knowledge that they would certainly be apprehended forced them to wait until nightfall before starting through the straits for Oakland.

It was flood tide on a day of mellow sunshine, and the west wind was blowing strong and true. To sail up the Sacramento River was an immediate decision. At Sacramento they fell in with a number of boys who were swimming in the river. Jack listened to them in amazement. They were "road kids," and as they talked, a new world, larger than that of the bay and the pirates and the fish patrol, opened up to him. His companion went back to Oakland, but Jack stayed with his new acquaintances to get his first taste of the road.

This group of young hobos had made their headquarters in Sacramento and was composed of boys who were victims of poverty-stricken and disorganized homes. In order to survive they ran in gangs and combined begging with petty thievery. During the several weeks Jack spent with them he considerably enlarged his vocabulary and knowledge of the world, exchanged his title of Prince of the Oyster Pirates for the moniker, Sailor Kid, and earned his right to be a full-fledged road kid by "going over the hill"—beating his way over the Sierras into Nevada and back. Much else he learned that was to be useful to him later when he returned to the road, but although he liked the life he soon wandered back again to Oakland and the water front.

He hunted up Nelson, worked as little as possible, and ran with the West Oakland hoodlum gangs. The ranch boy who had hungered for playmates, the friendless bookworm in the school-yard, now had companionship in abundance, and yet never before had he felt so alone. He was sociable enough, had no quarrels with any of the crowd, performed his share and more in its activities, but at no time did he feel himself even an integral part of things, let alone close to the center.

The years of solitude had been too many for him to shake off their effects now. He who had never learned how to play with children, who had made himself the hero of countless dream adventures, was unable to become a part of the rank and file of any group. His failure to be one with the others of the West Oakland gang hurt him, made him cautious in future relationships, and more prone than ever to fall back on himself. Years later when his retreat to the country, and its rationalization, was complete he dismissed his gang experiences a little contemptuously, asserting that they had first taught him to hate the city, for they had clearly shown him "the futility of life in such a herd."

In the midst of them, however, he was apparently completely demoralized, drunk much of the time, careless of the present and indifferent to the future. But the sense that something vital was lacking in his life was beginning to be stronger than his cynicism. But for this he might have remained a bum or, what was more likely, he might well have lost his life in some casual water-front brawl. His experiences had hardened him physically and mentally, developed his assurance and self-reliance. Bewilderment and frustration had culminated in his attempt at suicide, and that past, all the forces that made toward life, his youth and strength, his thirst for adventure and knowledge, his stubborn determination to live fully and deeply, reasserted themselves.

Through the aimless days and nights these forces were working in him, forcing him to grope slowly toward a decision. After a terrific orgy of drinking following a political torchlight procession when he came very close to death from alcohol and the drunken fighting in which he was willy-nilly involved, he made up his mind: he would cut loose and leave it all behind.

It was toward the end of the year. The fact that the sealing fleet was wintering in the bay determined his choice. In one of the water-front saloons he met Pete Holt, a harpooner, and after they had talked a while it was arranged that he would go with Pete as his boat puller, sailing on whichever ship Pete chose. A few days after his seventeenth birthday, on January 20, 1893, he signed the articles of the Sophia Sutherland and he was aboard her with Pete when she sailed through the Golden Gate for the sealing grounds off the coast of Japan.

The seven-months' voyage—the only time he ever sailed before the mast—gave him a badly needed breathing spell and permitted him to gain perspective. He remembered the ship as the Sophie Sutherland, but she appears twice on the lists of merchant ships of the United States for 1893 as the Sophia Sutherland, a three-masted schooner of one hundred and fifty-odd tons, built four years before in Tacoma.

Save that he was consciously careful, still sensitive from his experiences with the West Oakland hoodlums, in adapting himself to his new associates, and that he read the books he had brought with him in his sea bag, his conduct did not differ from that of his shipmates, who performed their duties aboard ship and got drunk in port. Nevertheless he was different. He was not going to continue to be a sailor, for one thing. When he set out he knew that with this voyage he was breaking definitely with the life he had led for the past two years. Long before he returned he had decided on his next move: to get a job ashore immediately and go back to reading and studying.

Some of the other sailors made plans, too. The difference between them and Jack was that he carried his out while they, forgetting their good intentions, drank up their payday at the end of the voyage, and when it was gone shipped out again. From this time on Jack would make plans, and insofar as it was possible he would carry them out, setting his conscious will against the chaos of life as he found it, and reducing what he could of it that was about him to order. Failure would discourage but not stop him; he would merely make new and better plans.

In the fo'c'sle he had opportunity to observe for the first time the results in himself of his years of reading outside of school and was sharply aware that he possessed, in contrast with the others, a large fund of information and a mind able and trained to think. Hand in hand with this, of course, was the pleased realization that he, again the youngest of them all, could work and fight and drink as well as any and better than some. So frequently in his writings recurs his chant of pride in brute strength in general and his own in particular, that one can scarcely fail to realize that this achievement must have been difficult and dearly bought.

With an eye to higher wages, and because of his confidence in his mastery of small-boat sailing, he had signed on as an able-bodied seaman. A certificate of such rating, granted to men at least nineteen years old only after proof by affidavit and examination of at least three years' service on deck, was not yet indispensable. Recommendations from Pete Holt and others of the crew whom Jack had met were sufficient for the sailing master. Aside from learning the names of a few ropes and how to steer by a compass, Jack found his knowledge ample for the requirements of a deep-sea vessel. His adjustments to his shipmates required more skill, but in this, too, he was successful, refusing, with ready fists to back up his determination, to become a door mat for the older men, performing his work well and cheerfully, and soon being accepted as one of them.

For fifty-one days they saw no land, except the island of Hawaii from the distance, until they reached the Bonin Islands southeast of Japan, now known by their Japanese name of Ogasawara Jima. Here the American and Canadian sealers put in for water and repairs before sailing north for the hundred days of hunting along the coast of Japan and Siberia to the Bering Sea. It was Jack's first foreign land, and tropical at that. As they dropped anchor in the small land-locked harbor every detail was just as he had expected it to be from the public-library books he had read. Primitive native canoes and Japanese sampans surrounded their vessel. Behind the village the land rose steeply, smothered with vegetation, to where jagged peaks thrust nakedly against the sky.

The sailors had told him much about the islands. They were volcanic, earthquakes were frequent, and small islands often rose suddenly out of the ocean only to disappear in a later cataclysm. The fishing was excellent, they had heard, and legend had it that beyond the village they would find great trees on the mountainsides, and palms and ferns and wild pineapples and strange tropical flowers in profusion.

Victor, a Swedish sailor, Axel, a Norwegian, and Jack talked things over and carefully mapped out their activities during the ten days the ship would be in port. They would explore the island (from the deck they could clearly discern the very path they would take), they would climb the mountains, they would go fishing. But when they reached shore they found that a rioting crowd of several hundred drunken sailors from the sealing fleet had taken over the village and were openly defying the efforts of the helpless Japanese constabulary to restore order. Axel, Victor and Jack, none of whom had tasted liquor for fifty-one days, viewed the uproar sympathetically but with no desire to join in it. They had other plans. But first, before they set out, why not have one drink?

That ended it. Before dark they had been engulfed by the mob and were drinking and shouting and fighting as enthusiastically as the rest. When they sailed out of the harbor ten days later they had not seen more of the island than the village. Purple passages, he would call such incidents when he wrote of them a few years before his death, bitter against his ancient enemy, John Barley-corn, but remembering these days and nights of his youth with mingled pride and self-pity. Re-creating them, clothing their shoddiness with hot and glowing words, he would fling them like a challenge to the bleak and empty thing his life was becoming. But that would be later; now he went his headlong way, under-standing little but learning much.

For three months they hunted seals in the gray, fog-smothered northern waters, each day very like its fellow, a methodical routine of slaughter and skinning and salting of hides. Then with a big catch they turned south for Yokohama. Sight-seeing plans were laid again, and again cheerfully abandoned as soon as they stepped ashore. The fortnight spent in the Japanese port was not a purple passage; his memories of it were mellow. The season's work done, shipmates and other sailors of the sealing fleets gathered in the water-front saloons, exchanging yarns, recalling shared dangers and triumphs, and drinking to all of them and to each other.

One exploit stood out in Jack's memory. As he told it a few years later to a chance acquaintance on the road, he had incurred the wrath of the port police for some infraction of Japanese rules and regulations. Pursued by them, he ducked, shoes and all, into a sacred temple or two and burst unceremoniously through the paper walls of several teahouses. Finally, chased to the water's edge, he jumped in and swam to the Sophia Sutherland a mile or so away. He did not know that the policemen had given him up as drowned, and was surprised by their awe-struck faces when they met him on the street the following day. The story was all over the water front by nightfall, and for a few days, until a fresh exploit took its place, Jack was something of a hero.

Noting the effects of liquor on others as well as himself, he was slowly beginning to learn about drinking. He always maintained that he drank first for companionship and then for the tingle, the excitement and heightened awareness. Discovering, however, that there was a limit to all these which, once passed, reduced con-scious pleasure to nothing, he strove to gauge and keep within it. Saloon drinking and debauches on bay pirate boats were all he knew. In Yokohama he extended this knowledge.

One afternoon he and the young son of the owner, himself aboard the Sophia, paid calls on some of the other ships in the harbor. Greeted courteously by one mate, they were offered a drink. A bottle of scotch, a bottle of water and tall glasses stood on a table. "Say when," invited the mate, pouring whisky into a glass for Jack. But Jack, never having heard the expression before, said nothing. "Say when," repeated the mate, looking at him curiously. It was quite a lot of liquor, Jack thought uneasily, but at the third "say when" he understood and gasped, "When!"

He returned to California in September, bronzed and stronger and healthier than ever before. This first taste of travel had made him eager for more, but not immediately. His vagabond years were over now, he was sure. He was going to settle down and make good. A job, books and study—that was the program.

CHAPTER

5

FOR A LONG TIME after the panic of 1893 many remembered the two decades that had intervened between the international depression of the 'seventies and the 'nineties as a sort of Golden Age and, forgetting the intermittent hard times, regarded the panic as a cruel accident that had brought it to an untimely end. Everyone had had jobs, great fortunes were made, and opportunity beckoned at every hand. Afterwards, although prosperity came and went as always, it seemed to those who mourned the past that American life had sadly changed. Mistaking symptoms for causes, and tilting at windmills, these people crossed over into the twentieth century without understanding what had taken place in their country and why there could be no return to the "good old times."

With the close of the Civil War the stage had been set in America not only for the 1893 panic but for its successors as well. Although competition grew ever fiercer and more brutal modern capitalism had set its feet firmly on the road it was to travel, and what has been called the "era of cannibalistic absorption" had begun. The signs were there for those who could read them. Inflation, the establishment of trusts and combinations, and the intensification of colonial expansion by the chief European countries—these especially distinguished the last five years as they moved toward catastrophe.

Results of genuine growth of industry and factors of the wildest speculation were combined in the wave of specious prosperity which preceded the crash. The land booms in Australia and other

54

countries which had recently been opened up were typical of the trend of speculation. By 1887 Canada, Australia, South Africa and other British colonies, as well as many South American countries, were building railroads, and Great Britain was filling their orders for capital goods. The need for steel products was enormous, but woolen goods and innumerable other commodities were also in great demand. Industry hummed and British workers entered an unexampled period of employment.

With typical aggressiveness British capital sought and found ever newer markets, reinvesting heavily in industrial enterprises all over the world and accepting foreign securities in payment for goods. Meantime competition with Great Britain by Germany and other European nations entered into the struggle for the trade of British and neutral markets.

The outstanding effect upon America of this international activity was the opening up of the West. Two events had cleared the way for this: England's repeal of her corn laws in 1846 and its conversion into an industrial nation, and the passage of the Homestead Act in the United States in 1862, which opened the public lands for settlement. To supply her insatiable demands for foodstuffs once her imperial march was under way, England had turned to the United States. At the same time, however, that young nation had begun to develop its own potentialities, and to this end extraordinary expenditures abroad were necessary. America's solution to her problem was the phenomenal and determined expansion of her agriculture.

Romantic tradition to the contrary, the settlement of the West was not voluntary, but dictated inexorably by the needs and ambitions of European and American capitalism. Railroads were thrust into the new lands, fences were built and virgin soil was plowed because American agriculture had not only to feed the growing millions of workers in Western European cities, but to provide her own bankers and industrialists with commodities which would help to pay the interest on foreign loans and buy what was needful to transform the country into a capitalistic one. Because of this the settlement of the West, though rapid, had little vitality of its own. Dependent on distant markets and obedient to its role in the national economy of a debtor nation, it lacked elements which would have made for stability and independent growth.

Many factors, closely interrelated, assisted in the Western migration. The railroads had penetrated the thinly populated regions of the South, Southwest and Northwest, and millions of acres of land in these sections had been thrown open on generous terms by both the government and the railroads. As early as the 'seventies the failure of wheat crops all over the world had sent many European peasants and American farmers in search of new lands. Now men who were sick of military service in the numerous European wars of the time, and others, equally sick of the endless poverty from which they could not escape, listened to the glowing propaganda of the transatlantic steamship companies, reread letters from friends and relatives who had gone before, packed their belongings and left the old world for the peace and prosperity of the American West.

For a little while it appeared that their dreams would be realized. The soil produced good crops, and prices for agricultural products were high. In addition gold was discovered in the Black Hills of Dakota and the cattle boom began on the great plains.

Meantime American manufacturing and commerce were making tremendous strides. The United States was building more and more railroads, and the demand for commodities for this purpose stimulated all lines of production. Increased employment resulted in further expansion of credit as well as larger importations of consumption goods. And, inevitably, speculation entered the scene, showing its head in the activities of promoters, stockbrokers and finance capitalists. With rapid industrial development feverishly demanding tremendous amounts of capital, the flotation of unmeritedly large volumes of securities and the oversubscription of stocks and bonds was common, and in the shape of joint-stock corporations, finance capital began to establish its dominance over industry.

England had become America's largest creditor. Between 1887 and 1890 over a hundred million dollars of the stocks and bonds of American railways were taken in the London market. More than half a billion dollars was floated in the United States itself in gas, electric light, street railways and Western land developments, and because of the adverse trade balance, many of these bonds went abroad as payment to foreign capital.

During the last few years before the crash it was very easy to float issues. Financial investments of every description, from Mexican railways and mines to American breweries, were on the market. South America, South Africa and other newly opened up countries were similarly involved in this period of inflation, while in Europe every capitalistically developed nation was in competition with the others for the privilege of issuing loans and taking over financial ventures which they would ordinarily have eschewed.

And then the false and artificially created prosperity began to topple. Loans fell off because the security had been covered and no margin remained. Argentina and similar countries had been permitted to increase their indebtedness out of all proportion to their industrial development. While the loans had been used to a great extent for this purpose, a substantial part of them had been pure swindle. With the curtailment of loans, trade fell off and could not be revived until a natural exchange of products took place between the debtor and creditor nations.

The prestige of the various financial houses had facilitated the milking of the investors. A loan floated in London by Baring Brothers and Murrietos had been subscribed to eleven times over. When Barings crashed consternation spread throughout the financial world. The failure of this gigantic British combine was due in large measure to its speculative investments in Argentina. But heavy importation of British capital had also brought about the overexpansion of American railroads, and when the railroads could no longer meet their carrying charges the bubble burst in the United States.

The retroactive forces involved in the false prosperity and the resulting depression, which linked the American panic of 1893 with the world depression, are very clear.

The South American crisis brought stagnation in the export trade. Australian loans based on English produce were cut off. The McKinley tariff in the United States destroyed the rough woolen trade of Bradford and then proceeded to act as a boomerang in America. Because Central and South American countries were no longer able to get credit in London, they were forced to lower their purchases in Great Britain. Various restrictive measures, tariffs and the like, by foreign governments competing with British imperialism caused a sharp decline in its foreign trade and further aggravated the depression in the United Kingdom. The effects were soon felt in America.

The temporary prosperity of the American farmers had already been threatened by the opening of new grasslands to cereals and meatstuffs in Canada, Australia, India and Russia. Restrictions applied against American meat, the increase of grain importations from Argentina and from India by way of the Suez Canal—these had exerted a strong influence on the world market, while good crops in Western Europe had reduced the price of cereals at Liverpool and necessitated a decrease in the exports of American breadstuffs.

The United States had been buying more than it could pay for, and its creditors had been accepting American securities in payment. Now British and other European interests, forced to withdraw part of the gold which they had invested in this country's enterprises, demanded immediate settlement of these debts in the only metal used in international trade.

High protective tariffs reduced government revenue, and the crisis was further prolonged by the government's policy of ordering the treasury to purchase silver. The bullion value of the dollar fell from eighty-one cents in 1890 to sixty cents in 1893. As in all depressions gold disappeared. In June 1894 the amount of it in the United States had dwindled to sixty-five million dollars. As the gold reserve decreased alarm grew, and there was a rush from every quarter for the redemption of treasury notes in gold.

Everywhere banks closed their doors, and this was especially true of the West and the South. The Erie, Union Pacific and Northern Pacific were among the hundred and fifty-six railroads that went into receivership. Between April first and October first, 1893, more than eight thousand commercial firms failed with liabilities of about two hundred and eighty-five million dollars, and depression gripped the nation.

Unemployment, augmented by European immigration, the disemployment of American workers as overproduction resulted from the growing use of machinery, and the tremendous number of laborers thrown upon the market by the cessation of railroad construction, was acute in the cities and in the agricultural areas as well. More than eleven thousand mortgages were foreclosed between 1889 and 1893 in Kansas alone, and in 1894 wheat was selling for forty-nine cents a bushel.

And while the country plunged ever deeper into the abyss, J. P. Morgan and another financial house reaped excessive profits from a loan of sixty-five million dollars of gold for government bonds. Thus finance capital made the best of the panic.

As the Western settlers stabilized their social status a certain ideology had begun to develop as a result of the peculiar conditions of their life in which uncertainty, hazards and struggle played prominent roles. Lacking the orderliness and conservatism ordinarily associated with group life, a strong sense of individualism and impatience of restraint became typical of these people. Solitude had produced more than independence and self-reliance. While nature was often unkind it was never implacable; but because each victory was singlehanded, the farmer came to believe that nothing was impossible and that a solution could be found to every problem. This belief was fertile soil for the growth of credulity, superstition and faith in panaceas. In one thing only was faith lacking, and that was in government. The West, young, isolated and without traditional ruts, did not regard the civil codes with the reverence bestowed upon them by the inhabitants of the more settled regions of the country.

The average farmer's ambition was to be a respectable and secure member of the middle class, to receive good prices for his crops, and with this money improve his farm so that he could get better prices for his crops and become an even more respectable and secure member of the middle class. To this end, as has been seen, he had joined various organizations of his fellows to fight against the railroads in particular and monoply in general, and for cheap money, free silver, government ownership of railroads and telegraphs, and a moratorium on mortgages, the initiative and the referendum, the direct election of United States senators, and similar reforms, certain that these would ensure and make permanent the return of prosperity.

With American agriculture's loss of a large share of the world market already keenly felt before the onset of the panic of 1893, the farmers' smoldering discontent blazed up. Armed with the latest versions of the old panaceas, the farmers' alliances and the Greenback and Populist movements reawoke to more militant activity than ever before.

As conditions grew worse the revolt spread widely. Hamlin Garland wrote: "As ten-cent corn and ten per cent interest were troubling Kansas, so six-cent cotton was inflaming Georgia." The Homestead strike fanned the hatred of big capital, and Mrs Mary Ellen Lease of Kansas told the farmers that "it was time to quit raising corn and begin raising hell!"

The People's party had been formed in May 1891, when over fourteen hundred representatives of reform groups met in Cincinnati, Ohio. A huge convention in Omaha on July 2, 1892, completed preparations for the entrance of farmers into the presidential election. Two days later the Populist party came into existence, demanding as solutions of the crisis the cessation of mortgage foreclosures, the free coinage of silver and more paper money. In November the Populists polled a million votes for General Weaver—three times the plurality of Cleveland over Harrison—and won twenty-two electoral votes. This was the first time since the birth of the Republican party that any minor party had won representation in the electoral college.

For a brief time this success of middle-class effort at political action, supported by broad strata of the working class, strengthened the idea of the efficacy of political reform through legislative means, but the coastal regions of the West were to give this movement a sharper edge.

Behind the startling news that the Commonweal of Christ— General Coxey's Army of the Unemployed—was to march from Massillon, Ohio, on Easter Sunday, 1894, to hold a monster demonstration on the steps of the national capitol at noon on May Day, were the mass movements of the unemployed in California since the 'seventies, and Carl Browne, friend and collaborator of Dennis Kearney during the great days of the Workingmen's party of California.

Until he joined Kearney's movement, Browne had been living quietly in Berkeley, across the bay from San Francisco, and for some years had been earning his living painting and exhibiting "panoramas." Once he had smelled the smoke of battle, however, his brushes and oils became secondary to his interest in journalism and politics. In 1880 he was using his paper, the *Daily Graphic*, to advocate the presidency of General Weaver. The Greenback movement held him for a few years, but by 1886 he was campaigning for the National Labor party, financing himself by a brand-new panorama of the Battle of Gettysburg. Shortly after this, he started the *Cactus*, a weekly cartoon paper which militantly attacked everything of which he disapproved, and which he published on and off for many years.

The death of his wife led him, he claimed, to the discovery of the new theosophical principle which he called "soul absorption." It was this extraordinary doctrine which he was to sell to Jacob

Coxey, the stone-quarry proprietor of Massillon, and which was soon to bear fruit in the Commonweal of Christ.

The World's Fair had drawn Browne to Chicago, where he occupied himself as a spieler for a fakir selling Kickapoo Indian Blood Remedy and agitating among the radical Populist groups to march on Washington. When he met Coxey at one of the silver conventions he promptly interested him in his idea, and when Coxey invited him to come to Massillon he accepted, knowing that Coxey was in a position to finance the movement.

"Humble Carl," as he called himself, had learned much during the years he had spent with Kearney. Although the "petition on boots" was a phrase used even in the Russian Populist movement it has been credited to Coxey. As a matter of fact it was Browne's, as was the "Commonweal of Christ" and its theosophy, the banners, the horses for the leaders of the army, and charts and other paraphernalia with which he traveled around the country in a wagon, spreading the message of Coxey's reforms. Astride a white horse, wearing corduroy trousers thrust in high-top boots, buckskin jacket, fur overcoat and huge sombrero, he commanded every eye; when he spoke his vivid language and quick wit gripped all who heard him.

Despite Browne's apparent charlatanry, his ability to impress even Samuel Gompers, and to persuade the national convention of the American Federation of Labor to endorse Coxey's plan to end unemployment by having Congress pass his "good-roads" bills, makes it impossible to dismiss him with any broad characterization. Neither his sincerity nor lack of sincerity enter into the question. He was effective.

His theosophy, while it was the object of much ridicule and satire, contained an element which dramatized the movement and gave it color. He maintained that Christ had been reincarnated through many human beings. Coxey was the cerebrum of Christ, while he, more modestly, was the cerebellum. And obviously by the time the army, through which the reincarnation of the rest of Christ was distributed, gathered in Washington it would contain such a large part of the son of God that all hell, let alone the subservient tools of Wall Street, could not stand before it! That Coxey accepted this, indicates Browne's influence over the "general."

His sense of advertising was superb. The army's banner was Browne's idea. Beneath a picture of Christ ran the inscription:

"Peace on earth, good will to men. He hath risen, but death to interest on bonds." This not only proved effective for enlistment purposes, but it provoked the Salvation Army into a controversy which resulted in Coxey's army being talked about over the length and breadth of the land. The fact that of all the armies of this period Coxey's is the best remembered is due probably to Carl Browne. It was certainly smaller than any of the Western industrial armies; a mere one hundred left Massillon on the scheduled date, with as many newspapermen as "soldiers" making the trek, and during the journey to Washington this number never exceeded three hundred.

Of the seventeen or more armies originating in various sections of the United States, the most efficient and militant, and those which contained the greatest number of bona fide workers were formed on the Pacific coast. These were never integral parts of Coxey's army. Long before its formation California workers had become accustomed to grouping together when unemployed, and Kearney had taught them to present their grievances physically. The proposed march of the Commonweal of Christ acted merely as the starting gun for them to organize for the long journey across the continent.

The panic, which had started earlier in Great Britain and other European countries, had become evident in New York in the spring of '93, and by June was being felt in California. Industry and agriculture came to a standstill. Two and a half million dollars in gold which had been sent from the East arrived too late to prevent banks from crashing. Six national and twenty-one state banks closed their doors. Thirty-five thousand men were out of work in San Francisco alone, and this number was swelled by the addition of the unemployed who had been driven out of the city limits of Sacramento and who had drifted helplessly to San Francisco and the East Bay. The situation was desperate. Every means of alleviation was resorted to, from soup kitchens to public wood-yards and street-sweeping.

In the midst of this the Western armies began to organize. The largest of these, and the one which was considered in many respects the most interesting, started from Oakland and was led by General Charles T. Kelly, self styled, as were all these "generals." This army was warmly supported not only by the labor movement, but by the middle class as well, because of the widespread and bitter hatred of the Southern Pacific. This same support was given to the American Railway Union in its strike a few months later against the Pullman Palace Car Company. Militancy and high spirits characterized the journey. For many it was a holiday such as they had never known before. Not until nearly the end did problems of food and transportation fail of solution. The resistance of the railroads and other obstacles were overcome by the pertinacity of the army and the enthusiastic support of the farmers and the townsfolk along the way. They were halfway across the United States and as strong as ever when in Des Moines Kelly heard that Coxey had been arrested in Washington. He always maintained that had the Western armies, better organized and with more support from the labor movement, arrived in Washington first, they could have changed the situation.

Although they had no definitely formulated program the armies attracted many men merely because they offered an escape from morbid conditions of poverty and unemployment. The Western armies in particular maintained discipline in their ranks, tried to exclude the professional hobo, and showed ingenious organizational ability. The threat of having from one to four hundred thousand unemployed in Washington demanding relief never materialized. No more than a thousand congregated there at one time. But the threat at least gave expression to a protest against the capitalistic character of the government.

Unsuccessful though they were, these marches symbolized an episode in American politics much greater than themselves. Offshoots of the agrarian rebellion which had dominated populism, they mirrored the grievances of the industrial workers as well. This period has been described as one of the most acute in the history of the labor movement. Certainly its events caused the most extensive use of troops since the Civil War. Capital was definitely on the offensive, and the trade-union movement received serious setbacks. The use of the injunction became regular, and Eugene Debs and other strike leaders found themselves jailed as a result of this effective means at the employers' disposal. In many states the object lessons the marchers were given in the identity of powerful railroad interests and state governments resulted in disillusionment with so-called impartial government.

Members of the Western industrial armies, which included young, unskilled workers as well as skilled craftsmen, could not fail to be affected by the nation-wide strikes of industrial workers and the activities of the Populists against the offensives of capital. Farmers' Alliances, the Grange, the Populist parties, trade-union locals, chapters of the Knights of Labor—all helped the armies in their marches. And social consciousness awoke in many of these workers as they came to realize that their personal predicaments were not unique but the results of conditions which affected their entire class.

CHAPTER

6

IN THE LIVELY PATTERN of Jack London's life the fall and winter of 1893 make a design that differs entirely from the rest and does not reappear. Circumstances as well as his own determination had made a clean break with the past. Most of his former companions on the water front were gone. Among several who were dead was Young Scratch, riddled by bullets in a drunken battle with the police; others were in prison or in flight from the law. Resolutely he turned his face toward the untried future.

John and Flora seemed older and more remote from him than ever, but they were undoubtedly glad to have him back. Money was scarce, John was often ill, and his pension was none too large. Jack was grown now and seemed willing to settle down at last. Flora was almost cheerful when, shortly after he returned, he went to work.

He found a job in the jute mills—ten hours a day at ten cents an hour. Surprised to discover that his labor was worth no more than it had been nearly three years before in the cannery, he consoled himself with a promised raise in the near future to a dollar and a quarter a day. The public library saw him again, and the Y. M. C. A., whither he was drawn before long in search of companionship. Here he found good, serious-minded boys who worked hard and found ample enjoyment in the physical exercise and other recreation offered by the "Y." Very earnestly he strove to adapt himself to them but failed. From both life and books he had learned infinitely more than most of them would ever know. In their company he was bored and even lonelier than before.

It was not a happy period he was going through. Neither direction nor purpose was clear. Much that he did was tentative, experimental. If it worked, well and good; if not, he would try something else. As always, he poured all of himself into every undertaking, undiscouraged by failure, sure that sooner or later he would find what he was seeking. Thus he regarded the winning of a writing contest conducted in November by the San Francisco *Morning Call*. When it worked he made up his mind to become a writer; when a few weeks later it failed to work he lost interest.

For some time the *Call* had been conducting amateur writing contests for young people. Flora noticed the "one week more" announcement of one which offered larger prizes than usual, and drew Jack's attention to it when he came home from work. Descriptive writing was wanted, word pictures. Jack, tired after the long day in the jute mill, listened without enthusiasm, but Flora was persistent. For several days the local papers had been carrying colorful stories of the wreck of the steamer City of New York, which had gone on the rocks just inside Point Bonita in a blinding fog. Everyone was talking about the wreck, argued Flora, why couldn't he write about something he had seen while on the Sophia Sutherland? She had captured his attention. He remembered the very thing!

Two thousand words was the limit set by the newspaper. Jack wrote more than four thousand in two sittings, spent a third evening pruning it down to size, made a clean copy, and Flora, hovering in the background, offered to take charge of it from then on. She took it across the bay herself and gave it to the editor on the last day of the contest.

Five judges unanimously awarded the twenty-five-dollar first prize to "Story of a Typhoon off the Coast of Japan, by John London aged 17." The second and third prizes were won by girls, students at Stanford and the University of California. One fault the judges found with Jack's manuscript: it had been written entirely in the present tense. Very conscientiously they bluepenciled the vivid description of the storm, the race of the small boats back to the schooner, the death of the bricklayer-sailor, slowing its tempo, robbing it of much vitality with "wases" and "weres" and "had beens."

Jack's production of this prize-winning narrative at this time is a matter of no little astonishment. It is well, even skillfully written, with a sureness that seems to betoken practice and experience. Did Flora know that Jack was interested in writing, had she seen previous attempts, when she suggested that he try for the contest? Or, as many who feel the pinch of poverty, did she think principally of the prize, with nothing to lose by a little effort, and twenty-five, fifteen or ten dollars to gain? There is no telling. One searches in vain either for earlier writings or intimations that an impulse to express himself in this way had been manifested before. He had, of course, written compositions in school, but the last of these had been done over three years before, and in the interval of oyster pirating, hoboing, drinking and sailing, it is doubtful if there was opportunity or inclination for writing.

Flora's words to the contest editor as she placed the manuscript in his hands furnish the sole clue: "Jack has often wished he could write about what he has seen." He had often wished, had wished enough to speak his wish aloud in a place where his thoughts were seldom uttered! It appears safe to assume, knowing that in a few years he would be writing regularly and purposefully, that the desire to write had been present and acknowledged for some time. What then was his equipment at seventeen?

He had seen and done a great deal; he had something to say. Further, Frank Atherton and others who knew him at this time have frequently mentioned his excellence as a storyteller. Even as a youngster, they recall, he could vividly describe events he had witnessed or shared. As the years passed this gift for narrative grew richer. But when he told a story, either something which had happened or an invented tale, his language was always very simple, and his dramatic powers and imagination relied for expression on his voice and mobile features, and his rare, wide gestures. He did not write this way. The writing vocabulary was quite different, larger, richer, more supple, and conveyed very efficiently what the lifted eyebrow and twisting mouth and quick movement of the hands had added to his spoken words.

Acutely perceptive, naturally articulate, he must have sought words hungrily long before he consciously recognized his need. When he sat down that night after work to describe the storm which he had witnessed and been part of but a few months before, his years of incessant reading, of storing away words in his memory, bore fruit. It was not easy. He worked for long hours, transmuting sensory impressions into words that would tell as precisely as possible what he had seen and heard and felt, but he worked with a certain confidence for he was using words that were part of his reading vocabulary to describe something which in turn was to be read.

Ever practical, his elation at having won was soon dominated by the wish to repeat the performance, not as an amateur contestant this time, but professionally. He had heard that newspapers bought special articles. Several more evenings went into the laborious composition of a second piece. But the editor who had been pleased to award him the first prize in the contest refused this contribution so quickly and so curtly that Jack's enthusiasm collapsed on the instant, and he abandoned further attempts for the time being.

At this juncture he met Louis Shattuck, who lived near by and worked in a blacksmith's shop. Louis had neither roamed the world nor spent time in the public library, but a friendship was quickly formed between them, for with Louis' advent impulses long struggling for expression in Jack were released. Louis was in love, not with any particular girl, but with all girls. Self-taught, he had refined his pursuit to what Jack considered the height of artistry, and which he desired to emulate.

The Queen of the Oyster Pirates and other girls he had known during his bay adventures, and exotic maidens in Oriental ports— these had meant the physical expression of sex. Its emotional expression he had entirely missed. Now, listening to Louis, he found himself likewise in love with love, prey to a baffling new sensation as painful as it was pleasant. His moon-calf days were brief, and he emerged from them little wiser than he had been before. He was to study and master much in his life, but knowledge and understanding of women would always elude him.

The boy, who at fifteen had been the talk of the water front because he had stolen French Frank's girl, at eighteen was overcome with shyness at the mere thought of conversing with any of the young girls who passed him on the street or worked near him at the jute mill. Poverty increased his lack of confidence. When Louis and he had paid for room and board at home and taken care of clothing needs and cigarettes each had less than a dollar left for weekly spending money. The girls they met did not expect costly entertainment. In those premotion-picture days a date rarely meant more than walking or sitting in the park. Nevertheless, before the evening was over some money had to be spent for refreshments, and there was the rub.

This ever present problem the boys solved to the best of their ability in comradely fashion, lumping their resources and on occasion permitting the one with the more important engagement to take most or all of the tiny hoard. Not until years later did Jack laugh at the spectacle of himself appalled at spending fifty or sixty cents in one evening and forgetful of the occasions when he had squandered a hundred times that sum in a single drunken night with the oyster pirates.

Through the warm evenings of late summer and early autumn and until the winter rain and cold drove them indoors, Jack and Louis prowled the streets, two eager-faced, shabbily dressed youths, seeking and finding answering eyes and shy smiles, for the same enchantment drew girls into the fragrant darkness to stroll, arms linked, along the sidewalks and through the public parks. Like Louis, Jack was always persuading himself that he was in love with the girl of the moment, but with only one did this really occur. He called her Haydee when he wrote of her long after, remembering with much tenderness his first glimpse of her at a Salvation Army meeting, how helpful Louis had been in bringing them together, the hours when, awkward and tongue-tied, he sat beside her on a park bench, the dozen or so kisses they exchanged.

The small episode stands by itself in his turbulent youth, connected neither with the past nor the future. When next he fell in love he would be older, moving unswervingly toward a goal whose importance to him would dwarf everything else, even love. One breath from the past touched the idyl at its very beginning. Following Haydee and her aunt from the Salvation Army meeting to discover where she lived, ecstatic with love at first sight, he had been hailed by a woman from the water front and turned regretfully aside to listen as she told him of Young Scratch, who had died in her arms. It was his last contact with the old associates for many years, except for Johnny Heinhold.

Haydee's visit to the city came to an end. As winter set in the nights grew chillier. No longer could Louis and Jack loiter at street corners. To spend the evenings in each other's homes was unthinkable. Remained only the saloons where there was warmth and cards and conversation.

Neither of them had any desire to drink; Jack had not tasted liquor since he returned from sea. But they had no choice. If they met no one they knew a glass of beer apiece lasted them through an evening while they played pedro and listened to the talk around them. The arrival of acquaintances or old schoolmates, however, was usually disastrous, what with the inevitable treating and possible losses at cards. More than once they were forced to spend several evenings on end huddled in their overcoats in a chilly, ill-lit livery stable, playing euchre and casino until next payday.

Times were bad. As the winter advanced, unemployment increased. The families of many workers knew hunger and cold, small tradesmen were terrified, and the daily papers were filled with reports of even worse conditions elsewhere. Jack often heard desperation in the voices in the saloon. Sometimes he lingered at street corners where knots of men had gathered and listened to their bitter words and arguments. The "bosses," "monopoly," "controlled government," the "proletariat"—these words crashed like cymbals in the speeches of many soapboxers.

Although he did not understand all that they said he recognized the sincerity of their passionate utterances. Long since he had noted and resented the extremes of wealth and poverty that existed in his own town. But, with misery all about him, he did not yet feel personally involved. He was young and strong, he had a job. True, it was not a good job, and he worked very hard for very little, but he would do better. It was just a matter of time.

The promised raise at the jute mill did not materialize. Disgusted, he realized that unless he made an effort to better himself he might be working for ten cents an hour for the rest of his life. Unskilled work would certainly get him nowhere, therefore he would learn a trade. Choosing electricity as the most fertile field, he considered ways and means to achieve his end. How to obtain training and earn his living at the same time? The answer was obvious: start at the bottom and work up.

At the street railway power plant he found the superintendent more than willing to give work to such a zealous young man. He was put at the bottom, as he desired—shoveling coal. Later, he was told, he would become an oiler, and still later he would learn to assist the mechanics who worked on the motors. After that he might go clear to the top; it all depended on him. With a vision of this glowing future before him, he set to work with a will. He shoveled coal for both day and night shifts, a job which was presumed to take ten hours, but which in reality took nearly thirteen. Every thirty days he had one day off, and his salary was thirty dollars a month.

From the start it was a nightmare of back-breaking toil which demanded all the resources of his splendid vitality, as well as his courage and determination, to perform. And it was all for nothing. Weeks went by, however, before he learned that he had taken over the work of two men, each of whom had received forty dollars a month. A decade later he could remember the superintendent with grim humor: "I thought he was making an electrician out of me; as a matter of fact, he was making fifty dollars per month out of me." But at the time it was no laughing matter.

When exhaustion and anger had run their course he found himself again at a dead end. His earnest striving to learn to run in harness had brought him precisely nowhere, and in the process his revulsion against the lack of direction in his life and the impulse to settle down had spent themselves. At first his lovesickness had numbed his impatience of restraint and dull routine; later he had deliberately curbed it, hoping that it would pass as he moved higher up the ladder toward success. Now, hot with resentment at realizing anew the merciless exploitation of his strength whenever he tried to sell it for wages, he was mastered by the determination to be his own boss.

Remembering the free days and nights on the bay, the clean wind and fog, the spaciousness of sky and water, he turned in revulsion from the thought of ever returning to the cramped and filthy quarters where he had labored for long hours at machine or with coal shovel. But what to do now? Where to go? One thing was clear: there was nothing to hold him longer in Oakland.

Since the beginning of the year Coxey, the "good-roads" bills and the Commonweal of Christ had been widely discussed in the daily papers, saloons and street-corner meetings in Oakland. Early in March news came from nearer home. General Lewis C. Fry was organizing an industrial army in Los Angeles, and on the sixteenth it set out, six hundred strong, on the three-thousand-mile journey to Washington. Rumors and contradictory reports flew excitedly from mouth to mouth. Bitterness against the Southern

Pacific, which opposed the army with every means at its disposal, was shared by middle and working class alike, and sympathy with the industrials grew from day to day. A week later, right across the bay in San Francisco, Colonel William Baker began to organize a second Western army. The Commonweal of Christ had left Massillon on schedule, on Easter Sunday, March 25. Two days later the mayor of San Francisco refused point-blank to aid Baker's men in reaching Sacramento, but after a week of parades and speeches, applauded by great numbers of San Franciscans, he weakened and donated twenty-five dollars to ferry them across the bay.

The mayor of Oakland protested hoarsely, threatening dire consequences if they did not leave town before dawn. The Southern Pacific continued to deny their request for free transportation. Although sympathizers provided them with food and energetically raised two hundred dollars to pay freight charges for them as far as Sacramento, resentment of the attitude of the city and railroad officials was uppermost. In the midst of the excitement Charles T. Kelly, thirty-two years old, compositor by trade and identified with several local labor organizations, took over the leadership which Baker proved unable to maintain. From then on this group was known as Kelly's army.

All day the men wandered in small groups about the city, airing their grievances to all who would listen. Jack, following in their train, made up his mind to join them. The march, promising adventure and a chance to see the country, was the very escape he had been seeking. John and Flora could get along without him for a while; he would not be gone long. And when he came back? That question he put out of his mind. Hurrying home, he made feverish preparations to leave, for the latest news was that the army would leave about seven the next morning.

He did not know, in bed that night for the last time in many months, that the army had been roused at two in the morning by a general fire alarm and marched to Sixteenth Street station by the fire and police departments, as well as a number of hostile citizens hastily deputized for the purpose; that Kelly, protesting, had been arrested and then released as soon as the authorities saw that the temper of his men would not stand for it; and that they had been unceremoniously bundled into boxcars and started on their way to Sacramento before sunrise. Jack was among many who had been left behind.

Unwillingly using part of his small stake, he took the afternoon train to Sacramento, arriving four hours after the army, its ranks swelled by new recruits, had departed for Ogden. His experience on the road two years before now stood him in good stead. He caught the eastbound overland that night, and "held her down over the hill" to Truckee. Confident that the army could not be far ahead, he pushed on as rapidly as possible, being ditched from one train only to grab the next, riding blinds, bumpers and rods, passing coal when necessary, and "throwing his feet" in small towns when he wanted to eat.

Hundreds of others were traveling east as he was. Although the railroads were making it more than usually difficult for these men to ride Jack was struck by the comparative ease with which food was obtained. Throughout the country sympathy was being kindled by the spectacular march of the unemployed and expressed by individuals and communities in practical ways. Noting this, as well as the number of men on the road, united in purpose and undaunted by the organized opposition of the railroads, Jack began to perceive, dimly at first, then more and more clearly, that his problem was not an entirely personal one or his predicament unique. Conscious analysis of his experiences and observations was still to come, but identification of his lot with that of others had begun. He did not appreciate the meaning of unemployment as most of his fellow travelers did for he had never been laid off and had but recently thrown up a job, but the pace he had been forced to take and the amount of work expected of him became significant. He drew no conclusions, remained objective, took mental notes, observed and absorbed and enjoyed himself thoroughly.

Late one afternoon, about ten days after Kelly had left Oakland, eighty-four men, the "after-push" of the army, were lying on the straw-covered floor of a refrigerator car at Ames's monument at the summit of the Rockies. Outside a blizzard had blotted out mountains and sky, but inside it was warm and almost comfortable.

Two men climbed into the car. H. R. Lytle, who had been elected lieutenant of the detachment, remembers that one was a Swede, and the other a young man of about twenty, with "round features and dark curly hair. He wore a chinchilla coat, a novel in each pocket, and a cap pulled well down over his head. His flannel shirt, shoes and trousers had seen better days." Like the

Swede, he was traveling light, without either blankets or extra clothing. When he enlisted and was asked his name he told them that he was called Sailor Jack, but that his real name was Jack London.

Jack never forgot his introduction to the army, for he had no sooner entered the car than he became acquainted with the "threshing machine." It was almost dark and there was little floor space. Stepping accidentally on a recumbent man, he was abruptly propelled through the air, landing heavily upon another. Resentment and action were simultaneous. For several minutes until he unexpectedly found a bit of free space, he was tossed back and forth. When he caught his breath he discovered that the threshing machine had been his initiation and welcome. And while they rode east through the blizzard they wore the afternoon and night away telling stories that had never been told before—good stories they were, for the threshing machine awaited a failure.

Now the going was easier. The sympathetic citizens were becoming very practical. It was more sensible to feed eighty-six hungry men once and help them on their way than to permit them to linger and be forced to feed them many times. When the detachment reached a town it was met by police who escorted the men to restaurants and brought them straight back to the car.

In this fashion they reached Omaha, where a special platoon of police hurried them across the river to Council Bluffs. It was two o'clock of a cold, rainy morning. Kelly's army was camped at Chautauqua Park, six miles away. Jack and a few others elected to seek shelter in town and go to camp by daylight. He found an empty saloon, raised on stilts and resting on rollers preparatory to being moved, but neither warmth nor cheer was available there that night and he did not stay long.

His first sight of Kelly's army was through a driving rain. Sixteen hundred weary men who had covered two thousand miles in less than two weeks were camped in six inches of mud. Shivering in wet, ragged clothes, they were huddled around small fires which struggled vainly against the rain, sending up dense smoke and no heat. A little distance away a large, dry Chautauqua amphitheater, which had been promised to the army, was filled with militiamen.

Jack readily found his fellow travelers, now known as Company L of the Second Division. During inspection one of their number was found to be only eighteen and was refused, as no one under twenty was permitted in the army. Jack's age was not questioned, although he had celebrated his eighteenth birthday but three months before.

That day, led by Kelly on a big black horse, the men marched seven miles through pelting rain to Weston. Their flags and banners were as sodden as their clothes, but the journey was yet young and their spirits were high. Two thirds of the distance from San Francisco to the capital was behind them. Ahead was a friendly, thickly populated region where they were sure they would be fed generously and helped on their way. And when the marrow of their bones began to ache with the cold they would remember the railroads and the militia, and anger would warm them again.

Supper was eaten in the midst of rain, sleet and hail. At nightfall the north wind, which had lashed them mercilessly all day, grew fiercer and more bitter. Unable to face another night in the open, the men scattered in all directions to find shelter. Jack was among those who spent the night in a hayloft.

Three days they lingered at Weston, and every day the opposition of forces and the relative strength of each became more evident. Kelly's demand for transportation from the railroads was peremptorily refused. Eastbound traffic had completely stopped. Then, while the army waited, the railroads began to move all their empty rolling stock east as rapidly as possible. The regular trains went through well guarded by Pinkertons, and the railroads issued ultimatums concerning the seizure of trains. Despite this the indignant citizens of Omaha and Council Bluffs joined forces to assist the army, stole an engine and several boxcars and rode out to pick up the men. Unfortunately the train was too small, and before a larger one was obtained the army decided to move on by foot.

All along the ten-day journey to Des Moines the men received generous gifts of food and wagon transportation. The weather broke at last, and pale spring sunshine lay over the land. Each campground was immediately invaded by friendly sight-seers. Townsfolk and farmers, young ladies dressed in their best and mothers with children clinging to their skirts came to look over the army, noting with pleased surprise how "well behaved and gentlemanly" the men were, staying late to sing songs and listen to speeches.

Company L contained several talented amateurs who needed

little urging to put on a show of songs and dances which brought many nickels and dimes from the visitors. One man with gifted hands fashioned and sold miniature furniture of pins and feathers. Jack, lacking the ability to sing, dance or make furniture, evolved an original and effective racket which he worked to the limit. Seated near the campfire, a despondent, homesick expression on his face, he would suddenly look up and remark in a heartbreaking tone, "If I had a postage stamp I would write a letter to my mother." Bystanders were immediately all sympathy. Even his companions, who knew the graft, were often shaken by the misery in his voice. Stamps or money to buy them were always forthcoming, and Jack, looking properly grateful, would scribble furiously until his benefactor and the witnesses had moved on, when he would repeat the performance. Sometimes he would collect as much as a dollar and a half a day.

As the army advanced, the enthusiasm with which it was received began to diminish. Curiosity rather than sympathy brought visitors to camp. Disputes and complaints within the army never ceased, although as time went on hatred of the Pinkertons, who continually harried them and even entered their ranks as provocateurs, was a strong unifying force.

The rivalry that had existed between Kelly and a certain George Speed almost from the beginning broke out into the open on several occasions. Colonel Speed had organized the Sacramento contingent and was in command of the Second Division of the army. The men in its several companies were almost all from Sacramento and were intensely loyal to their leader. Henry Vincent, official historian of the Commonweal of Christ, described Speed as "a sort of socialist agitator," who had recruited in Sacramento by soapboxing on street corners. But one of the members of the Second Division remembers him as a sincere, dependable man who knew something of Karl Marx, and a practical revolutionist whose only concern all his life was to better the conditions of the working people. The devotion of Speed's men in the Second Division was typical of situations that were to be repeated often in the next thirty years.

When circumstances forced a showdown between Kelly and Speed a few days out of Weston, fully one third of the army backed Speed. Kelly hurled charges of mutiny, accused Speed of violating disciplinary rules; Speed demanded an accounting of several thousand dollars which had been donated to the army.

Reducing Speed to the ranks was worse than useless. His supporters stood firm and immediately made him general of a separate army. In the end a compromise averted a split: in the future the staffs of the divisions were to work more closely together, and the accounts were to be open to inspection.

Jack watched the fight from the side lines, interested but unaware of its significance. "In the afternoon the little troubles were all made up," he wrote in his diary on April 25. He was much more concerned with his feet than with quarrels between the leaders. His shoes had worn out, and for several days he had walked barefooted when he could not get a ride. When the commissary finally supplied him with another pair he was footsore, and the new shoes promptly raised blisters.

The number of wagons was always insufficient. "Of course our company walked," Jack wrote, and on the next day, "As usual our company was walking while the S. F.'s rode." But Lieutenant Lytle noted that one member of his company did very little walking on the trek across Iowa, and that was Jack. "He rode the day before, he rode today, and he would ride tomorrow," Lytle recalled. "Jack was always opposed to violent exercise." Nor did Jack take kindly to camp work, hauling wood and water and washing. In one thing, however, he excelled, and that was in "throwing his feet."

Clothing that had been ragged when their owners started on the march soon wore out in the constant exposure to weather. The commissary was not equipped to supply the vast need for wearing apparel, and many of the men suffered keenly from the dampness and the raw spring winds. More than once during the time he spent with the army Jack disappeared from camp immediately after breakfast, returning in the late afternoon, looking like a perambulating secondhand clothing store. Straw and derby hats he brought back, and summer, sports and winter suits, underwear, shoes, socks and cravats, starched collars and cuffs. The camp roared with laughter and rude jests as some of the men paraded around afterward in discarded long-tailed evening clothes and large-checked gambler's suits. Jack maintained that there was no secret to his success, that he simply went straight to the best residential section and rang the doorbell of the largest and most elegant house. Company L's final judgment was that "Jack was no piker when it came to throwing his feet."

At night as they ate supper and prepared for bed, or sat about the campfire on fine nights, the men engaged in endless discussions. Everyone had something to say, and every variety of panacea, from single tax to astrology, was offered to solve the depression. There were numbers of trade unionists in the army, many chronically unemployed hobos, a sprinkling of Socialists and even a few declassed members of the petty bourgeoisie. Jack listened to them all.

The trade unionists were essentially unskilled and semiskilled workers, and therefore not members of the aristocracy of labor who regarded the wage system as final. Experience of unemployment had shaken their faith in this system, and consciously or unconsciously, some of them were approaching a class consciousness. Although the American Federation of Labor was well under way at this time the labor movement was definitely on the defensive, and these men, finding themselves unemployed, were beginning to see the limitations of trade unions as a solution to their problems, and to grope for a united action more efficacious than their efforts as craftsmen had been.

Their present plight as a result of the panic was not only shaking them into social consciousness but was widening the scope of their interest beyond that of populism. Facts were accomplishing what soapboxing and preaching had failed to do. There were those in the army who already regarded their immediate demands —relief from their present position—as merely provisional. With only a dim idea of their final aim, they were nevertheless eager to support and choose leaders who declared themselves opposed to capital, and they had begun to regard with skepticism any suggestion which identified the interests of capital and labor. The new orientation toward a more-than-wage system and the abolition of classes was often indicated in the campfire discussions. In the midst of the ferment of ideas Jack was most favorably impressed with the point of view of the Socialists, who although few in number, clearly revealed to him their more fundamental understanding of sociology.

Walking, riding in wagons whenever possible, the army reached Des Moines on the twenty-ninth of April. The difficulties that had been encountered had robbed it of its earlier brave appearance. Health, not always robust after months of unemployment and privation, had suffered. Sometimes as they straggled along, discarding tattered blankets and worn-out clothing on the way, they looked more like soldiers retreating from a disastrous battle than

Kelly's Industrial Army marching across the country to present its demands to the government at Washington.

At Des Moines the army marched to the old stove works, sat down and announced that it would walk no more. They ate, slept, played baseball, rested and waited serenely for some means of conveyance to be arranged. Spring, full bodied and warm, was upon them. Jack lay contentedly in the new grass, reading, feeling the stir of growth about him, watching the army's activities with remote amusement.

The citizens of Des Moines grew uneasy, then desperate. Their sympathy and desire to co-operate did not imply their willingness to continue indefinitely to feed twelve or thirteen hundred men three meals a day, but the army did not seem to realize this. Finally General Weaver, the hero of the Populists, assisted by local labor leaders, saved Des Moines from civic disaster by a plan which turned Kelly's army into a navy. They would build flatboats and float down the shallow Des Moines River to where it joined the Mississippi. In the same fashion they could proceed to Cairo, and then go up the Ohio to Wheeling, West Virginia, where they would be only a few hundred miles from their destination.

Money, lumber, carpenters and tools quickly appeared, and Kelly's "shipyard" at the junction of the Raccoon and Des Moines rivers resounded with activity. Jack was delighted with this turn of affairs, laid aside his books and worked with the rest. The boats were eighteen feet long, six feet wide and one foot deep, and in three days a hundred and thirty-four of them were completed. On the morning of May ninth Des Moines enthusiastically waved good-by to the men it had been feeding for eleven days.

One of the boats had been christened the Pirate, and in a short time it was living up to its name in a thorough-going manner. Sailor Jack was its unofficial captain, and his nine men were as irrepressible as he, high spirited, independent and determined to take advantage of every opportunity to turn the march into a glorious holiday.

Superior handling of their boat over dams and through rapids brought them well in front, and for the greater part of the nearly three hundred miles to Keokuk on the Mississippi, they stayed in front. There were excellent reasons for this. The army was living off the countryside, but the commissary always trailed far in the rear. Jack's small vanguard managed to skim the cream of the produce that was offered, half out of goodness of heart and half to keep the invaders from lingering, and set up their own strictly private commissary. They took not only the best of everything, but a great deal of everything. They even eschewed water for making coffee, boiling it instead in milk—"pale Vienna" Jack called it.

Meantime the main body of the army was often very hungry. In vain Kelly ordered the "pirates" back and threatened them with discipline. No boat could keep up with them, and they had not the slightest intention of foregoing the abundance of food and tobacco that was so easy to obtain. Then Kelly hit upon the plan to send two horsemen ahead to warn the farmers. Overnight it became impossible to get food, and hunger drove the "pirates" back to the army.

But when they rejoined Company L, Captain Gorman, outraged by their behavior, would neither recognize nor feed them. Lieutenant Lytle, who had intervened for them, promptly found himself elected Captain of Company M. Both Kelly and Speed objected, but the "pirates" and the ten men in Lytle's boat stood firm, and the revolution was finally ratified. Prudently deciding to keep his eye on his new command, Lytle had a blacksmith make two stout iron hooks and four staples. When his boat was firmly secured to the Pirate the combination was thirty-six feet long with twenty men at the oars, and nothing but a steamboat could have caught up with it.

Whenever they encountered rapids the advantages of the double boat were spectacularly demonstrated. Jack developed an ingenious scheme. As soon as the lead-boat was caught he shouted an order, and the ten men leaped into the rear one. The first immediately floated free and moved forward. Another order brought the twenty men into the lead-boat and the second one cleared the obstruction. While the rest of the boats, including Kelly's police boats, hung up in bad water they seesawed gaily ahead. In smooth water they made even faster time by rigging up a mast and using blankets for sails. The police boats were always behind, and once again they lived off the fat of the land.

Several times other boats challenged their lead. Lytle remembers one five-mile spurt, the men rowing like mad, with Jack at the stroke oar, urging them on to victory. When they won he was as excited as a child; "Jack talked all day about the wonderful race." In the end Kelly washed his hands of Company M and

placed Colonel Speed aboard. Thus they entered the Mississippi—
the first of the fleet.

This was the last of the fun. For some time there had been
much dissatisfaction. Kelly's discipline was growing lax, and the
men were losing confidence in him. Desertion marked the final
phase of the march of the Industrial Army, although some went
doggedly ahead and actually reached Washington. The change in
the morale was partially due to the news they received in Des
Moines of Coxey's arrest at the capital on May Day, but the
processes of disintegration were already at work. The men were
hungry, and the movement was showing itself unable to survive
with any degree of success the impact of the social forces lined
up against it. Its aim had never been clear, and many who joined
had thought of it merely as an escape from the discomforts of
poverty and unemployment. Now they were still poor and unemployed, and their discomforts were even greater than before.

Jack had grown tired of the aimlessness of the march as well as
its discomforts. He had seen enough of the country to want to
see more, and his experience as a hobo made him know how easily
this might be accomplished. On the eighteenth of May he wrote
in his diary: "We passed a miserable day on the water with a
chilling wind and driving rain. In the afternoon we camped in
Missouri where we passed a miserable night." A week later he
deserted at Hannibal, Missouri.

CHAPTER

7

HE LEFT the army lightheartedly, careless of whether it would reach its destination or not, and pushed on alone. In part his attitude was a reflection of the sense of futility and discouragement which was coming over the men as the movement went to pieces; in part it was the result of the genuine detachment he had felt from the beginning. He had gone along, that was all, with neither convictions nor determination to right his or anyone else's wrongs. As long as there had been excitement and fun he had remained. But the prospect of pushing on under more and more unpleasant conditions to the bitter end did not attract him. There was too much else to see and do.

He had no immediate plans. Sooner or later he would return to California, but first he would see more of the country. Summer was just beginning, the railroads would take him wherever he wished to go, and he was second to none at "throwing his feet." A pampered son of the rich, setting out to see the country with letters of introduction, checkbook and luggage, would have been no better, although differently equipped.

Chicago was his first destination, for Flora had written that a little money and several letters were waiting for him there. She also begged him to take care of his health, not to fall in the water with the paper money she had mailed him, and to avoid being sent to jail. He wanted to go to Chicago for another reason. Having been an interested visitor to the San Francisco Mid-Winter Fair before he left Oakland, he was curious to see the widely discussed World's Columbian Exposition in Chicago. It had been closed

since the beginning of the winter, but as soon as he had picked up
his mail and bought a secondhand outfit of clothing he made his
way to Jackson Park and spent the rest of the day wandering
through the grounds and gazing at the buildings which had made
architectural history.

A day or two later he turned up in St Joseph, Michigan, to pay
a visit to one of Flora's sisters. Mary Everhard welcomed him
warmly, eager to know the son of the little sister she had not seen
for so many years. Although no friendship grew between him
and his cousins he found his aunt a sympathetic listener and
confidante. He showed her the diary he had been keeping, ampli-
fying the bare jottings with running comment as he went along
and bringing strange pictures before her startled eyes. Almost before he knew it he was telling her of the prize he had won the
preceding autumn and of his slowly forming decision to write
again. Mary Everhard's encouragement of this ambition was important, coming as it did in the midst of his uncertainty about
the future in general and next steps in particular, and it sustained
him for months after his return to Oakland.

He was very comfortable at the Everhards'. He ate and rested
and talked with Mary and explored the countryside. Later the
sand dunes of this part of Lake Michigan's shore line, as well as
the name of one of his cousins, Ernest Everhard, were to appear
in *The Iron Heel*. But neither comfort nor Mary Everhard held
him long in St Joseph. In a few weeks he was on the road again.

With his usual thoroughness he explored New York from end
to end. Its undeniable beauty, its towering skyscrapers, the bridges
flung across the rivers, the pulse of traffic-laden streets, all its
potentialities for progress and civilization, as well as all its evils
and corruption—these struck him forcibly. But his deepest and
most abiding impression was of the distress of the poor. When he
saw fire escapes, parks, the Battery, filled all night long with men,
women and children unable to sleep in stifling tenement rooms,
emaciated children and hungry-eyed men and women, it needed
but little imagination to picture their suffering during the bitter
winter months. Neither time nor improved circumstances altered
this reaction. He hated and feared New York. When he had become a successful author he went there only when it was absolutely necessary and, acutely aware of what the city meant in
terms of suffering and deprivation, he never stayed longer than
business demanded.

Jack was beginning to think, and to think hard. He had gone a long way toward identification of himself with his class, but thus far his experiences had permitted him to retain the belief that he was an exception, luckier or perhaps better equipped by "nature" to meet exigencies than most people. Disillusionment on this score was to come soon.

He left New York to see Niagara Falls. Returning in the early morning from a second view, he was arrested in Buffalo, charged with vagrancy and, after witnessing the complete disregard of the legal rights he had assumed were his, was sentenced to thirty days in the Erie County jail. He was always able to remember the approximate date of his arrest—toward the end of June—because a few days later the great American Railway Union strike broke out.

Prison bit deeply. He described it in *The Road*, as in other books he described his brief experiences with the oyster pirates and fish patrol, and the gold hunters in the Klondike, as if he had spent years there instead of a few weeks. As far as the thirty days in prison was concerned, his faculty for absorbing the experiences of others and living them in imagination succeeded in scaring him, to use his own word, into thinking through to a conclusion the problem that had been more and more clearly set before him. He grasped the spirit of the law, based on class difference and property rights, and saw how it operated. The working class lived under a system which rendered it helpless. Mere superiority in numbers did not matter. Unemployed, the workers had organized themselves into armies whose marches had accomplished nothing. Arrested, they were denied their rights and sent to prison. Awareness that he was a member of this class became knowledge, and everything that he learned stimulated him to learn more.

In order to survive he swiftly adjusted himself to prison life. After two days of hard labor in the yard he became a "hallman." Night and morning he served bread to the prisoners in their cells, and at noon assisted the head hallman in placing the bread rations on the convicts' trays as they filed through the hall. It was an easy matter for the hallmen to obtain extra rations, and these they later peddled to the prisoners in exchange for chewing tobacco. This was merely one of the many grafts within the walls of the prison.

Scenes of brutality were constantly in evidence. As a boy and youth, Jack had always been quick to defend with words and fists the underdog in an uneven struggle. One night when he was still with the army he had even defended the rights of a mother cat and her kittens to share the hayloft in which several of the men were passing the night. Now he was forced to stand by, unable either to do anything or to betray his feelings, and witness the manhandling of convicts and even worse degradations. When he wrote of this experience he described much of what he saw as not only unprintable but unthinkable. Some of his readers have drawn back in horror from the brutal realism of his stories. Such people knew neither the depths of his knowledge of brutality nor all that he meant by the often repeated phrase, "Man's inhumanity to man."

A prison acquaintance who had taught him the ropes when he first entered expected him to return the favor by joining him outside in a career of petty crime. They discussed this very seriously and laid many plans, but not for one moment did Jack actually consider it. His thirty days in the penitentiary were enough to make him go out of his way to avoid the remotest chance of being returned there. The day they were released he adroitly eluded his companion, caught a southbound freight and left Buffalo.

Through the warm days and nights of August he roamed across Pennsylvania, following the whim of the moment, hopping freights, loitering in pleasant spots, pausing to look more closely at what interested him. His bed he made under the stars and paid for his meals with gay tales of adventures. Frequently he met men who earlier in the year had been part of the various industrial armies. From them he heard the inglorious end of the movement. Small groups of tired men had straggled into Washington all during July, going into a camp on the outskirts of the "city" which had been established by Coxey's men after the May Day fiasco. Congress ignored their plight, while the waning attention of the headline readers was soon drawn to the A.R.U. strike. Food donations were scanty and irregular, and the men were often hungry. For a while they picked and sold blackberries which grew wild near by, but the season was short. One after another their leaders left them. In the end a kindhearted merchant and the commissioners of the District of Columbia arranged to transport the remnants of the armies back to their homes.

Throughout his life Jack often encountered and received letters from fellow wanderers during this year. With the publication of his tramping experiences, scores of hobos whom he had never seen suddenly remembered the author, and to prove it told yarns which eventually became part of the Jack London legend. At the time of his death a prisoner in the Columbus, Ohio, penitentiary broke into print as a friend of Jack's hobo days. They had met in a Memphis river-front saloon, he recalled, had tramped together all over the South, and Jack had planned to visit him the next month. If Jerry's story shortened his sentence Jack would have been glad. He had never denied acquaintance with any of these men. "Who am I to say nay to their stories?" he always asked.

Some of the leaders of the armies he would likewise hear of again. For years Coxey was good copy for the newspapers as a candidate for office, a bitter critic of William Jennings Bryan whom he charged with the destruction of the populist movement, and as leader of a second, although unsensational march to Washington in 1914. Years after Jack's death Coxey was advocating still another petition on boots. Carl Browne's name bobbed up from time to time for the next twenty years. Failing to make a fortune by inventing a flying machine, he devoted the remainder of his life to Coxey's reforms, trying especially to persuade the Socialist party to support him. Kelly, back in California, basked in past glory for a long time, fancying himself a great labor leader, but when, inspired by Coxey in 1914, he sought to duplicate his earlier performance his arrest before he was scarcely under way cured him. As for George Speed, Jack was to meet him again, and soon, for when he returned to Oakland and joined the Socialist Labor party he discovered that Speed was an old-time member of the San Francisco section.

Meantime Jack wandered happily. Laughter bubbled easily to his lips, as witness his unforgettable memory of the seven-up game with the moon-faced Negro and other hobos beside a railroad track near the Susquehanna, when he laughed "till it seemed the top of my head would come off." As the weeks passed his sense of physical and mental well-being was fortified by the fact that out of the events and experiences of the past years was emerging an understanding of life and of his place in it. From knowing only what he did not want to be or do, he was coming to know what he did want and how to set about obtaining it. And while he traveled leisurely back to New York and up to Boston he was perfecting his plans and developing his point of view.

The diary which he kept more or less regularly during this

time indicates his varied interests, as well as the growing impulse
to make notes and put his thoughts on paper. He wrote down
what he saw and did, current slang and hobo argot, words of
popular songs that struck his fancy, the latest jokes, and in the
midst of these, quotations from some of the books he read en
route. In the public libraries of many towns he spent long hours
satisfying his curiosity about subjects mentioned in casual conversation with fellow travelers or encountered in the shabby
volumes he picked up for a few cents in secondhand stores. He
seems to have read a great deal of poetry, and quotations from
several poets on the subject of death are interspersed with statements of desires and ambitions whose articulation marked his
rapidly approaching maturity.

The thought of death as annihilation, the cessation not only of
living but of consciousness and individuality, constantly intrigued
him. His youth and unscarred love of life made this solution very
remote, but all of his life it was to be his ace in the hole, the one
sure escape when frustration, disappointment and confusion had
become finally unendurable. At the same time his deep-seated wish
to find his place, to become stabilized and bring order and purpose into his life was expressed in a sudden, unexpected desire for
fatherhood and its attendant joys and responsibilities. He was
eighteen and he did not intend to marry until he was twenty-six
or twenty-seven, but from this time on marriage and fatherhood
were to have a definite place in his plans.

When he came to Washington he conscientiously visited all the
points of interest, from government buildings to Civil War
cemeteries. He was not much impressed with the capital. Afterwards he recalled it chiefly as the one city in the United States
and Canada in which he had gone down to defeat trying to beg
clothes. For two weeks he rang doorbells in vain, asking for shoes.
Later, in Jersey City, he succeeded almost immediately in obtaining a pair.

In Baltimore he fell in with several hobos of a type he had not
met before. Although he would always be cordial to all tramps,
never turning any of them away empty handed, his preference
was for the educated, professional hobos. If he were prone to
sentimentalize about these vagabonds it is understandable. He
had chanced upon them at a time when he was beginning to be
aware of the extent of his ignorance, and in a sense they were his

first teachers. Some of them were brilliant men, trained in various professions, widely read. They not only spoke fluently but with an easy familiarity on subjects of which he knew next to nothing, and drove him to the libraries again and again for further information. From one of this special brotherhood, Frank Strawn-Hamilton, he was soon to learn much.

The Baltimore group held his interest for days. In Druid Hill Park they argued from morning until night about philosophy, science, sociology, economics and revolution. Often, horns hopelessly locked, some of them invaded the public library to obtain factual information with which to batter down opponents. Encountering another gentleman hobo in Boston the next month, Jack ventured to air his newly acquired knowledge. All day they sat on park benches in the mellow sunshine, discussing Kant, Spencer, Karl Marx and others whose names and ideas were still unknown to Jack. He found the experience intoxicating, but his desire to prolong it indefinitely, to spend day after day in this pleasant fashion, was checked by the realization of how little he yet knew compared with what he needed in order to hold his own even with these itinerant scholars.

He must study, become educated and learn more of these subjects which enthralled him. Just how this determination was to be realized, he was not yet sure, but nothing would deter him. His first step was to go home. Once there he would reconstruct the routine he had followed successfully while in grammar school—so many hours for eating, sleeping, working and studying. It had worked before; it would work again.

The New England autumn nights were growing chilly. It would be well to start West before the winter weather began, especially as he had decided to return across Canada to Vancouver. He would need warmer clothes and a small sum of money for emergencies. The clothes could be begged en route, but the money? A daring thought occurred to him. Perhaps he could write something and sell it to one of the Boston newspapers or magazines. He had succeeded before, why not a second time?

Maitland Leroy Osborne, for many years connected with the *National Magazine*, remembered very distinctly his first meeting with the man who some years later became a valued contributor to the periodical. He met Jack one morning on Newbury Street. Jack was probably "making the stem" for his breakfast; at any rate the two men fell into conversation. Osborne learned that Jack had slept on a bench in the Public Garden the night before, that he had been on the road for many months, that he was a writer, and that right then he had a story to sell.

It happened that the predecessor of the *National*, the *Bostonian*, was placing its first number on the stands in October of that year. Osborne, impressed by Jack and fired with enthusiasm by the thought of providing the magazine with an unusual feature, hurried him to the editorial office. When Jack left Boston for Montreal he was richer by the ten dollars which Mr Chapple had paid for his article.

Many cold nights later while he was thawing out in a sand house near Rogers in the mountains of British Columbia, he met another young man who entered the sand house for the same purpose. He was also bound west, and their acquaintance began, Jack later recalled, when Smith, the newcomer, remarked that he had been "pounding his ear." Jack, despite his wide knowledge of slang, was mystified until George explained that it meant "dossing," "kipping," or sleeping. They took an instant liking to each other and stayed together for nearly two weeks, traveling to Kamloops and then to Mission, where they lingered a few days before parting.

From Smith's recollection of that fortnight it is possible to obtain a fair impression of Jack at the end of his aimless years, homeward bound to go back to school. He was almost nineteen years old then, a strong, taciturn young chap, diffident, even suspicious of chance acquaintances—"ginks" he usually called them—but gay, friendly and confiding once he had come to like an individual.

It was Smith who "held her down" with Jack over the most difficult stretch of the Canadian Pacific—the hundred and ten miles between North Bend and Mission. One by one other hobos who were attempting it the same night were ditched; only Jack and Smith reached their destination. The train stopped frequently, and at each halt the crew chased them off, but when it pulled out both men were back. It was blind baggage, rods and rear platform of the Pullman all the way. Twice Jack took the rods. Only once and for a brief time did they ride the same spot together. They taunted the brakeman until he was nearly in a frenzy, but when they reached Mission he had acknowledged defeat and was pleading with them not to ride his train into Vancouver.

"Smithy, you're a pretty good gink! I like you," was Jack's

comment. And when he caught a train for Vancouver a few days later he regretted that Smithy had decided to go South rather than accompany him to Oakland.

There is no doubt that the year 1894 was a most significant year in his life. He said later that he had been shocked into thinking at this time, and it is true that among the influences that shaped him were many which acted as blows. ". . . I was down in the cellar of society," he wrote nine years later, "down in the subterranean depths of misery about which it is neither nice nor proper to speak. I was in the pit, the abyss, the human cesspool, the shambles and the charnel house of our civilization. This is the part of the edifice of society that society chooses to ignore. . . . I shall say only that the things I there saw gave me a terrible scare . . ."

The months of eluding railroad detectives on the road, his outrage at his arrest, the swift disillusionment of his boyish ideals and of his heretofore secure belief in the inviolability of his rights as an individual, and the prison experience itself undermined forever for him the so-called "sanctity" of the law. He developed a consciousness of it which, while it never became articulate, was at once contemptuous and respectful. He would obey the law, not because it was the law, but because it was stronger than he and because he knew at first hand the penalties of disobedience. His contempt included all who were associated with the law—policemen, detectives, district attorneys, judges, guards and jailers—and because they did the bidding of forces antagonistic to him and all who belonged to the propertyless class, he regarded them as enemies.

Class consciousness had been forming within him for some time. As newsboy, factory hand, pirate, patrolman and hobo, he had witnessed and felt personally the injustice of society as it existed. The various elements he had encountered in Kelly's army, especially the class-conscious trade-unionists and Socialists, had contributed much to his awareness of the social forces and of his own position in society. The contrast between the West and the crowded industrial centers of the East threw this into high relief.

He knew now that he was a member of the working class. He knew further that, without training, he could at best be sure of employment only as long as his muscles remained strong. But from what he had observed of the number of declassed elements in Kelly's army—unskilled workers whose muscles were still good, and skilled workers whose knowledge of their crafts had not saved them from unemployment—he realized what little reliance was to be placed on selling either muscle power or skill to earn a living. He was young and strong, but so were many others whose youth and strength found no buyers. And one thing was sure: he was not going to be one of the thousands of helpless and unfit he had seen everywhere in the land. His proximity to the fate of these members of his class terrified him. Carelessly, unthinkingly, he had walked straight into the trap, but before it was too late he would get out. His decision was made: in the market where muscle and skill were dirt cheap he would display and sell, and for fancy prices, the products of his brain.

When his thinking had gone this far he knew that he must educate his brains, but it went further. His situation was a common one. There were millions of other young men, and women, too, whose hunger for a richer, fuller life was as great as his. All of them were caught in the same trap. It was a big trap and a powerful one. He and a few others might be able to escape. The rest, for all their youth and courage and bright visions, would grow old and die in it, frustrated and embittered. Why not destroy it once and for all, so that no one would ever be caught again?

Thus did the problem pose itself to him at the start. And when he went back to school to engineer his own escape by training his brains he was determined to learn more as soon as possible about the larger but equally challenging question of escape for all.

8

HURRY! Faster, faster! This, the dominant characteristic of Jack London's activity until the end of his life, was immediately evident as he entered his nineteenth year and the Oakland high school at approximately the same time. He had arrived late at the starting point. He must hurry, drive himself mercilessly until he caught up, and even then he must not relax but push on ahead to the foremost ranks. There was no time to do things slowly and thoroughly. Find the short cuts, cram in the book knowledge, then try it and see what happens! If it worked, well and good. If it did not work cram in more knowledge and try again. Meantime keep at it, study, push ahead!

It was as if a powerful motor were getting under way. All the parts were new and tight. It sputtered badly in the beginning, and adjustments were made with ignorant, impatient hands. It must go quickly and once there it must not falter. Nor did it for more than two decades when, worn out by what had developed into a senseless mania for speed, it was abandoned.

When he began the first of the two years of study which were to provide him with his only formal higher education his determination was to spend the next seven years in high school and college. Fortunately John London's health had somewhat improved, and for the time being he and Flora could manage without Jack's financial assistance. Jack was free, therefore, to get part-time jobs to support himself, and attend regular high school rather than to go only at night, which would take him much longer. Knowing, however, that this favorable arrangement could not last indefinitely, he was prepared to make whatever changes would be necessary, short of giving up his project. He was convinced that a university degree was indispensable to earning his living by his brains, whether as a writer or in another capacity, and nothing would swerve him from his purpose.

But while insofar as it was possible he was dictating the circumstances of his life, deliberately placing himself in an environment of his own choosing, he was totally unprepared for what that environment would do to him. He was far from being formed. His early years had hardened him, but principally to their own hardness. In the new, softer environment he approached at this time the rough wisdom of the streets and the road seemed useless. Sometimes in the beginning it seemed as if he had learned nothing worth while during his nineteen difficult years. His values, so clear and precise before, were confused. How to tell gold from brass when everything dazzled his unaccustomed eyes?

Plastic though he was, however, he did not yield passively. Full bodied, a tragic sense of social inferiority had sprung into being, which, while it permanently warped his judgment nevertheless made him defiant rather than submissive toward the influences he was encountering. Even before he realized how deeply impressed he was by the new environment he had set about to impress it as deeply with himself, and in the resultant struggle both his strength and his weakness were fully developed.

In the 'nineties the world of book knowledge and higher education was essentially the world of the middle class, and although he did not know it then Jack crossed its threshold when he entered high school. From the first day he found most of his schoolmates hostile, critical, unwilling to accept him as one of them. He was so obviously different. His manner was rough and uncouth, his clothes shabby, his general appearance careless. He was not much older than they, and yet he was a man while they were juvenile and inexperienced. And he had become a man unlike any they knew personally, but like some they had heard about, seen from a distance, and been warned against.

One of his schoolmates, a young lady who grew up to become the wife of one of his friends, always remembered her first sight of him as the French teacher, Mme Grand-Pré, attempted to call her class to order at the beginning of the term. Jack, slouched in his seat, was smiling contemptuously at the childish uproar.

Georgia Loring noted his tousled hair, his wrinkled, ill-fitting blue suit, the flannel shirt open at the neck, and later, when he stood up, the long, baggy trousers with "spring bottoms," a style affected by toughs and hoodlums and in striking contrast to the neat short pants of the other boys.

His attitude toward learning French was one of apparent indifference, nor did this change as the classes continued. He always regretted later that he had been unable to master any foreign language. When called upon to recite he would only half rise from his seat, bending forward and grasping the desk with both hands while he answered rapidly in a nearly inaudible voice. As soon as he had finished he would quickly slump down again. When school was over for the day he left immediately, pulling his rumpled cap from his pocket before he was out of the classroom.

They thought that he was unsociable and never guessed that, although he would have died before he admitted it, their own unfriendliness had cut him to the quick. Sometimes he would stand on the outskirts of a small group, listening to their talk, his eagerness to be included visible even to them. But when, as casually friendly for the moment as they were casually cruel at other times, they addressed him, he would stiffen, answer them rudely and stride away, swinging his shoulders irritably.

They also thought that he was conceited. He had joined the Henry Clay Debating Society, and in discussion and debate they resented his positive manner and radical opinions. Furthermore they were disconcerted by the way he flaunted facts in their faces, ignorant not only of the years of reading and studying alone which had enabled him to assemble his tiny hoard of information, but frequently of the facts themselves.

It was not pleasant at first. At the time he did not know that he minded it. He was too busy. School work, extra reading, odd jobs after school and on Saturdays, and later janitor work in the school itself, hours spent trying to apply to his writing what he was learning—these filled every available moment. But the impact of the stupid snobbishness that walled him around nevertheless stimulated him to assert himself. In conduct and activity he accentuated the differences between him and his classmates, his poverty and working-class origin, his wider experience and maturer, more capable mind.

He submitted stories and articles to the school paper, the *Aegis*, and they were published week after week, a notable series to be found in such a periodical, for they were drawn largely from his hobo and sailing experiences. The little middle-class boys and girls had never seen anything like them—hunks of raw life hammered into words, inexpertly, but with undeniable effectiveness. They did not like him, he was not one of them, but they came to respect him. By his very difference he had impressed them.

He had crossed the threshold and entered the vestibule of the middle class, and there he stayed. No doors were opened to him. At all times, of course, he had access to the great body of middle-class culture and learning. As long as he could earn his keep he could find what he sought in schools and libraries that were open to the public. And he might have gone his way with serene indifference to the class itself if it had been indifferent to him. Its hostility challenged him. He would show them! That he succeeded was unfortunate. Long after they were sitting at his feet in supine admiration and paying him handsomely for the privilege he was still showing them, unaware that he was not victor but victim.

There was another possibility. Had all the doors remained closed he might have entered the radical movement sooner, given himself to it wholly, and found in it the answer for his social and cultural needs. It attracted him strongly. As soon as he returned from the road he had begun to read the books he had heard discussed, Spencer, Darwin, Bellamy; street meetings drew him whenever he had time to linger. But unexpectedly a door was opened.

Two friendships grew out of Jack's frequent trips to the public library during this year. One, more or less negative, was nevertheless to have a definite influence upon him for some years, but the other was destined to dictate the course of his life.

The library had undergone a great change with the recent arrival of Frederick Irons Bamford, once assistant librarian of the Mechanics Library in San Francisco, more recently professor of English literature at Hesperian College near Sacramento. His task was to develop the long-neglected reference department. A Canadian gentleman by birth and education, a Christian-Socialist by conviction, he brought to the provincial little library all that he could of the gentler cultural tradition of the late nineteenth century. Visitors found him a small, frail man with eager, kindly eyes, greeting them from behind a desk on which a librarian's paraphernalia was flanked by a vase of flowers, a bit of statuary and a tastefully arranged group of the latest books. He solicited requests for information, and as soon as a question was put to him he would scurry across the room, or up the stairs to the narrow balcony on the west wall where there were no windows and the shelves rose nearly to the ceiling, to return smiling and triumphant with the desired volumes.

He was greatly interested in young students, placing himself wholly at their disposal and searching always for a spark which he might fan into a blaze of devotion to knowledge for its own sake. Jack's pursuit of information about literature and the latest developments in science and sociology soon brought him under Bamford's approving eye. He talked with the boy, ascertained his background and ambitions, and set about to assist him in every possible way. Their common interest in socialism brought them even closer together.

But life had given Jack a realistic approach to the movement such as Bamford would never have. The existence of classes, the class struggle, the merciless exploitation of workers, the need for their organization and education along militant socialistic lines, the inevitability of force as the sole means of dethroning the masters of society—Jack had not learned this from books. Gentle Bamford disapproved of force, did not think it was necessary, relied on the ballot and the "improvement" of man by education. He felt, furthermore, that there was a much more important side to socialism. Marx was the giant of them all, of course, but Jack would benefit more right now from reading books by men Bamford considered to be disciples of Marx in the aesthetic, cultural field: Ruskin, Carlyle, Arnold and Morris.

Staggered sometimes by his ignorance as each turn in the road revealed new vistas of which he had never heard before, Jack listened and read obediently. There was so little time! How would he ever be able to encompass everything he needed and desired to know? He accelerated his pace, cut down his hours of sleep, and still the unread books mounted higher and higher.

He had fallen into the habit of studying in the library whenever possible. His small, bare room in the cottage in East Oakland, which he had fitted up as a study with a kitchen table for a desk, was splendid, of course. He preferred to write there. But there was something about the big, book-walled reference room that was relaxing and conducive to study. The quietness was never silence; the rustle of the turning page, hushed voices, a quick, light step across the floor, made him feel less alone, warmed him. And there was that young fellow who worked in the library, Fred Jacobs, with whom he frequently chatted and who more than once had given him a helping hand with his English assignments. Fred, a slightly built, blond, studious-appearing boy, was also going to school and hoped to enter the university the next year. He had been working most of the time since he finished the grammar grades. By going to night school he had managed to acquire a number of university credits, but now, having saved enough money, he intended to finish everything up in a year at a "cramming joint." Jack was puzzled; Fred dressed, talked, and although he was a little older, even looked like the boys in the Oakland high school, but he was cordial, and they were not.

As the weeks passed their acquaintance progressed. Fred was easy to converse with, interested in what Jack had to say, shy, but willing to talk about himself. Chemistry was his field. In a practical way he already knew a great deal about it, and had read all the books he could find on the subject, but he was impatient to get into the university classes and laboratories. His blue eyes shone behind his spectacles. And was Jack interested in photography? He had been working at it for some time, taking, developing and printing his own pictures. He would like to show Jack some of his best work.

Thus encouraged, Jack awkwardly confided something of his own interests. Socialism left Fred cold. He knew and cared nothing about it, and Jack did not mention it a second time. But working one's way through school—Fred understood and appreciated that. He would be glad to help him. And Jack should certainly get acquainted with Bess Maddern, because not only was she good at mathematics and even taught it privately, but she, too, was going to night school in order to enter the university. And there was Jim Reed and the girl he was going to marry as soon as he had his sheepskin, and Ted and Mabel Applegarth. Ted would be entering college in the fall; Mabel was already taking special courses there. Jack must meet them. He would like them.

Meantime Fred had told his friends about Jack and they were curious to see him. Bess thought that his name was familiar and finally recalled that a John London had won the prize story contest in the *Call* which they had discussed two years before. It must be the same boy. Ted Applegarth, lingering purposely in the library one day, was the first to meet him. Ted rather over-whelmed Jack. He was so plainly a "gentleman," with his formal manner and English accent, but his friendliness was genuine. Jack began to hope and to fear that he would meet the others.

One Saturday evening he found himself at loose ends, too tired to study or read or write, and hungry for companionship. He had no friends. When he came back from the East he had not hunted up Louis Shattuck, and besides, in his present mood nothing would be duller than picking up a girl and sitting with her on a park bench. He wished that Frank Atherton were in town. On his rare visits from Los Gatos he and Jack nearly always went to the theater or opera in San Francisco. Sometimes they would drop in afterward at the Bella Union where they watched the antics of the underworld over ten-cent mugs of beer, and talked about life and their ambitions.

Too restless to stay at home, he went downtown and was stand-ing indecisively at the crowded corner of Twelfth and Broadway when someone hailed him. It was Applegarth, and with him was a slender, black-haired young woman whom he introduced as Miss Maddern. They were at loose ends, too, explained Ted, and for lack of a better idea were on their way to attend a Salvation Army meeting for the fun of it. Wouldn't Jack join them?

Jack fought down his shyness and assented. But a Salvation Army meeting was very uninteresting. He knew because he had been to many of them. Couldn't they think of something pleasanter? Bess remembered that there was a concert that night at the Congregational Church. How would that do? Jack thought that it would be fine, and Ted was agreeable.

And she, too, was friendly, he realized happily. She had heard about him from Fred, it seemed, and how he was working and studying hard to go to college. Fred and she had been hoping to enter in the fall of '96 so that they would be in the first class of the new century. It looked as if Fred would make it since he had decided to go to the University Academy, Anderson's School in Alameda, where Ted was going, but that was too expensive for her so she would have to enter later.

Jack forgot his shabby clothes, even forgot to watch his speech, and they did not seem to notice; at least, she did not. Ted looked up sharply once or twice at a swearword or a bit of hobo slang, but said nothing. After the concert—he had not paid much attention to it, because little as he knew about music he knew even less about the astonishing pleasure of being with young people like these—Bess asked him to accompany them to her home to raid the pantry, but he awkwardly excused himself. He had to be up early the next morning to study and write but, sure, he would be glad to come some other time. The ice was broken. When Fred told him soon after that he was invited to the Applegarths' for Sunday-night supper he needed but little urging to accept.

The face of Jack's world changed so radically and so quickly that afterward he did not quite know how it had happened. For months he had doggedly pursued his lonely routine of school, work and study. Now, suddenly, he was welcome in two homes and participated regularly in all manner of activities initiated by this group of old friends who had accepted him wholeheartedly.

At first the difference between him and them made him very uneasy. They seemed always to have known and taken for granted much that he was now consciously striving to acquire. And even in matters which he himself had taken for granted they differed. Speech, manners, customs—all were slightly foreign to him. It was as if he had lived all his life in a far, isolated province and had just arrived in the capital of the country. It was not the capital, of course, merely the suburbs, but he did not know that.

None of them were well to do, but their houses reflected a grace and leisure of living that was new to him. The Applegarths' flat was elegant in a late-Victorian way, the Madderns' big house was serene and comfortable, and in both he met generous hospitality. He had neither time, equipment nor temperament to be critical. Also, before he had his bearings, he fell in love with Mabel Applegarth, and as a result viewed everything through a rosy mist for a long time.

The Applegarths had come to Oakland from England, the father being a mining engineer, and the transplanted family retained most of its British middle-class characteristics. They might be a little short on finances but they were very long on British culture, refinement and tradition. With Mr Applegarth frequently absent for long periods, the household had become one which revolved about its women. Furniture, food, conversation and much else reflected their tastes and interests.

Mrs Applegarth, small, delicately built, with finely chiseled features and a wealth of glossy brown, beautifully dressed hair, concealed beneath a yielding femininity many of the traits of an astute commander in chief. A gesture, gentle but precise, was law; a half-uttered request was granted without further discussion. As chaperon for her daughter, she zestfully shared in all the activities of the young people. No bicycle trip was too tiring, and at picnic suppers neither bugs nor wood ashes in the roasted potatoes and broiled steaks disturbed her. Jack, who had never met her like before, found her unexpectedly good company, charming, witty and tactful as well as sympathetic with his strivings.

She had reared Mabel carefully as a typical young English girl of good family but, youthful and attractive herself, she would not permit her to forsake her role of ingénue. It never occurred to Mabel to question her, and besides, she fitted the role perfectly, with her soft, golden curls, appealing blue eyes and beautiful hands. She was the oldest of the group, but none of them seemed so young and inexperienced. Her habitual langour was no pose; she had never been strong.

Jack idealized and worshiped her. For him she embodied all the grace and charm of young womanhood. The laces, embroideries and trimmings of the day, the narrow waists and long, sweeping skirts enhanced her fragile beauty. She played the piano, quoted poetry, "knew" English literature, and had positive although unoriginal opinions on a number of subjects of which he knew very little. Her correct British speech was a constant reminder of the slovenliness of his own, her perfect manners demanded and received miracles from him, and her pitiful lack of strength and vitality (perhaps the most striking difference between her and her mother) evoked in him tenderness and an old-fashioned gallantry.

So entranced was he with the Applegarths that he scarcely noticed how much more at ease he was with Bess and Fred, and that a quiet, dependable comradeship was growing among them. For many reasons they were closer to him than the others. About them was a definitely sulphurous odor of rebellion against their environment. Determined to escape, they were working their way into and through college without assistance from their parents, and with no sense of drama or heroics were slowly but surely attaining their objectives. He liked them both enormously, and was pleased when he learned that they were sweethearts and planned to marry as soon as Fred had graduated from the university.

In almost every way the contrast between Bess and Mabel was extreme. Bess was several months younger than Jack, slender and athletic, with vigorous, blue-black hair and hazel eyes. For several years she had been earning her living by tutoring, but her manner of sturdy independence, which Jack admired even while in thrall to Mabel's helplessness, was deceptive. Few knew that it was a gallant mask for unsureness and a lack of self-confidence which assailed her whenever she stepped outside the limits of her knowledge. Calmly and efficiently she would have explained an algebra problem to the President of the United States himself, or ridden a bicycle to the North Pole and back without a tremor, but confronted by a discussion on literature, which she dearly loved but felt she did not properly understand, she was struck dumb.

Because the Madderns regarded higher education as a waste of time except for the rich, "who put on airs and wasted their time anyway," Bess had gone to business school as soon as she completed the grammar grades. Her mother, Melissa Jones, came from generations of plantation and farming people who had done very well without college degrees. Although Henry Maddern, last of an ancient, once-wealthy Cornish family whom hunger had finally driven to America, had been raised a "gentleman" and destined to be an organist, he had bowed to circumstances in order to earn a living and become a plumber. Pride in family name and traditions, training in music if it were desired; for the girls, instruction from their mother in homemaking; for the boys, the opportunity to learn the plumbing business from him—this, he believed, was sufficient equipment for his children.

But Bess thought otherwise. To study bookkeeping had been the compromise of a long struggle for permission to go to high school. She mastered its tedious intricacies in short order, then, rather than enter an office, looked about for bookkeeping pupils. She was barely seventeen when she realized that she must buy the privilege of planning her own life. Extraordinarily gifted as a teacher, and despising bookkeeping, she energetically sought and found primary and grammar-grade students who for various reasons were unable to attend school, and before long was fully occupied every day. Her family vigorously objected, but in the face of board and room paid promptly each week they could do nothing, not even when she began to go to night school and speak of the university.

When Jack met her she was more than halfway to her goal and gaining confidence as, month by month, study increased her knowledge. Slow but thorough, anything she learned she could teach, and Jack benefited greatly from her mastery of algebra and English grammar. Sometimes, watching her vivid, mobile face and sensing the control in her tense voice, he was struck by the thought that she might have been an actress. Once he spoke of it and learned that only family disapproval of the stage for any of its daughters had kept her from being on the stage long before as a protégée of her cousin, Minnie Maddern Fiske.

One branch of the Cornish Madderns had rebelled against threadbare gentility a generation before Henry brought his mother and sisters to the new world, and had chosen to become strolling players across the length and breadth of England. Migrating to America, some of them had joined one of the many Mississippi showboat companies. Minnie Maddern had been born in New Orleans at the end of a season's run. On the boards from childhood, she was well known on the New York stage while still in her 'teens. Bess had long been a favorite cousin. On frequent tours to the coast Minnie observed her critically, and about the time she graduated from grammar school she suggested that the young girl be placed in her care to train for the stage. Henry and Melissa refused for various spoken reasons, and Bess remained at home. Years later Minnie was to ask for one of Bess's daughters for the same purpose, and again to be refused.

Before he came to know the group Jack had considered his schedule overfull, and had wished for more time to devote to interests which could not qualify because of the rigid requirements of his needs. Nevertheless it accommodated itself quite easily to his new activities. He continued his school work and outside reading; the hours spent earning a living did not decrease; as before, he turned out stories and articles from time to time. But Saturday evenings and Sundays, and now and then week nights, found him at the Applegarths or the Madderns, on bicycle trips into the hills, picnic suppers, or sailing on Lake Merritt.

Mabel and Bess believed that he should learn how to dance, and many evenings were spent in the Madderns' large living room, with Mabel at the piano, before the girls gave up in despair and agreed with him that he would never be a dancer. Other evenings he worked late with Bess over algebra problems, learning to savor the quiet satisfaction that comes from correct mathematical reasoning and ultimate solution. This was part of Bess's gift to him; the rest came from her appreciation of his aims and his fight to attain them, from her own example of perseverance, from her reverence for struggle itself and her scorn of supine acceptance of "things as they are."

Mabel and her mother gave him music and the British nineteenth-century poets, with the exception of Browning, and table manners and old-fashioned courtesies. Mrs Applegarth persuaded them to organize a club which met regularly at her flat to review books and discuss literature—the French Club, they called it, not because it was even remotely concerned with French culture, but because they could not pronounce the elegant name Mrs Applegarth had given it—Fin du Siècle. Other gatherings were less intellectual, as witness the pie-eating contests on Sunday evenings when Jack, who loathed desserts of any kind, downed incredible quantities of Mrs Applegarth's cherry pies.

Ted taught him chess, and often on late afternoons he would come straight to the flat from his janitor work at the high school, his hands still swollen and moist from mopping floors and washing windows, to spend an hour before supper with Ted over the chessboard. Mabel, who did not care for the game, frequently interrupted their concentration, and never failed to reprove Jack when discovery of a disastrous move brought emphatic profanity to his lips. All of them were startled by Jack's colorful language, but Mabel gave every appearance of being severely shocked. Often Jack's embarrassment was covered by the shouts of laughter caused by Mabel's antics.

Throughout this period he did not drink at all, not even when he went to the First and Last Chance Saloon to borrow a few dollars in an emergency from Johnny Heinhold. Johnny not only appreciated what Jack was attempting to accomplish, but had great faith in his success. There is no doubt that he would have helped the boy anyway; Johnny was a good friend to many besides Jack whose destinies were not so spectacular. The money was always promptly returned, and for several years Johnny's generosity at trying times was one of the few dependable factors in Jack's life.

The oyster pirates and roistering seamen, his companions on the road and fellow convicts were far from him now. Sometimes it was hard to believe that he had actually been one with them. Recalling his experiences to his new friends, he was careful to tone them down. During the summer he camped with the Applegarths in Yosemite Valley while Mabel convalesced from a serious illness. Sitting about the fire at night, he remembered other campfires only a little over a year before in the mud and slush of Iowa. He described to the Applegarths what he thought would amuse and pleasantly horrify them, but much that he remembered he kept to himself and thought over when he was alone.

To the ordinary observer, Jack's life during this period might have seemed full, happy and very satisfying, but this was not entirely the case. He had not broken with his past when he entered the middle class; he could never do that, although later he would try. Poverty of the stark, working-class variety walked with him daily, and his responsibilities had not lessened. His family silently hoped that he would soon come to his senses, give up his mad idea of a college education, get a job and settle down. He did not blame them, understanding their terror as age and failing strength increased their dependence on him, but he was sure that he was on the right track, that events would soon justify his course. In time both parents even came to share his confidence to a certain extent, John because he was fond of the boy, Flora because she began to see that if Jack were to realize his ambitions, she might once again know the pride and security she had lost so many years before when she left Ohio.

Their attitude did not concern him one way or another, however, although he was glad when they did not worry. What did concern him was the why of the whole situation—why it had been so much harder for him to find himself than Mabel and Ted, for instance, and even Fred and Bess; why boys and girls of his own class, equally and often more talented than his middle-class friends, would never have a chance at all. Realizing this, he was appalled by the frightful waste of intelligence in a world that obviously needed all it could get of it.

And so he was not, could not be content. The more he saw of what he later was to call the parlor floor of society, the more poignantly he remembered the cellar. He wished that his new friends might share his interest in the social problem, but their dismissal of it as something with which they need not concern themselves did not affect him. During the first of the two years he was in their group none of them knew that a part of his life was hidden from them. When it finally came to their attention they considered it merely another eccentricity of this boy who was odd in many ways. But Jack's gravitation toward the socialist movement, and his eventual participation in it, was perhaps the most important phase of all his activity at this time.

CHAPTER

9

AS CAPITALISM approached maturity in the 'nineties fundamental changes already operating under the surface of American life began to be felt and seen. The escape to the land having been cut off by the closing of the frontier, cities developed rapidly, and the urban influence spread in ever widening circles until it affected the entire nation.

Few were more than superficially aware that a new era was well under way, welcoming as pleasing novelties the flood of new inventions which sooner or later altered almost every phase of their existence, but missing their significance. During the last two decades of the nineteenth century appeared, one after the other, the telephone, bicycle, trolley car, fountain pen, arc lamp, cash register, phonograph, linotype machine, glucose, incandescent lamp, chemical fire extinguisher, oleomargarine and much else common today but new then. Meantime the accomplishments of inventive skill were steadily increasing the productivity of labor.

The average American scarcely noticed even the change coming over the home as it yielded helplessly to the demands of the factory system. In previously unheard-of numbers women began to earn their living, leaving the home for the office or factory and deserting the country for the city. A generation earlier women had become factory workers, but their daughters now aspired, and successfully, to positions as stenographers, saleswomen and librarians, while their untrained immigrant sisters entered factories and domestic service. As industrial activity and increasing population turned towns into cities, land prices within the city limits rose sharply, and apartment houses and hotels began to replace the single-family house. Charlotte Perkins Gilman said later, "the home was being lifted clean off the ground—yardless, cellarless, stairless, even kitchenless."

The metamorphosis of the American home was paralleled by the metamorphosis of the school. As early as 1895 John Dewey was proclaiming that the school was "life, and not a preparation for life." Everywhere courses of study were being radically adjusted to the requirements of the new industrial day. Even state boards of education recognized the need for vocational training and accepted the responsibility of providing it. The high school, formerly a mere stepping stone for the favored few into the hallowed halls of university learning, sprang into prominence because additional education was now required for employment, and vocational schools of every variety came into being.

That the majority of those who heard Mr Dewey's prophetic utterance either did not understand or were not interested in understanding his message, and that other so-called educated people who patronized libraries and read books were blind to the social drama being enacted beneath their very noses is evidenced by examination of available library circulation figures for the period. In 1893, for instance, Americans were reading, in order of preference, *David Copperfield, Ivanhoe, The Scarlet Letter, Uncle Tom's Cabin, Ben Hur, Adam Bede, Vanity Fair, Jane Eyre* and *The Last Days of Pompeii.* Mark Twain was thirteenth below Dickens on the list of favorite authors, F. Marion Crawford fifteenth and William Dean Howells, who of all the newer school of American writers was reflecting most clearly the themes and tempo of his day, was twenty-sixth. There are significant omissions: the leaders of the local-color school which, a generation later, was to fill high school textbooks; the younger English novelists, Hardy, Meredith and Stevenson; the French and Russian writers—Zola and Tolstoy, to mention but two. The indictment seems more or less complete.

In the face of nation-wide indifference, however, signs of the times were on every hand, revealing the maturing process of capitalism and the clarification of class lines which had up to then been blurred and indistinct.

Philanthropy, for instance, became organized in the larger cities during the 'nineties, nearly one hundred charity organizations being in full swing by 1893. Their objectives were to institutionalize philanthropy, abolish public outdoor relief and check mendicity; in other words, the "covering-up" movement, which would nobly attempt to meet the demands made upon it as decade after decade America's standing army of unemployed increased, had begun. This period saw the genesis of the professional, trained social worker. The larger organizations maintained elaborate filing systems, and through these the cataloguing of dependents into "worthy and upright poor," "willing paupers," and "voluntary dependents" was off to a good start. Organized, philanthropy was much more efficient than before, but aside from superficial efforts at relief, it ignored the grosser social and economic injustices.

Great changes had already taken place in journalism, but others more spectacular were to come. Inventions were making possible the printing of larger newspapers with vastly improved make-up, and the two major news-collecting agencies, the Associated Press and the Scripps-McRae, were beginning to extend the field of journalism. The 'seventies had witnessed the passing of the earlier great leaders of the press, Greeley, Bennett, Bowles and Bryant. In the next decade appeared the first of two figures who were to dominate American journalism well into the twentieth century.

Joseph Pulitzer had arrived in the United States in 1864, a penniless, seventeen-year-old Hungarian-Jewish boy. Nineteen years later, already proprietor of the St Louis *Post-Dispatch*, he bought the moribund New York *World* from Jay Gould for $346,000 and proceeded to play ducks and drakes with the traditions of conservative journalism. Not only did he brighten the pages of his paper with pictures, dish out local scandals and pulpy romances and play up crimes, but he used his editorial columns to fight against local corruption and other abuses. The *World* became the voice of the urban masses, and circulation leapt from sixteen thousand to one hundred and sixteen thousand. In a short time men like Godkin of the *Nation* and Dana of the *Sun* were completely eclipsed.

But another man now entered the field who was to beat Pulitzer at his own game. In 1895 William Randolph Hearst bought the New York *Journal* and, assuming the role of a soapboxer for the people, ran up his circulation to four hundred thousand. He was the only New York editor to support Bryan during the 1896 campaign. First to introduce feature writers in the daily papers, he met competition as others followed suit by ruthless overbidding. Homer Davenport, Frederick Opper, Winifred Black, Bruno Lessing, Alan Dale—these were among his early choices. Later he was to buy Jack London. The new century was scarcely under way before Hearst was secure in the saddle as the boss of yellow journalism, and nothing would challenge his sway until the advent of the tabloids.

The 1896 presidential election took place in the midst of unprecedented viciousness and ferocity between Bryan democracy and the Republican party. A glance at the cartoons of the time and perusal of the political speeches show the snarling bitterness of the campaign. Propaganda material issued by both parties aimed haymakers. Theodore Roosevelt is credited with saying that the silver men might well be "stood up against the wall and shot." John Hay, a man not easily perturbed, wrote about Bryan to Henry Adams in London, "The boy orator makes only one speech—but he makes it twice a day. There is no fun in it. He simply reiterates the unquestionable truths that every man who has a clean shirt is a thief and should be hanged, and there is no goodness or wisdom except among the illiterates and criminal classes."

Populism and Bryan democracy made a high-water mark of incoherent revolt. Bryan's popularity may be explained by his quack remedies for checking the growth of monopolies and the domination of finance capital. The secret of his success lay in his ability to simplify the complexity of causes by reducing and dramatizing the conflict into the biblical struggle between the powers of good and evil, and by making his enemies personify all that was bad, vicious and oppressive.

Before 1896 had fully run its course, however, the tide of the depression turned. The failure of Indian wheat crops that very year and the shortness of the European wheat crops the following year brought about a rise in the prices of agricultural staples. Due to the rapid advancement of large-scale production, more manufactured articles entered into foreign trade, thereby releasing the strain upon gold for the balancing of international payments. And finally the world's gold supply was substantially increased by the opening of new mines in the Klondike and on the Rand in South Africa, and by the invention of the cyanide process for extracting gold from low content ores.

It was not long before the dire and gloomy prophecies of the silver orators appeared unduly exaggerated. The American farmer, whose noisy discontent had fed the fires of populism, ceased to be an enraged revolutionist and settled down as a responsible citizen and dependable producer. Suddenly the movement he had so lustily espoused was hopelessly out of step with the times.

The economic development of the United States after the Civil War can be explained principally by the replacement of cotton and wheat by coal, iron and steel. By the end of the nineteenth century the United States led the world in the production of these commodities. The greatest range of ore, the Mesabi in Minnesota, was opened in 1892. The Merritts, who had developed it, were wiped out in the 1893 panic, and John D. Rockefeller, already king of the lake ore ships, acquired the range.

Lacking a social base in this developing industrialism, populism and Bryan democracy were doomed. Despite the fact, however, that the Populists were defeated nationally in 1896 their influence had considerable effect in the states for some time.

The main issue in the campaign had apparently been the old monetary one: remonetization of silver *versus* retention of the gold standard. But underneath, as evidenced even in the Republican party, the real cleavage was between great wealth on the one hand and the middle and working classes on the other; 1896 marked a high point in the crystallization of this class conflict, and from then on the struggle was to be openly acknowledged not only in sectional but in national politics. The great corporations came to be considered the embodiment of all evil, as one after the other legislative investigations exposed some of their ruthless practices to public view. As time went on the urban lower class found an ally in the working class in the fight against what they termed the common enemy.

Not even the strenuous and effective labors of Marcus A. Hanna, while preparing the Republican party convention, had been able to insulate it against this political division. Despite the large majority acceptance of the platform which opposed free silver, and its reported demonstrative approval, the vote on the financial plank had shown one hundred and ten delegates firmly opposed to its acceptance. After their defeat this contingent withdrew from the convention, declaring, "The people cry aloud for relief; they are bending under a burden growing heavier with the passing hours; endeavor no longer brings its just reward . . . and unless the laws of the country and the policies of the political parties shall be converted into mediums of redress, the effect of human desperation may sometime be witnessed here as in other lands and other ages."

In similar vein, but bearing the inimitable stamp of the silver-tongued orator, is a portion of Bryan's speech at the Democratic convention: "You come to us and tell us that the great cities are in favor of the gold standard. I tell you that the great cities rest upon these broad and fertile prairies. Burn down your cities and leave our farms, and your cities will spring up again like magic. But destroy our farms, and grass will grow in the streets of every city in this country."

Nevertheless the curtain had rung down for bimetallism. Between, roughly, 1895 and 1907 three movements became noticeable: the organization of capital, the organization of labor, and the growth of coercive interference of government in the struggle between the two camps in favor of capital.

The 1896 defeat of Bryan democracy established the industrial and political domination of the great trusts. At once they demanded world markets and the powerful navy necessary to achieve them. Looking apprehensively eastward, the United States witnessed the partition during 1897–98 of China's profitable market and riches by European powers. Their intent rivalry irrefutably established the fact that commerce was the backbone of all political interests, that diplomacy was merely the instrument to maintain foreign markets and extend trade relations, and that armies and navies were essentially accessories for attaining these ends. As a matter of fact the United States had not been a disinterested spectator of the last insurrection against Spanish rule which had broken out in February 1895. At least fifty million dollars of holdings in Cuba were in the hands of Americans, and at the beginning of the insurrection America's commerce with the island amounted to a hundred million annually.

In the midst of all this, of course, the little competitive capitalists' political power diminished alarmingly. Finding it almost impossible to exist in the domestic market alongside of the trusts, let alone compete with them in the foreign markets, the little capitalists energetically opposed all imperialistic manifestations. As a debtor class they also wanted a depreciated currency, but their efforts to obtain this were no more successful than their attempts to halt imperialism. The curtain had rung down for them, too, but they did not know it.

The destiny of the working class was far different. The extending application of machinery was causing greater concentration of capital, and the immense, growing combines created vast armies of workers who sweated together elbow to elbow in the early modern factory. The conditions of their employment and the increase in their exploitation sharpened class lines, and then began to solidify the workers' class ideology. As a result the struggle between the growing labor movement and the big capitalists in their ever-demanding drive for a higher rate of profit, took on greater and greater proportions, and each open conflict added an uncompromising bitterness to both sides.

The Buffalo Railroad strike and the one at Homestead against Carnegie and Company in 1892, the bloody struggle in Coeur d'Alene in 1893, Cripple Creek in 1894 and the Pullman strike the same year, Leadville in 1896–97, Salt Lake and again Coeur d'Alene in 1899, the recurring strikes in the coal region of Tennessee—from these and others, workers in many industries throughout the nation learned much which was later to be revealed in their organizations and tactics. Those who were organized represented only an insignificant portion of the working class and were in the main skilled workers. They advanced toward trade unionism slowly and painfully, continually harried and often outwitted by the bosses. Between 1898 and 1904 Hanna's National Civic League did them untold damage. Aiming at the inclusion of influential labor leaders in the camp of the employers, this flanking movement was so successful that the half a dozen years have been called a "honeymoon period of capital and labor." But, like many honeymoons in which the basic ingredients of agreement and harmony are lacking, it was not to last, despite the matchmakers.

The working class produced leaders faster than the employers could steal them. Free at last of the agrarian movements which had sidetracked it and squandered its strength again and again, rooted now in its proper sphere, the virility of its growth organizationally was astonishing. Not the least of the events of the cataclysmic 'nineties was the release of American middle-class idealists and intellectuals from their long absorption, first in the movement for free land and the abolition of slavery, later in the futile agi-

tation against the land monopolists. Now, with these causes relegated to the past, the best of the middle-class idealists turned
to the working class, finding their places in it, as their European
counterparts had done long since, and working side by side with
its proletarian leadership.

The history of the Socialist Labor party from 1877 to 1897 is
the history of American socialism for the same period. Emerging
with its new name from the second meeting of the Workingmen's
party of the United States in 1877, its zigzags during the next two
decades graphically mark in red the growth, development and
weaknesses of a young working class striving for manhood.

European refugees had brought with them some Marxian, but
mostly pseudo-Marxian ideas, to a country in which they were
foreigners both ideologically and traditionally. Their inability to
apply Marxian principles to American conditions was due, in the
main, to ignorance both of the country and of the principles.
Confined within their own sectarian circles, their behavior politically was more like that of an esoteric group of scholars than of
builders of a mass political party.

Until the 'nineties the Socialist Labor party had developed
slowly in numbers as well as ideas. Foreigners, especially Germans, made up the largest part of its membership, its central organ
was published in German, and its influence among American
workers was practically nil. But with the entrance into the party
at the beginning of the 'nineties of the Columbia University law
professor, Daniel De Leon, the whole course of the party
changed.

De Leon was born in Venezuela in 1852, the son of a prosperous
physician. Educated abroad in Germany and Holland, he came to
America, after receiving his university degree at the age of
twenty, to study law at Columbia. Upon completion of this
course he was retained there for several years as assistant professor of international law. His popularity with both faculty and
students as well as his obvious capabilities put him in line for a
full professorship, but life intervened.

De Leon's vigorous mind could not long be penned within the
comfortable and secure boundaries of the university. Probing beneath the surface to discover the causes of various unacademic
phenomena of American life, he fell under the influence of Henry
George and, for a short time, was interested in Edward Bellamy.

The immediate result of the appearance of Bellamy's utopian novel, *Looking Backward*, had been the so-called Nationalist movement. Bellamy, ignorant of Marxian socialist philosophy, advocated "an industrial army for maintaining the community precisely as the duty of protecting it is entrusted to a military army." With the apparent reasonableness which was to bring him many disciples, he inquired, "What inference could possibly be more obvious and more unquestioned than the advisability of trying to see if a plan which was found to work so well for purposes of destruction might not be profitably applied to the business of production now in such shocking confusion?"

Rejecting the class struggle and advancing no laws for socio-logical development, Bellamy was a social improviser. His ideas were so simple, however, and appealed so strongly to the under-dog that in a short time a movement had patterned itself upon his superficial remedies.

The first organization in this movement was the Bellamy Club of Boston, which soon changed its name to the Nationalist Club. By 1891 there were a hundred and sixty-two such groups. Bel-lamy's explanation of the term "nationalist" throws light not only on his opinions but on the confusion of isms through which the early radical movement was groping: ". . . This is called Na-tionalism because it proceeds by nationalization of industries, including the minor application of the same principle, the munici-palization and state control of localized business. Socialism implies the socializing of industry. This may or may not be based upon the national organism, and may or may not imply economic equality. As compared with socialism, Nationalism is a definition, not in the sense of opposition or exclusion, but of a precision rendered necessary by a cloud of vague and disputed implica-tions historically attached to the former word." Sometimes the clubs co-operated with the Socialists and more frequently, with the Populists; occasionally they ran independent candidates, but essentially they were propaganda groups.

De Leon rejected nationalism in short order. Henry George's single tax theory held him longer, however, and led indirectly to the next and most important step in his search. Although the Socialists gave active political support to George during his mayoralty campaign in New York in 1886 they differed with his ideas. Accepting his criticism of the production of wealth and its distribution, they disputed his analysis of causes. Against the single taxer's consideration of landownership as the fundamental factor in modern society, they placed factory production. To the single taxer's belief that the only form of economic exploitation was rent—the return made for the use of land—they retorted that the source of all value was surplus value—the unpaid part of the workers' labor—and that from it "rent-interest-and-profit" were drawn.

The single taxers saw in the private ownership of land the root of all evils; the Socialists saw it in the private ownership of the means of production—machinery and the like—as well as land. The single taxers believed in competition in industry, the Socialists in collectivism. The single taxers proposed to abolish the landlord and monopolist of "land values," but did not oppose the continued existence of capitalist and wage worker; the Socialists proposed nothing less than the abolishing of all classes and the establishment of economic equality. The single taxers claimed their theory to be universal and applied it to all times; the Socialists maintained that theirs was an outgrowth of modern economic conditions, i.e., capitalism, and that socialization was the logical next step in the growth of concentration of capital and large-scale industry.

Between the single taxers and the French eighteenth century physiocrats there was much similarity. The Frenchmen had based their principal analysis upon a nonindustrial society; the followers of Henry George sought to retain the individualism of a pioneer period and preserve it in the face of growing industrial conditions. The movement, financially assisted by Fels, the soap manufacturer, had a mushroom growth but went to pieces with the death of its founder in 1887. Only the year before he had polled sixty-eight thousand votes for mayor, and this was in an old New York whose eligible voters would not equal the number now franchised in the borough of Manhattan alone.

De Leon followed closely the sometimes acrimonious attacks and counterattacks of the two groups with an increasing disillusionment in the single tax and a growing interest in socialism, and turned finally to make a thorough study of Marxism. Here he found what he had been seeking. In 1890 he joined the Socialist Labor party and because of his ability soon gained a leading position. And as the history of the Russian Bolshevik party when it was based upon Marxism is identified with the biography of Lenin, so was that of the Socialist Labor party identified with the life of De Leon until his death in 1914.

Before the advent of De Leon there had been two tendencies in the Socialist Labor party's attempts to entrench itself in American soil. One believed in concentrating on socialist propaganda during elections and left the trade unions to their own devices; the other centered all its activity in the trade-union movement and ignored politics. De Leon opposed both and, rejecting tempting short cuts, started the movement on the performance of its historic task.

De Leon's stand was clear cut and uncompromising. He believed that the socialist revolution would occur first in the United States because, due to the absence of feudal restrictions, it was a country of classic capitalism where the highest capitalistic relations existed, and where the objective conditions were more nearly ripe for the socialist revolution than in any other country. From this he took the position that it was necessary to awaken the class consciousness of the working class as quickly as possible and attack the capitalist fortress. Those thus awakened and organized into the revolutionary Socialist party would become the advance guard—"the head of the lance," or "the head of the column."

He once said concerning the function of the party, ". . . as in storming of fortresses, the thing depends upon the head of the column—upon that minority that is so intense in its convictions, so soundly based on its principles, so determined in action that it carries the masses with it, storms the breastworks and captures the fort. Such a head of the column must be our socialist organization to the whole column of the American proletariat, the head of whose column must consist of the intrepid socialist organization that has earned their love, their respect, their confidence."

Against the reformism that appeared in the party he initiated an unyielding struggle. He considered reforms to be merely a change in the outer form while the inner substance remained the same. As he put it, a poodle may be shorn to look like a lion, but it remains a dog. Pointing out that the capitalist politicians were keenly aware that reforms acted as safety valves, and that reformists could be easily enticed by concessions, he thundered, "The tiger will defend the tips of his mustache with the same ferocity that he will defend his very heart."

As the last of the 'nineties approached, the changing conditions of American life impressed themselves more deeply upon the Socialist Labor party, and it was not long before it was again in the throes of bitter factional warfare which was soon to end in a split. Leading those who resisted the orthodox and revolutionary socialism of De Leon were Morris Hillquit, Abe Cahan and other opportunists. Their oppositions were based upon a program of adaptation to the new conditions in America, not as intransigeant revolutionaries, but as practical politicians and parliamentarians emphasizing chiefly immediate demands. For their example they took the mass social democratic movement in Germany which had departed in many fundamental ways from revolutionary socialism and centered its activity upon fulfillment of parliamentary ambition. The American counterparts of the German leaders sought to ape even their servility to the trade-union bureaucracy and orientation to the middle class.

The issues between the opportunists and the De Leon intransigeants were many. They accused De Leon of being fanatically severe in the enforcement of discipline. De Leon believed that relentless opposition against intellectual individualism was unavoidable in order to strengthen proletarian discipline. On this question his conception of party organization and even his tone closely resembled Lenin's.

His blunt rejection of "gentleness" and "tolerance" as inconsistent with a logic which demanded "intolerance" and "irreconcilability" above everything else, his refusal to sacrifice quality for quantity, principle for numbers, and his insistence on a party-controlled press further angered his opponents. He condemned "parliamentary cretinism," seeing in parliamentarism itself only an instrument for revolutionary propaganda, and decrying ballot reforms, referendum schemes, the initiative, the election of federal senators by popular vote, as "so many lures to allow the revolutionary heat to radiate into vacancy."

Out of the debates on the question of autonomy or centralization came De Leon's famous simile of the mountain and the plain. He pointed out that the United States was young and vast and not uniform. Capitalism developed in every direction, but because of the youth of the country, primitive possibilities were bound to crop up unexpectedly. Proletarian elements still attached by the umbilical cord to bourgeois interests would obviously not be so strongly welded together as those among whom such connections had been sundered. Lacking their homogeneity and active sense of sacrifice, their efforts would be less focalized than a more fully class-developed revolutionary element. De Leon called the former the plain and the latter the mountain of the labor movement, and maintained that for the mountain, conducting its work in a concentrated manner, centralization was inevitable, while organization of the plain of necessity assumed an autonomous form.

De Leon left an indelible mark on the American trade-union movement. To him, a neutral attitude on the part of revolutionists toward the unions as to form of organization or methods of struggle was nothing less than a betrayal of the workers' interests and tantamount to neutrality toward the "machinations" of the capitalist class. He was equally outspoken in condemnation of certain phases of the labor movement, dismissing the American Federation of Labor or craft unionism as "pure and simple," and as a buffer of the existing order. "Labor fakirs" and "labor lieutenants of capitalism" were scornful epithets coined by him in the heat of battle against the leadership of the American Federation of Labor during his long fight for revolutionary industrial unionism, which he passionately believed in and fathered. In time he was to develop his ideas on this subject further and consider the unions the nuclei of the future society which, after the social revolution, would take over the direction of its economic life. In 1895 he abandoned the policy of "boring from within" the A. F. of L. and organized the dual union, the Socialist Trade and Labor Alliance, with a revolutionary socialist platform. Later Debs and other Left-wingers in the Socialist party took this same position.

In the light of subsequent developments in the radical movement here and abroad, De Leon's strength and weaknesses are clearly discernible. His very refusal to compromise on tactical grounds and his overestimation of the revolutionary possibilities in the United States eventually led the movement into sectarianism; his intolerance and tendency to exaggerate repelled rather than attracted workers. In 1900 party members were forbidden to hold leading offices in craft unions, and if officials in these organizations applied for membership in the party they were refused. This nearsighted policy resulted in an isolation that was tragic not only for the party but for the labor movement, which was left completely at the mercy of "fakirs."

On the other hand, at congresses of the Second Socialist International he was one of the first to oppose its high rabbi, Karl Kautsky, for his opportunism. "We are divided from them not only by a physical but also by a historical ocean," he said, explaining the coolness of the leaders of the Second International toward the Socialist Labor party. And then, unable to see how a revolution could break out in a relatively undeveloped industrial country, he voiced his faith in the immediate destiny of the movement in America: "They still live under semifeudal conditions while we are at the threshold of the Socialist Revolution!" It is significant that the leaders of the Second International were equally cold toward certain other revolutionary currents within the International: the Bulgarian "Tesniaks," the Dutch "Tribunists," and the Russian "Bolsheviks."

Lenin considered De Leon one of the greatest Marxian thinkers. "But," he asked, half in jest, half in earnest, "did not De Leon err on the side of 'sectarianism'?" De Leon anticipated an essential element of the Soviet system—the replacement of the bourgeois parliament by representatives from production units. Unlike the Bolsheviks, however, he did not see the inevitable transitional period between capitalism and socialism—the "Dictatorship of the Proletariat." Believing that with the revolution the state would be eliminated and socialism realized at once, he denied the need of a party after the revolution. De Leon and the Bolsheviks were very close to each other in many ways, however, especially in their determined and uncompromising fight against all forms of opportunism.

With the decline of the Knights of Labor and the rise of the A. F. of L. in the late 'eighties and early 'nineties, the Socialists had lost considerable influence in the labor movement. The new crop of leaders in the A. F. of L., many of whom had been trained in socialist ranks, chose to steer clear of politics. An open break was precipitated at the 1890 A. F. of L. convention by Gompers' refusal to grant a charter to the Central Labor Federation of New York because one of its component organizations was the local section of the Socialist Labor party.

De Leon's dual unionism, "doctrinal orthodoxy," insistence on strict party discipline and party-controlled press, did not help the situation. Trade unionists remained at a distance, distrustful and uneasy. The Hillquit-Cahan opposition and the Volkszeitung group determined to take matters into their own hands. With an avowed position of neutrality toward the "fakirs," they looked around for opportunities for broader mass activities as well as parliamentary possibilities. Before long the inevitable split with De Leon occurred—a noisy one at that, which landed in the courts before it was over—and for a time there were two Socialist Labor parties.

The bitter industrial struggles of the time, disillusionment with populism following its abject surrender to Bryan, and impatience with the Socialist Labor party's refusal to offer immediate solutions or panaceas resulted in the development of a new current outside of the main stream of the radical movement. Clamoring for a "new deal" in radicalism, it based itself on utopian colonization schemes that were to be characteristic of the American movement for decades. Even forty years later the tragicomedy was recostumed and played again. In the midst of the depression which followed the 1929 crash, when Lenin's Third International had become a mask for a bureaucratic growth even as his embalmed body was serving as a proletarian icon, Upton Sinclair, blithely ignoring the lessons of the past and the stark realities of the present, not only launched another of these fantastic schemes, but enrolled thousands of desperate, frightened people under the banner of EPIC.

The *Coming Nation* was founded in Greensburg, Indiana, by J. A. Wayland in 1893, and proceeded at once to "Yankeefy" socialism. The movement, essentially a brand of Left populism, was very similar to Bellamy's. Offering simple, ready answers to the average man's problems in life, unaccompanied by historical analyses and perspectives, its advantage over De Leon's socialism in winning members was tremendous. When the attempt to demonstrate the feasibility of this new brand of socialism on a thousand acres in Tennessee ended in dissension and Wayland's forced withdrawal from the colony, he started the *Appeal to Reason*, first in Kansas City, and later in Girard, Kansas. The paper's propaganda was opportunistic, superficial junk, but it nevertheless soon rolled up a huge circulation.

Still another anti-De Leon movement appeared in Milwaukee with the appointment of Victor Berger to the editorship of the Wisconsin *Vorwarts*. This was a socialism based on a revision of Marxism, deleting its revolutionary content, minimizing the ultimate goal, and basing itself on parliamentary activity and immediate demands. Berger differed with revolutionary Marxism but, not a complete enemy to theory, he also differed with those who came over from populism. In '94 he had supported the People's party, but when the Populists endorsed Bryan and free silver he had broken with them. Now, with the decrease of German immigration threatening his party with decline in Milwaukee, where its membership was mainly German, Berger was ready to co-operate with other reform groups.

In the meantime Eugene V. Debs, after campaigning for Bryan, had been converted to socialism when Berger visited him in the Woodstock jail following his arrest in connection with the American Railway Union's strike. Debs regarded Berger as his socialist "godfather," but a few years were to elapse before their paths ran together. Debs first embarked, with Henry Demarest Lloyd and Reverend Myron W. Reed of Colorado, on a utopian-socialist colonizing scheme, and became an organizer for this Brotherhood of the Co-operative Commonwealth.

When the A. R. U. was convened in special meeting by Debs in June 1897, it was immediately liquidated. Then, enlarging the meeting by the inclusion of representatives from groups of all shades of the rainbow, as well as a few free lancers, it reconvened. Out of this conglomeration was born the Social Democracy of America. Besides favoring many populist and Left populist demands, it accepted the colonization program of the Brotherhood of the Co-operative Commonwealth, which proposed to settle gradually one of the Western states until they could capture it and transform it into a socialist state.

At the convention the following year the organization split into two groups, the Socialists favoring political action, the anarchist and free-lance elements sticking stubbornly to colonization. Debs supported the Socialists led by Hourwich, who bolted the convention, and, meeting later with Frederick Heath of Milwaukee, organized the Social Democratic party of America. On the executive committee of this party, besides Debs, were Berger, Seymour Stedman and others who favored the revision of Marxian socialism. Their program, a combination of populism and revisionism, was close to that of the Hillquit-Cahan brand which, besides opposing dual unionism and centralization, was supporting Bernstein, the German revisionist of Marxism.

This anti-De Leon faction initiated unity conferences with the new Social Democratic party that led ultimately to an agreement to combine forces in the presidential election. Debs of the Social

Democratic party was to be candidate for president, with Job
Harriman, leader of the Hillquit-Cahan group in California, as his
running mate. A little later a merger of the two groups was consummated after some difficulties by a referendum vote, and the
Socialist party of America came into existence.

This immediately became the rallying ground for all groupings
who were opposed to De Leon and revolutionary Marxism. Later
from the Social Reform Club, an offshoot of the American Fabian
Society, came several important recruits, notably W. J. Ghent.

True to tradition, the West, whose peculiar conditions few of
the Socialist leaders knew or understood, contributed uniquely
to both the radical and labor movements. The Socialists of the
time who could see as far as west of the Rockies believed that the
accumulated pressure following the closing of the frontier would
immediately bring dire consequences to the capitalistic order.
Ignorance and overeagerness misled them. The class struggle
slowly grew sharper and more clearly defined, it is true, but it was
to be a lengthy, not a brief process. Irrigation and other untapped
resources extended the period of more or less peaceful development, and the West could and did accommodate many who
otherwise would have continued to revolt against their economic
misfortunes and suffering. The conflagration of class war which
the Socialists expected did not sweep the country; instead, it
blazed up from time to time in separate fires of varying scope
and intensity.

The Socialist Labor party in California, far from the parent
body and faced with problems that did not exist elsewhere, found
progress difficult. Isolated from the labor movement by De Leon's
policies, its efforts to serve it or clarify its confusion were usually
futile. The working and middle classes were still fighting the
"yellow peril." In the 'nineties Japanese began to replace Chinese
as the objects of white hatred. Again the voice of Dennis Kearney
was heard, but now it was only a hoarse whisper threatening to
drive them out. By 1895 their competition was being keenly felt
in the hop, beet and fruit industries, and when the re-enactment
of the Chinese Exclusion Act came up, the labor unions demanded that the Japanese be excluded as well.

During these trying times the California Socialist Labor party
did what it could to emphasize the larger aspects of the situation
and promote the class struggle, but, none too clear themselves,

their voices were drowned even by Kearney's. A few years later, after De Leon had lost the California party, he said bitterly, "There the party suffered most and freak-fraudom has held highest carnival."

A glance at the reading list given out by the Oakland section of the Socialist Labor party during the late 'nineties reveals its lack of Marxian character: *Looking Backward*, Edward Bellamy; *Cooperative Commonwealth*, Lawrence Gronlund; *The Soul of Man under Socialism*, Oscar Wilde; *Fabian Essays on Socialism* and *Woman, in the Past, Present and Future*, A. Bebel; *Paradoxes and Conventional Lies of Our Civilization*, Max Nordau; *Horace Greeley and Other Pioneers of American Socialism*, Charles Sothern; *Quintessence of Socialism*, Dr A. Schaeffle; *Reporter and Socialist*, A. Jones; *Socialism*, Encyclopedia Britannica. Not one book by Marx or Engels! The fact that only a very few books dealing with scientific Socialism had been translated into English is in itself a severe commentary on a movement which claimed to base itself on that Socialism.

Two kinds of socialist literature were being produced at this time, native and foreign. The native literature used an American vocabulary and addressed itself to an American audience, but at the same time it revealed the limits of the Americans' economic development, for it abounded with utopianism of all sorts, colony experiments (more pronounced in the United States than in any other country in the world) and a mishmash of muddled reform movements.

Aside from the translations of one or two of the Marxian classics, the foreign contributions were scholarly and scholastic, much more theoretically correct than the native brand but heavily pedantic. Couched in a vocabulary foreign to Americans, the lack of clarity and simplicity of these works veiled their accuracy and comprehensiveness. The average American found them over his head. What the literature of the movement urgently needed was the illustration of its principles by examples from American history. This method was effectively employed by many of the European socialist writers, but the Americans, still involved in learning the synthesis of German philosophy, English economics and French politics, failed to discover it.

But the class struggle did not wait for them. In the mining regions of the West, workers, unaided by the well-intentioned Socialists, met the mineowners in battles that exposed the nakedness and brutality of the war of the classes and corroborated in blood what Marx had foreseen. Farmers and others had not yet settled these regions and blurred the class lines in typical American fashion. With a comparative absence of the middle class, which vacillates between the two camps and finally adds its weight to the winning side, the miners and the owners faced each other and slugged it out.

The owners and their representatives were "quick on the trigger." Ignoring all pretenses of legality, they substituted concentration camps, called "bull pens," for the "due process of law." The miners were forced to resort to Winchester rifles and dynamite to defend their jobs and their lives. Although they were fighting for better conditions and higher pay without any conscious class philosophy, before they were through they had learned much and gone far toward a class-war ideology. Many of them became disillusioned with the function of government, and even with democracy itself, because of the role played by their government on the side of the owners.

In May 1893, after the '92 strike in Coeur d'Alene, Idaho, the miners formed the Western Federation of Miners, famous for its militancy and symbol of the most bitter struggles in the history of the American labor movement. It was this group which in 1898 organized and affiliated with the Western Labor Union in Salt Lake City, which in turn, after changing its name to the American Labor Union in 1902, merged with other radical unions three years later to form the Industrial Workers of the World.

This was the Western protest of the young labor movement against the aristocracy of labor in the A. F. of L. and its class collaborationism. As an organization, the Western Federation of Miners did not start out with a revolutionary program. Its revolutionary consciousness was preceded by revolutionary action.

CHAPTER

10

BESIDE the old city hall in Oakland was a tiny triangular park crisscrossed by paths and dotted with benches. On warm summer evenings the townsfolk used to gather there around the bandstand to gossip with their neighbors and listen to the concerts. Carriages moved slowly under the flickering gas lamps along the adjoining streets while their occupants took the air and caught snatches of music. At nine o'clock the city hall bell tolled curfew. Sometimes fire alarms drowned out the band, and the carriage audience would hastily make room for the noisy, horse-drawn fire engines.

The bustling 'nineties approached. Strolling in parks and listening to band concerts became outmoded. Traffic thickened on the wide path that connected Washington Street and San Pablo Avenue, and progressive citizens began to suggest that a little less park and a busy street cut through would benefit the city. To the members of the newly formed Socialist Labor party section, however, the crowded paths represented but one thing: a potential audience for their doctrines.

Like everyone else with a message, they had been soapboxing in Chabot Park, just behind the Oakland high school. Chabot Observatory had been given to Oakland as a "lecture room and astronomical station," but more lecturing had always been done outside under the trees than inside. Thanks to the city's decision to observe the spirit and intention of the gift, the small square became Oakland's Hyde Park, and remains so to this day.

City Hall Park offered a new field to the Socialists and less competition, but at first the hurrying people did not seem inclined to pause and listen. Max Schwind, the Oakland Socialist Labor party's financial secretary, and Frank Strawn-Hamilton, its most brilliant speaker, evolved a scheme that successfully met the problem. Standing on the steps of the city hall, they would begin to argue, raising their voices as they disagreed more violently. A curious crowd immediately gathered, hopefully waiting for opinions to be backed up with fists. As soon as a sufficient number were standing about, Schwind and Hamilton ceased to argue and, as Schwind said years later, "harangued 'em."

Jack passed the park and the city hall as he went to and from the free library, and he fell into the habit of stopping on the outskirts of the crowd whenever the Socialists were speaking. Before long his obvious interest attracted their attention. It was Herman Whitaker, better known to his friends as Jim, who first made Jack's acquaintance, greeting him in a comradely way that pleased him immensely, and inviting him to attend one of their Sunday evening lectures. Jack liked the gaunt Englishman at once, and a friendship began which was to last for several years.

Jim had been instructor of athletics and gymnastics in the British army. At the conclusion of his enlistment he had emigrated to Manitoba and there had suffered the anguish of defeat which was so often the lot of the settler. Completely beaten, he left Canada and came to California with his wife and small children. Matters mended very slightly. It was still almost impossible to make ends meet, and in his despair he turned, as so many Englishmen did in the 'nineties, to "socialism" as a cure for all human ills. But Jim's socialism sprang from different soil from that which Jack was beginning to learn. The English Socialists of the 'nineties were revivalistic and emotional, and their Bible was Robert Blatchford's *Merrie England*. This issued an inspiring call for the destruction of the upper classes of landowners and industrialists and the formation of a co-operative commonwealth by the masses of the people, but neglected to suggest any means by which this might be accomplished.

The co-operative commonwealth intrigued the California Socialists. They had come together in the Socialist Labor party by devious ways, most of them having been members of Bellamy clubs until the collapse of the nationalist movement. Knowing little or nothing about Marx, they welcomed the British evangelical socialism with enthusiasm. As early as 1895 the Oakland group put theory into practice by starting a co-operative grocery store, which benefited them a little, but saved Whitaker, who was soon placed in charge at a small but regular salary, from complete desperation.

More and more frequently Jack absented himself from the Sunday-night suppers at the Applegarths', drawn irresistibly to the party's public meetings and to the men he met there, especially Whitaker. The two had much in common at that time, despite the difference in their ages, and Jack benefited from the friendship in many ways. At Jim's invitation he began to stop at the grocery store during slack hours to discuss socialism, literature, life and ambitions, and to swap experiences. Jack told of the sea and the road, Jim of the brutal battles with hostile nature he had waged and lost in Manitoba. Even then Jim knew the desire to write of these matters, but the idea seemed too fantastic to acknowledge even to himself. One day this incredible dream would be realized.

Jim's physical skill and mastery of boxing and fencing appealed strongly to Jack. Often when the store was closed for the night they would draw the blinds and practice both arts. Jack never became as good a fencer or boxer as Jim, but he learned much, and his body gained greatly in suppleness and grace. The earnestness and sincerity of Jim's radical beliefs impressed Jack favorably. Nevertheless he realized that from others in the movement, Strawn-Hamilton, for instance, he could learn more of socialism. He did not feel ready yet to join the party; he was too busy, and he knew too little.

The end of his first year in high school was approaching. Visualizing two more years of it before he could hope to enter the university, he was appalled. In January he would be twenty years old. He wanted to write, but first he must be better educated; he wanted to know more of socialism, but that required time for study. With all that he desired to accomplish, it was absurd to move at this snail's pace. He knew that he could get through the high school courses more quickly than they were being taught. There must be a short cut.

In his dilemma he turned to Ted and Fred, but their only suggestion was Anderson's, the "cramming joint" both were attending. There he could cover the ground as rapidly as he wished, and if his work were recommended by the academy the university would accept him. The one drawback was the expense, for Anderson catered to the children of the wealthy and his fees were correspondingly high. The more he considered it, the more Jack was certain that this was the solution—if he could borrow the money. Such was his faith in himself that he did not doubt his ability to repay the loan with generous interest in a short time. He knew he would make good! All he needed was the chance.

Happily his sister Eliza was able to lend him the necessary sum, and the start of the spring semester saw him enrolled at the University Academy in Alameda and setting out to complete two years' work in four months. For five weeks, although he studied night and day, he knew the ecstasy of accomplishment. With excellent instructors to assist him he was fairly eating up the units the university demanded. By the end of the first month he knew that he was going to make it.

Most of his fellow students regarded his presence with disdain, but he paid them scant attention. That lesson had been learned at the Oakland high school. And he was too immersed in his studies to observe that after a few weeks their disdain was deepening into resentment. When he was summoned into Mr Anderson's office he was totally unprepared for the blow that awaited him.

Mr Anderson was very sorry. . . . Jack was an excellent, even an extraordinary student . . . but there had been talk, and dissatisfaction. After all, the school's reputation might suffer, and the university might even withdraw its accrediting if it learned that a student had been permitted to do two years' work in one semester. . . . He was returning in full the money Jack had paid in, and he wished him all the luck in the world.

Jack was stunned by the injustice. What was a "cramming joint" then if a student, having paid his fee, were not permitted to cram? And his progress had been approved by the school's own strict standards! Later he understood. Like everyone else, Anderson had his living to make, and he could not lose his wealthy clientele for the sake of one threadbare student. But at the time bitterness was uppermost. Was the only road to the university to be the long, slow one? Discouragement was only momentary, however. Defiance—of the dictum that sought to prevent his entrance into college in August, and of a society which permitted such criminal frustration of ambition and willingness to work for its achievement—flared up almost at once.

In one of Jack's early scrapbooks is to be found a small red booklet, a membership card issued by the American section of the

Socialist Labor party in Oakland to Jack London, signed by M. Schwind, and showing that Jack entered the party in April 1896. This was the first of two decisions which he made when he left the academy. The second set him to studying nineteen hours a day in order to take the entrance examinations at the university in August.

The summer months sped by unnoticed as he bent himself to mental toil more demanding of his resources than even shoveling coal had been. Lifting tired eyes from his books, aware for the first time that the deep night silence was broken only by the loud ticking of the alarm clock which mounted guard over the books and papers on the battered kitchen table, he would note dully that it was long after three. Sometimes it would be the clatter of the first milk wagons that brought him back from quadratic equations or the fall of Constantinople.

He would rise, surprised at the stiffness of his body, and stand briefly by the open window through which flowed the fragrance of gardens, and from further away the tantalizing odors of the marshes and the bay. In dawns such as this he had brought the Razzle Dazzle into the estuary laden with plundered oysters. But later, when the alarm roused him after a scant five hours of exhausted sleep, he would remember waking sullenly to go to the cannery. Stung by the difference in perspective then and now, he would spring joyfully out of bed, bolt his breakfast and hurry to his books.

Flora regarded him noncommittally. Years ago she had given up trying to understand her son. Settled in resignation, she no longer even fretted because they were so poor. Perhaps something would come of Jack's efforts, she thought unhopefully, with the fatalism that had attended her purchase of lottery tickets. Her boy's effort to make something of himself, however, affected her more than she was aware. Long abandoned ambitions of her own began to stir. Although she had been giving piano lessons intermittently for years, when the man called as usual to collect information for the 1897 city directory, she informed him for the first time that she was a music teacher, and that her son, John Jr, who had been listed as a "mariner" in 1894, and as a "commercial traveler" in 1895, was a "student." John, near the end of his life now, encouraged the boy. With implicit faith in perseverance and hard work, he was sure that Jack would not fail.

Driving ahead at full speed, eyes fixed on the road, Jack had no time to think of either success or failure. He was preparing for examinations in English, history, mathematics and physics, and out of these he hoped to garner a sufficient number of entrance credits to be admitted as a special student. To study physics without a laboratory, to fix precisely facts and dates in a year's course of history, to review elementary algebra and geometry and push ahead as far as possible into advanced algebra, to have grammar and composition at his finger tips, as well as knowledge of the masterpieces of English and American literature—this must be accomplished in a little over three months.

Bess and Fred stood by, ready to unravel tangles and smooth the way as much as possible. Without Fred, the physics would have had to be abandoned, and Bess's skillful coaching eliminated many of the mazes and pitfalls in the mathematics. But aside from this there was literally nothing they could do except to cheer him on. The Applegarths twittered excitedly about his ambitious efforts, and on the rare occasions he came to the house were amused and indulgent when he fell unexpectedly asleep after supper.

He managed to attend party meetings and lectures with fair regularity for two months, then regretfully postponed the pleasure of active membership, not only because of lack of time, but because his mind, stimulated by what he heard, returned reluctantly to his studies. Even Whitaker saw him but seldom.

When, nerves taut and strained, fatigued almost to the breaking point, he presented himself in the court of the Mechanics Building on the Berkeley campus on the morning of August 10, 1896, he faced the several days of examinations with almost his mother's fatalism. He plowed steadily through the tests, deaf to the scratching of other pens about him and unaware until later that the examinations were far stiffer than any of the samples he had looked over. The university, unable to care for the unprecedented influx of students during the last few years, had raised its standards without warning.

The last examination written, he was utterly spent. When he returned home he noticed as if for the first time the walls of his small room and the scarred table desk which had become so intimately a part of him. The sight sickened him. To get as far away as possible from all that had filled his days and nights for months, to forget, to rest, was what he urgently needed. Prescribing for himself, he turned to what he loved best, the bay, and then, deliberately for the first time in his life, to alcohol. Borrowing a small sailboat he fled.

At Benicia he chanced upon old friends, men he had known in the oyster-pirate and fish-patrol days and who were not remotely reminiscent of his more recent friends—not students, not ladies and gentlemen. He ate with them and drank with them—drank deep. That night he slept on the water, and the next morning received the splendid loan of a salmon boat for a few days. Companioned only by wind and water, he sailed on alone, revisiting the scenes so familiar—could it have been only four years before? —and returning by the end of the week, refreshed in body and mind, to learn the results of his examinations.

That year the opening of the fall semester was attended by more than the usual excitement. The university was in the midst of its first "boom." For a quarter of a century it had been plodding along, growing slowly and unspectacularly. The sudden increase in enrollment during the 'nineties caught it unawares with less than a dozen shabby, nondescript buildings and a small teaching staff. Overcrowded classrooms, courses withdrawn for lack of space and dearth of instructors, sharply raised academic standards and entrance requirements—one followed on the heels of the other, but could not stem the flood.

It may be that the success of the intercollegiate track team in 1895 drew attention first to the university and then to its plight; it may be that the general public itself had become college conscious. At any rate money soon began to pour in with which to transform the university. Architect Maybeck, then a young drawing instructor in the art department, interested an influential regent in a harmonious construction of the new buildings; the widow of a wealthy senator financed an international competition for the plans; and the students returned to a campus that was joyfully incredulous of its good fortune. The discomforts were easily borne now. Tents erected to accommodate the overflow were greeted hilariously, as was the news that the budget was too small that year to permit the library to be opened and lighted at night. Was not this the last year of poverty?

Rivalry between the freshman and sophomore classes was keener than usual. The first-year students not only outnumbered the second, but manifested an insufferable pride in their class numerals. The "naughty-naughts" they christened themselves,

painting a large "U. C. 'OO" on the slopes of Yerba Buena, then
Goat Island, even before they had signed the university roll, and
impatiently awaiting the freshman-sophomore rush.

Into this adolescent world, dominated by the youth of the leisure class, came Jack, shabby as ever, a little dazed that he should
be there at all, and prepared to take a full course and support
himself at the same time. The clamorous hysteria of class rivalry
meant nothing to him, possessed of a deeper excitement which the
strutting bantams could not have comprehended. Returning from
the road a year and a half before, he had strained toward a goal
so remote in time and experience that it had been difficult to visualize in actuality. Now the first objective had been realized, and
not only was it finer than he had dreamed, but from its eminence
he could clearly see how close he was to the accomplishment of
his ultimate aim.

Eight and a half units he had mustered for entrance credits,
more than half of what was required for regular undergraduate
standing. If he cared to he could make up the rest by passing
more examinations, and in four years gain a diploma, but that was
furthest from his intention. He did not want to be a college
graduate but a writer and a revolutionist, and apparently the university was going to assist him greatly. Turning the pages of the
announcement of courses, seeing science, philosophy, literature,
history, even foreign languages within his reach, he waxed Ba-
conian, taking all knowledge for his province and deploring the
limitations of time and the university regulations which kept him
from taking a dozen courses each semester instead of five.

Eagerly he pored over the booklet. The "history of Europe
during the middle ages, a study of political institutions and movements on the continent from the fifth to the fifteenth century"—
he would take that, and at the same time the "political history of
the nineteenth century." Next year he would sign up for a course
on economic theory which was even more intriguing; a "critical
study of writers and systems and discussion of unsettled problems
of political economy, socialism, etc." With what was to be
learned on the side from books and discussions of socialist economic theory, he would soon have a thorough knowledge of the
subject!

When he looked over the English courses he knew that he had
been right in coming to college. There was no doubt that by the
end of his first year he would be making a good living at writing,

for here he could learn everything needful. He selected three: one that taught effective writing by "training in composition and in methods of investigation and presentation of results"; a second which covered the history of English literature; and a third, which seemed the best of the lot, "Composition, based principally upon the reading of nineteenth-century writers on science—Darwin, Tyndall, Huxley, Spencer and others."

The first few months were singularly pleasant. Still enthusiastic about his studies, secure in his small circle of friends, and active once more in the Socialist Labor party, for the moment he was content. Campus activity outside of class did not interest him; he preferred to observe. Several times Bess and Mabel persuaded him to join their group at dances in the college gymnasium, where he watched them benevolently from the side lines. Afterward they walked the five miles home, two by two along the quiet streets.

Jack made no stir in campus life, not even as a radical. When less than five years later he became famous many of his fellow students tried to recall John Griffith London, ex-'oo (thus, in an unexpected burst of formality he had signed the university roll), and failed. His name does not appear in any of the campus publications during that semester. But in Oakland the newspapers began to know him. As the presidential campaign moved toward November, the *Times* and the *Item* published several letters from Jack London which vigorously opposed the doctrines of the single taxers and Populists with socialist arguments and propaganda.

The campus reflected in miniature the nation-wide ferment. The semester had scarcely begun when calls were issued for the formation of Republican, Bryan and Gold Democrat clubs. The pros and cons of the silver question were debated by student organizations and informally discussed everywhere. In the midst of the excitement a certain Edlin, known as the "Freshman Socialist," challenged the Republican and Bryan clubs to public debate, and Professor Plehn diplomatically lifted the lid from the steaming kettle by asking the young man to air his views to the class in political economy.

As Jack watched, his earlier amusement changed to contempt. These students and professors, reputed to represent the best of the middle class, were neither intelligent nor honest. Even their passionate political opinions were spurious. The day after the election the issues of the campaign dropped into limbo and the

Thanksgiving football game with Stanford became the burning question.

Everything Jack observed was strengthening his revolutionary outlook and driving him away from the university. Toward the end of the year he faced his wavering faith in the benefits of a college education. His courses were not living up to expectations. Comparing what they promised with what they actually gave, he grew angry, as one who had been deceived by a glowing advertisement. He was not learning anything that he could not dig out of the books himself, and more quickly. On the other hand, he was spending much precious time on work that was utterly useless for his purpose. In this connection he was shocked by his teachers' apparent abhorrence of the present, of ideas that were alive, of books that grappled with contemporary problems and experiences. The bitterness he expressed toward universities throughout his life is the measure of his original confidence and ultimate disillusionment.

One other event contributed to the unhappiness Jack usually associated later with this period and that was receiving the unexpected and gratuitous information that John London was not his father. Jack had never been popular with some of his numerous steprelatives, but for some reason his effort to obtain an education inspired their active dislike. They told him an ugly, garbled story and then they taunted him with it.

Incredulous, he went straight to Flora. One glance at her strained, tight-lipped face was sufficient. He did not press her for details other than the name of his father, and they did not speak of the matter again.

The shock caused by this knowledge cannot be overestimated. Jack brooded over it for months, and until the end of his life the scar it left was sensitive. In old files of the San Francisco papers he read the story of his mother's attempted suicide, then set about to get in touch with Chaney. This task did not prove difficult. Chaney's reputation as an astrologer still lingered in the West, and after a brief search Jack learned his Chicago address from one of his fellow astrologers. Using the Applegarths' address for a reply so that Flora would not be further upset, he wrote to Chaney, asking for the truth.

Chaney's reply, disclaiming any relationship, was an even more staggering blow than the first inkling of the situation had been.

Several letters passed between the two before Jack, sick at heart, abandoned the correspondence. Just why Chaney chose to deny his fatherhood is not easy to say. He stubbornly stuck to his story, but every phase of his denial was suspicious, its vehemence, its slanderous attack upon Flora, even the time-worn excuse of temporary impotence dragged in for proof. Flora's few friends of the time have given ample testimony of her loyalty to Chaney during their short marriage. Chaney, on the other hand, has erred many times, for reasons best known to himself no doubt, in recording facts in his writings. One finally gives up the enigma.

What is significant is that Jack was deeply hurt by the affair at a time when his self-confidence needed bolstering, not shattering. He lived at a time when illegitimacy was regarded with horror except by the enlightened few. It also seems probable that this knowledge determined his attitude toward his mother for the rest of his life. He was gentler to her thereafter, but he never quite forgave her. At the same time his affection for John deepened.

As his interest in his college work waned, the financial strain grew more noticeable. He had resolved to complete at least a year's work before he began to break trail alone, and had even registered for the second semester, when suddenly the game was no longer worth the candle. On February 4, 1897, he was granted honorable dismissal and his college days were over.

He found that week's meeting of the Socialist Labor party devoted to a fiery discussion of a certain city ordinance which had been resented by the Oakland radicals for nearly two years. Ordinance No. 1676 forbade speaking at any public meeting on any public street situated within the fire limits of the city without the written permission of the mayor of Oakland. This, claimed the Socialists, violated the rights of free speech and public assembly guaranteed the citizens of the United States by their constitution. For some time the pros and cons of making a test case had been argued back and forth. Now Abraham Lincoln's birthday was approaching—a holiday and an excellent opportunity to draw crowds. To invite arrest in order to test the constitutionality of the ordinance was unanimously decided upon.

Jack had listened to the discussion with great interest. He was new to the movement, but a test case sounded like something very significant. Besides, Abraham Lincoln had long been one of his heroes. When a volunteer was called for Jack stood up. It was a good choice. His letters to the *Times* and the *Item* had given him a little notoriety. He was a known Socialist. And the older and more experienced comrades knew that when youth protested the violation of liberties the public was generally favorably impressed. Jack was a poor soapboxer. He gave it up long before he overcame his dismay at the thinness of his voice in the out of doors and the resultant absence of passion in his tones and gestures, as well as the shyness which almost strangled him. He turned to Herman Whitaker. "Come with me?" he asked, and Jim agreed.

When Jack mounted the soapbox on February twelfth the usual crowd collected, and, as usual, Jack found himself tongue-tied. Summoning all his courage, he jerked out a few inadequate sentences. The crowd cheered, faintly and ironically, then began to move away. Jack glanced despairingly at Whitaker. Jim was not a much better speaker, but he had at least more experience. They exchanged places, and Jim managed to hold the crowd until he heard the hoped-for cry, "Hi, the cops!" Jack pushed him aside, remounted the box and was haranguing away in the best manner when he was hauled off the box and marched to jail.

The trial resulted in an acquittal. The constitutionality of the ordinance remained unchallenged, but Jack had earned his first socialist laurels. Thus did he celebrate his rejection of the bourgeois academic life with a gesture whose sincerity outweighed its futility.

The impulse that had sent him racing through high school and into college spent itself in a few frenzied weeks of writing. Poetry, short stories, essays and articles flowed from his pen as he sat hunched over the kitchen table from early morning until late at night. Everything he had learned during the past two years went into them. In no sense of the word was he pouring out his soul; he was writing in order to make a living, in order to feed and clothe and shelter himself and his parents without returning to machine or manual labor.

He knew no one who had ever published anything. Ignorant of form and markets, he blundered on alone. The borrowed typewriter, which possessed only capital letters, was balky. "Weird," he later described the appearance of the manuscripts which he confidently mailed to various editors. The few which still exist are collectors' items today, but in 1897 the editors would have none of them.

For a short time he persisted, hoping against hope for one acceptance. The textbooks he had bought with hard-earned money were sold to buy paper and postage stamps; he borrowed a few dollars wherever he could, and tried to forget that John was carrying the full burden of the household. Then he gave up, not defeated, but convinced that he would have to study and practice more before he could expect success. Manuscripts and notes were packed away, and he went out to look for a job.

Spring found him working in a small steam laundry at Belmont Academy, a boarding school on the peninsula south of San Francisco. After installing the latest machinery, the owner had discovered that it was humanly possible for two strong youths to do all the work. Jobs being scarce, it was easy to secure such young men, work them long hours at top speed for six days a week, and pay them thirty dollars a month and board.

Thirty dollars a month—that had been Jack's top wages since he was fifteen years old. The board represented the only increase in the value of his labor power in six years, although he was stronger and more skillful, not to mention being better educated. This realization, far from discouraging him, was merely added proof of the correctness of his decision to earn his living by brain instead of brawn. And the experience undoubtedly made him an even more passionate Socialist than before. His keen interest in national developments as well as his limited understanding of their significance is revealed in a letter to Ted Applegarth when he heard the news of the formation of the Social Democracy of America in June 1897: "Organized labor, headed by Debs and beginning with the American Railway Union, has commenced a change of front. The old method of strikes and boycotts to obtain shorter hours and better pay has been abandoned. They now strike for political power, their openly avowed goal being the co-operative commonwealth. That is, the socialist propaganda in the United States is assuming greater proportions."

At first glance the laundry work seemed a remarkable solution of his immediate problem. He could not only send money home to the old people, but save up for a new writing spree. Besides, every evening and all day Sundays he would be free to read and study. The first week completely disillusioned him on this score. It was impossible to study or even to read light fiction after working all day at the pace demanded by his employer, and on Sundays his mental efforts were confined to dozing over the newspaper. It proved easy to save money, however, for he was always too tired to leave the grounds to buy even a glass of beer. When the academy closed for the summer he returned to Oakland and opened a new offensive against the magazines.

His self-confidence lost the joyousness that had marked it during his campaign to obtain an education, grew stern and unyielding. The objective was as clear as ever, and more desirable, but since the university had failed him the way was obscure. Watching his tiny hoard melt away, he knew that soon he would have to get another job. Apparently that was the way it had to be: to sweat for months in order to buy a few weeks in which to write and study, and then, just as he began to get the hang of things and know that he was making progress, to find his money gone and more months of manual labor ahead. So be it! He accepted the exasperating prospect grimly, but he did not know how near he was to the end of his patience.

CHAPTER

11

AFTER the turmoil of the presidential election the first half of 1897 seemed very placid. Few noticed either the gradual easing of the long depression or the war clouds that were beginning to form. But in the middle of the summer news of an event that had occurred nearly a year before threw the country into a fever of excitement which was to last, despite the Spanish-American War, for more than two years. Before the first of August the rush to the Klondike was on.

Reports of the gold strike found Jack at the end of his resources and wearily searching for another job with which to buy a few more months of leisure in which to write later in the fall. With every repetition of how a few Alaskan prospectors had walked off the SS Portland with three quarters of a million dollars in gold dust, his conviction grew that he, too, could make a fortune in the Klondike. Unfortunately, however, a decision to join the rush could not be carried out so simply as when he had gone off with Kelly's army. This time he would need an outfit and money.

Jack's frantic efforts to be grubstaked were like those of thousands of other impecunious young men throughout the nation. But the unprecedented madness which gripped young as well as older Americans at this time cannot be entirely explained by their lust for gold. Unexpectedly a new frontier had appeared. "There being no new oceans to explore," writes a poet, "the cry 'Bonanza!' roused the world-old zest!" Jack listened ardently. For two years and a half he had stayed at home, his wanderlust submerged in the grueling struggle to obtain an education and learn how to write. Now as he listened to tales of hardship and danger he saw the adventure path before him once more and knew that he must go.

His friends were scandalized that he should abandon his carefully laid plans in this fashion. A note from Mrs Applegarth beseeched him for all their sakes to change his mind. Flora received the news stoically, but John, already bedridden with his last illness, was enthusiastic and regretted only that he could not go himself. In his urgent but futile search for a backer, Jack even called at the home of Joaquin Miller, only to learn that the poet had already departed to cover the gold strike for the newspapers. Then help came from an unexpected quarter. Captain Shepard, his sister Eliza's elderly husband, caught the fever and gladly grubstaked him in exchange for his company on the trip. When the SS Umatilla, laden with gold seekers, left San Francisco on July twenty-fifth, they were aboard.

It was long before either the argonauts or those who stayed at home learned how the rush had started. Even Jack, writing in 1899, spoke more than once of "MacCormack's strike" in August 1896. To most Americans Alaska was "Seward's Folly," an unknown territory which for some inexplicable reason had been acquired by the United States from Russia shortly after the Civil War. Echoes of a boundary dispute with Canada appeared in the newspapers from time to time, but few were interested. Reports that the land contained gold, silver and copper, as well as certain valuable fur-bearing animals, were duly noted and forgotten.

Even in Alaska its fabulous wealth was almost as unguessed as in the days of Russian exploitation. Although it controlled every natural resource, the Russian-American Company had developed only the fur trade, crisscrossing the silent land for seventy years, blind to the gleam of precious ore, slaughtering walrus and seal on the "golden sands of Nome." Persistent rumors of gold lured a small but steady stream of American and other prospectors during the 'seventies and 'eighties. Although the strikes they made were not spectacular most of them played their "hunches" and stayed to become the "sourdoughs" that were celebrated later in song and story.

One of this number was George Washington Carmack, who had left his job on the Vallejo-San Franciso ferryboats when he heard of the Juneau discoveries in 1880. He found little gold but he, too, stayed, prospecting once in a while, but depending on hunting, fishing and trading for livelihood. In contrast with other miners who earnestly sought gold through many years of purposeful wandering, Carmack seems to have been singularly indifferent. Certainly his great discovery was purely accidental. In the summer of '96 he was hunting moose and caribou in the Upper Yukon country with two Indian companions when he heard that the long-awaited salmon run had begun in the Klondike River. Turning back, he encountered another old-timer, Robert Henderson, who had just made a small strike near by and advised him to locate beside it. This done, Carmack and the Indians followed an unnamed creek—soon to be called Bonanza—down to the Klondike, where he camped to catch salmon. And here, resting beside the river on a warm August afternoon, his eye was caught by the glitter of strange colors on the bank. Legend has it that with two fry pans the three men panned out seven hundred thousand dollars in dust and nuggets before their claims were recorded.

Word of the strike spread quickly down the Yukon to Forty-Mile and Circle City, and in a short time the old-timers had staked the Bonanza and adjacent creeks. When gold was found at bedrock, the last skepticism vanished. Before snow fell the new town of Dawson had come into existence on the wide, spruce-covered flat at the junction of the Klondike and the Yukon rivers. During the following spring and summer the remainder of the new El Dorado was quietly prospected and located by small efficient stampedes. When the first "chekakos" arrived the sourdoughs had the situation well in hand, and most of the newcomers were destined to get little besides the trip for their hardships, suffering and money.

In later years Jack London often quoted the old miner's adage that "two dollars go into the ground for each dollar that comes out," and observed that the Klondike was no exception. The approximate quarter of a million gold hunters who started for the North during the two big years of the rush spent in the aggregate a staggering sum for transportation, equipment and supplies. The rigors of the trip from salt water over the passes to the Yukon discouraged many. A scant fifty thousand reached the interior. An infinitesimal percentage of these brought back fortunes of varying sizes; among the less than one seventh who actually found any gold at all, a few broke even.

Jack found no gold in the Klondike. Winter closed in before he

scarcely prospected at all. He performed no feats and had no adventures, save that of managing to get in before the freeze-up, for
it came early that year and many were stranded en route. But
from the time he landed on the beach at Dyea until he floated,
scurvy ridden, down the Yukon on his way home the following
spring, he was amassing a store of impressions of things heard
and seen, which were to yield him a fortune during the succeeding years.

The saga of Jack London's trip over the Chilkoot to the Yukon in the fall of '97 is the saga of the thousands who came then
and later on the same errand. The steamers dumped their passengers and freight at low tide on a long sand spit opposite the
Indian village of Dyea, and departed as quickly as possible. Long
before all the boxes and bundles could be separated by their
owners and lugged ashore through the shallow water the tide
rose. Thousands of helpless argonauts and tons of baggage clut-
tered the beach. Behind them reared the snowy Coast Range
Mountains which must be crossed, and immediately, if they hoped
to reach Dawson that year. The small number of Indians and
horses that were available could pack but a fraction of the stuff.
They went to the highest bidder, and for the average man the
price was soon out of sight. Many gave up without even trying,
sold their equipment and took the next steamer home. Others
started out manfully only to turn back, defeated.

While still aboard ship Jack and Captain Shepard had formed
a partnership with three others. In the midst of the confusion
they brought their outfit safely ashore, pitched camp and laid
plans for the next move. Of the two passes, White and Chilkoot,
the latter was the more difficult but appreciably shorter. Their
choice was quickly made: they would start up Chilkoot in the
morning. At this point Captain Shepard remembered that dis-
cretion was the better part of valor, and after listening to vivid
descriptions of the difficult journey ahead, decided, much to
Jack's relief, to return.

The trail led across several snowy plateaus, which grew
rapidly steeper until inexperienced men, laden with packs, scrambled upon hands and knees to the foot of the pass. Many maintained that the Chilkoot was in no sense of the word a pass but
a mountain itself. Those who ascended its precipitous thousand
feet in two hours made excellent time. At one point the Indians

had cut a thousand steps in the ice, but otherwise there was no path. From the top it was possible to coast down a short distance, then a new type of trail began which "Scotty" Allan, famous Alaskan dog driver, described as "a series of flats, mountains, hills, water, mud, quagmires and bogs from one end to the other."

Jack toiled zestfully with the rest. Daily he increased his load and knew pride when he could pack as well as the Indians. Even then, perhaps, he was beginning to be conscious of a personal ideal which later, after exposure to Nietzsche, would dominate much of his work. He visioned a certain type of white man who could equal the physical prowess of the finest specimens of primitive man, and outdo them, as well as his less favored white brothers, in intellectual power and achievement. As the years passed this became an obsession. Failing to realize it in himself, he began to weave his wish into his stories, where accomplishment was easy and sure.

On the Klondike trail in '97, however, he succeeded. In record time the four men reached Lake Linderman, the smallest of five glacial lakes which they would follow to the Lewes River and thence via the Pelly to the Yukon. Trees were felled at Linderman, cut into boards at the single small sawmill, and a boat was quickly constructed.

Jack had never been part of a struggle against such tremendous odds. The swift, sure approach of winter was daily more evident. The bitter winds against which they fought their way across the long lakes could not prevent ice from forming in sheltered pools, and no one could predict when the freeze-up would occur. They wasted no time in weighing their chances. Hour by hour they pushed forward, overcoming each obstacle as they came to it. Jack's skill in handling a small boat stood them in good stead, for the sail they rigged up, despite the weather, saved them many hours of rowing.

Linderman, Bennet, Tagish and Marsh—four of the lakes and their connecting passages were behind them when they entered Fifty Mile River which at two points narrowed precipitately into the dreaded Box Canyon and White Horse Rapids. Because portage would consume valuable time, Jack ran the boat through both of them, avoiding disaster in the whirlpool of the first and shooting down the foaming, wavelike crest of the second. They knew that now they were past the worst dangers, but at Lake Lebarge they encountered a storm which forced them back for three days in succession. On the fourth they made it, fighting across inch by inch and watching the lake freeze behind them.

Dawson had been their destination, but when they reached the Yukon word of a recent strike at the mouth of the Stewart River, seventy miles short of Dawson, determined a change of plans. On October ninth, two and half months after they left San Francisco, they made camp on Upper Island, between the Stewart and Henderson Creek. And there, in one of several cabins which had been abandoned by Bering Sea fur traders, Jack's active participation in the gold rush came to an end.

As the long winter locked Alaska in the silence which would last until spring a large proportion of the citizens of the United States proceeded to lose their heads over the gold rush in thoroughgoing fashion. Newspapers and magazines stimulated the hysteria and incidentally increased their circulation; promoters, inventors, manufacturers and others set out to reap a golden harvest at home.

As soon as the rush began, warnings had been sounded of inevitable suffering and privation during the Alaskan winter, but they were universally disbelieved. Even Joaquin Miller, veteran of many earlier stampedes in the West, dismissed them scornfully as an old trick to frighten people off. His newspaper assignment was to gather information about the trip, especially for the poor men who hoped to go in the spring, and he promised to dispose of such lies in short order. But before he reached Skagway he realized that the insufficient food and equipment that were being taken in would exact a heavy toll from the thousands spending their first winter in Alaska.

Miller and others repeated the warnings, but they went unheeded. Klondike enthusiasts listened to little that did not paint in ever brighter colors the golden hoard they coveted, or tell them how to obtain it most easily. The sudden revival of the boundary dispute with Canada irritated them exceedingly. They were very possessive now about "Seward's Folly," and during the next two years they avidly discussed the question. It was not finally settled, however, until the fall of 1903, and by then the intense popular interest in the Klondike had long since diminished.

The agitation which news of the discovery brought to the Pacific coast was soon duplicated in the Middle West and East. Within ten days after the arrival of the Portland, the exodus of old-timers from the Mother Lode country had threatened the closing of the California mines. In the cities many, long unemployed, rejoiced as they took the places of workers who had unceremoniously quit their jobs, drawn out their savings and departed. A mass meeting of streetcar employees in Tacoma, Washington, chose and outfitted nine of their number to prospect and locate claims for the benefit of the rest.

As the fever spread this practice became common. Hundreds of the participants in the '98 rush were grubstaked by small groups of individuals, or represented the many "Mining Cooperatives," "Placer Syndicates" and "Poor Men's Chances" which had sprung up during the winter. An exotic variation was the company formed by a number of Chicago spiritualists. The prospector they dispatched to the Klondike was equipped with the maps and directions for locating rich claims which the mediums had received from their spirit guides. The idea was apparently no novelty. A lady clairvoyant seeking backers for a similar company claimed that she had already successfully found hidden deposits of precious metal in both California and Colorado.

Those were banner years for promoters. Anything which bore the name "Klondike" was sure to sell. Wall Street was cautious, but the man in the street and on the farm, and women as well, blithely bought mining stocks, good, bad and indifferent. Ignorance and enthusiasm were fertile soil for various schemes to shorten the long journey into the interior. When a citizen of Kalamazoo announced that he was establishing a balloon route to Dawson, reservations for the first flight poured in from all over the country. Shortly after news came that bicycles had proved useless over the passes and that hundreds of abandoned machines could be bought for a fraction of their cost at Dyea and Skagway, a New York syndicate began to advertise a "Klondike" bicycle—a combination bicycle and four-wheeled vehicle capable of carrying five hundred pounds of freight. Another intriguing combination was a boat sled equipped with sails and oars, as well as flat plates to cover the keel for land travel.

Dyea, Chilkoot, Lake Lebarge, Forty-Mile, Dawson, Bonanza Creek; panning, sluicing, lays, benches and placers—a curious jargon penetrated the American speech. Many who had never ventured outside of their home state glibly reeled off the number of miles from Seattle to Dawson, or named unerringly the tributaries of the Yukon.

Women were nearly as excited as men. Numbers of them dabbled in mining stock or assisted in various promotion schemes, but those who could made their way to Alaska. The winter of '97 found quite a few women in the various camps and towns. Most of them sought their gold in the saloons and dance halls, but some were wives who had persuaded their husbands to take them on the venture, and there were even a few courageous young women who had come unaccompanied. In the spring rush hundreds more arrived.

Rumors of the staggering sums being earned by seamstresses in Dawson, Juneau and other new towns agitated the rebellious heart of many a spinster who longed to escape the dullness and poverty of small-town life. Others, who believed that women could prospect as successfully as men, inserted personals in the newspapers, offering to accompany gold seekers in any capacity for a grubstake. A midwife guaranteed a yearly income of fifty thousand dollars to a partner who would invest five hundred in the hospital she wanted to open in Dawson.

One old lady, remembering American colonial history, tried to persuade the officials of the North American Transportation and Trading Company to send a shipload of young women to become wives of the miners. And when a lady sociologist announced her plan to transplant at least four thousand working girls from factories and sweat shops to the Klondike mining towns, thousands of applications, but no funds, poured in.

The enthusiasm evoked in the United States by the gold rush ebbed very slowly. Just as it began to diminish in the Klondike gold was discovered on the long narrow beach at Nome, and a new stampede began. Americans clung somewhat wistfully to their last frontier, and for a long time any mention of Alaska brought a flood of reminiscences from all who had shared in the adventure—the few who had actually gone, and the many who had remained at home. Thus, long before Jack London's Klondike tales took form a vast audience of men and women were eagerly awaiting them.

In later years Jack was fond of saying, "It was in the Klondike that I found myself. There nobody talks. Everybody thinks. You get your perspective. I got mine." The Klondike gave much to Jack London, but it was the speech and not the silence of his companions that enriched that gift. Night after night during the long winter months of enforced idleness men gathered together in the small warm cabins and talked. And Jack listened.

At the time he did not know that what he was hearing, combined with what he saw with his own eyes during visits to Dawson and in camp on Upper Island, was story material. Only toward the end of his stay did it occur to him that he might be able to sell a few articles to the travel and outdoor magazines. He listened and egged on the old-timers to further yarns because he was as interested in the new land as any of the great audience at home. And while he satisfied his curiosity the characters, scenes and incidents of scores of short stories and several novels were being stored away.

Two months in Dawson during the early winter netted him much. The raw frontier town appeared often in his later books. And out of Dawson came Buck, the hero of the first and greatest of his dog stories. He was fascinated by the color and bombast of the mining town, so like those that had flourished in his own state nearly half a century before, but it was during the months in camp that he came to know the old Alaska of the sourdoughs and the Indians.

It was midwinter when he returned to Upper Island. On the shortest day of the year there were two hours of sunlight. Intense cold and what he was to call the "white silence" hemmed in the small group of men who awaited the coming of spring so that they might determine the worth of the claims they had staked near by. The camp was a cross section of the new life that was pulsing through Alaska. Many were newcomers, some from farm and city in the States, others chronic wanderers who had been in the South Seas the year before and might turn up on the docks of Liverpool the next. There were several who did not speak of their past and none asked them, but most were eager to swap experiences in the nightly gatherings.

Louis Savard's cabin, the largest and most comfortable on the island, was the favorite meeting place. Louis' French-Canadian accent so delighted Jack that he drew him into conversation at every opportunity. That accent runs musically through many of his stories and Louis himself appears, while Nig, his sled dog who so cleverly evaded hard work, became one of Buck's teammates in *The Call of the Wild*. There Jack met Elam Harnish who, endowed with the qualities and exploits of a dozen other real and imaginary Alaskan heroes, was to swagger through *Burning Day-*

light. Out of many men, especially Emil Jensen, and Jack's conception of himself as a sourdough, emerged Malemute Kid, the central figure in several of his early Klondike tales.

He listened avidly to the adventures of men in their quest for gold, but whether on trail or in camp, it was the land itself that most deeply impressed him and man's not always successful struggle to exist in it. Here the ancient battle for survival was expressed in its simplest terms. Hushed primeval forests and snowy wastelands, the austere blaze of the aurora borealis, the vast impersonal force of a land inimical to life—these dominate his first stories, and through them move those who had learned to survive in the pitiless environment, the Indians and the old-timers. Were it not for this awareness of man's ceaseless struggle against overwhelming odds, these would have been merely mediocre tales in which one-dimensional figures performed somewhat incredibly against a painted backdrop.

The gold rush of which he was a part did not interest him, then. It was motivated by, and was bringing with it, much that he most despised in civilization. Eagerly he questioned the old-timers, and slowly the picture of Alaska in the days of the trail breakers grew in his mind. The early prospectors did not know that they were breaking trail. They had come, as they had often come before to far places, in response to the rumor of gold. Its promise, ever renewed, had held them fast through years of toil and suffering. Inured to hardship, else they would not have stayed, they had adapted themselves to the country, to its climate and its people. Many had married Indian women.

That their coming had brought change to the Indians' immemorial way of life, few realized. Alaska was large enough for both races; there need be no conflict. Nature alone was the enemy, indifferent to their strivings and dealing death impartially to all who relaxed their vigilance. And Jack, listening, saw the quiet years come and go; saw the toil-hardened miners and thrilled to the tale of their unsung deeds; saw the childlike Indians and felt himself profoundly moved by their tragic destiny.

He did not consciously deplore the coming of the new, but his admiration for the outmoded old was tinged with regret that such fine things should pass. Sick of civilization as he had found it, life in the brief years before Carmack's discovery seemed Arcadian. Then, courage, strength and intelligence, not a bank balance, had determined the status of men. Weakness, cowardice and greed, protected and perpetuated by wealth in civilization, were swiftly eliminated by nature, Indian tribal law and simple frontier justice. As he recalled life in the States his conviction grew that in the wilds men bulked larger as men than when penned in cities, were freer, nobler, more admirable.

And yet, although it flowered in cities, he knew that civilization was inherently good, not bad. Through it man had escaped his long thralldom to precisely what he was witnessing in Alaska, the endless, full-time struggle against nature just to keep alive. It was bad now because of capitalism. Once the producing class rose in its might, destroyed its masters and won to socialism, life would be fair beyond dreams. But now? And in the meantime? He drew back, shuddering, from the trap whose teeth he had seen and felt.

Thus, imperceptibly at first, the problem he was never to solve for himself took form during the winter on Upper Island. If he had come to Alaska before he had "opened the books" at all, or if, instead of too much Rousseau and too little Marx and large hunks of undigested Darwin, he had been well grounded in both science and socialism, the impact of the frontier would not have thrown him off balance. As it was, the widening of his horizon brought confusion rather than greater clarity.

He was a simple, direct man, and his need for simplicity was urgent. Things were good or bad, black or white, and thus he chose. But when he was confronted with a third choice his indecision was painful. He had aligned himself on the side of socialism rather than accept capitalism, and had been content. Now in the Klondike he found a third possibility which seemed to offer an escape from the evils of civilization by a return to nature.

What he feared and hated under capitalism did not obtain on the frontier. Its simplicity attracted him enormously. Furthermore, it already existed, was tangible, did not have to be attained by bloody struggle through many years. It had its drawbacks, but could they not be remedied by judicious borrowing of efficiency and comforts from civilization? And could not one fight for socialism even more effectively when his strength was not dissipated by close contact with capitalism's festering cities? Certainly, he would rationalize enthusiastically, the virtues of the frontier, doomed to perish under capitalism, should be preserved, and how better to accomplish this than by celebrating them out of one's own intimate knowledge?

He was never to frame these questions nor openly make the decision they posed, but from the time he returned from Alaska until the end of his life, he sought with growing desperation to reconcile his revolutionary principles and belief in the class struggle with his personal desires and preferences. The actual conflict was bitter and brief. In less than a decade the fatal combination of his spectacular rise to fame and affluence, his incomplete knowledge of Marxism, and the backwardness of the American socialist movement spelled defeat for his principles. Thereafter preference ruled, brilliantly rationalized, but transparent finally even to himself.

But as he emerged from the Klondike in the spring of '98, ill, penniless, and facing new responsibilities at home, no foreshadowing of future glory or ultimate disillusionment marked his bleak horizon. He had intended to remain in the North at least through the summer. If his Henderson Creek claim failed to pan out he would seek elsewhere. But long before spring released the land for prospecting he had been gripped by scurvy, which grew steadily worse until a return to fresh vegetables became imperative. Furthermore, the first mail in the spring had brought him news of John London's death the preceding October, and he knew that Flora would need him. Early in June he left Dawson with two companions, and in a rowboat floated fifteen hundred miles down the Yukon to salt water, and thence by steamer, stoking, to Seattle. On the last leg of the journey he returned to the road, beating his way, sharply aware of the absence of the exhilaration that had always accompanied similar feats in the past, on fast passenger trains to Oakland.

He was in no cheerful state of mind on the return trip. Here he was, twenty-one years old, and no nearer his goal than when he had entered high school three years before. Instead of staying at home and hammering away at the writing game, he had irresponsibly cut loose and gone off to the Klondike. It had been an exciting year, but a wasted one, no doubt about that. He would salvage what he could of it in short stories and articles. In the meantime he must buckle down and work harder than ever to make up for lost time. Long before he reached Oakland the old Spartan regime had been re-established in his mind: a job, a minimum number of sleeping hours in order to obtain a maximum for writing, and for further acquisition of knowledge, the public library and the Socialist party.

CHAPTER

12

THE NEXT FEW YEARS mark the most intense period in
Jack London's life. He entered it poor and unknown; he emerged
from it with success and fame assured. At the start two activities
absorbed his entire attention: the effort to learn how to turn into
salable fiction the rich store of experiences in his possession, and
the continuation of his education along socialist lines through contact with the party. The influence of the socialist movement upon
him at this time cannot be underestimated. However imperfect
may have been its interpretation of American affairs and his grasp
of it, the socialist viewpoint was his basic approach to an understanding and evaluation of what was occurring during these years
in the United States and abroad.

Just as it is impossible to fix the moment when night ends and
day begins, so it is impossible to determine precisely when
America embarked upon the course which was to lead her to a
predominant position in the world. At the turn of the century it
was still neither day nor night; nevertheless, the dawn of imperialism for the United States had begun.

Indications of this development could be observed even then in
the change taking place in the economic structure of the country
and in the concomitant effects this had upon social and political
life. Monopoly was moving forward in full stride now, withering
competition and speedily replacing small, decentralized units with
large-scale production. On the Continent and in England industry,
evolving from the Middle Ages, had acquired patterns which were

handed down from generation to generation. But America, lacking such traditions, was able to advance quickly and even to skip many stages. Experimentation and constant improvement characterized the building of the modern factory, and inventive ingenuity was free to achieve greater mechanization as rapidly as possible.

By 1900 American industry was no longer based on personal relations. The productive unit of the artisan and his family had already disappeared. Now the paternalism of the small factory owner toward his hired help was passing. Swiftly and surely the management and control of a large portion of industry was shifting from the producer to the banker and nonresident stockholder, and as this was being consummated, wealth was concentrating in fewer and fewer hands.

Seven of the greater trusts were formed between 1898 and 1901. And as the twenty-one major combinations which occurred in iron and steel to pave the way for the greatest of them all, the United States Steel Corporation, exposed the new role and growing control of banking capital, so did events in the railroad industry.

Ninety-five per cent of the higher grade mileage fell into the hands of six of the most powerful of these groups. The Vanderbilt, Moore, Pennsylvania, Morgan-Hill, Rockefeller, and Harriman and Kuhn-Loeb interests, each representing a capitalization of over a billion dollars, soon controlled a hundred and sixty-four thousand miles out of a total of two hundred and four thousand. Worn-out or unprofitable roads were ignored, but those either in the black or about to become so were closely watched, and large blocks of their stock sooner or later ended up in the possession of one of the major combines. In a short time the rails were to come even closer together.

Like the Rockefellers and the Morgans, the "big three" in the insurance field, Mutual, New York Life and Equitable, also had their trust companies. What was forbidden to the insurance companies themselves was accomplished by means of satellite banks, and the accumulated savings of small policy holders went into various speculative enterprises. Some of the money also trickled into the hands of insurance officials for private speculation. And on the boards of their trust companies sat representatives of the Rockefeller, Morgan and other banking groups.

For a long time the United States had been able to develop independently, thanks to her abundance of raw materials, the enormous labor supply provided by immigration and the widespread railroad lines that linked together the far-flung sections of the country. As soon as agriculture had piled up sufficient surplus the development of a huge domestic industrial economy began. With a population constantly spreading and thickening over a vast territory, America shortly found herself in possession of a large home market, unhampered as were European countries by conflicting currencies, sharp differences in customs and tastes, numerous trade regulations and other barriers. Many nations eyed this market greedily, and America, seeking to stave off British competition, which she could not yet meet, and to shelter her young industries, reared the high walls of the protective tariff.

Matching their wits against those of their rivals abroad, American industrialists were soon in the thick of the world-wide scramble for markets and more raw materials. Eager to assume as much as they could of the "white man's burden," they set out to inspire the backward peoples with a desire for neckties and underwear as a prelude to the further cultivation of their tastes. As commodities of ever-increasing variety poured from her factories and plants America's trade outlook began to cover the world. The value in round numbers of her manufactured goods had been one billion dollars in 1849; in 1899 it was eleven billions and moving steadily toward the sixty-one-billion mark it was to reach in 1923.

After 1893 America's balance of trade had been favorable. And when manufactured articles began to take foremost place in her exports her international status underwent a change. As an agrarian nation she had lived in smug isolation; as an exporter of manufactured goods and capital she commanded the attention of every country.

It was not long before American businessmen, actively scouring the world market, announced their dissatisfaction with their government's slipshod manner of extending trade agreements. Their influence in Washington promptly resulted in a number of reforms. Recognizing the importance of foreign trade, President McKinley initiated a reorganization of the consular service. With the exception of a few men of letters, such as William Dean Howells, the agents had been generally insignificant and incompetent men who could not meet the growing demands of American commerce. McKinley replaced two hundred and thirty-eight of the two hundred and seventy-two members of the service. The

Department of Commerce was established in 1903; in 1905 trade commissioners were appointed; and the following year the obsolete consular code of 1856 was completely revised.

As the twentieth century opened, America's foreign investments totaled more than five hundred millions and were mounting toward the nearly three billions they would attain in 1914. Capital had begun to flow from the United States to the backward countries. Despite the huge capital demands of her domestic market, America had sufficient surplus to send into Mexico, Cuba and Canada. Although she was not able to repurchase the investments of foreign capital in her own country until during and after the World War, the beginnings of this imperialism were unmistakable at the start of the new century.

In the Dingley tariff law, enacted in July 1897, the protection principle had been raised to the highest point. But as soon as big business felt the effects of retaliatory measures taken by foreign countries it decided that abstract theories of government could not longer block the opening up of new markets. The long struggle between the pros and cons of colonial expansion came swiftly to an end with colonies becoming a part of the "currency" of the United States.

America's "big-brother" role was well rehearsed and smoothly performed. While her statesmen loudly proclaimed their interest and concern for the small countries in Central and South America and reiterated their desire to join with them in a union of equals, they were quietly acquiring Porto Rico, the Panama Canal region and the Virgin Islands, making the Caribbean into an "American lake," and establishing actual if not formal control over Panama. The teamwork was excellent: diplomacy soothed the victims while imperialism skillfully took what it wanted.

To Germany the collapse of the Spanish empire offered a splendid opportunity to acquire urgently needed Pacific possessions, but England, determined to check Germany's growth as a world power, encouraged the expansion of the United States into the Western ocean. With this support America climaxed her initial efforts at colonization with a five-months' war against Spain in 1898, and emerged as one of the lesser world powers with island possessions in the Caribbean and the Pacific.

Sugar had brought the Hawaiian Islands under the control of the United States in the midst of the war with Spain. Then, despite opposition at home to the acquisition of colonies, she divided the Samoan Islands between herself, England and Germany by a treaty signed in 1899. To Tutuila with its harbor of Pago Pago were then added Wake and Midway islands, potentially valuable naval stations. Porto Rico was annexed and a protectorate established over Cuba. An American-made revolution and an artificially created republic in Panama, promptly recognized by the United States, resulted in another protectorate. Toward the Dominican Republic and Haiti, which comprised the most populous and the richest of the West Indies, the United States first adopted a policy of penetration and direct intervention in their political administrations, then moved adroitly toward the assumption of protectorates.

To what extent the interpretation of the Monroe Doctrine had broadened was evidenced when Great Britain was forced to submit to arbitration in her dispute with Venezuela. It was clear that thenceforth Europeans were to keep their hands off all regions in the Americas which the United States intended to control.

Participation in the Chinese situation could no longer be delayed. A few years before, the United States had watched from the side lines while the imperialist nations had partitioned China. Now she bent her efforts to halt their piracy and to preserve as much as possible of China as a free country and potential market for herself. Her declaration of the "open-door" policy, her dispatching of troops to China in 1900, ostensibly to co-operate with the other foreign nations in the relief of the legations in Peking, her ultimate decision to retain the Philippine Islands as a vantage point in making her influence felt in the Orient—these were shrewdly conceived, carefully executed steps in her advance toward world sovereignty. And when Japan entered the scene, advocating the open-door policy for the same reasons as her own, America did not hesitate to use the maneuver she had learned a few years earlier from England, fostering the expansion of the new power in order to impede the progress of more immediate rivals.

The United States navy not only distinguished itself during the Spanish-American War, but by 1900 it was outranked in strength only by Great Britain and France. Twenty years previously it had occupied twelfth place, and it was commonly believed that Chile's two modern cruisers could easily demolish the wooden hulks of the American fleet. A naval war college had been established in Newport in 1885. Before long the slogan, "a navy second to none," had superseded the Congressional discussions on "sea-going coast-line battleships."

Elihu Root became Secretary of War in 1907 after a front-page scandal involving the War Department had ousted his predecessor. Inefficiency, political appointments and corruption in the purchase of food and other supplies had been some of the more damaging charges. The war with Spain revealed among other things the necessity of field artillery, smokeless powder and high-powered rifles, as well as the importance of having on hand a large supply of the best war materials. Root pushed through a number of significant changes in the department to equip the United States for her new role, establishing a general staff in 1903 and an army war college in 1907.

A splurge of unusual prosperity immediately followed the Spanish-American War, and an era of gigantic capitalization and inflation began which was to continue until the next bloodletting —the panic of 1907. As usual, the war stimulated trade, large-scale destruction having created a heavy demand for producers' and consumers' goods and capital. And as usual, drafts on the future in the form of an increased national debt partially met this de-mand.

The war had come as a relief to a great many Americans wearied by decades of economic struggle. Beneath the artificial conditions created by the war, however, were operating the same processes that patterned American economic development, as all capitalist developments, in the cyclical elevations of inflation and dips of depression which had marked the nineteenth century. The respite, although exciting, was brief. The nation acclaimed its new heroes, Hobson, Dewey and Roosevelt, and rose to heights of indignation over the "embalmed beef" and War Department inefficiency scandals. Soon, however, the old problems of unemployment, rent and profit returned.

By the end of the nineteenth century tendencies just manifesting themselves in 1870 were in vigorous operation. The population, which had doubled its thirty-eight and a half millions in those thirty years, were moving cityward at a rapid rate. Already one third of the people were urban, and on every hand industry was founding new cities and accelerating the growth of old. Not provincial Concord, but Pittsburgh, with its dirt and noise and smoke of belching furnaces, typified the new America. The metropolis, whose outlines had been glimpsed in the 'seventies, had arrived.

To many it was an age of miracles. The gas stove was replacing the coal range. Soon farm life would be fundamentally changed by electric power and the gasoline engine. As steam had brought greater speed and ease to travel in the first half of the nineteenth century, so now were electricity and gasoline spectacularly shortening the distance between two points. The Niagara Falls had been harnessed by the start of the century, and water became one of the cheapest sources of power.

The enthusiasm invoked earlier by canals and railroads was transferred to street-railway systems. Boston completed the first unit of her subways in 1898. In 1901 the first electric elevated trains ran in New York and a little later in Chicago and Boston. The automobile was becoming a commercial utility instead of a "plaything of the rich." And in 1903 Orville Wright "flew" for twelve seconds at Kitty Hawk on the North Carolina coast. The next day Wilbur Wright stayed in the air for fifty-nine seconds. For the first time in world history a machine carrying a man had raised itself above the earth by its own power, sailed forward without reducing speed, and landed at a point as high as that from which it had started.

Despite its swift development the United States was a young nation. At the beginning of the twentieth century her population was still a combination of the pioneer and the immigrant, but even then these were coalescing to produce what were later to be fondly regarded as "typical" Americans. By 1900 the number of native-born whites of foreign parentage showed a marked increase, while the foreign-born group had slightly diminished, and the proportional relation of the Negro to the rest of the population had declined.

Pittsburgh's foreign-born workers, who hailed from the Mediterranean and Baltic countries, were typical of the new immigration. Germany's industrial expansion, improved conditions in England and a more liberal British agrarian policy in Ireland reduced the flood of emigration from these countries to a mere trickle. But only twice between the end of the Spanish-American War and 1914 did the yearly immigration figures fall below seven hundred thousand, for the poverty-stricken Italian peasant, the oppressed Slav from Austria-Hungary and the relentlessly persecuted Russian Jew took the place of the German,

English and Irish. America's apparently inexhaustible need for
workers during this period was widely exploited by agents for
steamship companies and land-grant railroads, as well as by labor
contractors whose illegal operations remained unchecked for a
long time.

The destiny of the twentieth century immigrants differed
significantly from that of their predecessors, who had been
readily absorbed by their communities. Almost two thirds of the
newcomers settled in the big cities where the nature of their work
as well as their alien speech and customs resulted in their segrega-
tion in various colonies in the slums and working-class districts.
Wage slaves were wanted now, not Americans. And so the melt-
ing pot, which had served the country well in the past, gradually
ceased to function.

Taking the country as a whole, workers were better off in
America than in Europe, but in New York and other large cities
their poverty equaled if it did not surpass that of European
workers. Two thirds of the male workers over sixteen were receiving less than twelve dollars and fifty cents a week in 1900.
Throughout the nation the average wage was less than two dollars
a day. Although beef was seventeen and a half cents a pound,
fresh pork fourteen, eggs twenty-one and a half cents a dozen,
potatoes a dollar and fourteen cents a bushel, and an excellent
suit of clothes could be bought for twenty dollars, the income of
the average wage earner could not meet these prices.

Judging the polarization of the population as determined by
wealth, the figures clearly indicate that even as early as 1890 seven
eighths of the families held but one eighth of the wealth, while
one per cent of the population owned more than all the rest put
together. It had become fashionable for a handful of this minority
to dole out a pittance of their booty to the mass of the people in
the form of charity. But that it was possible for a few to accumulate tremendous sums, while the vast majority grew more and
more impoverished was the basis for the indignation of the reformers and radicals who were soon to become outspoken.

It was surprising that their voices could be heard at all. The
glittering era of city civilization and great fortunes overshadowed
humble living and the growth of slums. An ideology of confidence
and a booster psychology characterized the surface of American
life, devitalizing even the natural class impulses of the brutally
exploited workers. Along with his particular product, the unique

American salesman sold his firm belief in America's greatness. The absence of social castes and traditional pauperism contributed largely, no doubt, to the acceptance of middle-class standards of living and a lack of interest in hoarding. Americans spent their earnings, sometimes with abandon. Andrew Carnegie was the bright and shining example for all young men, and Henry Ford was to become his successor. The widely publicized careers of Rockefeller, Frick, Carnegie and Schwab inspired the farm boy, factory hand and clerk to place no reliance upon petty savings as the means of acquiring a huge fortune, but to hope for a fortuitous benevolence from a newly rich friend, sheer luck, or a gargantuan coup. When oil might be found in an empty lot or in one's own yard, why spend energy and time with tedious savings?

The government, patterned upon the same design as the ascending power of capitalism, benignly approved and blessed its progress through the prevailing doctrine of laissez-faire. The development of the new industrialism's philosophy of individualism can be easily traced in the later interpretations of the Fourteenth Amendment, which had been proclaimed in 1868 and adopted presumably to protect the interests of the newly emancipated Negro.

After the late 'eighties this amendment became the judiciary's sharpest instrument in the defense of property as against human rights through the inclusion in 1886 of a corporation in the wider definition of a "person." Between 1888 and 1918 the amendment was invoked in seven hundred and ninety cases to protect property against "oppressive" state legislation. The courts never attempted to explain, however, precisely where the state's interference in matters of health, morals and the like ended and confiscation of property began. Most of the outstanding decisions for private property and against human rights were handed down during the 'nineties when a number of state legislatures were controlled by Populists who were fighting for relief from the railroads. The twentieth century found precedent to all intents and purposes become law.

After the 'nineties labor faced a new enemy quite as menacing as the courts with their injunctions and the militia: the state constabularies. The rangers were created in Arizona in 1901; Connecticut followed suit two years later; in 1905 the mounted police were established in New Mexico; an emergency force was organized in Nevada in 1908. Of them all, the most significant was

Pennsylvania's state constabulary which was legislated into being in 1905. Labor named its members "American Cossacks" and denounced it as solely a strikebreaking tool of capitalism. Although others championed these armed men as an effective agency against rural crime and industrial outbreaks, their presence during strikes evoked the enmity of labor, which charged them with savage brutality.

While the big guns of capital drove confidently toward their predestined goals of greatness and international power the opposite was the case with the workers. It was an excellent study in antonyms. The beginning of the century saw a labor movement confused, politically immature, and influenced by extreme forces which ranged from reform politics through the disillusioned hope of creating a producers' commonwealth to revolutionary Marxism. But while interest in the fate of unskilled workers, farm laborers, Negroes and other oppressed groups reached a new low, strata differentiation within the class became marked.

Still dependent on a middle-class outlook, the skilled craftsmen organized themselves in the American Federation of Labor, which had emerged a decisive victor from its struggle against the Knights of Labor without, and a weak revolutionary tendency within. Conscious only of its own narrow interests, it faced the future with an understanding merely of the limited function it would fulfill and not of its strength and potential power. As the favored section of the working class, it could well afford to rationalize its lack of concern for the unfavored majority. Thus the extremities of the giant of labor were chained.

The American Federation of Labor had profited greatly from the mistakes of its forerunners, the National Labor Union and the Knights of Labor. In defining the position of its skilled membership in the new industrial society, it rejected the class struggle and participation in it as the vanguard of the entire class. Instead, aping the conservatism of the British trade unions, it sought to achieve a sort of junior partnership with capitalism and endorsed class collaboration lock, stock and barrel. The pariahs of the labor movement, the casual and migratory workers and the Negroes, were left to shift for themselves, while the small, selective group of organized craftsmen met the class-conscious Fricks, Carnegies and Rockefellers with no equipment save job consciousness and contempt for their own class.

Workers and farmers had been restive during the 'eighties and 'nineties because of low wages and declining prices. The first decade of the twentieth century was scarcely under way, however, before the middle class began to complain, and was soon uproariously protesting "machine politics," the "system" which had been introduced by monopoly, and its attendant economic and social injustices.

Trustification of industry and the growth of specialization was undermining the basis for the skilled craft unions. Meantime the importance of the unskilled and semiskilled workers grew in proportion to the wider application of the machine and the extension of mass production. Realization of the obsoleteness of the craft union and of the need for industrial unionism existed only among the small group of progressive elements in the labor movement. Yet this was to be the issue which would divide not only the organized labor movement but its radical sections as well.

The American Federation of Labor was very strong in the building trades, where the skilled craftsmen were well entrenched and where rationalization was making but small inroads. But in trustified industry it was emphatically repulsed and before long its spasmodic attempts to organize ceased entirely. The era of trade agreements and legislative effort began. In politics the Gompers' formula, "Reward your friends and punish your enemies," became the Federation's strategy to protect the interests of the skilled workers and to beat off antilabor legislation. Spontaneous movements toward organization by unorganized workers, instead of being welcomed, were always viewed with alarm by the Federation.

While organized and unorganized labor was coming to grips with capitalism, here learning from mistakes and growing stronger, there retreating disastrously, the Left and Right groupings in the American radical movement took shape.

The extraordinary success of the presidential campaign conducted in 1900 by the Social Democratic party, and those who had seceded from De Leon's Socialist Labor party, overcame all obstructions to unity. Disputes over a party name and location of headquarters could not long endure in the face of the nearly ninety-eight thousand votes which the two groups had polled for Debs and Harriman, and on July 29, 1901, the Socialist party of America was formed. The Socialist movement was now divided into Right and Left camps: the Socialist party, a mixture of heterogeneous and conflicting elements, and the Socialist Labor party, which represented revolutionary socialism. But Left and Right groupings were soon evident within the Socialist party itself. These become known as the "Impossibilists," who, lacking De Leon's theoretical clarity, inclined toward his position but were opposed to many of his tactics, and the "Opportunists," who supported a leadership basing itself essentially on a mixture of Bernstein's revisionism of Marx and Left populism.

The Right wing, led by Berger, Cahan and Harriman, believed in municipal socialism, government ownership and parliamentary reform, and was anti-class struggle. An agrarian tendency originating in some of the Middle Western sections added its cheap money schemes and peculiar utopianism. The Right wing also received the support of a certain number of officials in the trade-union field because of its "hands-off-the-trade-union" policy and its collaboration with the leaders of the American Federation of Labor.

Slightly to the left of this group, but working closely with it, and united in a common struggle against the Left wing, were those who believed in Marxism theoretically but tempered it with "practical" application. This tendency, led by Morris Hillquit, opposed the brazenness of the Right wing's "post-office socialism." Later the World War was to bring out a more serious difference, but during these years the discrepancy between the word and the deed which characterized its position kept it near the Right wing.

The composition of the Left wing was fairly uniform, consisting in the main of workers, mostly unskilled and immigrants, and with few intellectuals as compared with the Right. For over two decades it was led by men like Haywood, Trautmann, March, Titus and Hagerty. And its most influential spokesman, often unclear, and by no means its theoretical leader, was Eugene Debs. His defection in the Left wing consisted principally of an unwillingness to unite with it in organizational struggles against the Right, but his espousal of its position and its ideas gave it tremendous prestige both within and without the party.

The Left wing fought for the class-struggle revolutionary policy instinctively rather than with theoretical consistency and perspective. It did not believe in the peaceful transformation of the government into a socialist one. As against government purchase and ownership of industry, it proposed nothing more or less than the Marxian concept of overthrowing capitalism and expropriating the expropriators without compensation. It rejected absolutely any of Gompers' class-collaboration policies, and waged uncompromising warfare against the "labor lieutenants of capitalism." With equal vehemence it advocated industrial as opposed to craft unionism, and urged active participation in all the daily struggles of the workers.

This group contained a number who represented definite syndicalist tendencies. Their conception of the future society was one in which the state played little or no role. Strongly anti-parliamentarian, they considered the industrial union of greater importance than the political party. Placing considerable emphasis on a passive "don't-work" general strike as a means of bringing about the revolution, they were inclined to ignore the fight for immediate demands. At the same time they were prone to underestimate the capitalists' active resistance to their plans. Finally they failed to take into consideration the peculiarities of American life, as expressed in traditions and ideologies, or to appreciate the role of the Negro and the lower stratum of the middle class and farmer.

From the beginning, the Socialist party was controlled by the opportunist leadership of Hillquit and Berger. The Right wing elements were especially gratified as its vote total leapt upward yearly. That this success was due in large measure to the failure of progressives to lead either of the major parties, as Bryan did in 1900 and 1908, as well as to the fact that many voted Socialist because they believed the party's banner signified merely such reforms as the curbing of corporations and direct popular control of officials and legislation, was not considered then. Instead, a wave of optimism and parliamentary ambition swept the party. Only later was it to become clear that the auspicious beginning had not ensured a similar ending. The years 1905, 1912 and 1919 were to become signposts in the development of the Socialist party of America, prophesying and finally revealing the failure of opportunism.

During the early years of the new century it was still possible for a large number of workers to escape into the middle class. Compared with European countries, with the exception of England, there did exist a great amount of freedom of press and assembly, as well as the rights to strike and to be elected to public office. Yet, despite this blurring of class lines and the sanguinary hopes of the new party of emancipation, increasing exploitation and the inevitable sharpening of economic conflicts would soon show that the rank and file of the working class were sounder in their instinctive reaction against capitalism than were the leaders of the Socialist party.

CHAPTER

13

WHEN Jack returned to Oakland late in July 1898, after a year-long absence in Alaska, he had determined to abandon his head-long rush toward a writing career and proceed slowly and methodically. During the long months of enforced idleness in the Klondike he had evaluated the results of the two and a half fever-ish years that had elapsed since he returned from the road. The unanimous rejection of his writings by magazine editors forced him to conclude that something was unquestionably wrong with his work. To discover what this was and correct it was to be his immediate task, and for some time he intended to study much more and write much less.

Up until now circumstances had offered him only the long, slow way of realizing his ambitions, and short cuts had been ac-complished through sheer determination. Now that he was re-signed to a slower pace, and even desired it, circumstances con-spired to force him ahead at breath-taking speed.

He found it impossible to re-establish the old routine. There were no jobs. Weeks of searching turned up nothing but washing windows, cutting lawns and trimming hedges, which meant long hours of manual labor for a pittance. During August he indulged in one last fling at prospecting when rumors of new gold strikes in the California mountains drew a small stampede from the bay region. In a short time, disillusioned, he was home again, and still unable to find a regular job, turned to writing while he waited for something to turn up.

He was richer than even he knew in material. Intense work and a rare period of keen self-criticism purified and strengthened both style and structure. And finally widespread interest in Alaska guaranteed him a hearing. Five months later his first Klondike story was published, and he was launched on the career he had chosen.

Many changes had taken place while he was away. The old crowd was scattered, even his mother was different. John's death, while not unexpected, seemed to have shocked Flora out of her long apathy. The brisk, businesslike woman of twenty years earlier had returned. By the time Jack reached Oakland she had increased the number of her music pupils, and on the income from this teaching and her small pension was managing her affairs very capably. While Jack was away she had taken into her home, and then into her heart, the little son of John's younger daughter. For a second time a small "Johnnie" was a member of her household. Moved by his helplessness and loneliness, she lavished on him the affection which bitterness and memories she could not forget had kept her from showing her own boy. Little Johnnie Miller contributed much to Flora's late flowering.

Of Jack's old intimate friends, none were left in Oakland but Bess Maddern. The Applegarths had moved to College Park, forty-odd miles south of Oakland, shortly before Jack went to the Klondike. And Fred Jacobs, seeing an opportunity to obtain practical experience as a chemist, had enlisted during the Spanish-American War and was on his way to Manila. Jack did not envy him the experience, not because of the hardships, which would not compare with what he had endured himself in the North, but because of what he felt Fred would have to take from his superior officers.

"A soldier's life is a dog's life at best," he wrote to Ted Applegarth, and then proceeded to state his attitude toward the war itself, an attitude which reveals his limitations at that time as a socialist thinker. Satisfied with the belief that "political democracy" must precede "industrial democracy," he hailed the results of the war as a step forward, and failed utterly to see that the colonial peoples whose destinies had been involved had been freed from monarchy only to be exploited in any way that capitalism saw fit. "As to the war," he told Ted, "I was in favor of it, and socialistically, too, strange as it may seem. While contractors and speculators may have made money out of it, I feel sure that money was not the motive power. As all the institutions of men are but the transient guises or rather formulas of evolution, it is easily apparent that political democracy must come before industrial democracy. The Hispano-American, or as some call it, the Yanko-Spanko, War was but a stroke against monarchy and for political democracy—the latter gradually grows into industrial democracy—and there it is, perfect political and industrial democracy combined are really what?—Socialism."

A few weeks later a newspaper article, reporting the arrival of a troopship in Manila, announced that one man had died of fever en route—Fred Jacobs. In November the news was finally confirmed: Fred had been buried in Manila with military honors. "So be it," Jack commented sadly to Ted. "He has only solved the mystery a little quicker than the rest of us."

The loss of Fred and the scattering of the old crowd brought Jack and Bess, the survivors, much closer to each other. For Jack, Fred had been the one friend with whom candid discussion of everything, including each other, had been possible. Bess was working harder than ever since Fred's death, filling empty hours with renewed efforts to enter the university as soon as possible. Occasionally they went bicycle riding, or Bess would prevail upon him to come to supper, but months elapsed before their friendship ceased to be merely a link with a shared past that held dear memories and began an independent growth.

Jack did not go often to College Park. It was a long trip and the rough road was hard on worn bicycle tires. Besides, his last illusion of love for Mabel had vanished in Alaska. He realized very clearly now that she had been the embodiment of an adolescent ideal which he had outgrown entirely. Her reaction to his radicalism and essential disbelief that he would succeed at writing, adroitly concealed but nevertheless felt by him, awoke his first doubts. Socialism brought him the intellectual rejection of all that Mabel had symbolized, while the frontier gave him a new ideal, who, Indian or white, was the heroine of his stories for some years. This was a woman whose beauty lay in strength, not in fragility, who could endure hardship and conceal sorrow, and whose loyalty to her man was no less than her reverence for him and the wisdom of all his acts.

If Mabel was hurt and puzzled by the change in Jack's attitude toward her she tried, and with fair success, to hide it and accepted him graciously in his new role of "only Jack." It was not easy. He had been in love with her and she knew it, but no one, she least of all, could have guessed it from his letters to her during this period. Life was not to be generous to Mabel but, considering her equipment, she met its rebuffs with a fortitude as great as any of Jack London's heroines. All that she knew was at his disposal as always. At his request she continued to criticize his manuscripts, and if the advice she gave him was wrong advice her wish to help him was sincere.

Desperately seeking work, Jack had chanced upon a notice of a civil-service examination for mail carriers and presented himself on the appointed day. If a vacancy occurred soon such a position would solve the problem of a steady income. It was Flora who persuaded him to abandon his frenzied job hunting until he heard the results of the examination some weeks hence. She was making enough to feed them, the pension paid the rent, and other matters could wait. Jack compromised by doing odd jobs at intervals with which to buy tobacco, stamps and manuscript paper, and to rent a typewriter, and sat down at the old kitchen table in his tiny bedroom to write.

Since everyone was talking about the Klondike he felt sure that firsthand information would be welcome. Accordingly, he set to work at once on a description of his trip down the Yukon from Dawson, and when it was completed he mailed it to a San Francisco newspaper, confidently expecting a check for ten dollars in a few days. Then he queried the *Youth's Companion* for the usual length and number of chapters in its serials, and as soon as he received an answer, turned out a twenty-one-thousand-word yarn in one week. By mid-September he was driving ahead intently in order to accomplish as much as possible before an appointment as a mail carrier reduced the number of hours he could devote to his trade.

The most striking phase of his work was the purely professional attitude with which he approached it. Writing was to be not a means of self-expression but a livelihood. In a certain sense this attitude was typically working class, and for a time bore its limitations. He used to tell his socialist friends at that time that if he could write and sell a thousand words a day at one cent a word he would consider the resultant ten dollars an ample daily wage. But in this he was pretending a nonchalance which he did not feel. Ten dollars a day was an incredibly high wage to him then. He did not guess, however, that his standard of living would always keep pace with or exceed his earning power, and that in a few years he would not only refer to his "wage" as an "income," but that, earning fifteen or twenty times that once-desirable sum, he would be always in debt.

He was concerned only with selling his wares. Perhaps his most significant discovery was the discrepancy between his friends' unvarying praise of his stories and the brutally prompt rejection slips. Lacking confidence in his own judgment, he had depended on Mabel and Ted Applegarth and one or two others who, unfortunately, knew far less about writing than he did, and nothing at all about the modern trends in style and subject matter which were already heralding the literature of the new century. Abruptly he rejected their well-intentioned applause and turned to what had never failed him in the past—the public library.

For weeks he ransacked the book shelves and magazine files for the very latest short stories, and pored over them until late at night, analyzing them, comparing them with his own, seeking the trick, the secret of their salability. Chancing on writers' magazines, he bore them home in triumph and studied them eagerly. The practical advice for new authors and the market tips which now fill such magazines were almost entirely lacking then, but what little they offered was useful. Besides, Jack was working out his own method of attaining successful authorship, a method as valid today as then.

In high school and college English courses he had met "masterpieces" on every hand, and, without realizing it, these were what he had been attempting to write. But the magazines were publishing and paying good money for stories which were clearly not masterpieces at all. The more he read, the more astonished he was to find many published tales which, despite their superficial cleverness, were essentially dull and commonplace. That, he felt, was unnecessary and inexcusable. Excitedly aware of the stories he could tell which would not be commonplace, he made the resolution which he was later to put into Martin Eden's mouth: "Hack work and income first, masterpieces afterward."

In any case, style and technique must be acquired. Like a first-year medical student he began to dissect the stories in the current magazines, taking them apart, tracing their nerves and sinews, and striving daily to reproduce the articulation of their joints.

Technique was not difficult to learn, but style evaded him. What was it, in the first place, and how might it be acquired? The problem was eventually solved by rule of thumb. Everyone was praising the vigor and originality of Kipling's style, therefore he would imitate it. Laboriously, in longhand, and for days on end, he copied page after page and story after story by Kipling. In a short time he noticed that his speech was becoming Kiplingesque, and when at last he sat down to write a story of his own it was in a fair imitation of the Englishman's style. But the device had worked! Style was many things—rhythm, cadence, choice of words, point of view and, more than anything else, the clearest emanation of one's self, as distinguishing as gait, scent or tone of voice. Slowly, but with increasing certainty, Jack London's literary style came into being.

Early he discovered the inadequacy of his vocabulary. Time and again a picture or bit of action stood vividly in his mind's eye, but he could find no words with which to set it on paper. For a long time he had used the dictionary haphazardly; now he organized a simple but effective system of vocabulary building. The definition and pronunciation of every unfamiliar word encountered in his voluminous reading or in the speech of his socialist comrades were written down on slips of paper. These he thrust into the frame of the mirror on his dresser, or pinned to the wall above his table, to be memorized. Longer slips dangled from a wire strung over his bed so that he might review them the last thing at night and the first thing in the morning. He used the new words as often as possible, welcoming the correction of any error. As the words on each slip were mastered and made his own new slips were put up. Again the device worked, and he rejoiced as the increasing vocabulary became supple and strong.

During this period when he learned the essentials of all he would ever know about writing, he sought always the principle, the "how" and "why" of technique which produced stories that would sell. The magazines were reflecting the battle-to-the-death between the moribund literary mores of the closing decades of the nineteenth century and the harbingers of the twentieth. He did not understand the issues of the conflict, which was unfortunate. His sense of timeliness, while acute, was for the superficial in writing, not its perspectives. An enthusiastic exponent of the new style and technique, he soon became a pioneer of American "realism." He broke every writing tradition long revered in

America, seemed (and was damned for it) ultramodern and shocking. Nevertheless, with one all-important exception, his subject matter constantly announced its nineteenth-century origin.

He observed, as he stated later in *Martin Eden*, two schools of fiction: the God-man and the clod-man. The old school placed too great emphasis on man's spiritual nature and potentialities, the new practically denied their existence, and both he believed were wrong. His determination to blaze a trail between the two betrayed at once the weakness and the strength of the epoch which produced him. It is not often that the voice of a transitional period is so loud and clear, but Jack London was nothing if not positive and vigorous. With one foot in the past and the other in the future, he noisily straddled the two centuries, last of the writers to celebrate the American frontier, first to trumpet the battles on the frontier of social justice.

Only his socialistic writings—some of the essays and especially *The Iron Heel*—were to catch and powerfully follow through the perspectives of an era in which romantic frontiers and frontiersmen yielded their place on the literary stage to cities and city men, and the struggle between man and nature and man and man resolved itself into the larger and more brutal class struggle. That he was able to see this at all was due in large measure to his closeness to the socialist movement but, although his socialism was at best muddled once or twice he saw further and more clearly than any of his comrades, and in this lay his one bid for a fame that would outlast his generation.

For the rest, on the one hand, he popularized what he understood of two nineteenth-century doctrines, socialism and evolution, unskillfully applying them to contemporary problems; and on the other, pandered to an audience which first regretted the passing of the frontier, and then came to regard it as a pleasant, although vicarious escape from urban life in which the struggle to survive was becoming ever more difficult.

With his decision to set masterpieces aside, he applied himself to potboilers and soon reduced them to the formula which, basically unchanged, but with less honesty and forthrightness, today dominates magazine fiction and motion pictures. As he explained it in *Martin Eden*, the formula consisted of three parts: "(1) a pair of lovers are jarred apart; (2) by some deed or event they are reunited; (3) marriage bells," or in other words, "boy gets girl." Tragic endings, fine writing, subtleness of thought and feeling were prohibited, but hypocritical sentiment of the sort that brought gallery applause and tears in the theater was mandatory. The only change in forty years is in adaptation to the growing sophistication and cynicism of the gallery, which has likewise demanded better writing, a little subtlety, and, tougher skinned, no longer objects to a few tragic endings.

Jack even worked out a forerunner of today's plotting devices. Realizing that although the third part of his formula was fixed, the other two were capable of infinite variation, he made several stock forms, which, as he described them in *Martin Eden*, were "like the cunning tables used by mathematicians, which may be entered from top, bottom, right and left, which entrances consist of scores of lines and dozens of columns, and from which may be drawn, without reasoning or thinking, thousands of different conclusions, all unchallengeably precise and true." During the next few years his potboilers lived up to their name, for the percentage of sales of the "machine-made" stories was sufficiently high to keep him going while he worked on better stuff—that is, stories that would bring greater financial reward.

One other indication of his businesslike methods was the bookkeeping system he initiated. He not only knew where each manuscript was at any given moment, and what magazines had previously rejected it, but he could tell to the penny the net profit of each sale by deducting the amount of stamps it had consumed before being accepted. Thus he "retired" a manuscript when the stamp outlay was about to exceed the sum he might hope to get for it.

"Dig is the arcana of literature," he wrote to Mabel Applegarth toward the end of the year, "as it is of all things save being born with a silver spoon and going to Klondike." A few months later, writing to Cloudesley Johns, a new friend which the publication of his first stories in the *Overland Monthly* had brought him, he amplified this statement: "There is no such thing as inspiration, and very little of genius. Dig, blooming under opportunity, results in what appears to be the former, and certainly makes possible the development of what original modicum of the latter one may possess. Dig is a wonderful thing, and will move more mountains than faith ever dreamed of. In fact, Dig should be the legitimate father of all self-faith."

Armed with this belief, and pressed constantly by lack of

money, he began to experiment with every type of writing that
might sell. He was perhaps in a more deadly serious frame of
mind than ever before in his life, but he turned out dozens of
humorous verses and plain, everyday jokes and mailed them out.
Then he overhauled the box of old manuscripts that had been
stored away. A pseudo-scientific horror story, composed during
one of the writing bouts after he had left the Belmont laundry,
seemed to have possibilities. He refurbished it and mailed it to the
Black Cat Magazine. When the San Francisco *Examiner* announced a prize short-story contest he promptly submitted several manuscripts. As election time approached the aristocratic
Fifth Ward Republican Club offered prizes for campaign songs,
essays and poems. He sent off contributions in each category.

Meantime he resumed the studying which had been neglected
since he left the university nearly two years before. Mr Bamford
advised and suggested, and Jack brought home from the library
many volumes on political economy, biology, history, literature
and everything else both thought he should know. Sleep was
again reduced to a minimum of five and sometimes four hours
nightly, and he arranged his waking hours into a rigid schedule
which he broke reluctantly only when he needed money to buy
stamps, tobacco or writing supplies. Then he washed windows
or cut lawns in furious haste, and hurried back to his writing.

One luxury he allowed himself for a short time, and that was
to continue the study and practice of verse writing on which he
had embarked just before going to the Klondike. Appreciation
of poetry had come to him for the first time during the crowded
two years at high school and the university, and it was not long
before he attempted to write verse himself. But he, who was so
readily articulate in prose forms, found himself tongue-tied and
frustrated when he sought to fix his thoughts and impressions in
meter and rhyme. Neither textbooks nor daily practice helped.
When his poems were done, each properly accented and rhymed,
they were poor, lifeless things which gave back not the faintest
glow of the ardor which had gone into their composition.

Years later, commenting on a verse written by his twelve-year-
old daughter, he reiterated his faith in his own method of master-
ing the elusive art: "An hour's teaching and a good textbook
would equip you to go ahead and learn all that is to be learned."
Then, remembering that the vaunted method had failed to work
for him, he quoted sadly from Browning, " 'But all the play, the

insight and the stretch—Out of me, out of me!' Read that *Andrea del Sarto* some day," he added. "You'll find what a heaven's for, anyway."

To the end of his life he remained passionately fond of poetry, but only once or twice was he tempted to try his hand at it again. That he achieved now and then in his stories lines of poetical prose which were surpassingly beautiful did not satisfy him. It was probably a long time before he even realized their excellence, for in his early writing days he was cruelly self-critical and dissatisfied with everything he did.

During the autumn of 1898 he labored long over heavy-footed sonnets, triolets and ballads, fondly polishing and repolishing them, and explaining to those who questioned his preoccupation with this unprofitable type of writing that this experimentation would help his prose style. The same period saw the production of the first of his Alaskan tales which he set down in rapid longhand, fifty to three hundred words at a time, and then, after allowing them to "set" for from one to fifteen minutes, typed into the manuscript to be submitted. Revision, he protested, was impossible for him, except for minor changes as he typed the final draft. Yet while he wrote lengthy letters to Ted Applegarth about poetry, and proudly exhibited his efforts to all who would read them, he dismissed with a sentence the poignantly beautiful story which first brought him to the attention of Eastern editors. To Mabel Applegarth he wrote in February 1899, "I was sick at heart when I read printed 'White Silence,' and I yet fail to see anything in it."

Jack had no inkling that the Klondike stories would make his fortune. He wrote them because he could not help himself; they clamored for utterance. Privately he believed that they were the best he had written so far, but he would recognize no confirmation of this opinion unless it came in a small, thin envelop containing a note of acceptance and a check.

As October and November passed, however, the confident mood with which he had begun his prodigious labors began to desert him. He had become inured to having his manuscripts returned with insulting celerity. Now the opposite was the case. He mailed them and they vanished into the void, and for months no word of their success or failure came back to him. He had had great hopes for the serial he had mailed to the *Youth's Companion* in September, and the suspense was hard to bear.

The newspaper to which he had sent the article neither accepted nor rejected it. He must have cherished this first "piece" about the Klondike. In a letter written in February 1901 to Professor J. C. Rowell of the University of California, he included it in his brief list of published material as "a travel article, 'From Dawson to the Sea.'" It did not appear in print, however, for many months after it was written.

The announcement of the awards in the Republican Club contest brought a ray of hope, for Jack had won two of the six prizes of ten dollars each. To him this money would be like rain on parched soil, and he joyfully planned its spending, but it did not arrive. On November twenty-seventh he wrote to Mabel Applegarth, "Everything seems to have gone wrong—why, I haven't received my twenty dollars for those essays yet. Not a word as to how I stood in my Civil Service Exs. Not a word from the *Youth's Companion,* and it means to me what no one can possibly realize."

After much dunning, the Fifth Ward Republican Club disgorged twenty of the sixty dollars it had promised to pay out and thereafter ignored all demands for the remainder. Finally the indignant prize winners met to discuss the matter. At Jack's suggestion they assigned their claims to him, and he brought suit against the organization. The following year, having been publicized not only as a rising young author but a militant socialist, Jack was twitted good-naturedly in the local press for this action.

The rejection of his contributions to the *Examiner* short-story contest was a blow to his determined confidence, but his reaction was one of anger rather than discouragement. "Enclosed you will find the successful *Examiner* story," he wrote to Mabel. "Please keep it, remembering that strength of narrative and originality of plot were demanded by those in charge of contest. Some day, when the mss. I submitted are published elsewhere, I shall forward to you so that you may compare. Also, in the successful story I send you, please endeavor to find what plot there is, if any, or if it is a study, or pseudo-study."

He could not have been a pleasant companion during these months. His letters to Mabel are tinged with bitterness which often yielded to a sort of snarling defiance. Recalling false starts and wasted time because he had blindly believed the praise of uncritical friends, he accused, "I was a fool—and no one to tell me!" And because she had been one of those who had most strongly urged the benefits of a college education, he announced vindictively, "I have learned more in the past three months than in all my high school and college."

He was staking everything on making a financial success of writing, unwilling to consider any other alternative in his frenzied desire to escape from being a laborer for the rest of his life. Sometimes, on black days, he would entertain the possibility of failure, look it in the face and torture himself with the vision of living and dying in Oakland, his dreams and appetites perpetually renewed and perpetually denied satisfaction. But there was always the ace in the hole, he would remember immediately. In such a mood he wrote to Mabel, "As long as my mother lives, I would not do this; but with her gone tomorrow, if I knew that my life would be such, that I was destined to live in Oakland, labor in Oakland at some steady occupation, and die in Oakland—then tomorrow I would cut my throat and call quits with the whole cursed business."

But later in the same letter, the ace in the hole was forgotten and his defiance reasserted itself: "The time is past when any John Halifax, Gentleman ethics can go down with me. I don't care if the whole present, all I possess, were swept away from me —I will build a new present; if I am left naked and hungry tomorrow—before I give in I will go naked and hungry."

Over and over again recurs the tight-lipped phrase, "So be it." But there were times when he admitted, not the possibility of failure, but his loneliness. Poverty and poverty's goad which forced him to long hours of writing and study of necessity isolated him from friends and companions. "Have received a letter from Bess," he wrote Ted Applegarth, "but have not the clothes to pay her a call." Most often he missed Fred Jacobs who, more clearly than any other, had seen his goal and appreciated his urgency in reaching it as soon as possible. Now there was no one with whom he could engage in fierce discussions or share confidences as young man to young man.

Even when he neither missed nor desired companionship, however, he was uneasily aware of aloneness, a sense of something incomplete in his life that would remain even if he were to become successful at writing. In retrospect, the vagabond years seemed an arid, empty waste studded at rare intervals with gaudy purple passages, and he drew back at the thought of their repetition. Recognition of his need of stabilization was compounded as much of his determination to waste no more time as of his healthy, normal maturity. His old longing for fatherhood revived, and his thoughts turned more and more to the contemplation of a wife and a home of his own.

The prospects were discouraging enough, to say the least. Putting his domestic dream into words in a letter written on a bleak Christmas Day, he suddenly caught himself up short: "Ever feel that way? Fred dreamed of it, but never tasted; I suppose I am destined likewise. So be it." But the woman he sought as wife and mother of his children remained always in the back of his mind, growing clearer as he described her type over and over in his Alaskan tales.

He wrote and studied, typed his manuscripts and sent them out, ears atune for the first assurance that he was on the right track. But when it came he did not recognize it. About the first of December he opened a small, flat envelope from the *Overland Monthly* and learned that the editors were not only greatly pleased with his story, "To the Man on Trail," but that, despite a large stack of manuscripts on hand, they intended to publish it immediately in the January issue. His heart leapt. The *Overland Monthly* still glowed with the prestige of its founder, Bret Harte, and was indisputably a first-class magazine. What Jack did not know was that it was likewise a poverty-stricken magazine, and as he finished the letter his elation collapsed. They regretted exceedingly that they could offer him only five dollars for the story.

Five dollars for three or four thousand words, for a story that was manifestly what a first-class magazine desired! But he was writing for a living! Obviously there was no living to be made this way. Where had he got the idea that the good magazines paid well, at least two cents a word, and on acceptance? There was no check in the slim envelope. For a moment he was tempted to give up but, considering the alternatives, he shrugged his shoulders resignedly and decided to stick it out a while longer.

A month later, hope worn thin and brittle, he opened another slim envelope, this time from H. D. Umbstaetter, editor of the *Black Cat*, concerning his horror story, "By a Thousand Deaths." Umbstaetter was definitely interested in purchasing it. Since Jack was unknown he asked for references, and appended a routine list of questions concerning the story's originality and previous submission or publication in whole or part. Jack was vastly intrigued, and reported it to Mabel in a relaxed and jovial mood, "Wonder what they'll pay?"

They paid him forty dollars, and promptly, for the story and permission to cut it in half, and Jack's spirits rose even higher. In *Martin Eden* he indicates the importance to his morale at this time of the *Black Cat* acceptance, and although he belittled the story when it was published it was included in the list he sent to Professor Rowell. Some years later, in an introduction to *The Red Hot Dollar and Other Stories*, culled from the *Black Cat* and published by Mr Umbstaetter, Jack wrote, "I was at the end of my tether, beaten out, starved, ready to go back to coal shoveling or ahead to suicide. . . . Literally, and literarily, I was saved by the *Black Cat* short story."

Now, when it no longer mattered, he received the long-awaited result of his civil-service examination. His percentage was 85.38 and he stood first on the eligible list for carriers. It would be something to fall back upon, of course, but he hoped that he would be able to avoid it. Questioning his postman, he discovered that he had a good chance for appointment, first as an extra man at about forty-five dollars a month, and then after six months as a regular at sixty-five, but, to his relief, he learned that a year might elapse before a vacancy occurred.

The *Overland Monthly* had accepted "The White Silence" for its February number. His judgment in the course he had set for himself having been confirmed by the *Black Cat* check, he was able now to listen quite reasonably to James Howard Bridge, editor of the *Overland,* in an interview they had in the middle of February. Making clear to him both the magazine's financial limitations and its national prestige, Bridge made him a proposition: he would contract for six more stories from Jack, to appear successively in the *Overland*, at the rate of seven dollars and fifty cents apiece; to counterbalance this admittedly low figure, Bridge guaranteed him a prominent place in the magazine and plenty of publicity from critics and reviewers in newspapers and other periodicals, which would soon bring him to the attention of those publications which could afford to pay him what he was worth. It was all Jack needed. He found that he could consider with equanimity even the possibility of not "arriving" for a long time. He was on his way and he knew it.

CHAPTER

14

" 'MARTIN'S after career, not culture,' " says a character in *Martin Eden*. " 'It just happens that culture, in his case, is incidental to career.' "

This was almost precisely the case with Jack London, and his pursuit of culture had not only led him to the public library and high school and college, but was one of the factors which kept him close to the socialist movement. The sincerity of his socialist convictions, especially at this time, is unquestionable. But the sections of the Socialist Labor party in San Francisco and Oakland would scarcely have held him long had they not also offered what was bread and meat to his career.

A Socialist Labor party meeting in those days was composed of grave, well-disciplined men and women, for the most part middle aged, and nearly all of them bearing the marks of people with regular standing in regular communities. If the proletariat proper was conspicuous by its absence, the number of intellectual members and sympathizers was gratifyingly high. In addition to these, the audiences generally included highly skilled artisans, a sprinkling of musicians, several connected with the printing trades, a few clerks with their wives and sweethearts, a university student or two, who had been sent by a professor to observe this new social manifestation, a handful of elderly New England relics from the Civil War period who had been fiery Abolitionists in their youth, and to whom the Civil War was the last word and Lincoln the last incarnation of the deity, and odds and ends of middle-class people who had drifted in from the street or had been attracted by the name of the speaker.

The meetings were decidedly not agitational but educational; in fact, the Socialist Labor party was at that time conducting a very distinguished cultural campaign. The cream of the Bay region intellectuals attended more or less regularly, liberal professors in the near-by universities welcomed invitations to speak, and both San Francisco and Oakland were on the itineraries of a large number of traveling scholars and speakers. The grade of discussion was therefore very high.

Jack, greatly matured during his long absence, felt that his old comrades, and even the movement itself, had changed for the better, were more vital and purposeful. They believed the same of him and welcomed him warmly. For the first time he began to take an interest in abstractions and in knowledge for its own sake, and strove to supplement in his reading what he learned during the discussions. "To his keen, young mind," comments Austin Lewis, "the debates at the Socialist Labor party section meetings were matters of the greatest importance. The lecture of the preceding Sunday was a grave affair which lasted all week and was the subject of lively controversy and discussion in the little group to which he belonged."

In the beginning this group had been drawn together more by physical than intellectual sympathy. Upon Jack's return he and Jim Whitaker resumed their boxing and fencing bouts, as well as the long talks during slack hours at the grocery store. In these activities they were now joined by Tom Booth, a machinist and a member of their section. Booth was a man of great physical strength, and the loss of both feet in a railway accident some years before did not prevent him from being a skillful boxer, even on artificial feet. He could not compete intellectually with Whitaker, but he was endowed with a bulldog tenacity, and although his socialism was tinged with the religiosity typical of the newly class-conscious British proletariat from which he had come, his courage and devotion to the movement were inspiring.

Booth and Whitaker were Jack's closest friends for some time. Later, Jane Roulston and Anna Strunsky were to become part of the group. "All of these," recalls Austin Lewis, "were essentially honest, upstanding people with no nonsense about them, and who told the truth to Jack even to his face. They were all fine people, too, in their way, and unusual enough. Jane Roulston was a

Wellesley College graduate, Anna Strunsky a student at Stanford, outstanding for her work in college debates. They were of enormous value to Jack London in his formative period, and from all of them he got something, either physical, as in the case of Booth and Whitaker, or intellectual, as in the case of the two women." Jane Roulston, a woman of great force of character and intellectual integrity, was ten or twelve years older than Jack. Although her attitude toward him was more or less maternal she never hesitated to express her opinions and criticism of him. Jack's admiration for this woman, retiring, almost old maidish in her ultrarespectable, typically Eastern bearing, was tremendous. In a few years, however, they unfortunately drifted apart. For a while her influence upon him continued through Anna Strunsky, with whom she had formed a close friendship. Jane Roulston remained loyal to the Socialist Labor party when the split came, while Jack went with the majority. After 1906 she made New York her home, and their paths rarely crossed. Nevertheless Jack never forgot her, and she appears in *The Iron Heel* as Anna Roylston, the Red Virgin, fascinating, lovable and a genius, whom all men desired, but whose devotion to the Cause was so all-embracing that she denied herself love, marriage and motherhood.

Outside this small group of close personal friends were three men whose influence on Jack at this time was inescapable: Austin Lewis, Frank Strawn-Hamilton and George Speed. Of the three, he was most intimate with Hamilton and least with Speed, but it was Austin Lewis who knew and understood him best.

Jack and George Speed, despite the twenty-two years' difference in their ages, had much more in common than their experiences as private and colonel in Kelly's army. Meeting again in the Socialist Labor party, their reactions to the group were practically identical. Each, by virtue of his own life experience, knew exactly how much real working class there was about the Socialist Labor party. As Austin Lewis says, they were very much like the augurs of Rome who could not pass one another without smiling. And yet George Speed and Jack London were never close friends.

Born in the working class, life had soon made both sharply aware of the abyss of the lumpen-proletariat into which they might be forced at any time. Youth and a bowing acquaintance with the middle class, thanks to Flora, had thus far saved Jack;

Speed had maintained his position without that dubious aid. With this background they found themselves part of a group of people who had never belonged to the proletariat and had no intention of ever doing so, and yet who not only spoke on its behalf, but preached a philosophy that predicted its triumph. This triumph, however, was wholly dependent upon the working class itself, with which none of these people were acquainted. But Jack London and George Speed were.

Despite the sentimentality of bourgeois agitators, the one thing a proletarian desires more than anything else is not to be a proletarian. There are two ways of accomplishing this: to climb out of the working class, or to abolish it entirely. The first depends on extraordinary luck or unusual ability. The second is a long, slow process which demands from the individual unswerving faith and complete selflessness. Jack possessed the special gifts which could lift him out of his class; George Speed might have long since effected his escape.

But Jack had neither a particularly strong faith in the proletariat as a combative group, nor an active belief that the socialist state would be achieved within his lifetime. He grew a little desperate at the thought of remaining poor and a worker to the end of his days. His hatred of the conditions under which he had labored in his youth invoked in him the determination to put a safe distance between him and them forever, if possible.

He had evolved a sort of Darwinian conviction of the victory of the strong. With one or two exceptions, the proletariat as he knew it was not yet strong. Even the workers in the movement were not only inexperienced as fighters for the cause they had espoused, but so gripped by the fear that they might somehow be precipitated down the black slope of poverty and unemployment into the hell of casual labor and degradation of the lumpenproletariat, that they clung to the status they had achieved with all their might. A new machine, the substitution of the linotype for hand setting, the thousand and one changes, large and small, which occurred in industry during the 'nineties, worried and depressed them. Despite their brave, socialistic talk, they were very timid.

George Speed, uncorrupted and incorruptible by petitbourgeois fears and ambitions, stood alone, and Jack's admiration, envy and resentment of him were equally mixed. In Speed and in Speed's way Jack recognized the heart and the guts of the movement he believed he believed in but, although it tempted him at times, he could not bring himself to take that way. Between him and Speed lay on the one hand Jack's loathing of physical labor, and on the other the lure of the socialist intellectuals, the "brains" of the movement, and these were the stronger. As the years passed Jack preferred to forget his one-time comrade. Only in *The Road* does his name appear at all, and then it is rarely mentioned.

While Jack, fighting tooth and nail, exploited his talents and climbed out of his class into the security and ease of the one above, George Speed to the end of his life kept his remarkable powers and abilities at the disposal of the working class. From his valiant defense of the Chicago anarchists, who went to the gallows in 1887 as a result of their fight for the shorter workday, until his death in 1931, he remained a revolutionary worker.

He had come to Daniel De Leon and the Socialist Labor party via the Knights of Labor and the Kaweah Colony of the Co-operative Commonwealth movement. Later he left the Socialist Labor party for the Industrial Workers of the World, of which he was one of the founders in 1905. For almost a quarter of a century he participated in every major strike of the I.W.W. He was to be a class-war prisoner in the jails of many states, and to be indicted with the Chicago I.W.W.s during the World War and sentenced to Leavenworth Penitentiary. In his middle sixties when he was released, he went forward undaunted. Hearing in 1927 that the Colorado miners were in trouble, he set out at once to assist them, beating his way over the Rockies, a seventy-three-year-old man with an aging body but an indomitable spirit. When he died at seventy-seven, Jack London, worn out and disillusioned at forty, had been dead for fifteen years.

Strawn-Hamilton was one of the itinerant socialist scholars, a nonproletarian by origin and experience, an intellectual by birthright and inclination. Jack's description of him, written not long after their meeting, is slightly exaggerated, but it indicates how deeply Hamilton had impressed him. ". . . a remarkable man, college-bred, qualified to practise law in all the courts, spilling over with the minutest details of every world-philosophy from Zeno to Nietzsche, deeply versed in political economy and sociology—in short, a genius of extraordinary caliber."

Hamilton was very secretive about his past, but it was obvious that his background had been one of wealth and culture. A student at one of the best Eastern universities, he had left in disgust before graduation, and yet by the time Jack met him his learning was far beyond that of the average college professor. Some university of the day was the poorer for not having obtained his services. He had all the requisites of a great teacher, and in addition possessed a vocabulary and a genius for exposition not often met.

He was an indefatigible reader; nothing seemed to escape him. Most of all, he was attracted by the "nebulous sinuosities" of philosophy. A profound student of Marx, he had a fundamental grasp of the intricacies on which theorists loved to spend their time. Looking back across the years, Austin Lewis recalls him as an utterly un-American product: "One sees his type in certain small restaurants in Geneva, just as, twenty-five years ago, one might have seen Lenin, with his little pile of books, his strained, anxious face, and that absorbed look which told that the mind was far from the bodily surroundings. At his best, one might have wished for a portrait of Strawn-Hamilton to perpetuate him as the typical humanist thinker."

Few on the Pacific coast had met anyone like him. He had none of that physical robustness which Jack, for instance, admired and demanded, and none of that pushing, personal drive which is part and parcel of the West's conception of success. Hamilton's lack of "success" was as conspicuous as his extreme poverty. Many, failing to understand him, roundly condemned him for wasting his talents, and for his disquieting carelessness of dress and appearance. But they came to hear him speak, and they listened to the end.

His mind was far too complicated and his views too deep to entertain the ordinary frequenter of street meetings, and the soapbox saw him rarely. But he dazzled and delighted the audiences who heard him at the party's public discussions, and at section meetings he was invaluable. Here was someone who knew the trend of modern life, who spoke authoritatively on the philosophical controversies of the day. He could bring Jack to an appreciation of theories and statements in a brief conversation, notwithstanding the fact that Jack had spent fruitless hours endeavoring to understand these matters by himself.

"Whatever his other qualities," says Austin Lewis with some authority, for he was Jack's critic, mentor and friend in those days, "Jack could not be classified as intellectual in any real sense. He was a poor debater, even in private, and his brain was not of the rapid or active variety. Strawn-Hamilton gave him, painlessly, far more than he could have obtained with tremendous effort from a complete course of philosophy in any university."

Hamilton's poverty was acute. That he survived the privations and tortures of his California life is nearly incredible. Even his closest friends never knew where he slept or how he kept body and soul together. When they could they helped with a bit of change, but most of them were poor themselves. In the end he became what few of his type ever did, a sort of mendicant, who by reason of his keen mind and charming personality found access to the homes of people who were attracted to him. But when he eschewed the bourgeois society in which he had been born he unfortunately also eschewed bourgeois soap and water. Time and again his outraged hosts, too well bred to explain why, ejected him from the house to which a short time before they had warmly welcomed him.

Jack understood Hamilton's kind of poverty; he had been on the road himself. Between them, he and Flora could always manage extra meals and a bed. Nor was Jack squeamish about insisting that he bathe. As neither cleanliness nor dirt mattered in the least to Hamilton, he would graciously comply with the whims of his host.

They spent much time together, the tall, rangy philosopher and his younger, sturdier disciple, and Hamilton, applauding Jack's struggles to write, sometimes recalled and spoke of his own, forever to be denied, ambitions. Writing would probably have come to him as effortlessly as speaking. But refusing to compromise with his rejection of the bourgeois world, and unable to making a living in any other, he had been hopelessly crippled by poverty. Its gifts—ill health, weakness and instability—made it impossible for him to elaborate his ideas in written form; a typewriter was an undreamed-of luxury. Warmed with food, he would relax and talk with Jack for hours, sometimes wittily, often profoundly, and occasionally poetically, while Jack listened in rapt attention.

It was not long before Hamilton had infected Jack with his own enthusiasm for Herbert Spencer. Unfortunately, Jack not only gobbled Spencer whole but, more or less illiterate in philosophy, he failed to gauge the value and significance of Spencer in relation to the intellectual movement in which he was a cog. The situation was even more serious in regard to Nietzsche. Temperate by reason of his greater knowledge, Hamilton could take both philosophers in stride without losing his perspective; Jack promptly became intoxicated. While Hamilton was tolerant of Nietzsche, weighing his worth very precisely, every prejudice, and what today might be termed "complex" in Jack responded violently to the Nietzschean doctrines. In time Hamilton might have put him straight on this and a number of other ideas; in time he might have read himself back to sobriety. But success came too soon, and with it the end of time for studying.

The name of Strawn-Hamilton appears in *Martin Eden* as one of the radical intellectuals whom Martin met through Russ Brissenden. Of the fictional Hamilton, Brissenden said: "There's no end to the possibilities in that man—if he weren't so insuperably lazy." But it was Brissenden himself who embodied the best of the real Hamilton. In a glowing passage which describes Brissenden's speech, those who knew Strawn-Hamilton find him again: "Living language flowed from him. His thin lips, like the dies of a machine, stamped out phrases that cut and stung; or again, pursing caressingly about the inchoate sound they articulated, the thin lips shaped soft and velvety things, mellow phrases of glow and glory, of haunting beauty, reverberant of the mystery and inscrutableness of life; and yet again the thin lips were like a bugle, from which rang the crash and tumult of cosmic strife, phrases that sounded clear as silver, that were luminous as starry spaces, that epitomized the final word of science and yet said something more—the poet's word, the transcendental truth, elusive and without words which could express, and which none the less found expression in the subtle and all but ungraspable connotations of common words. He, by some wonder of vision, saw beyond the farthest outpost of empiricism, where was no language for narration, and yet, by some golden miracle of speech, investing known words with unknown significances, he conveyed to Martin's consciousness messages that were incommunicable to ordinary souls."

As proletarian-socialist and intellectual-socialist, two greater contrasts than George Speed and Strawn-Hamilton could scarcely have been found, but in their belief in the destiny of the proletariat, they were one. The faith of both men was unshakable; in the ultimate victory of socialism they saw all the beauty and glory of life. Jack could trust Speed's faith in the working class; he rejected only the course of action it implied. But Hamilton's serene faith in something about which he knew nothing made Jack skeptical. Under the spell of his enthusiastic words Jack would see workers indisputably endowed with all the qualities one would desire for the Revolution and the new society to come and, rejoicing, would fetch up hard against the realization of the proletarian as he knew him.

Thus early did the contradiction arise between Jack's belief in the destiny of the working class and his lack of belief in its ability to achieve this through its own efforts—a contradiction which he would eventually solve by relying wholly on the activity of individual leaders, who shared his attitude toward the masses, to bring about the triumph of the proletariat and the reign of "Brotherhood." Instinctively he felt the danger to the American socialist movement which lay in the dominance of such men as Hillquit and others of the professional and literary types, and his distrust of middle-class, "respectable" Socialists deepened into dislike. Six years were to elapse, however, before he came into open conflict with them.

Writing to a friend in April 1899, Jack stated, "Job Harriman is considered to be the most popular socialist speaker on the Coast; Austin Lewis the best historical, and Strawn-Hamilton the best philosophical."

Of the three men who stood between Jack and escape from the working class, Austin Lewis was the most formidable. His brain was as fine as Strawn-Hamilton's, his learning as profound, and more catholic since it was not confined to the philosophers, his ability as a speaker as great, and his origin as irreproachably non-proletarian. On the other hand, like George Speed, he was not content with merely talking and theorizing about the class struggle; he worked for it.

When strikers and their revolutionary leaders hurled themselves against the massed front of capitalism and wound up in jail, Austin Lewis' task began, for he was that rare thing in those days, a labor attorney. And when, in the confusion that rocked the radical movement at the turn of the century, clarification of issues was necessary, and the why and wherefore of the strife was demanded, it was Austin Lewis who explained, for he of all the Western comrades was the one who not only knew the his-

tory of socialism and the socialist movement, but how to tell it
so that all would understand.

Like Speed and unlike Hamilton, Lewis earned his living. More
than that, he earned a living for a wife, four children, a sister
and an aging father, not a luxurious living or even a comfortable
one, to be sure, but Austin had his own severe standards and they
were met.

More understanding of middle-class psychology than either
man, more warmly human than Speed, who made himself into a
revolutionary weapon, or Hamilton, who was all intellect, Austin
appreciated Jack's problem from the beginning so well that as the
strain grew Jack became embarrassed and uneasy. But that was
later. During the period that preceded his catastrophic success
Jack recognized none so devoted and eager to help him as Austin
Lewis.

An Englishman by birth and education, Austin had come to
California at the beginning of the 'nineties. While his father conducted an academically excellent but unprofitable preparatory
school in Marin County, Austin, already a Socialist, set to work to
organize the movement on the Pacific coast and to establish himself as an attorney. He founded the first Socialist Labor party sections in the Far West, and his ability at the law soon made his
name known. Escape from the working class was unnecessary for
Austin, but how easily might he have avoided the privation and
poverty that was the lot of a socialist labor lawyer. The bourgeoisie would have paid him well for exercising his abilities on its
behalf, but he chose to remain loyal all his days to the principles
he had adopted in his youth.

At that time access to a considerable number of the works of
Marx and Engels was denied those who did not read German.
Austin took upon himself the important task of making available
as many of these as possible. In his spare time, which was less than
that of most people, for he was very active in the movement, he
translated *Landmarks of Scientific Socialism*, or *Anti-Duehring*,
by Frederick Engels, as well as Marx's appreciation of Alfred
Feuerbach. Austin had no patience at any time with language
barriers when they might be removed with a little effort. German
and French he knew well. Later, when he was aiding the Magon-
ists during the Mexican Revolution, he learned Spanish. And still
later, following closely the events in revolutionary Russia, he obtained an excellent reading knowledge of Russian and ceased to

await the appearance of tardy and often inadequate translations. Some of this disciplined, determined approach to the acquisition of knowledge he sought to impart to Jack, but although he admired Austin's methods, Jack felt that he could not take the time to put them into practice. A devout believer in short cuts, and with access to the stored-up knowledge in the minds of generous friends, he postponed serious study to a time when he had begun to earn a living at writing and could slow his pace. Austin was among the most generous of these friends, and it is to be regretted that Jack's mania for speed prevented him from benefiting as much as he might have from this source.

Thus he never understood the significance of the crisis which occurred in the Socialist Labor party. He took no part in any of the disputes which racked the party locally as well as nationally, and accepted without demur the decision of the Oakland section of the Socialist Labor party to join the new group, although Austin remained with the older party. Austin, knowing the background of the controversies, could have explained them to him, and, listening, Jack would have learned much that he did not know about socialism itself. It was all politics to him and he was not interested, and he was too busy, anyway. That politics and the socialist movement could not be disassociated seems never to have occurred to him. Almost to the end of his life he kept his socialist dream untarnished by closing his eyes to every manifestation which he did not like. When at last he opened them he was bewildered by what he saw, and wept at the difference between the dream and reality.

While Austin succeeded to some extent during the early years of their friendship in making clear to Jack, or at least as clear as it would ever be, much of the theory and practice of Marxism, he was equally helpful in relation to Jack's career as a writer. He had a fine ear for prose, a keen story sense, and was one of the few amateur critics with whom Jack was acquainted who could give his reasons for an "I like" or an "I do not like." Austin was valuable, however, in a far more important way. Publication of the first stories in the *Overland Monthly* had convinced him that Jack was uncommonly talented. But Austin foresaw that public recognition of this talent was likely to outstrip its necessarily slow development, and he feared the consequences.

Here was a greatly gifted young man who might go far. But he was little better than half educated, and his values and perspectives were just beginning to emerge from the confusion wrought by his earlier experiences. He had known poverty and struggle all his days. Now he was on the verge of success, and of making more money than he had ever thought possible (and even Austin did not dream how much that would eventually be). Would Jack be able to keep his head?

Austin had neither the time nor the temperament to inject himself into the situation in any way, but in his frequent discussions with Jack he could and did stand uncompromisingly on his principles and beliefs. "I was always straight with Jack," he remembers. When his opinion was requested he gave it bluntly. So firm was the bond between the two that little speech was necessary. Jack knew without being told when Austin was pleased, or when he felt that Jack had failed to measure up to the standards on which they had tacitly agreed.

The first volumes of Jack London's short stories reveal the slow deepening and strengthening of his powers during these years. The little group of socialist intellectuals did their work well. More than that, they bound him with ties of friendship more closely and for a longer time to the movement than would otherwise have been the case. On the surface at least his life showed a unity of interests—work, friends, ideas and ideals—which had never existed before and would not again. He never learned much socialism, it is true, and politically he remained an ignoramus, but he gained a perspective which was to prove more valuable than he knew. The experiences of these years contributed so richly to his development that their vitality was not exhausted until long after replenishment from the source had ceased.

From day to day the movement stimulated him. The defiant words with which Marx closes the *Communist Manifesto:* "Workers of the World unite, you have nothing to lose but your chains and a world to gain," rang like a trumpet call, creating in him the feeling of emotional elation which he loved. Here was the promise of strife, a bitterly contested struggle with victory at the end. And the beauty and rhythm of the words themselves thrilled him, for he loved poetry with an intensity which most young men reserve for more material and tangible things.

There was always some excitement to keep him alert and anticipatory. As the movement grew, apostles became more active, and propaganda raged from platforms in dingy halls to soapboxes on the city streets. Arrests were more numerous; free-speech fights occurred from time to time, and the struggle went on unceasingly in the courts and churches, in the schools and the workers' halls. To belong to the Socialist Labor party was to belong to an international army that was battling on many fronts. Weekly came the story of conflict and imprisonment and death, and, listening, Jack felt himself one in comradeship and purpose with countless millions over the world.

"In 1899," writes Austin Lewis, "Jack London was young, vigorous, with a sure sense of emotional values and a mind which was beginning to show marks of cultivation and development. One would have predicted for him a wholesome, beautiful existence. But even then there were other concepts and theories of life attracting him, seducing him, destroying him, really. These concepts have destroyed much since his time, and have rendered the world unsafe. In 1899, Jack stood with one foot planted in the soil of social democracy, but the other foot was already being clogged in the morasses of the philosophical teachings from which have sprung fascism. As a matter of fact, there was much in common between Jack London and Mussolini. The latter, however, was by nature more ruthless. He brutally solved his contradictions in terms of his own interest. Jack was in reality much more tender. He broke under the contradictions. But 1898 and 1899 are the two eminently beautiful years of his life, for then he stood upright, and could wear that inimitably beautiful smile of his without a touch of insincerity."

CHAPTER

15

THE LAST YEAR of Jack London's struggle for success was under way, a year so rich in fulfillment and in promise of even greater rewards for the long years of unswerving purpose that it glowed in his memory to the end of his life. He entered it poor and unknown, although in his ears was ringing the first faint applause which greeted his series of stories in the *Overland Monthly*. He emerged from it with success assured, and with the privilege of thenceforth molding his life as closely as he wished to his heart's desires.

But in this too-swift achievement of the only ambition he had ever formulated—to make a living at writing and so escape forever from a life of working-class toil and hardship—lay the seed of the ultimate tragedy which was to overtake him, for he had no heart's desires that could not be bought. All that poverty had denied him he wanted, and an unkind fate was to grant his wishes with a prodigal hand.

Appreciating his gifts, his tremendous capacity for hard work, the driving power of his ambition, one is appalled that he did not even desire fame, except for the money it might bring him. In letters and conversation with friends he spoke warmly of his love of music and verse, of his enthusiasm for the socialist movement, of his slow, sure mastery of the craft he had chosen. But not once did he express a burning desire to accomplish something fine and enduring in any of his fields of interest, not once did he dedicate himself passionately, as young men so often do even though practical considerations later moderate their fervor, to an ideal whose realization was infinitely desirable and infinitely remote. And he was only twenty-three!

As he moved from obscurity toward the bright place in the sun that was to be his, he was sometimes uneasily aware that his victories were failing to satisfy him, that his hunger was yet unappeased. He could not understand it. Why did only the struggle seem good, while accomplishment was flat and tasteless? Restlessness would seize him then, and the old desire to escape would reassert itself. "I shall go to Paris!" he would announce. "I shall take passage on a big English windjammer and sail around the Horn!" Little by little there crept into his manner a positiveness and self-assertiveness oddly at variance with the unassuming modesty which had characterized him, as if by loudly stating his opinions and purposes he might still the doubts that fretted him. Once established, this tendency became permanent; in the end his manner was oracular.

But the struggle was good. Between the first acceptance by the *Overland Monthly* and the next one of importance by the *Atlantic Monthly*, lay seven months of intense work and study. Often he and Flora were hard put to make both ends meet. In the summertime Flora's pupils fell away. They could be sure only of her tiny pension and Jack's rejection slips, but they managed to survive, thanks to the small, irregular sales of his hack work and "machine-made" stories. Money for postage and paper was a constant drain, and it was disconcerting to note how their appetites increased as their finances diminished. Yet, recalling those days for his daughters, he would laugh gleefully.

He had three possessions: a bicycle, a decent suit of dark clothes and John London's mackintosh, and a fourth on which he paid rent, a typewriter. All were important, even necessary, to him. The bicycle saved time and carfare, for he hated to walk. The suit of clothes meant that he could call on his friends. When it rained the mackintosh protected his clothes on his daily trips to the public library. And the typewriter translated his sprawling longhand into clear type that the "silent, sullen peoples who run the magazines" could read. "If typewriters hadn't been invented by the time I began to write," he would chuckle, "I doubt if the world would ever have heard of Jack London. No one would have had the patience to read more than a page of my longhand!"

When all went well he worked, secure with his possessions around him and the rent paid on the typewriter. But when things began to go badly first the mackintosh, then the suit of clothes, and then, reluctantly, the bicycle went to the pawnshop. Last of all, the typewriter was returned to the shop, and he would sit at home, mackintoshless, suitless, bicycleless and typewriterless, the pile of scribbled sheets growing higher and higher while he waited prayerfully for the postman to bring him a slim envelope that would contain a check. Then he would redeem everything and start in again. "Am out of paper," he wrote to Ted Applegarth during one of these crises, "so have not typed it yet. Sent off 10 mss. and have 9 more ready to go as soon as I get stamps. Revised 3 more yesterday and today, and expect to revise another 5000 word one tonight."

"That's the way it is," he would sum up, fifteen years later. "You look back and see how hard you worked, and how poor you were, and how desperately anxious you were to succeed, and all you can remember is how happy you were. You were young, and you were working at something you believed in with all your heart, and you knew you were going to succeed!"

So confident was he that, growing impatient that he should have to wait at all, he somtimes permitted himself to luxuriate shamelessly in moods of self-pity and apparent discouragement. Thus he wrote to Mabel at the start of the last hard summer: "Well, well, plenty of dig, and an equal amount of luck may enable me some day to make perhaps a small livelihood out of the pen. But what's the diff.? I get so hungry sometimes, hungry for all I have not, that I'd rather quit the whole thing and lie down for the good long sleep, did I not have my mother to look out for. This world holds so much, and it takes but such a little to get a fair share of it. . . ." But this was only Jack, sure of the outcome, dramatizing himself in the midst of the closing scenes of his struggle, and exulting secretly as each day's work brought him nearer his goal.

It was at this time that he established the routine from which he was never to depart, writing a thousand words a day, six days a week. When by chance he fell behind his daily quota he conscientiously made it up the following day, but if the work went well and he surpassed his quota, the surplus could not be subtracted from the next day's stint. How precisely he kept track of those words! "Last week I finished 1100 words ahead of the required amount," he wrote to a friend. "Today I am 172 ahead of my stint."

The manuscript was written in longhand and then carefully copied on the rented Oliver typewriter. He went at the job with meticulous regularity, as one who was accustomed to reporting for work on time, and to doing work which would pass the test of a foreman. His attitude was reflected in his methods: he was producing wares that had to find their market. To all intents and purposes, he was a worker for pay.

To Mabel he wrote, apropos of a twenty-five-dollar offer for a story, "It stands for ten days' work, so I get two and a half per day for it. I notice in today's 'want column' of the *Examiner*, an ad., which runs to the following purpose: 'Wanted: a bright, intelligent well-educated young man, thoroughly competent at stenography and typewriting, for office work. References required. $4 per week to commence.' He who runs may read—he'd have to work nearly two months to get what I expect to get."

When the thousand words were written and typed the day's work was done. He planned new stories, took notes, sent off rejected manuscripts and then turned to studying. He kept abreast of current affairs by reading three daily papers, as well as the socialist periodicals, and pored over the magazines whose acceptances he coveted. Seeking to improve his writing, he worked laboriously through books on style and structure. Finally he read as much as he could of the radical literature of the time, not only the pros and cons of the Marxian theories, but the ever-increasing body of literature written by the disciples of Darwin and Spencer.

Although his time was fully occupied with these activities, plus regular attendance at party meetings and discussions, his loneliness persisted. Side by side he and Flora fought the common enemy, lack of money, but they had little to say to each other. Flora was behaving magnificently. Her determination that he should succeed was as great as his own. He could not guess what it would mean to her—the rehabilitation of her pride, a justification and reward for her hard life—and she did not speak of it to him. While not great, the disparity of age between the party members and himself prohibited intimacy. He began to yearn for the companionship of his contemporaries.

Slowly the character of his relationship with Bess Maddern changed. None knew better than she the long way he had come in the last four years, none rejoiced more at the first signs of victory. Her grave admiration of his achievements delighted him. When he was downcast she cheered him determinedly, rejecting the possibility of failure, and she followed with wistful wonder his extravagant flights of fancy when gaiety and confidence had their will with him.

Noting her sturdy independence, her gift for comradeship, the ease with which she adapted herself to his moods and demands while making no demands upon him, her generosity and loyalty, he knew himself no longer lonely. "We have such fun together," he told her the next year when, without warning, he asked her to marry him. "We had such fun together," he said years later to the children of that marriage, remembering how it had come about.

Apropos of the "very nice young lady" who accompanied him on his "far from conventional rambles," he wrote to a friend, "Last Sunday, threatening rain, we wandered off into the hills, cooked our dinner (broiled steak, baked sweet potatoes, coffee, etc., crab, French bread, and a patty of dairy butter), and were a couple of gypsies. Tomorrow we may jump on our wheels and ride off forty or fifty miles. And yesterday we may have taken in the opera and dined fashionably."

Perhaps the greatest boon to him that year was the correspondence with Cloudesley Johns, which began shortly after the publication of "The White Silence" in the *Overland Monthly*. Johns' congratulatory note was the first fan letter Jack ever received, his first tangible knowledge of any of the people who read the stories he fashioned in his little room. His eager thanks prompted Johns to write again, and in a short time letters were passing regularly between them.

The significance of this new friendship may be appreciated when it is realized that Johns was a contemporary, a struggling author himself, and likewise a Socialist. How zestfully they explored each other's minds, often impatient with the limitations of letter writing, but exploiting them, nevertheless, whenever possible in order to make a good impression. They exchanged life histories, personal problems and opinions on every subject imaginable, criticized each other's stories, rose to sublime heights of philosophical argument, and dropped to the mundane practicalities of story-market tips and the best way to persuade editors to pay for material after they had accepted and printed it.

Reading those letters forty years after they were written, one is struck by how much of himself Jack revealed. One sees him as he saw himself, putting his best foot forward, fearful sometimes of criticism but brazening it out; one shares his moods and listens to his opinions, applauds his triumphs and watches the change in him as success came.

To Johns, who had asked for a photograph of his new friend, Jack wrote, "You shall be one of a number of friends who wait and wait in vain for a likeness of yours truly." (A poor prophet, Jack; in a few years he would be the most photographed author in America.) "But I'll do this"; he continued, "tell you all about me. Twenty-three years of age last January. Stand five feet seven or eight in stocking feet—sailor life shortened me. At present time weigh 168 lbs.; but readily jump same pretty close to 180 when I take up outdoor life and go to roughing it. Am clean shaven—when I let 'em come, blond moustache and black whiskers—but they don't come long. Clean face makes my age enigmatical, and equally competent judges variously estimate my age from twenty to thirty. Greenish-gray eyes, heavy brows which meet; brown hair, which, by the way, was black when I was born. . . . Face bronzed through many long-continued liaisons with the sun, though just now, owing to bleaching process of sedentary life, it is positively yellow. Several scars—hiatus of eight front upper teeth, usually disguised with false plate. There I am *in toto*."

To this he added a further descriptive note a few months later: "Ha! Ha! You demand comfort in place of conventionality, eh? Ditto here. Tomorrow I shall put on a white shirt, and I shall do it under protest. I wear a sweater most of the time, and pay calls, etc., in a bicycle suit. My friends have passed through the stage of being shocked, and no matter what I should do henceforth would, I know, remark, 'It's only Jack.' "

The dominant note of the correspondence is one of increasing optimism and sureness as month by month he sold more stories and articles and at better prices. But as he progressed the joyful first realization of recognition and the freely expressed self-criticism, not only of his work but of his capabilities, which characterized the earlier letters, vanished before the defiant articulation of his determination to make money.

In the spring he was writing: "I sometimes fear that, while I shall surely develop expression some day, I lack origination. . . . Thanks for the tip to 'Western Press'; I have some of my earlier, immature work with them now. Suppose I'll some day call my present work just as immature. . . . How are you off for humor? To save my life, while I can appreciate extremely well, I cannot develop a creative faculty for the same. . . . When I have finished a thing I cannot, as a rule, tell whether it is good or trash."

When he discovered that Johns did not share his enthusiasm for Rudyard Kipling, he replied in a sentence that gives one pause, so precisely does it state his own literary destiny: "I agree with you that R.L.S. never turned out a foot of polished trash, and that Kipling has; but—well, Stevenson never had to worry about ways or means, while Kipling, a mere journalist, hurt himself by having to seek present sales rather than posthumous fame."

By September the change was beginning to be evident; ". . . it's money I want, or rather, the things money will buy, and I could never possibly have too much. As to living on practically nothing—I propose to do as little of that as I possibly can. Remember, it's the feed not the breed which makes the man." "How I envy you," he wrote a week later, "when you say that you do not write for publication. There is certainly far greater chance for you to gain the goal you have picked out than for me who am in pursuit of dollars, dollars, dollars."

Two months later he boldly announced his choice: "If cash comes with fame, come fame; if cash comes without fame, come cash." "Nay, nay," he protested the next month, "bankruptcy is not an ideal state, at least for me. It's too horrible for words. Give me the millions and I'll take the responsibilities." Shortly before his first book was published in 1900 he reaffirmed his belief: "Money? Money will give me all things, or, at least, more of all things than I could otherwise possess."

The deeper intent of his decision of five years earlier to make his living by brain rather than brawn becomes very clear. It was not a living he wanted to make, but money, and writing, for which he was aware he had a certain talent, was a convenient, readily exploited means to that end. Nor can any charge of insincerity be laid against him on this point. He gave fair warning of his intention from the start, and to the end of his career he reiterated to an unbelieving world his dislike of the work he had to do to gain the money he so desired.

Reading his personal letters and the interviews he gave to the press, recollecting conversations, in all of which he candidly expressed his attitude toward writing, it would seem that one is belaboring the obvious in stressing this point, except that it has long been the source of a large part of the misapprehensions concerning Jack London. Once one accepts his youthful avowal at its face value and examines other facts in its light, many of the contradictions of his subsequent career are resolved. Perversely, with a high disregard for tradition, he had chosen as a field in which to make money one which had hitherto been loftily dedicated to the finest expression of man's thoughts and aspirations with no thought of pecuniary reward. Even an openly expressed desire for fame was frowned upon. The twentieth century has changed all that; literature is only one of many formerly sacred professions which have been commercialized. But forty years ago Jack London's assault upon literature for the sole purpose of making money was universally disbelieved.

There was good reason for this. He had reckoned without his talent, refused to consider seriously the rich endowment that was his. During the early years while he pressed forward exultantly, demanding and receiving ever higher prices for his wares, he was exerting himself to the utmost, and his readers were dazzled by the splendor he offered them. Later, when devotees began to recognize the polished, and, toward the end, the all too frequently unpolished trash that appeared under his name, they felt that he had betrayed them, sold them out. But it was only that the businessman, weary of the game, was growing careless and indifferent.

Likewise he reckoned without the sincerity of his socialistic convictions, his belief in the splendid destiny of the working class which loomed beyond the blood and sweat of the class struggle. He was scarcely launched as a writer when he began to use his pen for the socialist movement. These writings, with few exceptions, were mediocre, but the passionate idealism which motivated them touched a spark in the hearts and minds of countless readers, who thenceforth believed in him and trusted him. Further, he could not confine his socialism to essays and pamphlets. It spilled over into his fiction work, ennobling many a thousand words that were pounded out merely to build a boat or a house or buy more acres for his ranch.

Jack clung naïvely to the idea that as long as he was honest about his intention of writing for money he was relieved of all responsibility. As he saw it, injecting socialism into fiction killed two birds with one stone: it was good propaganda, he believed in it; and because people seemed to like it, it sold more books and so brought him more money. Stubbornly he refused to face the real issue—the fact that certain phases of his work, whether he willed it or no, had created a loyal and devoted following to which, in all fairness, he owed integrity. Taxed with failure to give this, he would retort savagely, "What right have they to expect more of me than I give them? I made them no promises! More, I have made no bones about why I write."

His indignation over this point was showy. He set up straw dummies and brilliantly knocked them down: "I have never yet written a line for print that I would be ashamed for my two little girls who are growing up to see and read, and I never shall!" But he had not been accused of immoral writing, but merely of inconsequential slush. For a long time he would not see that his righteousness deceived no one but himself. How had such a situation come about? he would wonder, as knowledge of his helplessness bit into him. He had thought it would be so different.

As a poor boy dreaming of riches, he had visioned a beatific existence in which there would be time and opportunity for the enjoyment of everything desirable: luxuries and travel and study; the production of literary masterpieces, and the striking of mighty blows for socialism. Poverty, he believed, forced men to live like beasts, cowering in their holes, never lifting their eyes above a narrow beast horizon. Wealth, freeing man from cowardice and an animal preoccupation with the bare essentials of existence, would likewise free his mind and spirit for the pursuit of their own peculiar pleasures. Bread first and glory after, that was the formula!

He could not see that this attitude was incompatible with his socialism. He was living in a capitalist society. All about him men were getting rich, and not as honestly as he. Besides, he was exploiting no one but himself in the process of acquiring wealth. So he would beat the capitalists at their own game, he would show them!

Thus he argued, twenty-three years of age and on the threshold of success and, stepping forward confidently, walked straight into a trap of his own devising.

From the start his imperious demands for material possessions outstripped his earning power, and although the latter reached phenomenal heights, it always lagged behind his debts. To plan, to order, and then to work frantically to pay for the things he had

wanted—that was all that life was to permit him, inexorably denying him the joy and fulfillment he had been so sure would be his
once he possessed all he wished. Bound to the wheel of his debts,
but obstinately contracting new and ever greater ones, seeking
desperately to acquire at no matter what expense some one thing
which would bring him happiness, he staked his talent, his principles, and finally his life itself on the achievement of an infantile
ambition, and, winning, lost.

One phase of the legend which has grown up about Jack
London insists upon crediting him wholly for his sudden leap
from obscurity to fame, from poverty to riches. To believe this,
however, is to miss much of the drama of his career. With un-
canny precision his ripened talent and perspectives coincided with
an objective situation which made his phenomenal success almost
unavoidable.

He arrived on the scene just as American literature, no longer
able to resist the pressure of modern life, burst the shackles which
had bound it to the modes and mores of the past and leapt forward
eagerly to trumpet the new day. While the country pulsed with
the discontent of the 'eighties and 'nineties, literature had remained
decorously silent concerning not only the momentous changes
that were taking place, but the actual conflicts between the old
and the new. Clinging obstinately to its narrow sectionalism, it
failed to reflect the sweep of national life, the coming of industry
and the growth of cities, the emergence into the open of classes
and the class struggle. By the 'nineties, however, its determination
to remain cheerful, nonpartisan and innocuous broke under the
strain, and the pioneers of the new literature forged ahead.

Outworn traditions of gentility crumbled swiftly before the
vigorous portrayal of modern American life. Conservatives,
shocked by the noisy clamor, withdrew into ivory towers, but the
majority of readers and countless thousands who had heretofore
not been readers at all expressed their enthusiastic approval. In the
space of a few years America became a land of phenomenal book
and periodical sales.

Meantime a revolution had occurred in the magazine field. For
years *Harper's*, *Scribner's*, *Century* and the *Atlantic Monthly* had
held sway unchallenged, purveying cool tranquil fiction and essay-
like articles to an exclusive audience of cultured Brahmans. During the 'eighties, however, a few farsighted men began to see the

need for a new type of magazine. Of these, three were outstanding—Frank A. Munsey, John Brisben Walker and S. S. McClure. They were convinced that magazines did not appeal to a large audience, first, because they failed to provide vital reading matter, and second, because they cost too much. Technological improvements in printing and the manufacture of paper were greatly lowering production costs, while contemporary American life was crying out to be described and commented upon in another medium besides the daily press. Working separately, and coming to grips in the autumn of 1893 in brief but bitter competition, they finally succeeded, with *Munsey's*, *McClure's* and *Cosmopolitan*, in introducing the cheap, popular magazine, selling for ten cents a copy as opposed to the old twenty-five and thirty-five-cent rate, and replete with lively fiction and controversial articles. *Munsey's*, with keener understanding of what the American public wanted, took the lead and kept it for some time, but *McClure's* and the *Cosmopolitan* were close on its heels.

At the turn of the century these magazines and others which had followed their lead were in full swing. Their low price and exciting contents had attracted at least a half a million new buyers and probably two million new readers. Determined to retain and further increase this source of profit, the cheap magazines constantly exerted themselves to intrigue and titillate their audience. Never before were readers so pandered to! Whatever they wanted, whatever caught their fancy—that they should have. In a few years, led by McClure, who saw the possibility of exploiting the gigantic consolidation of Big Business which was taking place, this combination of editors, eager to please, well-trained staffs, and a wide circulation among readers whose appetites for the sensational had been sharpened for nearly a decade, was to inaugurate the era of muckraking.

Seeking quick returns for his time and effort, Jack London's first objective was the magazines. Books would come later, preferably after serial publication, for thus he could collect twice from the same work. Comparing the lists of his serial and book publications, one observes how successfully he applied this rule throughout his writing career.

The conclusion he drew from his close study of the current magazines placed him in the ranks of the iconoclasts. He had nothing but scorn for the old-fashioned periodicals. "Our magazines are so goody-goody," he wrote to Johns. "This undue care not to bring a blush to the virgin cheek of the American young girl is disgusting. And yet she is permitted to read the daily papers!" Considering his purpose, his selection of the markets he most desired to reach showed unerring judgment: *Munsey's* and *Mc-Clure's*. In the autumn of 1899 he wrote to Johns, "By God! if I have to dedicate my life to it, I shall sell work to Frank A. Munsey. I'll buck up against them just as long as I can push a pen or they can retain a ms. reader about the premises."

This ambition was never to be realized. He fared better with *McClure's*, however. The following spring McClure, ever alert to acquire significant new authors, saw in Jack London a talent which, properly nurtured, would return his investment tenfold. His financial support and encouragement brought Jack safely through a few years that might otherwise have been trying to one who was in such a hurry to succeed. Meantime he ranged wide for markets, driving persistently for those which would pay him best, eventually to find what he sought in the newspapers and magazines owned by William Randolph Hearst.

The welcome accorded his Alaskan tales as they were published monthly in the *Overland* during the spring of 1899 convinced him that he was on the right track. If Westerners were interested in these themes then they should be equally attractive to readers throughout the country, for the gold rush had involved the nation. Accordingly, he never ceased bombarding the Eastern magazines, choosing the better-class ones, now that he was surer of his ground, because he knew they paid better. He grew a little weary of the Klondike as time went on. "Many who know me ask why I, with my knowledge of the sea, do not write some sea fiction," he told Johns. "But you see I have been away from it for so long that I have lost touch. I must first get back and saturate myself with its atmosphere. Then perhaps I may do something good."

Many who visited him at this time are sure that they remember the five feet of rejection slips impaled on a sharpened wire which, they claim, was a prominent feature of his bedroom-study. Better proof of his industry, however, were the acceptances, which totaled twenty-four stories, articles, poems and jokes published during 1899, not to speak of work composed then and published the next year. When the long-awaited mail-carrier appointment finally arrived he had progressed too far toward successful authorship to be willing to lay it aside for a small although dependable income, especially as Flora, who could burn bridges with the best of them, approved his decision.

The *Cosmopolitan*, pursuing its policy of encouraging discussion of sociological problems, announced a prize contest, offering the sum of two hundred dollars for the best article on "Loss by Lack of Co-operation." Jack felt himself peculiarly fitted to try for the prize by virtue of his association with the Socialist Labor party and the socioeconomic reading he had done. With ample time to meet the deadline, he set to work on an essay entitled, "What Communities Lose by the Competitive System," planning it carefully from beginning to end, and writing it over a period of months. "Hammering away at that *Cosmopolitan* essay at intervals," he wrote to Johns at the end of July. "Am thoroughly satisfied, as far as I have gone, which is saying a good deal for me—am usually sick at this stage, and it's such dry, dissertative stuff after all."

The progress he had made both in understanding and the ability to convey it since he had pounded out sociological essays during the period of feverish composition after he left the university elated him. But his enjoyment of this type of writing did not kindle any desire to do more of it immediately. For the time being he proposed to stick closely to his plans. A discussion of this possibility with Johns evoked one of the clearest statements of his attitude toward writing: "As for my writing histories and works on economics—I may, some day—but I have little ambition to do so. The same may be said of any kind of writing under the sun. My only wish that way is the all-needful—it seems the easiest way. Had I an assured income, my ambition would be for music, music, music. As it is, impossible—I bend."

He did not really expect his *Cosmopolitan* essay to win the prize. It had been as socialistic as he could make it. When a year later he received the announcement and the two-hundred-dollar check, he laughingly told his socialist comrades, "I guess I'm the only man in America who is making money out of socialism!" But although he soon began to write other socialist essays, it can be truthfully said that their prime purpose was never to make money.

Toward the end of July arrived the significant acceptance from the *Atlantic Monthly*. Sitting at the kitchen table with the letter before him, Jack suddenly remembered that it was just a year since he had reached Oakland, ill and penniless, from the Klondike. Now a story which had been then but a glimmer in his brain had been accepted by a magazine whose literary standards were the finest in America! How right he had been all these years, he exulted, and how wrong all the others who had sought to dissuade him from his purpose! And although he had fashioned the story, "An Odyssey of the North," with all the skill of which he was yet capable, it was only a beginning. He would do more and finer ones!

Concealing his jubilance, he wrote nonchalantly to Johns, "Did you ever write a yarn of, say, twelve thousand words, every word essential to atmosphere, and then get an order to cut out three thousand of these words, somewhere, somehow? That's what the *Atlantic* has just done to me. Hardly know whether I shall do it or not. It's like the pound of flesh."

Not do it? He set to work immediately, fully aware of how publication in the *Atlantic Monthly* would affect his status as a writer. Furthermore, he had realized instantly that now it was possible to launch a project over which he had been hesitating for some time. His next letter to Johns casually announced the result of his decision: "Yes, I cut the story for the *Atlantic*. . . . Have also sent Houghton, Mifflin & Co. collection of tales." His apprenticeship as a writer over, he was ready now to publish his first book.

Heart high, eyes on the future, he pressed forward during the closing months of what was probably the happiest year of his life. The bleak days of proletarian servitude were far behind him now; everything was encouraging and full of promise. "Society will never injure me," he voiced his optimism. "The world calls too loudly for that!"

CHAPTER

16

NOT THE LEAST of the effects of the acceptance of "An Odyssey of the North" by the *Atlantic Monthly* was the abrupt change in the attitude of certain Socialists towards its author. Jack's friends in the movement were not especially surprised by his casual announcement of the great news; they had been following his work closely and knew the strides he had been making. But the day of the socialist opportunists was dawning, and it was they who, suddenly discovering a nearly full-fledged celebrity in their midst, began to exploit him "for the Cause."

The party was in the throes of the struggle between the De Leonites and the Cahan-Berger-Hillquit group. Although the majority of the California Socialists were being swayed by the oratory of Job Harriman, the activity of Austin Lewis and a few others, who stanchly supported De Leon, produced discussions which were often bitter and acrimonious. Jack, ignorant of the issues involved, was confused and unhappy. What, he argued, did a political fight for power between rival factions have to do with socialism? And, and most immediately, was he himself a Socialist?

Jack was going through a period in which, and with good reason, he was doubting his socialism. Certain reading he had done in the past year had undermined what had been a too-facile acceptance of the tenets of Marxism. He had relied on second and third sources and listened uncritically while this one and that, forgetting his meager equipment, had expounded their understanding of Marxian theories. Further, like most laymen of his time, he really knew very little about modern science. Now it appeared to him that "evolution" and "biology" might upset the whole edifice of Marxian thought.

More than once during this period he confessed, "No, I am not a revolutionist or Marxist. I've read too much Spencer for that." Or, unwilling at other times to abandon his belief entirely, he would qualify it, "I am still a Socialist, but an evolved product, possessing a faith in humanity equaled only by a conception of its frailties and faults."

His examination and testing of his beliefs had scarcely begun, however, when they were cut short by an unprecedented event: the party asked him to deliver a speech. A poor speaker, his efforts had been confined for the most part to rare outbursts on the soapbox three years before. At that time the intellectual prestige of the Socialist Labor party was very great. And it had asked him to speak! He did not realize for some time that the request was due almost entirely to the fact that he had sold a story to the *Atlantic*, and that the local papers, continually egged on by the *Overland*, which had faithfully carried out its promise of publicity, had been frequently mentioning him in what he called "divers newspaper puffs." He accepted gladly.

Discussion of a general topic would permit him not only to assume a more active role in the party, but to avoid taking sides in the controversy. And the long months of unremitting toil at writing had tired him, made him eager for more and wider contacts with people. "Haven't addressed an audience for three years," he wrote Johns, telling him of the speech he was preparing for the Oakland section on the twenty-fifth of November. "It'll seem strange." But the strangeness vanished in the face of people eager to see and hear "the distinguished magazine writer," as the San Francisco section billed him early in December.

Although the local papers said, "He spoke with more earnestness than eloquence," as far as his exploiters were concerned, Jack London's career as a socialist speaker was a success. It publicized the movement and brought financial returns. But its effects on Jack were very bad, and again one regrets the swiftness of his rise to fame. Not only did he cease to question his socialism, but no one else questioned it either. Thus he was permitted to write and speak an amazing amount of nonsense which passed for socialism and was not.

His presence on platforms became more and more an object of interest among a set of people who had no connection whatsoever with working-class politics or organization. Clubwomen and others who always flutter around a celebrity came to the Socialist Labor party public meetings to hear him talk revolution. And they were well rewarded. Young, strong and good looking, and wearing his unconventional soft shirt, he made a very attractive appearance. In increasing numbers during the next five years, the middle-class fringe of the radical movement, as well as those who had no interest at all in radicalism, flocked to hear him, and paid for the privilege.

His years of obscurity having been lengthened fantastically in his mind by the fierceness of his ambition, this sudden eruption into the limelight played havoc with his perspectives and values. Not only did his socialism wander unchecked into strange, un-socialistic channels, but the flattery of those who attended his lectures, and particularly the flattery of the feminine portion of his audiences, aroused in him a new sort of egotism and developed a personal vanity which had not heretofore disclosed itself. Austin Lewis, in the thick of the fight to preserve the principles of revolutionary socialism, had time to note and to convey to Jack what was taking place. Unfortunately Jack did not heed him.

"The very frank admiration of the more honest," remembers Austin, "and the subtle flattery of the more sophisticated, each had its share in the production of a state of mind. The truth of this conclusion may be readily demonstrated by referring to his writings, but it was much more evident in his bearing and in his attitude toward those whom he soon began to regard as his inferiors. This public admiration of the personal kind was the origin of a curious sort of snobbery which he afterward developed to an extraordinary degree—not the unconscious snobbery of the parvenu, who must have something to look up to, but the conscious snobbery of one who has found himself an object of personal attention, and, who, at the same time, has a notion that people who are admiring him are, in some respects at least, his social superiors. The whole of his life later at his country house in the Valley of the Moon is eloquent of this state of mind. Of course, the tendencies manifested themselves slowly, but the seeds were sown during those early lectures and public appearances."

Because Jack had always found it difficult to speak extemporaneously, and because he knew that he might be challenged by the one or two in his audience who really understood Marxian socialism, he carefully composed and wrote down his speeches.

These became the nucleus of the collections of socialist essays which were later published in book form, notably *Revolution* and *The War of the Classes*. Examination of their contents, however, especially the essays written between 1899 and 1904, reveal much of the genesis and growth of the particular ideas, or, more properly speaking, the prejudices for which Jack London was later to be noted.

Darwin, Spencer, Nietzsche and Marx—these have generally been considered the sources of Jack London's so-called philosophy. Many, seeking to gloss over his chauvinism, have regretted that he was more impressed by Nietzsche than by Marx; others, weary of his monotonous twanging of the "struggle-for-existence" theme, have wished that he had followed more closely the modifications science made within his own lifetime of the Darwinian concept of evolution.

As a matter of fact these four thinkers did not influence Jack London as greatly as has been supposed. He read very little of any of them, and studied none. Darwin and Spencer were gobbled in one excited reading, although he later returned to Spencer and read him more carefully. His knowledge of Nietzsche was derived largely from listening to Strawn-Hamilton, and when he did turn to Nietzsche's own pages he was so enchanted by the philosopher's vocabulary and slogans that he noted little else. "The blond beasts," "the glad perishers," "the Superman," "Live dangerously!"—these were more potent than wine.

As for Marx, only the first volume of *Das Kapital* was then available in English; Socialists who could not read German were to wait until 1906 for Ernest Untermann's first complete English edition of "the entire Marxian theories of capitalist production." There is no evidence, however, to indicate that Jack studied even the one volume. His exacting schedule had always been based on the rapid acquisition of knowledge. If a subject could not be so acquired, and if he could find no short cut, it was put aside until that future date when, his ambitions realized, there would be time for everything. So Marx, save for *The Communist Manifesto*, went by the board, although, in all fairness, it must be stated that letting Marx go by the board was not an uncommon practice among American Socialists in those days.

Remembering Jack London's lifelong dependence for knowledge on books written by other people, one looks further afield for the principal source of his ideas, and thus stumbles upon a name and a handful of books which, forgotten today, would forty years ago have been a first and most obvious choice.

In 1894 Benjamin Kidd burst from obscurity into world-wide fame with the publication of a book entitled *Social Evolution*. Son of an earlier Benjamin, described as "sometimes of the Royal Irish Constabulary," and denied all but the barest educational and social advantages, Kidd had been granted a civil-service post at the age of nineteen and had entered the Inland Revenue Department at Somerset House. There he remained for seventeen years, faithfully fulfilling his duties, but at night he studied, alone. Groping toward the largest possible grasp of knowledge, he came upon *The Synthetic Philosophy* of Herbert Spencer, the first part of *Principles of Sociology* having been published the year he became a civil servant. Thenceforth, during years in which writing at night gradually took the place of study, Kidd was an ardent, unquestioning Spencerian, little dreaming then that one day, a celebrated man, he would deliver the annual Herbert Spencer lecture at Oxford.

The instant success of *Social Evolution* freed him forever from the Department of Internal Revenue. In the six years following its publication it was translated into German, Swedish, French, Russian, Italian, Chinese, Czech and Danish; in 1913 it appeared in Arabic. Kidd made a great stir for some years, but although his last book, *The Science of Power*, was published in 1918, two years after his death, he was practically forgotten by the outbreak of the World War.

Why then his vogue at the turn of the century? Merely because, while the Marxians dismissed him as a reactionary, and academic circles refused to take his works seriously, a large number of enlightened laymen saw in his doctrines a reconciliation between religion and the profoundly disturbing theory of evolution. As a popular philosopher he was well endowed. His awareness of the great issues involved in social and political history, and his conviction of the importance of his message were conveyed to his readers in a vigorous, journalistic style, ornate with rhetoric but undeniably effective.

Kidd's social philosophy has been described as "a mixture of antirationalistic strains of romanticist philosophy with the teachings of evolutionary biology." The phrase with which Spencer enriched Darwinism, "the survival of the fittest," had unlocked for

Kidd the mystery of life, and early he decided that the fundamental law of social progress was Darwin's principle of natural
selection. Ignorant of the work of De Vries in mutations, as well
as of Kropotkin's brilliant exposition of the superiority of mutual
aid against mutual struggle as a factor in progress, Kidd eagerly
applied the principle of natural selection to society, only to conclude that the mass of man must consent, in the interests of
progress, to yield to the few superior individuals who will be
selected to rule society and to keep it at the maximum of efficiency.
His next step was to see how this might be brought about.
Against human initiative and individual reason which, unchecked,
he believed might destroy society, he posed group restraint to
compel individual selfishness to subordinate itself to the common
good. Then, seeking a force to combat the dangers of rationalism,
he found in the Christian religion the "ultrarational sanction" for
conduct most conducive to progress. To justify his conception
of social causation and of progress he turned to history and skillfully fitted facts to theory. Out of this emerged the most seduc-
tive phase of his work—the glorification of Western civilization in
general, and of the Anglo-Saxon's contribution to it in particular,
because the Anglo-Saxon "has been deeply affected, more deeply
than many others, by the altruistic influences of the ethical system
upon which our Western civilization is founded."

Faced with the fact that, despite his altruism, the Anglo-Saxon
has been the most effective exterminator in history of the less
developed peoples with whom he has come into competition, Kidd
bowed before "a destiny which works itself out irresistibly." The
extermination had not come about by fierce and deadly wars, he
maintained, but "through the operation of laws not less deadly
and even more certain in their effect. The weaker races disappear
before the stronger through the effects of mere contact."

The briefest survey of Jack London's essays, personal letters
and interviews yields a mass of internal evidence linking his
convictions so closely to those of Benjamin Kidd that one cannot
but conclude that the effect on his thinking of *Social Evolution*,
and later of *Principles of Western Civilization*, was profound.
Passing by innumerable superficial borrowings—how zestfully
Jack seized upon Kidd's phrase, "the shrinkage of the planet," for
instance, playing with it in his earliest essay, "The Question of the
Maximum," written in 1898, and developing it more fully later in
the essay entitled "The Shrinkage of the Planet"—one turns di-

rectly to what has mystified many: Jack London's celebration of
the Anglo-Saxon, a dominant note throughout all his writing,
and fused by him almost from the beginning with his conception
of socialism.

Kidd's conviction of the destiny of his race had fallen upon
ground prepared to receive it. From babyhood Flora had told
Jack that as Americans of original British stock they were vastly
superior to their Italian, Portuguese and even Irish neighbors.
Furthermore, Jack grew up in California in the midst of the
antagonism against the Chinese and later against the Japanese.
Reading Kidd, he found not only a justification of his early
prejudices, but a thrilling explanation of his own survival through
experiences and adventures which had brought death to many
others. He had survived because he was fit, and he was fit because
he was a member of a mighty race!

"And by Anglo-Saxon," he defined it, "is not meant merely the
people of that tight little island on the edge of the Western ocean.
Anglo-Saxon stands for the English-speaking people of all the
world, who, in forms and traditions, are more peculiarly and
definitely English than anything else."

To Johns he wrote, "I do not believe in the universal brotherhood of man. . . . I believe my race is the salt of the earth. I am a
scientific socialist, not a utopian, an economic man as opposed to
an imaginative man." And again, "An evolutionist, believing in
Natural Selection, half believing Malthus' 'Law of Population,' and
a myriad of other factors thrown in, I cannot but hail as unavoidable the Black and Brown going down before the White."

An interview early in 1900 reported him as believing in an
ultimate democracy to be achieved by all peoples whose institutions, ideals and traditions are ethnologically Anglo-Saxon. "Not
that God has given the earth to the Anglo-Saxon," he was quoted
as saying, "but that the Anglo-Saxon is going to take the earth
for himself." A half year later he revealed the extent to which
he had accepted Kidd: "Socialism is not an ideal system, devised
by man for the happiness of all life; nor for the happiness of all
men; but it is devised for the happiness of certain kindred races.
It is devised so as to give more strength to these certain kindred
favored races so that they may survive and inherit the earth to
the extinction of the lesser, weaker races. The very men who
advocate socialism may tell you of the brotherhood of all men,
and I know they are sincere; but that does not alter the law—they

are simply instruments, working blindly for the betterment of
these certain kindred races, and working detriment to the inferior
races they would call brothers. It is the law; they do not know it,
perhaps; but that does not change the logic of events."

In "The Yellow Peril," an essay written in 1904, he completely
affirmed his belief in the essentially ethical character of the Anglo-
Saxon and of Western civilization: "Back of our own great race
adventure, back of our robberies by sea and land, our lusts and
violences and all the evil things we have done, there is a certain
integrity, a sternness of conscience, a melancholy responsibility
of life, a sympathy and comradeship and warm human feeling,
which is ours, indubitably ours, and which we cannot teach to the
Oriental as we would teach logarithms or the trajectory or
projectiles. That we have groped for the way of right conduct
and agonized over the soul betokens our spiritual endowment.
Though we have strayed often and far from righteousness, the
voices of the seers have always been raised, and we have harked
back to the bidding of conscience. The colossal fact of our history
is that we have made the religion of Jesus Christ our religion. No
matter how dark in error and deed, ours has been a history of
spiritual struggle and endeavor. We are pre-eminently a religious
race, which is another way of saying that we are a right-seeking
race."

And that to the end of his life he believed that the mass of men
must be ruled by the few is amply demonstrated in the short
story, "The Bones of Kahekili," written five months before his
death: " 'I will answer you,' said Hardman Pool. 'It is because
most men are fools, and therefore must be taken care of by the
few men who are wise. Such is the secret of chiefship. In all the
world that has been have there ever been chiefs, who must say
to the many fool men: "Do this; do not do that. Work, and work
as we tell you, or your bellies will remain empty and you will
perish. Obey the laws we set you or you will be beasts and without place in the world. You would not have been save for the
chiefs before you who ordered and regulated for your fathers.
No seed of you will come after you, except that we order and
regulate for you now. You must be peace-abiding, and decent,
and blow your noses. You must be early to bed of nights, and
up early in the morning to work if you would have beds to sleep
in and not roost in trees like the silly fowls. This is the reason for
the yam-planting and you must plant now. We say now, today,

not picnicking and hulaing today and yam-planting tomorrow or some other day of the many careless days. You must not kill one another, and you must leave your neighbors' wives alone. All this is life for you, because you think but one day at a time, while we, your chiefs, think for you all days and far days ahead." ' "

This, then, was the foundation, contradictory but infinitely adaptable to his changing moods, upon which Jack London built his social and personal philosophy. For a long time it met every demand he placed upon it, rationalizing his race prejudice and sense of superiority over the great mass of men, and at the same time permitting him to preach the class struggle and to sign his letters, "Yours for the Revolution." During the years that his desire to be a socialist propagandist was active, however, his philosophy took on the coloring of the socialist movement. There were times when race barriers went down before his enthusiasm for the Cause, and when, dazzled by the extent and militancy of the struggle, he lost his distrust of the working class and called all men Brothers and Comrades.

His reputation as a Socialist grew out of his writings during those periods when he was carried away by the drama of the situation and joyously reaffirmed his belief in the social revolution. At such times he was completely sincere, forgetting his Anglo-Saxon superiority, his determination to beat the capitalists at their own game. And when, again the businessman, he pushed forward ruthlessly toward financial success he justified his course and strengthened his self-deception by invoking the Anglo-Saxon myth and the creed of the "survival of the fittest" in the "tooth-and-nail" struggle for existence.

Jack London's self-confidence, without which he could scarcely have pulled himself out of what he called "the cellar of society," became a belief not only in his destiny but in his ability to accomplish anything he wished to do. "The ultimate word," he used to say, "is I LIKE." Thus he refused to see that sooner or later he would have to choose between being a socialist writer, and a professional writer determined to make money. He wanted to be both, so he would *be* both! Even when he actually chose, and isolated himself from the movement, he denied that he had chosen. It was not he who had failed the movement, he charged, but the movement which had failed him!

Now, feted and admired, he indulged himself for the first time during all the Spartan years with being entertained. He spoke at socialist meetings in Oakland, San Francisco, Alameda and San Jose on "The Expansion Policy," "The Struggle for Existence," and "The Question of the Maximum." He accepted invitations to dinners and "evenings." And when the Ruskin Club of Oakland asked him to become a member he joined with alacrity.

This group of East Bay intellectuals had been organized by Frederick Irons Bamford, Jack's old friend and adviser at the public library and a fellow member of the Oakland section of the Socialist Labor party. They met together monthly at dinner, at first at the Metropole Hotel in Oakland, later in the old club-house in Piedmont Park, Bamford making all the arrangements, and seeing to it that host, discussion leader and speaker were appointed for each meeting.

Since the majority of members were Socialists the subjects never ranged far from what Bamford, whom Austin Lewis has described as a "protestant evangelical Socialist," called "the sacred cause." David Starr Jordan of Stanford University, Jacques Loeb and several other professors from the University of California, a liberal minister or two, and whatever outstanding itinerant Socialist might be available—these were typical of the outside speakers, while Austin Lewis, Edwin Markham and Jack London were among the member celebrities who entertained the quiet well-bred little gatherings.

For some years before it finally faded out of existence the Ruskin Club was a bright but not a brilliant spot in the social life of a community which was for the most part indescribably philistine. Very earnestly it discussed the "many phases of socialism," but at best its connection with the movement was tenuous. Andrew Furuseth, head of the Sailors' Union of the Pacific and making labor history in those days, adroitly summed up the Ruskin Club. Refusing an invitation to speak, he wrote, "It would be of no purpose. You men see life from a parlor, I see it from the hold of a vessel."

From the beginning of Jack's association with Bamford's pet project the relationship between the two underwent a significant change. Jack, grateful for the older man's many kindnesses, had always looked up to him and respected his intellect. Now their positions were reversed. The pupil had surpassed the teacher, and Bamford, formerly the mental master, was transformed into a sort of mental valet and court retainer—a position which ultimately did a great deal of harm to both.

After a lifetime of serving dull, inconspicuous people, Bamford suddenly found himself the valued assistant and friend of a literary lion. As a result he not only met a great many others whom he regarded as people of importance, but he began to acquire a small, local fame himself. He cannot be blamed for striving to retain this favorable position, but he became, nevertheless, the first of the group of "yes men" by whom Jack was gradually surrounded.

The loneliness which had plagued Jack for so long was beginning to disappear in the midst of such fine company. "Have not had an evening at home for nigh on to two weeks," he wrote happily to Johns, "what with suppers, speaking, functions, and last but not least FOOTBALL!" But while he enjoyed his new friends and acquaintances he clung loyally to the old, seeing a great deal of Bess, writing frequently to Ted and Mabel and visiting them often in College Park. That autumn he and Bess began to study English together, he for review, and she in pursuit of the ambition which was never to be realized—to enter the university. Also, having become interested in the photography which he had learned from Fred Jacobs, he spent many evenings with her in her small dark room, developing and printing the pictures they had taken on their outings. "Boy" and "Girl" they called each other now, and their friendship had become very dear to both.

Throughout this happy period he was increasingly aware of his desire for children. This theme recurred frequently in letters and conversations with friends. To Johns he wrote: ". . . the paternal instinct is so strong in me that it would almost kill me to be the father of a child not physically or mentally sound. Sometimes I think, because this is so very strong in me, that I am destined to die childless!" But marriage, without which he would not consider fatherhood, he still shied from. "Have never been rash enough to put out a sheet anchor in the form of a wife" was a favorite expression of his at this time, occurring as late as two weeks before he actually married.

It was in the midst of his heady first success as writer and Socialist that he met Anna Strunsky, whose friendship was to be the most profoundly disturbing factor in his life for the next three years. This was not because she was a woman whose personal charm and magnetism has become legendary; nor because of her intellectual brilliance, but because, instinctively loyal to certain principles and ideals, she saw the danger in much of Jack's philosophy and opposed with all her strength his socialism for the benefit of "certain kindred races," his belief that woman was inferior to man, that war was justifiable, that might made right, and his determination to use his talents for the sole purpose of making money.

"Our friendship can be described as a struggle," she wrote a few years after his death, "—constantly I strained to reach that in him which I felt he was 'born to be.' I looked for the Social Democrat, the Revolutionist, the moral and romantic idealist; I sought the Poet. Exploring his personality was like exploring mountains and the valleys which stretched between troubled my heart. They did not seem to belong to the grandiose character he was, or could, by an effort of the will, become. He was a Socialist, but he wanted to beat the Capitalist at his own game. To succeed in doing this, he thought, was in itself a service to the Cause; to 'show them' that Socialists were not derelicts and failures had certain propaganda value. So he succeeded—became a kind of Napoleon of the pen. This dream of his, even when projected and before it became a reality, was repellent to me. The greatest natures, I thought, the surest Social Democrats, would be incapable of harboring it. To pile up wealth, or personal success—surely anybody who was a beneficiary of the Old Order must belong to it to some extent in spirit and in fact!

"So it was that our ancient quarrel, and many, many others, took their rise in the same source—a doubt, not as to himself—I never doubted the beauty and the warmth and the purity of his own nature—but as to the ideas and the principles which he invited to guide his life. They were not worthy of him, I thought; they belittled him and eventually they might eat away his strength and grandeur."

Anna was one of a large family of Russian Jews who had come to America to escape the pogroms and persecutions of Czarist Russia. Although they were never very well off, their home in San Francisco soon became noted as a gathering place for interesting people. To Jack, whose Gentile environment had been more than usually coldhearted and dull, the Strunskys seemed like beings from another planet. Not even the Applegarths or the Maddern, happier families than his own, had been anything like this. Accustomed to "Anglo-Saxon" restraint, the Strunskys' passionate, readily articulated devotion to each other and to their friends startled him no less than the fervor of their ideas.

Anna, at nineteen, was an extremely idealistic young person whose social conscience was that of the newly awakened youth of the 'nineties, a conscience which took upon itself the responsibility for the social sins of the time, which was eager for self-sacrifice, and which made a religion out of the mixed medley of theory proclaimed by the socialist sects of the day. Nor was she content merely to speak of her social ideals. She belonged to the Socialist Labor party, and later to the Socialist party, and although she was a student at Stanford University she attended meetings as often as possible and marched enthusiastically in processions, carrying a banner and being good-naturedly hustled by San Francisco's Irish policemen. Anna was likewise a most attractive young woman of unusual charm—a fatal charm it has been considered by many, who felt that had she not been constantly surrounded by love and attention, she might have developed her not inconsiderable talents. But Anna's charm rose out of what was to be a lifelong interest in other people and in their ideas rather than her own, and only when her principles or intellectual integrities were involved did she forsake her role of sympathetic spectator and become a protagonist.

From the beginning Jack roused this sort of opposition in her, at first an indefinable resistance, later an open struggle. There is little doubt that they fell in love early in their acquaintance, but their basic differences on which neither would compromise proved as strong as their mutual attraction. The contest came to no conclusion. Each withdrew, frustrated but undefeated. Their love, never consummated, endured, however, enriching a friendship which was one of life's few gifts treasured by Jack.

They met early in December 1899, at a Socialist Labor party meeting in San Francisco, and within a few weeks were seeing each other frequently and a correspondence was in full swing. Neither had met anyone before with so much in common—youth, the movement, love of poetry and ambition to write, for in those days Anna fully intended to become a writer.

Strongly attracted by her, Jack reached impetuously for the friendship she offered him, only to be completely baffled at every turn. In his first letter to her, he ventured to describe the impression she had made upon him: ". . . a woman to whom it is given to feel the deeps and the heights of emotion to an extraordinary degree; who can grasp the intensity of transcendental feeling, the dramatic force of situation, as few women, or men either, can. But this question at once arose: Has she expression? By this, I mean simply the literary technique. And again, supposing that she has not, has she the 'dig,' the quality of application, so that she might attain it?

"In a nut-shell—you have the material, which is your own soul, for a career: have you the requisite action to hew your way to it?"

But the inevitability of a brilliant future for Anna had never before been questioned, and she was startled. "Somehow it is a new note to me," she replied, "that of being seen as 'aimless, helpless, hopeless,' and I am uneasy under it all." In his second letter Jack, fearful lest he had wounded her in his "blundering, roughshod" way, and explaining his implied criticism entirely away, was in full retreat: "Take me this way: a stray guest, a bird of passage, splashing with salt-rimed wings through a brief moment of your life—a rude and blundering bird, used to large airs and great spaces, unaccustomed to the amenities of confined existence. An unwelcome visitor, to be tolerated only because of the sacred law of food and blanket."

But the better he knew her, the more he was sure that he was right on this point. Months later when they had become truer if less emotional friends, he repeated the warning: "Anna, you have a good brain, also magnificent emotional qualities (this you have doubtless been assured of many times), and insofar you are favored above women in possession. But carry Strawn-Hamilton before you. No system, no application. But carry also Mr Bamford's quoted warning from Watson's 'Hymn to the Sea.' Don't apply what you have, wrongly. Don't beat yourself away vainly . . .

"But, Anna, don't let the world lose you; for inasmuch that it does lose you, in so much you have sinned."

For a month or so after their meeting his lyrical outbursts continued, then, suddenly dropping "Dear Miss Strunsky" for "Dear Anna," his self-consciousness disappeared and he began to write her in a more casual comradely manner. Seeking to understand this change of attitude and tone toward Anna, one comes upon evidence of a larger and apparently deliberate change in him which began to manifest itself shortly after the first of the year.

Some time during those happy winter months he had pulled himself up short, aware that his carefully planned life was getting somewhat out of hand. The persistent, purposeful drive had vanished from his daily work, and its quantity had been sharply curtailed from the time he began to accept invitations to speak and dine and be lionized. More than that, he was in an emotional turmoil which was interfering with his work.

Very coldly he faced the facts: Houghton, Mifflin had accepted his collection of short stories, *The Son of the Wolf*, for mid-spring publication, and McClure had evinced a definite interest in his stories and essays. Not only must he produce more and better material in order to follow up his first success, but he must immediately make some money, for his finances had gone from bad to worse. In January he wrote to Johns, "Have pawned my wheel, bought stamps, and got things in running order again . . . have jumped my stint to 1500 words per diem till I get out of the hole."

As for his emotional problem, its solution can be found nowhere in his books, usually so frankly autobiographical, nor in his personal letters. Subsequent events are the sole proof that he did solve it. But one can see him, unable to understand why such an impasse had been reached, but resolutely putting it out of his mind as a threat to his ambition, now so nearly realized. Nothing was to stand in the way of that!

After the joyful winter the spring seemed bleak and unpromising. Although his sales picked up and the future was brighter than ever before, writing became a detestable task. "Am hard at it," he wrote Johns at the end of January. "Have not missed a day in which I have turned out at least 1500 words, and sometimes as high as 2000 . . . Sometimes forty-eight hours pass without my even stepping foot on the ground or seeing more of outdoors than the front porch when I go to get the evening paper. Hurrah for Hell!" Ten days later, "Have lost steerage way in the matter of writing. Have done twenty-two hundred words in 5 days, and gone out every night, and feel.as though I can never write again." A month later, "I am only averaging about 350 words per day, now, and can't increase the speed to save me."

He might have left for Paris. There was money enough now,

with *McClure's* paying him generously and other markets available. But Paris, so desirable less than a year before, no longer interested him. In any case he knew that to cut loose and go anywhere right then would not only be fatal for his career—once free from the daily grind of writing, when would he bring himself to return to it?—but that it would in no way still his deep, inner dissatisfaction. There was one thing he wanted. Slowly he groped toward a decision.

CHAPTER

17

THE next few years were to provide a testing ground for two of Jack London's theories which most closely touched his personal life: how to become a successful author, and how to achieve happiness and fulfillment in marriage and fatherhood. Jack determined the truth or falsity of any idea by putting it into practice. When he found that it worked he went ahead confidently; when the results he had expected failed to materialize he abandoned it, not gladly, but because there was no room in his life for things that did not work. In this case the first of the two theories triumphed; the second went down to defeat, leaving wounds that never healed.

He had grown up in an environment which had not only discouraged sentimentality but taught him to regard any of its manifestations with contempt. The period of his submission to the agonies and ecstasies of adolescent love had been very brief. Except for this and his adoration of Mabel Applegarth, he had had a sex life, not a love life, and his sex life had been the unmawkish, spontaneous activity of a healthy young proletarian unburdened by the inhibitions of his more favored brothers in the middle class. Now, as growing success led him deeper into that class, he came into contact not only with its ugly sex moralities, but with its saccharine-sentimental and soul-probing ideas of love which had come into full flower during the mauve decade.

Listening, Jack was first incredulous, then embarrassed, and finally indignant that intelligent, cultured adults should prattle like irresponsible, lovesick youths about subjects as significant as love and marriage. He spat his disgust in endless arguments with Anna Strunsky, a proponent of romantic love, and out of their fundamental disagreement grew eventually *The Kempton-Wace Letters*, which embodied in full the theories he tested for himself.

Forty years later, one can only wholeheartedly applaud his courageous assault on the time-honored and convention-bound attitudes which, he believed, made a mockery of these vital subjects. On the one hand, he maintained, marriage was not something extraordinary but a most normal and common occurrence; on the other hand, as an "institution necessary for the perpetuation of the species," it should be considered with the utmost deliberation and forethought by all intelligent people.

Love, as understood by the romanticists, he defined as "a disorder of mind and body . . . produced by passion under the stimulus of imagination," in order that the human type might be perpetuated and developed. For himself, he defined love more precisely as prenuptial, romantic or sexual love, and postnuptial, by which he meant conjugal affection and sex comradeship. The former was nature's trick to assure procreation, the latter was what romantic love, if the marriage endured, evolved into once the "impelling madness" of sexual love had spent itself.

He had no use for madness of any sort. He had a brain and he intended to use it. Nature might have to trick the average man into procreation, but not him. He was eager for children. Therefore, avoiding prenuptial romantic lovesickness in which his reason could not function, he would take a short cut, choosing for a partner in marriage a young woman for whom he already felt affection, and who would be strong, healthy and capable of producing strong, healthy children. "No, I am not in love," says his protagonist in *The Kempton-Wace Letters*, who is about to marry. "I am very thankful that I am not . . . I am arranging my life so that I may get the most out of it, while the one thing to disorder it, worse than flood and fire and the public enemy, is love."

Tracing the evolution of his attitude, he placed women in two categories. There was the wanton, "wonderful and unmoral and filled with life to the brim," and there was "the perfect mother, made pre-eminently to know the lip clasp of a child." The first he called the Mate Woman, and with her might be achieved, from the "strictly emotional and naturalistic viewpoint," the perfect love. The second was the Mother Woman, "the last and highest and holiest in the hierarchy of life." And it was this type which he married in his twenty-fourth year, "choosing a mate, not in the lust of my eyes, but in the desire of my fatherhood."

He did not have far to seek, for he knew but one person so qualified: loyal, generous and affectionate, a true comrade during nearly five years of friendship, and pre-eminently fitted for motherhood. *The Son of the Wolf* was published on April 7, 1900. On the same day Jack London and Bess Maddern were married.

The rise of Jack's fortunes during the next two years may be traced by the changing neighborhoods and types of houses in which he lived, the ever-increasing amount of entertaining in which he indulged, and the growth of his fame.

A few weeks before his marriage he and Flora and little Johnnie Miller left the cramped cottage for a two-story, seven-room house on East Fifteenth Street near Twenty-third Avenue—a more elegant house but in the same lower middle-class section of East Oakland. Not since she was a girl in Massillon had Flora lived in so fine a dwelling. How right she had been to encourage Jack! Now she would be able to share in his life, preside at dinner parties for his friends, and meet interesting people for the first time since those brief years in San Francisco so long ago.

But Flora's joy was short lived. They were scarcely settled when Jack brought home his young wife to be mistress of his household. Flora hid her chagrin as best she could, which was not very well, tried to efface herself and be helpful; Bess, who knew the story of Flora's difficult life, did her utmost to be daughterly, but the situation was more than either could handle.

Because she had gone to work so early, Bess had missed much of Melissa Maddern's training in Yankee-style housekeeping. Faced with a large house to keep in order and three people whose living habits she knew nothing about, in addition to the secretarial assistance she was used to rendering Jack, she was dismayed. Gladly would she have permitted Flora to run the house while she continued her teaching, but she had been brought up to regard housekeeping, whether she cared for it or not, as an indispensable part of her wifehood. Hiding her qualms, she set out to overcome its difficulties, and Flora was thrust willy-nilly into the background.

Within a few months of the marriage Flora and Johnnie moved to a cottage in the next block and matters began to mend. Flora did not preside, as she had dreamed, at Jack's dinner parties, but she was usually present, a small, silent figure, listening avidly and completely astonished that she understood so little of what they discussed. And whenever there were steaks to fry Flora was summoned to take charge while Bess watched, eager to learn the secret of Flora's artful hand with dry skillet and plain-boiled coffee. As time went on a touching friendship grew between these two women who were destined to be pushed aside as Jack's career advanced, a friendship that survived every test for more than twenty years. Chary of pretty phrases, each rendered the other her due in typical fashion. "You're a good women, Bessie," Flora used to say. And Bess told her daughters, "Grandma was loyal to me when it most counted, and ever since. There aren't many others who were."

Jack, meantime, had swung into work with renewed vigor. Now that everything was arranged to his satisfaction—and by summer he knew that his long desire for fatherhood would be realized in January—he was certain that the unhappy, frustrated years were behind him. Marriage had simplified his life enormously. Not only was there more time for work, but for play as well. Ten days after the wedding he wrote to Cloudesley: "Got settled down to work today, and did the first thousand words in three weeks, and hereafter the old rate must continue." And early in May he and Bess began their "Wednesday nights," which were to last as long as their marriage and brought together each week old friends and new for dinner and the evening. A few months later his routine was so well established that in addition to the Wednesday nights, Socialist party meetings and Ruskin Club dinners, he was able to find time for more exercise, swinging Indian clubs, jumping, riding daily on his bicycle, swimming several times a week, and looking forward to fencing, boxing and shooting in the near future with Whitaker.

Finances wobbled now and again that first year, and both were glad more than once that Bess had not entirely given up her pupils, but the outlook was generally very bright. McClure having proved a generous buyer of his stories and articles, Jack ventured to approach him that summer with an idea for a novel to be run serially in the magazine, and McClure promptly agreed to finance its writing as Jack had requested at the rate of one hundred and twenty-five dollars a month for five months, and longer if necessary.

Jack had scarcely begun *A Daughter of the Snows,* when he realized that his decision to write a sustained piece of work was premature. "Am winding up the first chapter of novel," he wrote Cloudesley in September. "I wish I were done." He had not yet learned how to put a novel together, and as the writing progressed he was appalled at the waste of good material. "I kept pouring in stuff and more stuff," he used to laugh ruefully, "and hoping that if I got enough in it would turn into a novel, but it never did." And it took unconscionably long to write. In February of the next year he told Cloudesley, "Well, I am on the home stretch of the novel, and it is a failure."

Although he had purposely asked to be financed while writing the book so that he might devote full time to it, he did other writing from the start, partly because it furnished escape from his dissatisfaction with the novel, partly because he needed more money, and partly because of his enthusiasm for the Kempton-Wace project. Work began on this in October of that year and continued irregularly until its completion in the summer of 1902. With the exception of a few short stories that approached the standard of those in *The Son of the Wolf,* he was contemptuous of his magazine work. "To tell you the truth, Cloudesley," he wrote in January 1901, "I haven't had any decent work published recently." And a year later, "Lord, what stacks of hack I'm turning out! Five mouths and ten feet, and sometimes more, so one hustles. I wonder if ever I'll get clear of debt."

And yet so certain was he of the correctness of his course that he refused to deviate. In December 1900, he received an offer which, had he accepted it, might have altered his subsequent career. The November issue of the *Cosmopolitan* had contained his prize-winning essay, "What Communities Lose by the Competitive System." The favorable comment it evoked prompted John Brisben Walker, editor of the *Cosmopolitan,* to write to Jack posthaste, offering him a full-time job at a yearly salary as editorial adviser and writer on special topics.

"Of course, I shall not accept it," Jack told Johns. "I do not wish to be bound. Which same you do think I am. No so. *McClure's* have not bound me, nor will they. I want to be free, to write of what delights me, whensoever and wheresoever it delights me. No office work for me; no routine; no doing this set task and that set task. No man over me." But before he sent his refusal he wrote to *McClure's* and received the assurance that his monthly check would continue, as well as his freedom to write as he pleased. As he pleased? Well, not exactly as yet, he admitted to himself, but soon. So he bound himself to hack work, sure that it would be a small price, and quickly paid, for freedom, and unaware that he would never escape its toils and achieve the liberty he so desired.

The new year began cheerlessly with tightened finances and heavier responsibilities. Both Mammy Jennie and Flora had to call on him for additional money, and friends turned to him for help. One of these was Jim Whitaker. Years of poverty, the dependence of seven children and a wife had failed to stifle Whitaker's ambition to become a writer. Watching Jack's climb to success inspired him to do likewise. Would Jack help him? With his own struggles fresh in his mind, Jack gladly agreed, and with a few other comrades and friends of Whitaker supplied the family each month with sufficient funds. For Jack, Whitaker's rapid advance was a source of both pleasure and astonishment. Within three months he had begun to sell to the same magazines which Jack had worked so hard and long to reach. Here was proof indeed of the excellence of short cuts, for Jim was benefiting from all that he had dug out for himself concerning how to write stories that would sell.

Even before the financial situation began to improve events occurred which brought Jack some measure of happiness and pride. In the small hours of the morning of January 15, 1901, his eagerly awaited child was born, a daughter, although he had counted on a son. "It," he called her unhappily the first day or two, until the morning when Bess, remembering one of the notes she had filed for him some months back and which listed names he admired for women, said, "Jack, will you bring Joan to me?" "Joan?" he asked wonderingly. "Joan! Splendid!"

There is no doubt that from then on his first-born who, out of her urgent need to understand the father she had known so briefly but so poignantly, has become this biographer, occupied a unique place in his life. She has lived more years since his death than those that went before. And because it is difficult to use the first person about someone as remote as the Joan Jack London knew, she shall be spoken of as Joan throughout this book.

Jack's fame as a writer had so increased that the local Socialists deemed him ripe for political exploitation. The Oakland section of the Socialist Labor party was no more; since May 1900, Jack's membership card had carried Social Democratic party dues stamps. A week after the birth of his daughter he was nominated by the party for mayor of Oakland, heading a full municipal ticket. His speech of acceptance revealed rather clearly not only his, but the party's brand of socialism.

He said in part: "So when we Social Democrats draft our municipal program we demand that which our national platform demands, that which we demand the world over, namely, equality of opportunity. True, our immediate demands partake of the nature of palliatives, but on the other hand, they are consistent with the great fundamental demand . . . For it is we, the Socialists, working as a leaven throughout society, who are responsible for the great and growing belief in municipal ownership."

Aside from a few speeches under party auspices, Jack made no campaign. When the election came in March he polled two hundred and forty-five votes against the successful candidate, John L. Davie. But, Jack laughed to his friends, that was not bad for an ex-oyster pirate and hobo. Throughout the year he continued to speak from time to time for the Socialists on "What the Community Loses under the Competitive System" and "The Question of the Maximum"; once he and Whitaker debated woman's suffrage. In February he appeared before a group at Stanford University as a literary man rather than as a Socialist, and gave his initial reading before a public audience with "An Odyssey of the North."

Nearly a year had passed since the publication of *The Son of the Wolf*. Although the novel was nearly complete, its publication was as yet months away. Feeling that a second book by Jack London should soon appear, Jack selected eleven of the numerous stories he had written in the interim for various magazines, and McClure agreed to publish them under the title of *The God of His Fathers*. The book appeared in May. "A second collection of Klondike stories—not so good as the first, however." Thus he described the new volume to Johns. Such a haphazard method of producing a book did not please him, and in order to avoid a repetition of it he began to plan a series of tales he had long wished to write, based entirely on Indian themes, and to be called *The Children of the Frost*.

Heavy spring rains which flooded the basement of the house on East Fifteenth Street and turned the yard into a lake coincided with an opportunity to live rent free in a very unusual house in exchange for boarding its owner. The middle of March found Jack, Bess and Joan installed in La Capricciosa, an ornate, pseudo-Italian villa recently erected on the shore of Lake Merritt by Felix Peano, a sculptor and member of the Ruskin Club. "Am much more finely situated now," Jack told Johns, "nearer to Oakland, with finer view, surroundings, air, etc., etc." Despite its rococo elegance, Jack was very proud of this house—a far cry indeed from the shabby West Oakland cottages of his boyhood. From its wide terrace he could overlook the scenes of many of his youthful adventures, the estuary and marshes, the lake, and against the sky the eucalyptus-clothed ridges of the Piedmont hills.

A Daughter of the Snows was finally completed in this house and sent off to McClure, to whom it proved a great disappointment. Although he rejected it his faith in Jack was such that he continued to send the monthly check. But Jack's subsequent stories equally displeased him; one after the other he rejected them also. Jack, shaken by realization of the mediocrity of his first novel, strove to justify not only McClure's faith in him but his own. "In its way," he wrote, almost prophetically, "the struggle for a man with a name, to maintain the standard by which he gained that name is as severe as the struggle for the unknown to make a name."

He was eager to fulfill his obligations to McClure, but he seems to have been spreading himself too thin to produce stuff of the desired caliber. At the beginning of the summer the San Francisco *Examiner* had asked him to write a special article on the arrival of the SS Oregon, and this was followed by other requests. The *Examiner* paid well and Jack could not resist the opportunity to make extra money, even though gathering material for the articles consumed valuable time and energy. In addition to these and the usual machine-made stories, he was working intensely on *The Kempton-Wace Letters* with Anna Strunsky and the new Indian stories.

When McClure wrote him at the end of the summer, sadly but firmly terminating their financial arrangement, Jack's self-confidence was severely jarred. Was all the long, heartbreaking struggle to become a writer to result merely in this, he asked himself, a flash in the pan, a promise never to be fulfilled? Was he

written out, or would he have to start in all over again and hammer his way to recognition? At this point he drew himself up
short. Defeated? Not he! He had "shown them" before; he would
show them again! But although he continued to work steadily and
speak enthusiastically of future plans the effects of this blow to
his pride and self-confidence were far reaching, and contributed
much to the alternating moods of dissatisfaction and melancholy
which were soon to dominate him, despite his superficial gaiety
at times.

The autumn and early winter of 1901 were lean and difficult.
Unfortunately, however, Jack's two books already published,
as well as his local reputation as special writer for the *Examiner*,
inspired tradesmen and others with confidence in him. Inviting
Cloudesley to pay them a visit, he said, "I am always hard up,
but I'll never again be as hard up as during your previous visit.
You see, I do not have to worry about grub from day to day.
I'm doing credit on a larger and Napoleonic scale. And gee! if
at any moment I should die, won't I be ahead of the game!"

Unwilling to lower his standard of living, which had risen
steadily since his marriage, he sank deeper and deeper into debt,
thus postponing even further the time when he would be free
to write what and as he chose. "The habit of money getting will
never become one of my vices," he used to say in those days. "But
the habit of money spending, ah God! I shall always be its victim!" When, coincidental with the last of the McClure checks,
it became necessary to leave La Capricciosa, he did not return
to the low rents in East Oakland, but defiantly chose a large,
almost luxurious house in a district in the lower foothills which,
although just building up, had already become a fashionable
neighborhood. It was at this address, 56 Bayo Vista Avenue, that
he was listed for the first time in the Oakland city directory as
"Jack London, author."

By this time he was heartily sick of the Klondike, but he
seemed unable to market stories with other locales and themes.
More and more often now he read books by other men about the
gold rush to prod his weary memory and imagination. He wrote
resentfully to Johns in November: "A man does one thing in a
passable manner and the dear public insists on his continuing to
do it to the end of his days." And the next month: "Am hammering away in seclusion, trying to get out of Alaska. Guess I'll succeed in accomplishing it in a couple of years."

Jack's defiance was shortly rewarded. In December he received an unexpected letter from the Macmillan Company, announcing its eagerness to publish his work and hoping that he had something to send on immediately. Two years, even a year before, such a communication would have brought him to the highest pitch of enthusiasm. Now, although easing the financial strain and promising ready publication for future books, it failed to lift his drooping spirits. Macmillan's acceptance of *The Children of the Frost* early in January 1902 was the beginning of a long association, only nine of the forty-three volumes published during Jack's lifetime bearing the imprint of other companies besides Macmillan.

In February the Londons moved to the last house they would occupy together, a large, rambling bungalow high up in the Piedmont hills where Jack and Frank Atherton had once hoped to slay wildcats with a slingshot. Five acres surrounded the house, half in orchard and half in fields that blazed each spring with California poppies, and although the center of Oakland was but a half-hour's streetcar ride away, Jack was more isolated and further removed from the city than he had been since his boyhood on the various ranches.

This point is not as trivial as it may seem. Nor does the exceedingly reasonable rent asked for the property explain his choice of it for a home; it merely made it possible right then. A change had been coming over Jack London, and what he called "the migration to the hills" was but an early symptom of that change. The Bungalow, his favorite of all the houses he ever occupied, was to see the end of one way of life for Jack, and its accompanying point of view, and the beginning of a new one, with an entirely different point of view.

Because of his eventual retreat into country life, the change in his attitude during this period toward living in the city is significant. During the first two years of his correspondence with Cloudesley Johns he was vehemently pro-city. "I have been isolated so much, that I can no longer bear to be torn away for long at a time from the city life," he had written in March 1899, and continued in similar vein from time to time:

"Think you could train yourself into becoming a hermit? For me that would be far harder than to train myself to become a suicide. I like to rub against my kind, with a gregarious instinct far stronger than in most men. A hermitage—synonym for hell."

". . . Outside of your own work what intellectual life can you have (in the country)? You are thrown back upon yourself. Too apt to become self-centered; to measure other things by yourself than to measure yourself by other things." "By all means . . . come somewhere and live in the center of things. In this day one cannot isolate oneself and do anything. Get you a big city anywhere, and plunge into it and live and meet people and things. If you believe that man is the creature of his environment, then you cannot afford to remain 'way off there on the edge of things."

But early in December 1901, after many months' silence on the subject, he wrote in the midst of the depression which had come upon him after his failure with McClure, "I am rotting here in town. Really, I can feel the bourgeois fear crawling up and up and twining around me. If I don't get out soon I shall be emasculated. The city folk are a poor folk anyway. To hell with them." In July of the next year he told Johns, "The world is made up chiefly of fools. Besides the fools there are the others, and they're fools, too. It doesn't matter much which class you and I belong to, while the best we can do is not to increase our foolishness. One of the ways to increase our foolishness is to live in cities with the other fools. . . ." And the following spring: "The city life is too unnatural and monstrous for us folk of the West. To hell with it. There's more in life than what the social shambles offer."

Throughout this entire period Jack's moodiness increased, manifesting itself in restlessness, a desire to be anywhere but where he was, self-pity, and a pathetic mingling of juvenile cynicism and despair. The boy would not, could not, perhaps, grow up. Nothing was turning out as he planned, he mourned, conjuring up pictures of the underprivileged lad he had been and reliving his struggles and privations. What was the use of trying to do anything? No one really cared! But then, his mood changing, he swore he would make them care, would make them sit up and notice him whether they wanted to or not, and would see to it that they paid him for the performance!

Money! That was the whip that lashed him forward, urging tired brain and body and nerves to the hateful task which, he stubbornly insisted, would one day buy him rest and leisure to enjoy the kind of life he was so dearly purchasing. He told Anna: "When the day comes that I have achieved a fairly fit scientific foundation and a bank account of a thousand dollars, then come and be with me when I lie on my back all day and read, and read, and read, and read. The temptation of the books—if you could know! And I hammer away at Spencer and Hackworth—try to forget the joys of the things unread." Debts crowded him with a nightmare insistence, and yet even when the pressure was greatest he could usually draw apart and look pridefully at the sums he owed. Surely he had come far to have been permitted that much credit!

To Anna, always sympathetic, he dramatized his soul struggles; to Cloudesley he wrote in a more cynical vein. Thus, describing his situation and gloomy state of mind to Anna early in January, 1902: "You look back on a tumultuous and bankrupt year; and so I. And for me the New Year begins full of worries, harassments, and disappointments." To Johns, on the next day, he wrote: "But, after all, what squirming anywhere, damned or otherwise, means anything? That's the question I am always prone to put: What's this chemical ferment called life all about? Small wonder that small men down the ages have conjured gods in answer . . . My dear boy, nobody can help himself in anything, and heaven helps no one. Man is not a free agent, and free will is a fallacy exploded by science long ago . . . Whatever we do, we do because it is easier to than not to. No man ever lived who didn't do the easiest thing . . . We are what we are, and we cannot help ourselves. No man is blamed, and no man praised."

The tone of most of his letters to Anna throughout this period reveal an emotional instability that must have been disturbing to both Bess and Anna; but Jack seems to have demanded and received in good measure great understanding from the women who were close to him. He was completely satisfied with his marriage, devoted to Bess and his little daughter and, not unmindful of the heavy burden Bess was carrying as wife, mother and hostess on slim means, looked forward to the time when servants, secretaries and nursemaids would relieve her of the drudgery and endless responsibilities which now filled her days. Nevertheless the comradely manner he had assumed toward Anna shortly before his marriage soon became a mask for much deeper sentiments, which persisted, unreturned save by friendship, until the book they had written together was completed and Jack had gone abroad.

But one wonders, in view of subsequent events, if Jack, bound securely to a marriage in which romance had played no part, did not like Ulysses, listen eagerly to the sirens' song, confident that his bonds would hold. That many women raised that song as his fame grew there is ample evidence, but he saw no danger to his well-planned scheme of existence. "Girl" and "Boy," he and Bess had called each other; now it was "Mother-Girl" and "Daddy-Boy," and these names symbolized a relationship that, of all things in his life, he was most positive would endure.

A too zealous search for the causes of Jack's deep unhappiness and dissatisfaction at this time lands one inevitably in the dangerous swamps of "psychology," where, lacking adequate data, one man's guess is as good as another's. But keeping on the firm ground at the edge of the swamp, it is possible to make certain observations that throw much light on the subject. That he was overtired is obvious. That he was nervously exhausted and exasperated by doing a great deal of work which he disliked intensely and persisted in doing because he recognized no pleasanter alternative, seems fairly safe to assume. In addition it is probable that he was more highly strung and sensitive than the average person, and possessed a generous share of the "complexes," "inhibitions" and "frustrations" which harass most young people at his age. Finally his tendency to exaggerate and dramatize his moods must not be forgotten.

Granting the above factors, and keeping in mind his avowed ambition to succeed at writing only in order to live well and enjoy leisure, his unreasonable reaction to disappointment and delay, however slight or temporary, is not astonishing. Something had gone wrong with his work. McClure's loss of faith in him had not been the result of a whim. Somewhere along the line he had failed to fulfill the promise of his early short stories. This must be remedied, and quickly, for he had no intention of remaining in poverty, however picturesque, much longer. By following trends and analyzing contemporary magazine fiction, he had first learned how to write salable stories. Now he would do it again, but this time he would push his investigation deeper to reach the very roots of the problem.

From the time Jack began to write for the San Francisco *Examiner* he was a target for the barbed reproaches of a San Francisco journalist whose by-line was Yorick. Commenting on one of Jack's articles, Yorick wrote: "I recommend it as a model of style and finish to all aspiring young magazine writers and yellow journalists serving their apprenticeship." And a few weeks later:

"But I fear that even Mr John London is on the broad highway
that leads down to wealth and destruction. He is reporting prize
fights for the *Examiner*, and that is proof that he is either starving
in a garret on the husks and crusts of magazine literature, or that
he has resolved to wear the purple and fine linen of yellow journalism and dine daily on mock turtle and the fatted calf à la
prodigal.

"Alas; and alack; and once more alas."

Although Jack joined in the laughter which Yorick's thrusts
provoked among his friends, he did not dismiss them lightly.
"Sordid necessities," he wrote to Anna. "For me Yorick has not
lived in vain. I am grateful to him for the phrase." But it was
"the purple and fine linen of yellow journalism" which intrigued
him most and turned his thoughts toward a possible solution of
the question he was soon to phrase as: "How and in what fashion
must he (the literary artist-aspirant with active belly and empty
purse) sing the joy of his heart that the printed speech thereof
may bring him bread?"

The results of the thought he gave to this question were embodied in several articles which, characteristically, he sold to various writers' magazines. In these his attitude toward the profession he had chosen received its clearest expression. Better acquainted now with the hazards of his undertaking, he charted the
course he would follow to his destination. "Popularity is the key-
note; popularity pays." These were his slogans, and he rationalized
them competently and unemotionally, and laid down the rules for
their achievement.

Ignoring the true poet, "who sings because he can't help it,"
he saw two types of writers driven by an ambition "to make
commodities of their written thoughts." The first was a small
group, "who have, or think they have, a message the world needs
or would like to hear"; the second was composed of "those whose
lives have been cast on hard ground and in barren places, striving
to meet the belly need." For these there was but one answer:
Cash. Laughingly, scornfully, he defied the dreamers and idealists who might be shocked: "We are the ones who suffer from the
belly need. We are joy loving, pleasure seeking, and we are ever
hungry for the things we deem the compensation of living. The
world owes us something, and we intend dunning until we get it."

For the past three years he had been dunning, and successfully
in that he had not been turned away empty handed. But it was

not enough; he wanted more. Somewhere in his voluminous reading he had come upon certain figures which tormented him: Daudet had received two hundred thousand dollars for *Sapho;* each of Kipling's *Barrack Room Ballads* had brought seven hundred and fifty dollars, and for some of his short stories he had been paid as high as one dollar a word; General Lew Wallace and Du Maurier had earned equally fantastic sums.

How? He demanded to know and, seeking the answer, he discovered what he called the paradox of the writing game: "that what the world prizes most it demands least, and that what it clamors the loudest after it does not prize at all." In other words, he had discovered that while the people who read magazines and books wanted merely to be amused and entertained, and had no concern with the ultimate appraisal of literature, the "critics" loudly hailed "worthy" writing and damned "balderdash" until their opinions were accepted. The poor little literary artist-aspirant thus had to serve two masters, the reading public and the critics, the one that he might live, the other that his work might live (and command fabulous prices because of its prestige); "and," commented Jack, "what the one demands most of all the other has little or no use for."

But Jack was not dismayed by this prospect; he thought he knew the solution. He had observed that yellow journalism was not confined to newspapers, and that magazine editors, in order to "bring the circulation that brings the advertisements that bring the cash," were choosing for publication material with the widest and most immediate appeal to the greatest number of readers. And this, he maintained, was as it should be. "The deepest values of life are today expressed in terms of cash. That which is most significant of an age must be the speech of that age. That which is most significant today is the making of money . . . (therefore) it is only fair that literature be expressed in terms of cash."

Clearly, all that was needful was to get a reputation, a name, and then everything one wrote would be printed, even those works which made a bid for posterity. And to accomplish this one must write for the great uncultured mass of people who, having been admitted into living by democracy, demand and pay for only what interests them. "The uncultured mass cannot become cultured in a twinkling of the eye . . . And wherever the mass is admitted into living, wherever the common men for the first time grip hold of life, there must follow a falling away from all

that is fine of tone and usage, a diminishing, a descending to a
something which is average, which is humanly average."

So he would write for these average, these humanly average
readers. He knew what they wanted—had he not been one of
them?—and how it should be presented to them. He had learned
much from writing for the *Examiner*. His stories would be timely,
colorful, vital and brief. Life had become complicated and moved
quickly. People had no time for superfluities. "The unpruned
shall be cast aside unread. What the race wants is the meat of the
matter and it wants it now."

Those who lived penned in cities or bound to the soil would
follow him in his fiction to far places, and in vicarious adventur-
ing would forget the drabness of their lives. Frank Norris knew!
Had he not cried, "Give us stories now. Give us men, strong,
brutal men with red blood in 'em, and women, too, that move and
have their being!" And if, without jeopardizing his chances for
material gain, Jack could give them more than that, he would do
so. "Let us be fire-bringers in a humble way," he wrote. "Let us
have an eye to the ills of the world and its need; and if we find
messages, let us deliver them. Ah, pardon me, purely for material-
istic reasons. We shall weave them about with our fictions and
make them beautiful, and sell them for goodly sums." But Jack
was soon to find the role of fire-bringer too expensive. After a
few attempts to play it he withdrew. "The bubbles of illusion,"
he said bitterly a few years later, "the paps of pretty lies are the
true stuff of stories."

Nine years later Jack described the state of mind which began
to manifest itself at this time as the "long sickness of pessimism."
"I had read too much positive science and lived too much positive
life," he wrote in *John Barleycorn*, that masterpiece of rationalization and self-justification. "In the eagerness of youth I had made
the ancient mistake of pursuing truth too relentlessly. I had torn
her veils from her, and the sight was too terrible for me to stand.
In brief, I lost my fine faiths in pretty well everything except
humanity, and the humanity I retained faith in was a very stark
humanity indeed."

But in a letter written to Johns in the midst of the "long sickness," his pessimism does not appear to be that of a young man
who had been terrified by the face of truth, but of one who had
sulkily admitted at last that he must walk, not run, toward the

attainment of his desires. "Concerning myself," he wrote on July 12, 1902, "I am moving along very slowly, about $3000 in debt, working out a philosophy of life, or rather, the details of a philosophy of life, and slowly getting a focus on things. Some day I shall begin to do things, until then I merely scratch a living.

"Between you and me, I wish I had never opened the books. That's where I was the fool."

CHAPTER

18

"I SHALL be impelled to strong drink if something exciting doesn't happen along pretty soon," Jack had written Cloudesley early in 1902. Except for the hope that his second child, whose birth was due in the early autumn, would be the son he longed for, the horizon of his days was flat and devoid of anything but routine work. The summer and Jack's patience were nearly at an end when, on July twenty-first, a telegram arrived from the American Press Association.

Seven weeks earlier the Boer War had come to an end with the signing of articles of peace at Pretoria, and the metamorphosis of the conquered states into British colonies had begun. Would Jack care to go at once to South Africa and write a series of articles on postwar conditions?˙Jack left the next afternoon.

A week later he sailed for Liverpool, having stopped in New York just long enough to meet George Platt Brett, president of the Macmillan Company, and discuss future publishing arrangements. On the train to New York, as he savored memories of his hobo days in the midst of the plush and polished elegance of a Pullman and looked forward with old-time zest to new scenes and experiences, a splendid project had taken shape in his mind. If time permitted he would lose himself in the London slums and try to see the structure and fabric of British life from the working-class point of view, as he had once seen it in America.

When he outlined his plan to Brett he met such an enthusiastic response that thereafter his thoughts were more concerned with it than the articles about the Boers. The day after he sailed he

wrote to Anna, "A week from today I shall be in London. I shall
then have two days in which to make my arrangements and sink
out of sight in order to view the coronation from the standpoint
of the East Enders, with their stray flashes of divinity." The cable
from the American Press which awaited his arrival on August
sixth and announced the cancellation of the South African series
left him in a precarious financial situation, but free to embark
at once upon his adventure in the East End.

On Coronation Day, August ninth, he stood in the rain in
Trafalgar Square, indistinguishable from the ragged poor around
him, and watched the procession that celebrated not only the first
coronation in England in sixty-four years but England's first great
imperial coronation. Seven weeks later he emerged from the East
End with a book describing what he saw there entirely written.

In after years Jack often said, "Of all my books, I love most
The People of the Abyss. No other book of mine took so much
of my young heart and tears as that study of the economic degradation of the poor." During the seven weeks of observation, personal experience and writing, he revealed his anguish in brief
notes to friends. To Anna: "My stomach will never forgive me
for all the filth I have put into it since my coming here, and my
soul for all the despair . . . I am worn out and exhausted, and
my nerves are blunted with what I have seen and the suffering
it has cost me . . . I am made sick by this human hell-hole called
the East End." To Cloudesley, near the end of his stay as well as
his nerves, he described the book he was writing: "It's rather hys-
terical, I think." And to Mr Bamford: "Things are terrible here
in London, and yet they tell me times are good and all are employed save the unemployable. If these are good times, I wonder
what bad times are like? There's no place like California and I
long to be back."

The basic effects of his experiences in the London slums were
slow to manifest themselves, but their immediate effect was to
render him appreciative for the first time of the personal life he
had been building for the past two and a half years and eager to
return to its security. In contrast with the poverty, squalor and
loneliness about him, his home in California, his wife and baby,
his well-planned life seemed nothing short of miraculous.

During the few weeks that remained of what was to be his only
trip abroad, while he traveled through Germany, France and
Italy, his thoughts were full of Bess. Only now did he realize how

well and under what difficulties she had played the role he had assigned her. To Bess, in the last month of her pregnancy, came the first and the only love letters she was to receive from him, letters which left her incredulous, yet daring to hope that for them both the difficult years were over at last.

Late in the afternoon of October twentieth Jack's second child was born, another daughter. But the cable announcing her birth found Jack in too happy a frame of mind to be greatly disappointed. He and Bess were only twenty-six; there would be plenty of time for sons. Now his holiday was over. Back to the Bungalow, to Bess and the babies, and a new kind of life for all of them!

Before he left New York for California he discussed future perspectives with Brett. He had now five books to his credit, the last three having been published in October. The Macmillan Company was to bring out two more, *The Kempton-Wace Letters* and *The People of the Abyss*, during the coming year. Except for certain tales in the three short-story collections, Jack was far from satisfied with his fiction. The novel, of course, was a failure, and the fifth volume, *The Cruise of the Dazzler*, was merely a juvenile, insignificant except in that it was destined years later to become Jack London's rarest first edition.

The release from hack work during the past few months had given him perspective and made him aware for the first time of the maturing of his powers. He knew past doubt that he was ready now to do his finest work. Anxious to ensure its performance under the best possible conditions, he spoke frankly to Brett, who not only agreed that he should thenceforth write much less and more slowly, but was glad to give the financial co-operation Jack desired. Jack returned to California secure in the knowledge that for two years the Macmillan Company would pay him advance royalties in the form of a regular monthly check of one hundred and fifty dollars.

Many who followed Jack London's career, appreciative of the social bias that marked much of his activity and some of his writing during several years, have wondered that he did not join, even briefly, the "muckrake pack" whose din filled the early years of the century. Tracing his progress, however, one is startled to discover how close he came to it, for Jack London was nothing if not timely.

Not long before the pack was turned loose the *Cosmopolitan* had offered him an editorship, and S. S. McClure, who inaugurated the movement, had kept a speculative eye on him for some time. Finally the manuscript of his one "exposure" book, *The People of the Abyss*, was completed and placed in his publisher's hands just as the first two muckrake articles appeared in *McClure's*: "Tweed Days in St Louis," by Lincoln Steffens and Claude H. Wetmore, in October 1902, and the following month, Ida Tarbell's first article on the Standard Oil.

The times were ripe, however, for sociological works. The same few weeks saw the publication by the Macmillan Company of W. J. Ghent's *Our Benevolent Feudalism*, a book which not only revealed a basic understanding of the state of affairs which the muckrakers and their readers were to find so shocking, but which was brilliantly prophetic of future developments. It made but a small stir at the time, even among the radicals, but it was destined to exert a powerful influence on the conception of Jack London's *The Iron Heel*.

Muckraking had no appeal for Jack. He was essentially a fiction writer, and turned to journalism only when financially necessary. Under no circumstances, especially after his sojourn in London, would he have abandoned his refuge in the Piedmont hills to dig up abuses and corruption in various cities and industries. And, ill equipped though he was as a Socialist, he was nevertheless well aware that mere exposure of evils would not correct them. But if he did not participate in muckraking he benefited by the movement enormously.

The voice of the muckrakers was the voice of the middle class, stifling its fear beneath outrage and bluster. It had stood by, unmoved, while the farmers and workers had protested their grievances during the closing decades of the last century. Now its turn had come. Small businessmen and manufacturers and many who were in the professions had awakened to the realization that America, the land of opportunity for everyone who sought it, had changed. Success, once the certain reward for effort, was no longer easily obtainable; often it was not obtainable at all. All about them now loomed a vast concentration of wealth, hemming them in, denying them growth. It was not right, it was unjust, it was illegal! Thus the middle class, and thus it turned an eager ear to the yelps of the muckrake pack.

Articles exposing and criticizing the evils of modern times were not new. Throughout the 'nineties they had been appearing in such magazines as *Harper's, Scribner's, Century, Atlantic Monthly, Nation, Forum, Arena, Review of Reviews* and *North American Review*. Some discussed "the coming billionaire," others held up for praise or ridicule the contemporary "prophets of unrest"—Henry George, Edward Bellamy, Henry Demarest Lloyd and others. But critical articles became muckrake articles because the frightened middle class recognized the menace of Big Business just as the new cheap magazines, having established their ascendancy over the staider, more expensive ones, began to look about for new fields to develop in the interests of circulation.

Of the various editors of these magazines, S. S. McClure was unquestionably the shrewdest. His sensitivity to those phases of American life which might be most successfully exploited in the type of magazine which he was publishing amounted almost to prescience. And yet when he began his search for topics with which to snare his readers' interest he did not know in the least what he was looking for.

A routine article he had commissioned on the Armour Institute of Technology at the time of the World's Fair in Chicago gave him his first clue. He had realized instantly that the few facts concerning Mr Armour and the packing industry itself with which the writer had rounded out his article were more vitally interesting than anything else. Why not, he thought, publish other articles devoted exclusively to various American industries?

This was the beginning of what was to develop unexpectedly into muckraking. McClure assigned Miss Ida Tarbell, who was acquainted with the oil regions of northwestern Pennsylvania and who was an excellent research worker, to the task of writing a history of the Standard Oil, planning to publish her first article in February 1897. Five years were to elapse, however, before the gigantic project was completed.

In the meantime McClure became more and more convinced that he was on the right track. For years Henry Demarest Lloyd had been writing forcibly about the trusts. Now others were beginning to speak of them. McClure neither approved nor disapproved of trusts, nor did he have any clear idea of their significance or how they had come into being. He described the phenomena simply as "business consolidation," but he was certain that it was the most important development, for good or bad, that was taking place in America.

As an editor, McClure could not fail to be aware, moreover, of the activity of what were then the professional molders of public opinion, who were damning discontent and praising the status quo from pulpit, sanctum, forum and college chair. In this crusade they were especially bitter against education. President Hadley of Yale believed that, in general, sociology, politics, civics and finance should not be taught for "they tend to prepare the minds of the next generation to look to superficial remedies for political evils, instead of seeing that the only true remedy lies in the creation of a sound public sentiment." Other "educators" went even further. One was convinced that girls would make better wives and mothers and housekeepers if they finished school at from fourteen to sixteen years of age, because, he maintained, further education would develop "ambition not compatible with the happiest homes." Another would have restricted education to the few: "For education means ambition," he wrote, "and ambition means discontent."

But McClure was a passionate believer in education. And as for discontent, he knew that if it were fanned instead of smothered in his magazine it would bring circulation. On the very eve of the muckraking era W. J. Ghent wrote: "Along with the morganization of industry steadily proceeds the munseyization of literature . . . Our popular magazines regularly keep before us a justification, actual or inferential, of things as they are." Muckraking must have caught Mr Ghent napping, for a year later the "popular" magazines were not only attacking, actually and inferentially, what Lincoln Steffens was soon to call "the System," and exposing its evils and corruption, but they had risen to incredible heights of popularity.

McClure, with a well-trained staff composed of writers of such caliber as Lincoln Steffens, Ray Stannard Baker and Ida Tarbell, easily led the pack, but other editors followed as quickly as they could make their assignments. Through 1903 and 1904 McClure watched circulation grow as thousands of new readers followed "The History of the Standard Oil" and Steffens' articles on municipal corruption. Ray Stannard Baker delved into the labor problem, discovering that not even labor organizations were free of graft, but turning up an amazing amount of material to the discredit of the employers. Not until the La Follette committee began in 1936 to investigate violations of civil liberties in industrial disputes would the spotlight of publicity again reveal so clearly to bourgeois readers the methods used by the bosses to crush the workers' struggle for better pay and working conditions.

By 1905 the pack was in full cry. *McClure's* was publishing Baker's "The Railroads on Trial," *Collier's* an exposure of the patent-medicine racket by Samuel Hopkins Adams, and the circulation of *Everybody's* was jumping from a hundred and fifty thousand to more than three quarters of a million while it fed to avid readers Thomas W. Lawson's "Frenzied Finance" and the results of Charles Edward Russell's investigation of the beef trust. That same year William Randolph Hearst acquired the *Cosmopolitan* and entered the fray with "The Treason of the Senate" by David Graham Phillips. Immediately muckraking, already influenced by Lawson's sensational manner of exposure, took on the strong yellow tinge of Hearstian journalism. With an eye to circulation most magazines promptly abandoned their approximation of McClure's sober, well-documented fact finding and followed the new leader.

Up to this time the literature of exposure had not yet received the name by which it was to be known. Phillips' series had angered Theodore Roosevelt and his attack on Chauncey Depew was the last straw. Denouncing the "lunatic fringe" of the magazine writers, Roosevelt quoted from Bunyan's *Pilgrim's Progress* the passage about the man with the muck rake who, unable to look any way but downward, ignored the celestial crown that was offered him and "continued to rake to himself the filth of the floor."

The President's epithet, which delighted both the muckrakers and the muckraked, as well as those who had taken sides in the controversies, stuck. The sanctimonious have liked to believe that Roosevelt's denunciation was a death blow, but muckraking continued without slackening for some years. Topics and problems heretofore never openly discussed became convenient spurs to circulation. Nice middle-class ladies and gentlemen, torn between embarrassment and curiosity, read about the "social evil" and the connection between "the System" and prostitution; *Pearson's* titillated them with stories of the New York underworld; Judge Ben Lindsay horrified them with unpleasant facts about juvenile delinquency. Even the *Saturday Evening Post* muckraked occasionally, though cautiously.

Muckraking was bad, indecent and should be stopped, everyone said, but each month saw the number of readers increase. Even

Roosevelt withdrew his opposition, not because he had come to approve of muckraking but because, being a shrewd politician, he saw a way to exploit it for his own ends. It was not long before he had become the symbol of opposition to the trusts, although, as Charles Edward Russell said later, "nobody could mention anything he ever did to oppose them beyond burning words uttered between large white teeth firmly clenched." As a matter of fact as a "trust buster," Roosevelt was a dismal failure. Between 1900 and 1908 the number of trusts in the United States increased from one hundred and forty-nine to ten thousand and twenty, and their total capitalization from four billion to thirty-one billion.

The end of muckraking came in a most logical manner. Thanks to the sensational content and form of the muckrake articles, circulation had boomed and advertising rates had steadily risen. But when Business, affronted by the attacks and exposures of its methods, suddenly withdrew whole pages of advertising, the magazines threw on the brakes and brought muckraking to a discreet stop. It was all over by 1912.

The seeds of destruction had been inherent, however, from the start. The collapse of the movement sooner or later was inevitable because of its limitations. Dedicated merely to exposure, it failed utterly to offer any solution or even the most superficial explanation of conditions. The majority of its readers, their taste for this type of sensationalism jaded, sought other fads; the remainder placed their hopes in legislative reforms and were content. As a record of a vanished period in American life, the muckraking articles are undoubtedly valuable, but in retrospect the movement appears to have been essentially a letting off of steam, "full of sound and fury, signifying nothing." If anyone gained it was Big Business, which thenceforth was careful to mask its maneuvers with greater circumspection and finesse.

It has been estimated that at the peak of the movement the total circulation of the ten magazines most active in muckraking was more than three million a year. But in addition to exposés, most of these magazines published a large amount of fiction. A glance at a bibliography of Jack London's serial publications reveals to what extent he, who was never a participant, benefited by the movement. Ever alert to earn as much money as possible from his writing, he made a generous portion of that rich fiction market his own. *McClure's, Collier's, Everybody's*, the *Saturday Evening Post*, and as time went on more and more frequently the *Cosmo-*

politan published his short stories and serialized his longer works. Small wonder that in a comparatively short time his name became a household word to millions of Americans who regularly read magazines but seldom read books!

Such was the sociological temper of the times that when Jack brought the manuscript of *The People of the Abyss* to Brett it was immediately accepted. The apt and dramatic title, generally regarded as among London's best, was not original, as he himself revealed in one of the footnotes in *The Iron Heel: "The people of the abyss*—this phrase was struck out by the genius of H. G. Wells in the late nineteenth century A.D." But from start to finish the book is uniquely Jack London's, and in many ways reveals its author much more fully than later, frankly autobiographical works.

While he was writing the book he strove consciously to be objective, to suggest no cure and to describe what he saw unemotionally, but in this he was far from successful. If by nothing else, his bias was betrayed by his choice of details, his chapter titles and the quotations with which he headed them. Pad his pages as he might with facts and figures from British sociologists or excerpts from police-court reports, his horror, and his deep-seated terror at what he witnessed dominated nearly every page.

Obviously this reaction added greatly to the effectiveness of the work in certain quarters, but elsewhere it evoked such comment as "yellow journalism" or "good story but poor sociology." The *Atlantic Monthly* considered it "deficient in the firmness and dignity of mood and touch which might have made it literature." But it was not his horror and sympathy which was condemned or misunderstood as much as his fear, and this by all odds was his most important reaction in that it had a lasting effect upon him.

The *Bookman*, reviewing *The People of the Abyss* early in 1904, accused its author of "snobbishness because of his profound consciousness of the gulf fixed between the poor denizens of the Abyss and the favored class of which he is the proud representative . . . he needs must assure the reader that in his own home he is accustomed to carefully prepared food and good clothes and daily tub—a fact that he might safely have left to be taken for granted."

But Jack London had escaped too recently from the squalor and insecurity of the working class to be able to take such a fact

for granted, and, by the same token, had far less need to assure his
readers of his comfortable status than himself. Scenes of his youth,
distorted by the ugliness he was seeing on every side, had returned to torment him, and only by reiterating the difference between his present good fortune and that of the dwellers in the
Abyss could he lull his panic at the thought that one day he might
be poor and a casual laborer again.

Taken by and large, the East End experience produced no
radical change in him, but it did emphasize and strengthen certain
tendencies which had already manifested themselves. With all the
sincerity of which he was capable he wished to see the end of the
regime which had produced such misery and degradation. But if
his faith in the ability of the working class to throw off its yoke
had formerly been weak, it had now practically ceased to exist.
British trade unions, even those with large memberships, had been
fighting desperately to keep wages up and hours down in the face
of chronic unemployment. But during his brief stay there he had
seen the labor market glutted with the thousands of soldiers who
were returning from South Africa and the hard-won gains of the
unions swept away.

Heartsick, his faith wavered not only in the possibility of
achieving socialism but in civilization itself. More urgently than
ever before he desired to escape from the festering cities to the
country and further, if necessary. Intellectually, Jack was in
perfect accord with the Marxian dismissal of Rousseau's back-to-
nature doctrines as atavistic and absurd, but under stress, when he
found modern society unendurable to contemplate, a desire to
escape from it always manifested itself. In the next few years this
tendency was to grow stronger, dictating the themes and locales
of much of his writing, as well as many details of his personal life.
"The unfit and the unneeded!" he wrote bitterly in *The People
of the Abyss*. "The miserable and despised and forgotten, dying in
the social shambles. The progeny of prostitution—of the prostitution of men and women and children, of flesh and blood, and
sparkle and spirit; in brief, the prostitution of labor. If this is the
best that civilization can do for the human, then give us howling
and naked savagery. Far better to be a people of the wilderness
and desert, of the cave and the squatting place, than to be a people
of the machine and the Abyss."

It would take the heart-lifting news of the outbreak of the 1905
revolution in Russia and the spectacular paper gains of the Socialist

party in America to rekindle his revolutionary spirit and confidence in the early victory of the working class for one brief last stand. But already in 1902 he had caught a glimpse of a different role which the proletariat and the "unfit and unneeded" might play in the not too distant future.

"The dear soft people of the golden theaters and wonder-mansions of the West End do not see these creatures, do not dream that they exist," he wrote of the slum dwellers. "But they are here, alive, very much alive in their jungle. And woe the day, when England is fighting in her last trench, and her able-bodied men are on the firing-line! For on that day they will crawl out of their dens and lairs, and the people of the West End will see them, as the dear soft aristocrats of Feudal France saw them and asked one another, 'Whence came they? Are they men?'"

And again: ". . . made desperate as wild beasts are made desperate, they may become a menace and go 'swelling' down to the West End to return the 'slumming' the West End has done in the East. In which case, before rapid-fire guns and the modern machinery of warfare, they will perish the more swiftly and easily."

Five years later, the failure of the Russian Revolution, Ghent's *Our Benevolent Feudalism,* Jack's scorn of the pacifism of the Socialist party leaders and disillusionment with his own slogan, "The revolution is here, now. Stop it who can!" would transmute this vision into the magnificent description of the Chicago commune in *The Iron Heel:*

". . . It was not a column, but a mob, an awful river that filled the street, the people of the abyss, mad with drink and wrong, up at last and roaring for the blood of their masters . . . Dumb apathy had vanished. It was now dynamic—a fascinating spectacle of dread. It surged past my vision in concrete waves of wrath, snarling and growling, carnivorous, drunk with whisky from pillaged warehouses, drunk with hatred, drunk with lust for blood—men, women, and children, in rags and tatters, dim ferocious intelligences with all the godlike blotted from their features and all the fiendlike stamped in, apes and tigers, anaemic consumptives and great hairy beasts of burden, wan faces from which vampire society had sucked the juice of life, bloated forms swollen with physical grossness and corruption, withered hags and death's-heads bearded like patriarchs, festering youth and festering age, faces of fiends, crooked, misshaped monsters blasted with

the ravages of disease and all the horrors of chronic innutrition—
the refuse and the scum of life, a raging, screaming, screeching,
demoniacal horde."

The People of the Abyss is not a great work, but its sincerity
places it among the handful of books Jack London wrote because
he wanted to, and not merely to make money. Its sale was not
large, and the serial rights netted him next to nothing, as it was
published in *Wilshire's*, a pseudoradical magazine. Jack was gratified by the small prestige it brought him among the serious reading public. Some hoped that he would continue to work along the
same lines, but the majority of his readers clamored for more
fiction. And because his determination to get out of debt and win
to financial security had been quickened by his new loathing and
fear of poverty, he was glad to accede to their wishes. Later, later,
he would write more about the people of the abyss and kindred
subjects.

CHAPTER

19

IN RETROSPECT it has seemed to some of Jack London's older friends that by 1903 he was an entirely different person. Beneath the surface, no doubt, the forces were already at work which were ultimately to produce the later Jack London, successful, wealthy and disenchanted with everything he had once held significant. Yet when he returned to Piedmont barely four months after he had left for England he was apparently the same, merely happier and surer of himself.

The first months of the few that remained of his marriage to Bess—and how incredulous he would have been then at the suggestion that this union would soon be terminated—were very quiet. His joy in his role of husband and father was so complete, and the fresh vigor with which he returned to writing so satisfying that in more than one letter to Cloudesley and Anna recurs the phrase, "I go nowhere and see no one." At Christmas he inscribed a copy of *The Children of the Frost* to Bess: " 'The first book of mine, all for your own,' you said. But what matters it? Am I not all your own, your Daddy-Boy?" And to Cloudesley, a month later, he wrote, "By the way, I think your long-deferred congratulations upon my marriage are about due. So fire away. Or, come and take a look at us, and at the kids, and then congratulate."

Jack's renewed enthusiasm for his family and his work lulled whatever apprehensions Bess may once have felt for their future together. Improved finances released her from domestic drudgery and made possible, for the first time since their marriage, companionship with her husband. In this brief summer of her life she moved forward confidently with the days, regretting the end of their solitude when once again they began to entertain, but unafraid.

It was during this quiet winter that he began, and finished in one month, the book which established his reputation internationally as a literary artist. The years of study and striving bore fruit at last in *The Call of the Wild*, of all his books the one conceived and executed with the least deliberation. He started out to write a short story, "a companion to my other dog story, 'Batard,'" he told Anna, and even when it grew to more than thirty thousand words he still believed that he was writing merely the experiences of a dog in the Klondike. After the tale was published and reviewers and friends alike pounced enthusiastically on the human allegory inherent in the dog's life-and-death struggle to adapt himself to a hostile environment, he reread his book with astonishment. "I plead guilty," he admitted, "but I was unconscious of it at the time. I did not mean to do it."

Neither then nor later, however, did he seek to understand what had impelled him to write such a book at this time. Its warm reception, assuring him thenceforth the long-coveted status of a popular and highly paid author, destroyed whatever curiosity he may have felt concerning his own motives and perspectives. As far as he was concerned this best seller was a purely fortuitous piece of work, a lucky shot in the dark that had unexpectedly found its mark. And again he congratulated himself on having joined the gold rush and amassed this fortune in story material.

But, despite its Klondike setting, *The Call of the Wild* stems just as certainly, though less directly, from his experiences in the East End as *The People of the Abyss* itself. And although it was his greatest purely literary achievement, it was also his first step, albeit an unconscious one, on a path that would lead him eventually toward something quite the reverse.

In *The Call of the Wild* he fled from the unbearable reality of the struggle for existence in capitalist civilization as he had witnessed it in the London slums to a world of his own devising, a clean, beautiful, primitive world in which, he convinced himself, the fit, be they man or beast, could and would survive. At the same time, forgetting his revolutionary principles, he affirmed his belief in adaptation as the sole means of survival.

There was always the man in the red sweater who wielded a club, he argued, and there were the fangs of one's fellows ready to rend and destroy. So he enunciated "the law of club and fang": adapt yourself to the club so that in learning to conform you may be beaten but not broken; learn every trick and device in using your own fangs before your fellows spring upon you and pull you down; and do all this so that in the end you may engineer your escape from both club and fang and be your own master and the master of others.

Such good fiction all this made! Never had Jack so thoroughly enjoyed writing, never had he written so well. The teeming slums, the filth, the suffering of people doomed to go down in unequal combat vanished as he re-created the primitive Northland that he loved and wrote on that most satisfying of all themes—success. Although he did not realize it, the story of Buck's triumph was the story of his own fierce struggle to rise from poverty and squalor to a position of growing distinction and security, the story of all strong people who use the cunning of their minds and the strength of their bodies to adapt themselves to a difficult environment and win through to live, while the weak surrender and die.

The few of his friends who ventured to criticize his philosophy in *The Call of the Wild* were abashed when he good-humoredly defended it, and dropped the subject. One of them, a woman with a frail body and a dauntless spirit, wrote him, "I respect the people who adapt, but I worship the brave souls that refuse to do so." He did not heed the warning. Later he would twice attempt, in *The Sea Wolf* and in *Martin Eden,* to prove that the strength of the strong individual was intrinsically worthless, that individualism itself was an anachronism and would disappear with other rubbish when capitalist society was replaced by a socialist one, but he was unconvincing, even to himself. Thereafter with rare exceptions he would avoid the issue and confine himself to characters and locales compatible with the philosophy both he and his audience found so satisfying.

Because his readers, seeking refuge as eagerly as he from the complexities and defeats of modern life, clamored for more tales of victories on the frontier, further progress on this route to popularity became doubly attractive. When in a few years his interest in the revolutionary movement had flared up for the last time and died he would turn deliberately in the direction that was so pleasant to travel and paid so well. For a long time, measuring his progress by the money he earned, he was able to deceive himself that this apparently triumphant march, whose gaudy banners and strident bugles were greeted on every side with wild applause, was not a retreat. When he realized the truth it was too late.

But banners, trumpets, applause and disillusionment were as yet in the unguessed future when early in 1903 he finished the manuscript of *The Call of the Wild* and sent it off, one copy to the Macmillan Company, another to the *Saturday Evening Post*. Although it had never previously been interested in his work, the *Post's* judgment of this story's appeal to readers was accurate, and a generous check accompanied its flattering letter of acceptance. Mr Brett, however, although personally enthusiastic, feared that the realism and beauty of the book would not be appreciated by "the sentimentalist public." Neither the magazine nor the publisher was satisfied with the title, and Jack did not insist upon it. Fortunately no one could invent a better, and the excellent original one was allowed to stand.

Publishing arrangements with Macmillan had naturally not been made for *The Call of the Wild*. Brett, dubious of its success, made a proposal: if Jack would sell the book rights outright for two thousand dollars the Macmillan Company would not only issue it in an unusually attractive form, but would spend quite a large sum on advertising it. This would also benefit his books already published, as well as those to come. Neither Brett nor Jack guessed what a gold mine *The Call of the Wild* would prove through many years. The proposal was a gamble for both. And Jack, his debts cleared by the *Saturday Evening Post* check, saw only that the two thousand dollars would enable him to purchase the Spray, a sailing sloop he had been wanting to own for some time. He accepted Brett's offer with alacrity.

The first edition of *The Call of the Wild*, ten thousand copies, was exhausted the first day. Throughout the country, book reviewers gave it unstinted praise. Those who from the beginning had resented what came to be known as Jack London's "redbloodedness" were temporarily silenced. A New Orleans reviewer, for instance, had dismissed one of the stories in *The God of his Fathers* with: "One might call 'The Great Interrogation' by Jack London a 'strong' story, just as one speaks of 'strong' butter." Nor did they speak any more of Jack London's "great promise." In *The Call of the Wild* he had more than fulfilled all his early promise. As proof of his mastery of his craft, what is probably the most beautiful prose passage Jack London ever wrote was frequently quoted: "In the fall of the year they penetrated a weird lake country, sad and silent, where wild-fowl had been, but where then there was no life nor sign of life—only the blowing of chill winds, the forming of ice in sheltered places, and the melancholy rippling of waves on lonely beaches."

What was more significant, *The Call of the Wild* brought to an end the comparison by well-meaning critics of Jack London's work with that of other writers. "As fine as Kipling," many had written of his first books. "He has only to go on to take the place perhaps of Stephen Crane," said others. Even Fred Lewis Pattee, revising his *History of American Literature* in 1902, had written in a footnote: ". . . Jack London, who with a few stirring tales had made himself the Bret Harte of the Alaskan gold fields." Now Jack London stood on his own feet as an American writer, daring, forceful and original.

One other important piece of work occupied his attention for a few days at this time, important not in itself but in its bearing on a later work. He reviewed W. J. Ghent's *Our Benevolent Feudalism* for the *International Socialist Review*, comparing it with *The Social Unrest* by John Graham Brooks, whose point of view was the antithesis of Ghent's. Four years later Ghent's prognosis of the slow, sure emasculation of labor by capital and the rise of the great industrialists and money barons to positions of absolute power and authority would reappear in *The Iron Heel*.

The period of intense activity in solitude drew to an end. The writing of *The Call of the Wild* had been sheer pleasure, but it had taken its toll in nerves. Imperceptibly at first, Jack grew tired of domesticity and his hermitlike existence and began to crave the stimulation of flattering friends and acquaintances. Bess neither praised nor flattered. Lifelong she retained her belief that if one did something well there was no reason why he could not then do it better. Jack's success pleased but did not surprise her. But Jack, with good work performed, needed congratulations, and the word went forth that the Londons were entertaining once more.

The Wednesday-night suppers at the Bungalow and the Sunday outings in the hills were a far cry from the first "Wednesday nights" in the house on East Fifteenth Street, when Bess had been often hard put to it to stretch an Irish stew among the dozen or so guests and wearily washed dishes late at night after everyone had gone. Now ample funds, two servants and a nursemaid for the babies under the watchful supervision of Mammy Jennie made entertaining the scores who came weekly as simple for her as it should have been pleasant. But the "crowd" had been changing in the last two years. Old friends were now far outnumbered by new, and Bess found herself hostess to numerous people with whom she not only was barely acquainted, but felt acutely ill at ease.

More gregarious than Bess, hungry for the praise so freely offered by his guests, and inordinately fond of the role of generous host, Jack uncritically welcomed all who came. But his growing fame had attracted types of people with whom he had had no experience. In truth, the ex-oyster pirate, -hobo, -poor student and -gold seeker could scarcely have encountered this horde of intellectual bohemians and bourgeois pseudo intellectuals unless he had achieved a startling success in one of the arts.

Naturally, not all these people were of the hanger-on type which usually flocks around a celebrity. Among them were some whose friendship was given to Jack and not to the famous young author, and others whose talents as writers, musicians or painters, while not great, were nevertheless genuine. But for the most part Jack's new friends were sycophants, well dressed, well mannered and glib. They fell roughly into two groups: those attracted to him as a new Socialist-evangelist, who today would be described as "liberals," and who, as they are today, were shunned by true Socialists; and those whose social orbits revolved about artistic and literary figures, and who, as today, made up the Greek chorus at studio teas and literary dinners.

The latter, endowed with large, supple vocabularies, prattled endlessly about literature and the higher criticism, the latest books and poems and plays, and Jack was often impressed by them, but the "liberals" bewildered him. At times he found himself literally besieged by spiritual aggressors who were full of the spirit of love and beauty. Such words as the "co-operative commonwealth" and the "reign of love" were on their lips, and in their eyes a gleam of hope when the growth of the socialist movement in Europe was mentioned.

When Jack asked these gentlemen of the white collar and broadcloth suit by what power they would bring about the transformations in the social state for which they apparently yearned they told him that they expected to get their heaven mostly through the revolutionary efforts of the working class, aided of course by the labors of men of good will like themselves. Jack was distressed; in a fashion he had rather looked up to these respectable, educated people. His contempt for the working class as he had known it was such that he had little belief in its power to do anything more than satisfy its most elementary cravings.

In the end, however, he was not deceived, understanding that behind all the humanitarianism of these good people was a very distinct ambition to take a leading part in the transformation of society and hence gain a position in the new society quite superior to that which they had enjoyed in the old. When not long after he discovered that this ambition was shared by many outstanding members of the Socialist party it proved a convenient bolster to his decision to leave the radical movement for greener pastures elsewhere.

Now, ill prepared for the flattering attention of the middle class, whose favor he had sued for in vain since his high-school days, Jack permitted his appeased vanity to blind him for some time to the essential shallowness and insincerity of most of his new friends. A decade later in *John Barleycorn* he exposed them, and those who had been added in subsequent years, with cruel vindictiveness when he described his reaction to "social intercourse with the glamour gone:" ". . . it was a torment to listen to the insipidities and stupidities of women, to the pompous, arrogant sayings of the little half-baked men." But as so often happened with Jack London, realization came too late.

Of the old intimate friends, Austin Lewis and Frederick Irons Bamford were the principal survivors. Jim Whitaker, nursing a real or fancied grievance, was no longer a visitor. Strawn-Hamilton's wanderings had taken him East; Tom Booth had long since dropped away. Anna Strunsky was in New York, and after Jack had left the Socialist Labor party for the new group Jane Roulston had seen him but rarely. Bamford was completely satisfied with Jack's progress and, watching him surrounded by his admiring, well-bred guests, would remember happily his own small contribution to the ultimate success of the shabby high-school boy he had once befriended. But Austin was not content. The Jack he knew and believed in was subtly changing, and he feared the consequences. As a matter of fact 1903 was to be the last year of their intimacy.

Many of the new friends were destined to remain close to Jack. Of these, two were significant: George Sterling, soon to be known as his best friend, and Charmian Kittredge, who in 1905 became his second wife.

A few years earlier, meeting Sterling when he began to be acquainted with fellow writers about the Bay, Jack had been greatly impressed by this poet, several years his senior and already well known locally, but intimate friendship with him had seemed inconceivable then. Nor did the ensuing two or three years bring them closer, although George was not only one of the "crowd," but after Jack moved to Piedmont, a neighbor as well. In the summer of 1903 Jack wrote him, "We have really never touched the intimately personal note in all the time of our friendship."

At the start the difference between the two men had been much greater than the likeness. In the interim, however, it was not George who changed, but Jack. Their lives had been completely dissimilar. Sterling came from a middle-class New England family, the son of a convert Catholic who had ardently desired to give one of his sons to the church. But in George the poet was stronger than the priest, and he abandoned his studies before they were completed.

Coming to maturity in California, his development as poet and man was circumscribed by his class, the limited cultural resources available, and the provincialism of the West. His was a true lyric gift, but at best he was merely a minor poet. Although he wrote continuously through the first two decades of the twentieth century he gave back no echo of the new tempos and themes so clearly caught by those who after 1912 brought about the renascence of American verse. When after many years his work finally transcended the boundaries of his adopted state, it was but a small note, lost in the full-throated chorus of the newer poets.

As Jack sought to escape from the class in which he had been born, so George. Jack was successful; George, failing, found refuge in Bohemia. It was a charming, old-fashioned sort of bohemianism that George assumed, and consisted chiefly of flouting social and moral conventions and behaving, when not working at his white-collar job, as if he were still a youth. Tall, slender and graceful, with a sensitively modeled face whose profile was so reminiscent of those on antique coins that Jack, with his passion for special names for people he loved, later called him "Greek," George was well suited physically to his role of poet-playboy. It was his misfortune, however, to possess a really excellent mind which, though long starved, functioned extremely well on the crusts it received. Too intelligent to be content with his compromises, too sensitive to endure the slow crumbling of his youthful ideals, George early hid his vulnerabilities behind a deceptive pseudo cynicism which served him well, until during the melancholy last years of his life it became genuine.

He mystified Jack for a long time. "Sometimes I conclude," he wrote George in the 1903 letter already referred to, "that you have a cunning and deep philosophy of life, for yourself alone, worked out on a basis of disappointment and disillusion. Sometimes, I say, I am firmly convinced of this, and then it all goes glimmering, and I think that you don't want to think, or that you have thought no more than partly, if at all, and are living your life out blindly and naturally."

As disappointment, and not disillusion so much as disenchantment, gradually took the place of Jack's enthusiasm, he and George found a common meeting ground, although Jack, with an ever-mounting yearly income, lived as a landed proprietor and never shared the attractions of George's bohemian existence. Their correspondence is curiously barren, however, of evidence of their intimacy. Their friendship grew and expanded in long hours of talk, usually over a bottle. Probably better than anyone else with whom Jack was acquainted, George understood what he meant by the "white logic" of John Barleycorn. And in many other ways George came near to being "the great Man-Comrade" for whom Jack had longed since adolescence and of whom he wrote:

". . . This man should be so much one with me that we could never misunderstand. He should love the flesh, as he should the spirit, honoring and loving each and giving each its due. There should be in him both fact and fancy. He should be practical insofar as the mechanics of life were concerned; and fanciful, imaginative, sentimental where the thrill of life was concerned. He should be delicate and tender, brave and game; sensitive as he pleased in the soul of him, and in the body of him, unfearing and unwitting of pain. He should be warm with the glow of great adventure, unafraid of the harshnesses of life and its evils, and knowing all harshness and evil . . . an all-around man, who could weep over a strain of music, a bit of verse, and who could grapple with the fiercest life and fight good-naturedly or like a fiend as the case might be . . . the man who could live at the same time in the realms of fancy and fact; who, knowing the frailties and weaknesses of life, could look with frank fearless eyes upon them; a man who had no smallnesses or meannesses, who could sin greatly, perhaps, but who could greatly forgive . . ."

Jack London had not been long dead when more than one critic, applying some of the rudimentary principles of Freudian psychology to the leader of the red-blooded school of American fiction, shocked and dismayed many of Jack's admirers with the suggestion of his latent homosexuality. Whether his writings reveal this or not is no longer of much consequence, but the quality of the affection which existed between George and Jack gives a certain validity to the conclusions of the literary analysts. In that relatively simple era before even the man on the street became Freud conscious, both George and Jack naïvely declared their love for each other. Both would have furiously resented and denied the inferences that would be readily drawn today from such a declaration, but it seems probable that the emotional interplay which continued between them for a number of years revealed this latent homosexuality of which neither was aware.

Among the women in Jack's circle of friends at this time, Charmian Kittredge was unique. Child of the late nineteenth century, she was in many ways a forerunner of a type of American woman of the middle class who would not fully emerge for nearly a quarter of a century. As a breaker of traditions, Charmian naturally made a number of enemies, but in an era when women's thoughts and actions were still narrowly circumscribed she managed to achieve extraordinary freedom without being socially ostracized.

Perhaps her greatest gift was her ability to adapt herself good-humoredly to unpleasant circumstances and sacrifice as few as possible of her desires and ambitions in the process. As a young woman, having been orphaned since childhood, she had not been pleased at the prospect of going to work. Music, books, riding and dancing, capped by the usual early marriage of the 'nineties, were much more to her taste. But by the time Jack met her she had been earning her living for some years as a competent secretary, and in addition was well read, an accomplished horsewoman and a dancing partner much in demand.

She had reached her middle thirties without being married. Many of the "crowd" who found her laughter a little loud, her horsemanship too spectacular, her eagerness to play and sing at the piano distasteful, did not fully appreciate that behind much of this exhibitionism lay a woman's very normal desire to attract a husband before it was too late. Beauty of face, according to those who knew her at this time, she did not have, but the years had taught her to display her good points to their best advantage. Small of stature, delicately built and very feminine, she wore the ribbons and ruffles and furbelows of the period with grace and charm.

Like the wives of many famous men, Charmian has been largely misunderstood. Friends and enemies have at once overrated and underrated her. She has been given credit that she did not earn, and blame that she did not deserve. As Jack London's wife she exerted little influence over him either for good or for evil. Throughout their marriage it was Jack who made the decisions and Charmian who concurred. Free of the legends that have surrounded her, she appears as a woman of average intelligence and more than ordinary courage, equipped with the usual complement of virtues and vices, who for eleven years made a better job of being Jack London's wife than anyone, knowing Jack, could have expected.

Jack had first met her in the spring of 1900 when her aunt, Mrs Ninetta Eames, was preparing an article about him which subsequently appeared in the *Overland Monthly*. A little later Charmian used her savings for a trip abroad, and it was not until some time after her return that Jack began to notice her as one of the "crowd," but markedly different. The growth of their friendship is best described in his own words, addressed to her: "And then You came, after your trip abroad, into my life. Before that I had met you quite perfunctorily, a couple of times, and liked you. But after that we met in fellowship, though somewhat distant and not so very frequently, and I liked you more and more. It was not long before I began to find in you the something all-around that I had failed to find in any man; began to grow aware of that kinship that was comradeship, and to wish you were a man. And there was a loneliness about you that appealed to me."

The discovery in Charmian of the "mate-woman" which Jack had once eschewed in his choice of Bess Maddern as wife and mother of his children took place during the almost hectically gay spring and summer that followed the completion of *The Call of the Wild*. He had already begun work on *The Sea Wolf*, his first attempt to use his seafaring experiences as fictional background, thus fulfilling the wish to write sea stories which he had expressed to Cloudesley nearly four years earlier. Many days were spent on the Spray, recapturing the feel of sail and wind and water, but ashore he devoted his leisure hours (and they were many, for he was doing little reading and studying) to play, and with as many playfellows as possible.

For a long time as part of his saga of success against great odds, Jack had mourned the playtime of which he had been deprived as a boy, especially the after-school hours and Saturdays when he had worked while most of his schoolmates played. Soon after he moved to Piedmont he had set out, aided and abetted by George and other Peter Pans of both sexes, to relive his lost boyhood.

How often as he delivered his papers he must have envied boys flying kites in the streets and empty lots! Now he surpassed their finest exploits, for in the deep, sun-warm grass of his poppy field he lay through many long afternoons watching huge, brightly colored box kites, six or seven of them in the air at a time, tugging fiercely at the lines which bound them to the heavy windlass. Boxing was practiced more zestfully with new opponents, men or women, skilled or unskilled. Many evenings were still devoted largely to music and verse and serious discussion, but more often as that last summer in Piedmont drew on, "rough house," practical jokes, and noisy, boisterous games predominated during the picnics in the hills or the bungalow parties. The "soda-cracker contest" was a typical diversion; while a jibing group watched, participants endeavored to masticate and swallow five large, old-fashioned soda crackers as quickly as possible and without the assistance of any liquid. Jack's laughter was louder than all the others.

In such fashion, Jack, on the threshold of the successful career he had longed for, celebrated the passing of his youth. But happiness, which he had confidently expected to accompany success, eluded him. Almost everything that he had wanted, wife, home and children, comforts and small luxuries, friends and money with which to entertain them, leisure for study and enjoyment, were his or within his grasp. What was wrong? he asked himself.

In sudden revulsion against the "crowd" and the silly, time-wasting diversions he had himself initiated, he thought of leaving the Bay region he loved and settling on a Southern California desert ranch with Bess and the babies until they were old enough to accompany him on long treks to the far corners of the earth. And even as he discussed this with Bess he knew that this was not what he wanted and that he did not know what he wanted, aside from making even more money at writing and continuing to serve the socialist cause as he knew it, in his own fashion.

He was twenty-seven years old, and the goal he had set himself had been reached too easily. A longer perspective at the beginning, or the vision to set new goals more difficult of achievement, once the old had been passed, might have kept him pushing forward exultantly for many years. Instead, he floundered helplessly, darted off at erratic tangents, and then sank slowly back. The strongest influence in his life, the revolutionary movement, sustained him longest, bringing to completion his one significant book before lip service to the cause he had once revered took the place of activity on its behalf. And in the end even the desire to make money became a compulsion, having been overpassed by what became almost an obsession to spread it prodigally before it was earned.

In the summer of 1903 he abruptly terminated that phase of his life which had begun when he returned from the road and entered high school. Having fallen in love with Charmian, he made his choice, though not easily, and left Bess and his two daughters.

CHAPTER

20

AFTER long preparation the curtain was about to rise on the
last and greatest historical event which was to affect Jack London's life and work: the 1905 revolution in Russia. Few American
Socialists knew very much about the revolutionary movement in
Russia, outside of the activity of the terrorist groups. Even Daniel
De Leon, better informed than most, consistently maintained
that a revolution could not possibly occur in a country whose industrial development had scarcely started. After it actually began
only meager reports of what was taking place reached the United
States, but the enthusiasm of the American radicals knew no
bounds.

Jack, who had been secretly disheartened for some time by the
Socialist party's emphasis on reform and parliamentary tactics,
found his instinctive belief in militant, revolutionary action amply
justified. In *The Iron Heel*, written in the midst of the pessimism
and reaction which followed the defeat of the 1905 revolution,
he would reiterate this belief and prove himself one of the few
American radicals whose revolutionary perspective was strengthened rather than weakened by this disaster.

In Russia the social forms were primitive and had been developing but slowly. With meager resources, and dependent upon an
archaic economic foundation, the country's social life reflected
this backwardness. In its struggle for existence the Russian state
outgrew its economic basis, until it came to absorb the largest part
of the national surplus, and even a part of that which was neces-

sary to maintain the Russian people. This terrific strain produced yawning crevices in the very foundation of the state, crevices in which it was later to be swallowed.

Economic development had been forced upon the country by bureaucratic measures. The growth of new trades, capital, machinery and large-scale production appeared artificial to the feudalistic economy of Russia, as sharp a contrast as that between the achievements of Russian science and the national ignorance. Only those measures of the state could survive, however, which corresponded to and accelerated the processes of the natural evolution of economic life.

The role of the state in the economic life of the country was tremendous. And when as a result of social development in Russia the growing native capitalist class began to manifest an interest in the more bourgeois democratic political institutions of the West, it came up hard against an autocratic state which, because it possessed a colossal army and other modern resources, was capable of protecting itself against internal enemies. It may have been unable to adjust itself to modern social relations, but as an instrument of oppression it was all-powerful.

The Russian autocratic state became a thing in itself and for itself, placing itself above all interests of society. In order to maintain its superior caste privileges and appetites, as well as an army to defend them, it increased its annual budget to astronomical figures. The Russian taxpayer was enslaved to European bank capital, and the Russian people were denied their most elementary demands by this Frankenstein. And although it was incompetent against foreign foes, to its own people it seemed invincible.

As the years passed the conflict between the requirements of economic and cultural progress on the one hand and absolutism on the other reached acute proportions. In the words of the Marxists, there was only one way to solve the problem: "to accumulate enough steam inside the iron kettle of absolutism to burst the kettle."

Until well into the nineteenth century few cities were industrial centers. The primitive industries were spread out in the villages and provided but auxiliary occupations for the peasants, while the cities were essentially administrative units with populations supported mainly by agriculture. Thus a prosperous, self-confident class of artisans was absent in Russian cities, and when modern capitalism appeared absolutism was perforce its handmaiden.

Overnight the large villages were transformed into modern industrial centers. But there was no middle class for these centers to build on, and, compared with Europe, the bourgeoisie played a very small role in Russian urban communities. Because a large part of the capital in Russia was imported and could thus bring pressure to bear on various European parliaments, the working class employed by this capital was able to exert its whole influence on Russia's political life. The poverty-stricken peasant and ruined rural artisan who became industrial workers and concentrated in large cities faced an absolutist state with nothing standing between them but a very small and very weak capitalist class, which was concerned only with profit, lacked historic tradition, was partly foreign in its derivation, and completely separated from the masses.

Thus on the eve of the 1905 revolution Russia was economically backward, with a politically weak capitalist class, but its working class had great strength. This apparent contradiction is resolved only when it is understood that there is no "immediate and direct dependence between the political strength of the capitalist and working class of a country on the one hand, and its industrial development on the other." As Leon Trotsky wrote, ". . . the struggle for the interests of Russia as a whole has become the task of the only powerful class in Russia, industrial labor."

Due to this correlation of forces, the combat against the strangling reaction of absolutism was made principally by industrial labor assisted by the peasantry. In 1903 the country was sharply agitated by strikes. During 1904 the first year of the Russo-Japanese war, there was a lull, but as the war continued the workers oriented themselves to it, and twelve months later put forward their demands in the street.

Japan had defeated China so quickly and decisively in 1895 that the European powers were taken by surprise. This victory ended all legends of a "renascence" in China. Backed by France and Germany, Russia forced Japan to satisfy herself with an indemnity, and Japan's victory failed to bring her the smallest piece of Chinese territory. To assist China in meeting her indemnity, a Russo-Chinese bank was established by Witte, the Russian minister of finance, with the co-operation of several large Parisian bankers. China's finances were to be straightened out at the same time.

The Siberian railway, on which work had begun in 1891 and whose cornerstone had been laid by no less a personage than Nicholas, then heir to the Russian throne, aimed at opening up new vistas for trade of which Russia sought to be the chief beneficiary. William II of Germany had suggested that Russia's future lay in Asia rather than in Europe; French loans made possible the eastward advance. But although the railroad would carry more German than Russian manufactured articles, Russia was not acting only as the tool of French capital and German industry. The East was the only way out for her, and an especially attractive one because of the apparent lack of opposition from the yellow and brown races.

Russia's metal industry was far more dependent on the state than her textiles, which were supported exclusively by the masses at home, and because of this the former had national influence on the country's policies. At the time of the coronation of Nicholas II in May 1896, a treaty was negotiated with Li Hung Chang by which Russia was granted the right to build railways in China. The Russo-Chinese bank immediately began to play an important role in this new phase of the expansion.

Although Russia was prevented by England from establishing a complete monopoly of railroad construction, she nevertheless made the most of the vast opportunities north of Peking. The original plan to connect the Siberian railroad with Vladivostok by running it through Russian territory along the Amur River was dropped, and it was proposed to cut across Manchuria which belonged to China. Through the railroad company, and on the pretext of safeguarding its interests, Russia then formally occupied Manchuria in a military manner.

In 1898 because of weather conditions and because Vladivostok was out of the reach of all the trade routes in the Far East, it was decided to head the railroad south and abandon Vladivostok as a terminus. Accordingly, Port Arthur and what is now known as Dairen, the two southernmost ports in Manchuria, were leased from China. Military occupation accompanied the lease, and Russia planned to make Port Arthur an impregnable fortress as well as a naval base for the Russian Pacific fleet, which was to be greatly expanded. Dairen was to be a commercial port.

The financial requirements of the Romanovs had multiplied spectactularly. Their money was being invested in business enterprises everywhere, and rumors persisted that they had even become the principal shareholders in Vickers, the British armament firm which supplied the Japanese navy in the war against Russia. Working through the czar's brother-in-law, a certain retired colonel whom Witte described as "a jobber of the lowest class," added more glamour to the rapidly becoming fashionable Far East by picturing Korea as a country of unlimited wealth and, what was even more important, a country not yet in the hands of foreigners. The Romanovs soon obtained a timber concession from the emperor of Korea, and Russians occupied the left bank of the Yalu, but this was merely a pretext for taking over the entire country.

Japan, however, was equally determined to control Korea, and between Russia and Japan Korea lost all semblance of the independence she had expected to enjoy after the Sino-Japanese war. Determined to "prevent the very rich mines of the Korean crown from falling into Japanese hands," Russia smuggled soldiers under disguise into Korea. From 1899 on war with Japan was inevitable. That Russia was preparing for war was evidenced by an increase in her war budget of forty-eight per cent between 1892 and 1902. No other European country was spending so much money for armaments. But, unknown to Russia, Japan was also arming feverishly.

Witte and Kuropatkin, the Russian minister of war, held out as long as they could against the threatening war. To Kuropatkin, mainly concerned with a war which would win Constantinople, Germany was Russia's sole enemy. Witte's commercial interest in Manchuria and Kuropatkin's desire to settle it were mainly responsible for Russia's refusal to evacuate the country. It was this conflict over Manchuria which was to place the United States dollar and the English pound on the side of the Japanese. War was further postponed by Russia because the Siberian railroad was not yet completed, Japan's maritime strength was still superior, and Port Arthur was far from being an impregnable fortress.

On the other hand, the Russian settlers rendered the situation increasingly critical by their abominable behavior toward the Chinese people. Russia was not the only foreign power, however, which behaved abominably toward the Chinese masses. When

Russia took Port Arthur the Germans seized Kiao-Chow and England laid hands on Wei-Hai-Wei. After the 1900 uprising in China of an outraged and indignant people against the "foreign devils," the movement quickly spread to Manchuria. There the finished parts of the railroad were destroyed. Manchuria was conquered by the Russians after indescribable atrocities were committed against the Chinese. Villages were looted and burned to the ground, and thousands of Chinese were sadistically drowned in the Amur. Forgetting the part played by Japan in the "pacification" of China, the Chinese turned to the Japanese in order to be freed of the Russians.

In Russia the internal situation was reaching threatening proportions. The method of waging pogroms against the Jews as a means of dissipating the revolutionary fervor which swept the brutally oppressed Russian workers and peasants was no longer of any avail. But a war against a foreign enemy like Japan, for the Japanese were not "Christians" but "heathens," would offer a splendid opportunity to turn the growing hatred of the masses for the Romanovs and their satellites away from revolution. The elements which favored war decided that the midget, Japan, would be an easily disposed of enemy. In governmental circles and among the nobility, they began to speak of the war as a "victorious little war."

Plehve, an energetic reactionary, became home minister in 1901. Witte, who tried to oppose his policies, was forced to resign in August 1903, and Plehve and Besobrasov, a guard officer and timber concessionaire in Korea, became the most influential people at court. Russia ignored the promise she had finally made in 1902 to evacuate all but the southern section of Manchuria. Recognizing the flow of events, Japan concluded an alliance with England.

By the beginning of 1904 there were about twenty-five thousand Japanese settlers in Korea. Practically all the shipping that came into Korea was under the Japanese flag; Japan operated the lighthouses along the coast; the railroads were being constructed and the utilities were controlled by the Japanese. That Japan could not lose Korea without being faced by a revolution at home was the opinion of even the Russian minister to Japan. In this crisis Japan was assured of financial support from the United States.

Japan determined to establish Russia's intentions in Korea with documentary proof during their negotiations. Japan proposed to recognize Russia's claims in Manchuria, if in turn Russia would recognize her claim to Korea. Russia's reply amounted to: "In Manchuria we are masters as it is; as for Korea, we shall see."

The anticipated war with Japan was being taken very lightly by Nicholas II's court in Russia, which believed that Japan would not dare to make the first move but would await the Russian attack. In the meantime, however, Russia was making very little effort to prepare for an immediate offensive. It is reported that in October 1903 Nicholas told the German emperor, whom he was visiting at the time, that no war need be expected in 1904.

But Japan was not waiting. Satisfied that further negotiations would be useless, and aware that more delay would permit Russia to complete her war preparations, Japan broke off diplomatic relations with Russia on the night of February 8–9, 1904, and her torpedo boats opened fire on the Russian squadron in the roadstead of Port Arthur.

This act added to the confusion of the startled Russian court, deluded by its "Japan-will-never-dare" attitude. The big Russian bear had been caught asleep. The army deemed necessary by Kuropatkin was estimated at three hundred thousand men, but only a little more than one hundred thousand were in Manchuria. The slightly superior Russian fleet was scattered among Port Arthur, Vladivostok and various Korean ports. Even distinctive signals for friend or foe were not established, and Japanese torpedo boats, under the guise of "friends," went into Port Arthur and blazed away at the Russian ships and their dazed officers. Three of Russia's battleships, two of them being among her finest, were disabled, and her superiority wiped away with one blow.

Port Arthur was blockaded, and, taking advantage of Russia's neglect, Japan established her own base at Elliot Island, a few hours' sailing time from Port Arthur, thus tying up the Russian squadron. Later, the flagship of the Russian admiral, Makarov, foundered with the admiral aboard, when it struck a Japanese mine during Makarov's attempt to break through the blockade on April thirteenth. After that the Russian fleet remained inactive.

Two Russian cruisers which had been forgotten in Korea were destroyed by the Japanese, and Japan proceeded to land troops on the continent unhindered. Once a firm footing had been established, Japanese soldiers moved into Manchuria, and Japan began to occupy the long-disputed territory. Japan sent her best men, while Russia kept hers for the enemy at home. For Japan, the war was a matter of life or death.

Toward the end of August the attack on Liao Yang was begun and resulted in a victory for the Japanese. This defeat for Russia was decisive, not in a military sense, but insofar as the opinion of the Russian people at home was concerned. On January 2, 1905, General Stoessel, the Russian commander of Port Arthur, started negotiations with the Japanese and surrendered, and with him the remainder of the fleet. The war was now definitely in favor of Japan.

The loss of Port Arthur was the spark which ignited the Russian revolution. In July 1904, just prior to Russia's defeat in the battle of Liao Yang, Plehve had been assassinated by the Social Revolutionaries. This killing of the powerful minister of the interior convinced the bourgeoisie and intelligentsia of the virility of the revolution. Liao Yang brought disillusionment, and defeatism swept the entire country. Shaken with fear, and lacking another strong man to fight the revolutionaries, the czar permitted a month to pass before naming Plehve's successor—Prince Sviatopolk-Mirsky, a man who believed in hoodwinking the masses with kindness rathen than relying on brute force. With the fall of Port Arthur, however, the bourgeoisie deserted the czar, and demands for a republic and a constitution were heard on all sides.

Bloody Sunday, January 22, 1905, marked in crimson the beginning of the revolution. Led by the priest, Gapon, thousands of workers, carrying icons and singing hymns, streamed from all parts of St Petersburg and converged in the square before the Winter Palace to submit a petition to the czar. ". . . We workers, inhabitants of St Petersburg, have come to Thee," said the petition in part. "We are unfortunate, reviled slaves. We are crushed by despotism and tyranny. At last, when our patience was exhausted, we ceased work and begged our masters to give us only that without which life is a torture. But this was refused. Everything seemed unlawful to the employers. We here, many thousands of us, like the whole of the Russian people, have no human rights whatever. Owing to the deeds of Thine officials we have become slaves."

After enumerating demands for civic liberty, amnesty, normal wages, the land to be gradually transferred to the people, and the convocation of the constituent assembly based on universal and equal suffrage, the petition closed with: "Sire, do not refuse aid to Thy people! Throw down the wall that separates Thee from Thy people. Order and swear that our requests will be granted, and Thou wilt make Russia happy; if not, we are ready to die on this very spot. We have only two roads: freedom and happiness, or the grave."

They asked to see the czar in person; they were met by the drawn swords of Uhlans and Cossacks. On bended knees, the workers begged to be permitted to go to the "little father," and the troops fired into the unarmed crowd. Over a thousand were killed and more than two thousand wounded. The revolution was on.

Russia's revolutionary movement at that time was made up of a handful of people derisively called a "sect" by the reformists. Lenin graphically described the revolutionary parties in general, and the revolutionary Social Democracy in particular, before Bloody Sunday, as consisting of a few hundred organizers and a few thousand members of local organizations, with a half a dozen revolutionary papers which appeared not more frequently than once a month, were published mainly abroad and smuggled into Russia under extraordinary difficulties and at the price of many sacrifices.

Within a few months great changes had taken place. The hundreds had grown to thousands and were rapidly becoming the leaders of several millions of workers. The peasantry soon added its dissatisfaction to the ferment, and the peasants' movement in turn affected the army, resulting in soldier uprisings and armed clashes between different sections of the army. This was how one hundred and thirty million people entered into revolution.

The 1905 revolution presented a striking peculiarity: in its social content, it was bourgeois-democratic; in the form of its struggle, it was proletarian. Demands for a democratic republic, an eight-hour day, and the confiscation of the vast estates of the nobility—measures which had been achieved by the French revolution in 1792–93—were not only what were being striven for, but what could be gained by the revolution's own forces.

The vanguard and main driving force of the revolution was the proletariat, and its most effective weapon to arouse the masses, and one which appeared with damaging regularity in the tidal waves of the decisive events, was the strike. The mass political strike played a most significant and extraordinary role for the first time during this revolution. Economic strikes were interwoven with political ones. In January 1905 nearly half a million people were involved in strikes, a larger number than during the entire preceding decade. Before the revolution came to an end nearly three million had participated in such action—twice the number of factory workers in Russia. Thus, due to the explosion of the latent energy of the working class in a revolutionary situation, was an apparently docile or acquiescent class transformed into a militant army of rebellion.

The first awakening of a political peasant movement took place in the spring of that year. When the condition of the Russian peasants at that time is realized—deluded by the czar's tool, the Orthodox Greek Catholic church, separated from each other by great distances due to the absence of roads, illiterate and poverty stricken, and only forty-four years' free from an intolerable system of serfdom—the impact of this movement takes on even greater significance.

Elements belonging to the Russian nobility had participated in the earliest revolution against czarism in 1825, and until the assassination of Alexander II in 1881 this opposition was led by middle-class intellectuals. The record of these intellectual revolutionaries commanded the attention of the entire world through their self-sacrifice and heroic methods of terroristic struggle against an even more viciously terroristic monarchy. Although these people failed to bring about a popular revolution their efforts to give the Russian masses a revolutionary education had not been in vain.

The strikes and the bitter lessons of the Russo-Japanese war were the main factors which propelled the slumbering Russian masses into action, and the strikes and the mass peasant movements succeeded finally in weakening the main prop of czarism—the army. When the soldiers and sailors were forbidden to attend any workers' meetings the workers in masses went to theirs. This joint action brought the armed forces closer to the workers. When officers who participated in these meetings failed miserably to influence the men under their command all meetings were prohibited.

The first and outstanding mutiny which shook the army and navy occurred on the Black Sea cruiser, the Prince Potemkin which, in control of the rebellious crew, later took part in the revolution in Odessa. In November 1905, Rear Admiral Pisarevsky peremptorily forbade any soldier, under penalty of being shot, to leave the naval barracks where a company of soldiers were stationed at the gates in full war equipment. Petrov, a sailor, immediately stepped forward and, loading his rifle in full view of everyone, shot and killed Lieutenant Colonel Stein of the Brest-Litovsk regiment and wounded the rear admiral. The order for Petrov's arrest was reluctantly carried out, but his release was soon forced by the roused sailors. All of the officers on duty were then imprisoned. After an all-night conference of the seamen the officers were released, but they were not permitted to enter the barracks.

The revolution reached its highest peak in the autumn of 1905. In August the czar was compelled to grant the so-called "Bulighin Duma," a "parliament" with an insignificant number of electors and possessing no legislative but only advisory powers. For the revolution, the proposed partial reforms meant only one thing: an effort to allay the people's unrest and slacken the workers' struggle.

Although the capitalists, liberals, and reformers were ready to accept the frightened czar's concessions the revolutionists of the Social Democracy issued slogans of "Down with the advisory duma! Boycott the duma! Down with the czarist government! Continue the revolutionary struggle for the overthrow of the government! Not a czar, but a provisional revolutionary government must convoke the first real popular representative assembly in Russia!"

Meetings multiplied, workers' and students' strikes and peasant uprisings increased, culminating finally in a great general strike which paralyzed all of Russia from October tenth to October fourteenth. The Bulighin Duma was swept away by the lava of the revolution and never came into existence. On October seventeenth the czar was forced to promulgate a new electoral law which recognized the legislative character of the duma, and increased the number of electors.

The rising flood of the revolution broke through all past traditions and regulations. In November alone over half a million workers were on strike. This number was swollen by several hundred thousand railway workers and postal and telegraph employees. Government power was rendered helpless by the general strike of the railroad workers. Universities which had previously been open only to the privileged became meeting places for the masses. Press censorship was ignored, and for the first time in Russian history revolutionary papers appeared openly in the principal cities and were freely distributed. In St Petersburg alone three Social Democratic papers were being published daily with circulations reaching up to one hundred thousand. The slogan of the St Petersburg workers was: "An eight-hour day and arms!" The conviction grew in the minds of greater and greater numbers of workers that only by an armed struggle would the fate of the revolution be finally decided.

In the heat of the revolution, to be precise, at the end of the general strike, a peculiar and significant mass organization sprang spontaneously into being: the "Soviets of Workers' Deputies," composed of delegates from all factories. Efforts were made to form soviets of soldiers' and sailors' deputies and to combine them with the workers' soviets. In several cities these soviets took on the character of the provisional government and became the organs and leaders of rebellion. In a few cities and for a brief time they were able to depose the state authorities and function as the regular government. Meantime over one third of the provinces became the scene of peasant riots and uprisings. At least two thousand estates of the nobility were taken over by the peasants and distributed among themselves.

A national movement for liberation spread among the oppressed peoples of Russia. Fifty-seven per cent of the population had been denied the right to use its native languages and forcibly Russianized. The millions of Mohammedans in Russia organized a league, and this was followed by many similar organizations among other nationalities. In Polish schools, Russian books and pictures of the czar were burned; in Russian schools in Poland, Russian teachers were driven out.

But the higher the revolutionary wave rose, the more viciously it was fought by the reaction, and it became more in the nature of a protracted civil war than a spontaneous uprising against the government. The Jews especially were made objects of persecution by the czar's forces. The December insurrection in Moscow brought the climax of the revolution. When this was crushed the retreat of the masses before the merciless "punitive expeditions" of the government began.

Geographically, historically and economically, Russia belongs to Asia as well as to Europe. Not only was the largest and most backward country in Europe aroused to revolution, but the movement encompassed the whole of Asia. Subsequent revolutions in Turkey, Persia and China revealed the imprint left by the 1905 revolution in Russia and the repercussions that were felt in the West.

The first Soviet of Workmen's Deputies, organized in St Petersburg, became an institution that was to shape the destiny of Russia, save for a brief interregnum, in the following decades. Although it lasted but fifty-two days it had been the revolutionary organ of the Russian people which had taken the leadership in political demonstrations, organized the masses, inspired political strikes and tried to arm the workers. But what distinguished it from other organizations which did similar things was its striving to become a "labor government." As "an organized expression of the will of the proletariat as a class," it fought for revolutionary power. Essentially it was in embryo the revolutionary government of the future.

Outstanding in the workers' movement in St Petersburg was a young revolutionist who, twelve years later with Lenin, was to organize and lead the successful Russian revolution as well as the Communist International—Leon Trotsky. He was only twenty-six when he became the recognized leader of the Petersburg soviet, and from then on he was acknowledged as a leader, theoretically and politically, by the revolutionary cadres of the Russian Social Democrats in and out of Russia, and among the Left groups within the Second International.

The revolution of 1905 has been called a dress rehearsal for the revolution of 1917. Moreover the problems created by the 1905 revolution accounted for the division then and in 1917 in the ranks of the Social Democratic party of Russia. It required the full force and power of a Lenin to whip into line such members of the "old guard" as Zinoviev, Kamenev and Stalin, and make them understand what had happened in 1905 and how to proceed in 1917. Subsequent events proved, however, that not even Lenin could teach most of them the lessons of the 1905 revolution. In the end Stalin became the embodiment of all the mistakes which Trotsky had fought relentlessly in the Social Democratic ranks.

The differences which developed were over the character of the 1905 revolution—was it bourgeois or socialist?—and the role of the working class in it. The Right wing of the party, known as the Mensheviks, considered the revolution to be bourgeois in character. They therefore strove to adapt the workers to play a role subordinate to and in harmony with the capitalist class against the monarchy. Plekhanov, one-time teacher of Lenin and outstanding champion of Marxism in Russia, could see in the revolution only a series of errors. He never failed to emphasize its bourgeois character and to insist that the Social Democrats be tactful in their relations with the Cadets, the party of the Constitutional Democrats, a liberal party of landowners and urban bourgeoisie led by Professor Miliukov.

Other leaders jettisoned the Marxist tactic in the revolutionary upheaval, maintaining there was no place for it and bowing to what they chose to call practical expedience. They spoke of the "carrying through of the revolution to the end," but by this they meant not the setting up of a "Workers' State" or a "Socialist Labor Government," but the achievement merely of the Social Democratic party's minimum program, after which capitalism would set in the rule under democratic relations.

But since a consummation of the revolution presupposed the destruction of czarism and the transition of state power to a revolutionary government, the question of what kind of a government was answered by the Mensheviks as "that of a bourgeois democracy." Russia, they maintained, would have to go through a capitalist development under a capitalist form of government, and the revolutionary party would, if possible, become a Left wing in such a government. In other words, since social conditions in Russia were not ripe for a socialist revolution, the Mensheviks believed that the taking of political power by the workers under the circumstances would be the greatest misfortune that could befall them.

The answer of the Bolsheviks, the Left-wing faction of the party, to the question of what kind of a revolutionary social power was to replace czarism, was "that of the proletariat and peasantry." They agreed that only the class struggle of the workers which established its leadership over the peasant masses would be capable of carrying the revolution to an end, and of triumphing in the bourgeois revolution. This coalition of workers and peasants they called the "revolutionary democratic dictatorship of the proletariat and peasantry." In this way they hoped to democratize the economic and political relations, although within the definite boundaries of private property.

This "democratic dictatorship of the proletariat and the peasantry" was not to be confused with the "socialistic dictatorship of the proletariat," or, more simply, the "dictatorship of the proletariat," as formulated by Trotsky. In 1905 Lenin did not want to formulate more than a "strategical hypothesis" to be tested in the immediate struggle. Therefore he did not determine in advance the political relations between the proletariat and peasantry in their democratic dictatorship. The Bolsheviks, believing then that to complete the socialist revolution was impossible, maintained that once the workers had succeeded to power together with the peasantry, they would become aware of the fact that their dictatorship had only a "democratic character." In the political self-limitation of the working class, playing a leading role in a bourgeois revolution, they saw an escape from the scissors of either a bourgeois or a socialistic government.

Trotsky, who belonged to neither group but worked closely with the Bolsheviks, took the position that a dictatorship of the proletariat could complete the revolution, a task which a bourgeois government neither could nor would do. As for the "democratic dictatorship of the proletariat and peasantry" of the Bolsheviks, he declared that such dual power was impossible, and that the question of which class the real dictatorship belonged to was one which could not be left unanswered.

Regardless of under what title the workers succeeded to power, he argued, they would be immediately confronted with problems in whose solution insistence upon the differences between a socialist and a democratic dictatorship would be of little help. For example, the new working-class government would have to give security to the unemployed in one form or another. This would provoke new economic struggles and strikes would increase. Meantime the capitalists would lock their doors and say, "Our property is under no threat of danger because it has been determined that the proletariat is concerned for the moment not with a socialistic but a democratic dictatorship." In the face of closed factory doors, a workers' regime would have to open them and start production again at the state's cost. And that, Trotsky pointed out, was the road to socialism.

Suppose, however, that the peasant party, standing beside the Social Democracy, would not permit security to be given to the unemployed and the strikers or the closed factories to be reopened at the state's expense? This would mean that at the very start, long before the tasks of the "coalition" could be even begun, a conflict would arise between the workers and the revolutionary government. The deadlock would be broken only by a taming of the workers by the peasant party, or a pushing aside of the peasant party by the workers—hardly a "democratic" collaboration in either case. Therefore, Trotsky maintained, the "self-limitation" of the workers' government would mean in the end the betrayal, in the name of the Republic, of the interests of the unemployed and strikers as well as those of the entire working class.

But Trotsky went further: Objective socialistic tasks would await a revolutionary government, but any attempt to accomplish them would strike a snag in the economic backwardness of the country. In the narrow mold of a national revolution there would be no solution to this contradiction. And if the workers' government were to content itself either with a revolution of this scope, or merely a democratic dictatorship, it would soon meet destruction at the hands of a united reaction.

Clearly, the workers' government must unite its forces with those of the socialist proletariat of Western Europe and the rest of the world. "World economy as a whole," he said, "and European economy in the first place, is completely ripe for the socialist revolution. Whether the dictatorship of the proletariat in Russia leads to socialism or not, and at what rate and over what stages, will depend upon the further fate of European and international capitalism."

Thus, early in 1905, did the "theory of the permanent revolution" take form in Trotsky's mind—an "uninterrupted" revolution which would pass over directly from the bourgeois to the socialist stage.

Later when Lenin formulated with clear precision the ideas which were to materialize and be applied by him in the 1917 revolution he and Trotsky found themselves in agreement on the significant issues which had been posed in 1905: the "dictatorship of the proletariat," and the permanent revolution. Even in 1917 there was disagreement on the latter point among the old Bolsheviks; today it constitutes the basic point of departure between those who consider themselves Leninists and those who are followers of the so-called Stalinist regime.

Not for many years were the details of the ideological struggles which grew out of the 1905 revolution available to American Socialists in any complete form. Nor was there much genuine appreciation of the little that did seep through to America in the period following the crushing of the revolution. Ignorance and apathy on the one hand, and the exciting game of building a national vote-catching machine on the other, soon brought forgetfulness of the tragic failure of the Russian revolutionists.

But for Jack London the event was of supreme importance, bringing him to full stature as writer and Socialist. Without 1905 *The Iron Heel* would never have been written.

CHAPTER

21

THE beginning of 1904 found Jack London nearing the completion of *The Sea Wolf*, on which he had worked steadily during the four difficult months which followed the separation from Bess and his daughters, and eager for at least a temporary change of scene and occupation. War between Japan and Russia was on the point of breaking out. With European and American war correspondents ready to depart for Japan at a moment's notice, Jack made inquiries. When the SS Siberia left San Francisco for Yokohama on January seventh he was one of the several correspondents aboard. "Could have gone for *Harper's, Collier's* and N.Y. *Herald*," he wrote Cloudesley, "but Hearst made the best offer."

None of the foreign correspondents distinguished themselves during the Russo-Japanese war, but few made more determined efforts to get to the front and report events than Jack London. As a writer he appreciated the opportunity to obtain the rich material the conflict would offer; as a Socialist he was equally desirous of witnessing the struggle between the two capitalist countries for the possession of Manchuria. Politely but firmly, however, the Japanese government enforced its opinion that correspondents belonged as far as possible from the scene of action. Jack believed otherwise and, as a consequence, for some weeks his stay in Japan and Korea was a stormy one. The zest with which he set out to overcome difficulties and delays marked a resurgence of the adventurous spirit which had been denied expression ever since the gold rush, and for a short time he enjoyed himself thoroughly.

Arriving in Tokyo on January twenty-fourth, he immediately became acquainted with the official attitude toward correspondents. But it was clear, even to an amateur, that only days would elapse before war was declared, and Jack had no intention of being caught so far from the scene. Four days later he was on his way to Chemulpho on the eastern side of the Korean peninsula and close to Seoul, the capital. From Seoul he planned to travel north by land to the Yalu River and on into Manchuria.

There being no steamer out of Kobe until February third, he made a fruitless trip to Nagasaki and then back to Moji, where he found a steamer leaving on February first. Five minutes after buying his ticket he came upon a picturesque street scene which he promptly photographed. Thereupon, just as promptly, he was arrested. Moji, unfortunately for Jack's plans to sail immediately, was a fortified town. He missed his steamer while the police questioned him as to the extent of his "spying" activities. Then they took him to Kokoura, requestioned him, tried and found him guilty, fined him five *yen*, and confiscated his camera for several days.

At Shimonoseki he arranged passage on the Kiego Maru, sailing on the eighth for Chemulpho, but on the sixth he learned that the Japanese government had taken the ship off its run. News that many Japanese battleships had been seen passing through the strait outward bound, and that soldiers had been summoned in the middle of the night to join their regiments touched his despair with desperation. War was at hand, and here he was still in Japan!

When he managed to catch a small steamer for Fusan, and another at Fusan for Chemulpho, he thought that his luck had turned at last. But on the morning of the ninth the Japanese government took over the ship and left its passengers stranded in Mokpo. Chartering a junk, Jack set out once more for Chemulpho, sailing up the "wild and bitter" coast of Korea, a stretch of land and water later to appear in one of the episodes of *The Star Rover*. A week later he reached his destination, where he learned for the first time that war had been declared.

At Seoul he outfitted and, on the twenty-fourth started on horseback for the Yalu. A fortnight later at Siu-Wan in Manchuria, forty miles from the front and the furthest north a correspondent had yet reached, he was ordered back, first to Pingyang, and then to Seoul. Here he fretted until the middle of April, when, having been assigned to the First Japanese Army in Manchuria, he once again started north. At headquarters, however, he found that he was still not permitted to see anything of the war. A note to Charmian early in May from Feng-wang indicated his irritable state of mind:

". . . I am well, in splendid health, though profoundly irritated by the futility of my position in this Army and sheer inability (caused by the position) to do decent work. Whatever I have done I am ashamed of. The only compensation for these months of irritation is a better comprehension of Asiatic geography and Asiatic character. Only in another war, with a white man's army, may I hope to redeem myself. It can never be done here by any possibility."

By May twenty-second he had made up his mind that if Hearst could not arrange for him to write up the war from the Russian side, an opportunity he scarcely hoped for, he would return to the United States. But before this decision could be acted upon Jack's growing bitterness against the Japanese culminated in an unfortunate incident. Confronted by an insolent groom who had been caught stealing fodder intended for his horses, Jack lost his temper and struck the Japanese. Threatened retaliation from the chief of staff of the Japanese army failed to materialize, but Jack left immediately for Tokyo on his way home to a "white man's country."

Jack London's scorn and loathing of the Japanese which he vehemently expressed on his return was a source of astonishment and pain to many who did not know how deeply rooted had been his prejudice before he ever went to Japan. Edwin Emerson Jr, a fellow war correspondent, summed up the attitude of the newspapermen toward Jack's behavior: "London's row with the coolie, and its prompt consequences, must have revealed to everyone, as well as to himself, his chief weakness as a news gatherer among a foreign people. London, according to his own professions, loathed and abominated the Japanese, and who has learned to appreciate their dominant trait of hiding their own feelings, cannot but realize that a man coming among them with such a disposition need never hope to get anything out of them. Not even true impressions."

If this was the opinion of a bourgeois journalist the reaction of Jack's socialist comrades may be easily imagined. Several years

ago Edmundo Peluso, in 1904 the youngest member of the San
Francisco branch of the Socialist party, recalled the autumn evening when Jack discussed his Japanese experiences at the socialist
headquarters in Oakland. Except for its sharpness, due, perhaps,
to the experiences of the three succeeding decades in the revolutionary movement, Peluso's account does not differ fundamentally
from those of others who were present.

"With evident pleasure," Peluso wrote in 1935, "he (Jack London) described the wilyness of these 'human burnt candles,' as
he called the officers of the Japanese General Staff, and used
stronger expressions with regard to them. But his gorge rose not
only at the Japanese General Staff; he cursed the entire yellow
race in the most outrageous terms. Some of the comrades present
were somewhat embarrassed. The struggle against race prejudice,
especially against hatred of the 'yellow' races, was part of the
daily work of the socialist branches on the Pacific Coast and it
was hard to conceive of Jack London, one of the foremost members of the branch, evincing rare chauvinism.

"Convinced that there was some misunderstanding, one of the
comrades began talking to him about classes that exist in Japan
as everywhere else. Another called his attention to the slogan
decorating the wall over the portrait of Marx: 'Workers of all
countries, unite!' But this did not touch him in the least and only
served to increase his passion. Pounding his fist on the table, Jack
met their arguments with, 'What the devil! I am first of all a
white man and only then a Socialist!' "

One wonders whether Jack, looking over issues of the *International Socialist Review* which had accumulated during his absence,
read an article by Sen Katayama which had appeared in March:
"I am opposed to this war," wrote Katayama in part, "but as a
Japanese I do not wish Japan to be beaten by Russia who in the
past treated the Jews as she has in Kishineff, and is still dealing
with Finns in the most brutal fashion, and moreover she has
shot down many laborers during strikes! And above all I wish
that the war may end as soon as possible, and I strongly desire
that the working classes of the two countries may realize the true
outcome of the war, and unite together to oppose the capitalist
governments that are the cause of all the wars."

Although Jack did not alter his opinion of the Japanese, he soon
confined open expression of his dislike to friends, and in public

utterance made an effort to keep his socialistic perspective. Thus the following spring in his lecture entitled "Revolution," he reported, "Only the other day, when Japan and Russia sprang at each other's throats, the revolutionists of Japan addressed the following message to the revolutionists of Russia: 'Dear Comrades —Your government and ours have recently plunged into war to carry out their imperialistic tendencies, but for us socialists there are no boundaries, race, country, or nationality. We are comrades, brothers and sisters, and have no reason to fight. Your enemies are not the Japanese people, but our militarism and so-called patriotism. Patriotism and militarism are our mutual enemies.' " But time and again, especially as Jack grew older, Benjamin Kidd had his way with him, and on numerous occasions he hailed as unavoidable "the Black and Brown going down before the White," because—he admitted it freely—he was convinced that otherwise the reverse might occur.

His essay, "The Yellow Peril," written at this time, clearly reveals his fear: "The menace to the Western world lies, not in the little brown man, but in the four hundred millions of yellow men should the little brown man undertake their management. The Chinese is not dead to new ideas; he is an efficient worker; makes a good soldier, and is wealthy in the essential materials of a machine age. Under a capable management he will go far. The Japanese is prepared and fit to undertake this management . . . Why may not the yellow and the brown start out on an adventure as tremendous as our own and more strikingly unique?"

His essential unwillingness, despite his acceptance of the Marxian point of view, to consider the possibility of these particular races overthrowing their "mutual enemies" and coexisting peacefully with the white race presented a contradiction not uncommon among Socialists of his time, nor even of ours. With an imperfect understanding of that which is usually called the dialectic, specific prejudices dissolve so deceptively in an abstraction! Essentially and intellectually, Jack believed in the solidarity of the entire international working class against its common enemy, capitalism. Visualizing the revolutionary struggle, he saw workers of all races as comrades and brothers. But in a specific situation, when for instance, the hated "little brown man" was involved, the abstraction vanished and the prejudice returned, tempered, and sometimes camouflaged entirely by subtle rationalization. Jack never admitted the contradiction; nevertheless his writing, both artistically and ideologically, was marred by this chauvinism.

Jack was in a far from happy mood when he returned to Oakland to pick up the tangled threads of his life which he had dropped when he sailed for Japan. All of his arrangements were temporary. He had destroyed the old plan; the new was no more than vaguely sketched; and to live without a plan was difficult for Jack. Between him and the new life he had chosen lay the shadow of divorce, which he hated and feared, not for himself so much as for Bess and Charmian. The century was very young and most people, he knew, were yet unwilling to accept the idea, let alone the practice, of divorce. He prepared himself to face censure, but the reality was to be worse than he expected.

Meantime he re-established himself in the flat in Oakland which he had taken upon leaving Piedmont, and for a few months Flora's ambition to preside as mistress of Jack's home was realized. Shortly after his return from Japan, Manyoungi, a young Korean who had been his servant in the Orient, arrived, the first of the personal servants—all Oriental—whom he was thenceforth never to be without. Manyoungi cooked and served excellent meals when Jack entertained, took full charge of his wardrobe and, in time, even dressed him. "It saves valuable time"—thus Jack explained this innovation to startled friends. But to Bess whom he saw frequently when he visited his little girls he revealed a disquieting satisfaction with this luxury. "Remember how shabby and unkempt I was when you first saw me?" he would exult.

Until the following spring when the outlines of his new personal life began to take shape, his mood of depression rarely lifted. During his absence Charmian had gone East to visit relatives and her return was still uncertain. More than once he seriously considered returning to Bess and the children and completing the once-cherished plan which he had abandoned just as its realization became possible. Intense activity—writing, speaking, entertaining and being entertained—partially allayed his dissatisfaction as time went on, and the excited comment which greeted *The Sea Wolf*, published that fall, was soothing. Having attained the long-desired pinnacle of fame, he was finding its rewards very gratifying.

Two of these furnish a significant contrast: the exclusive Bohemian Club of San Francisco, ever alert to leaven its preponderant membership of wealthy art enthusiasts with actual working artists, invited Jack to join; and the English Department of the University of California recommended *The Call of the Wild* as a model for classes in composition. The same period saw the publication of *Modern English Prose*, a textbook of rhetoric and English composition selected and edited by two Columbia University professors, George Rice Carpenter and William Tenney Brewster, and an excerpt from *The Call of the Wild* was included among the illustrative material culled from the works of many English and American authors long recognized as "masters."

Even Jack London's "brutality" was no longer openly attacked. Watching *The Sea Wolf* climb higher and higher in the bestseller lists, hearing praise from all types of readers, reviewers grew respectful of Jack London's indubitable power. Apropos of *The Game*, a short, beautifully conceived and executed novel about a young prize fighter which Jack wrote during the autumn of 1904, one reviewer wondered "whether he writes as he does because such themes appeal to him, or whether he does not rather do so from sheer delight in his mastery over words—a perverse satisfaction in ringing the changes upon some one of the baser human passions . . . and making his reader shrink and wince."

But neither of these was Jack's motive for the type of writing he was doing. "People find fault with me for my 'disgusting realism,' " he said during this period. "Life is full of disgusting realism. I know men and women as they are—millions of them yet in the slime state. But I am an evolutionist, therefore a broad optimist, hence my love for the human (in the slime though he be) comes from my knowing him as he is and seeing the divine possibilities ahead of him." As for style: ". . . remember that anybody, by hard work, can achieve *precision of language*, but that very few can achieve *strength of style* . . . What the world wants is strength of utterance, not precision of utterance."

And strength of utterance was what Jack London's readers were to receive in full measure for the next few years, while his sales mounted and his fame grew. Much that he wrote during this time was excellent; even short stories turned out rapidly for immediate cash. By the time he was thirty many were predicting for him a secure place in literature for all time. But there were some who declined to predict his future course. Even Julian Hawthorne, a great admirer, was cautious about "this 'prodigious youngster of twenty-eight' who is at once passionate idealist and brute materialist. The theme of his ambitious novel *The Sea Wolf* is just this conflict between idealism and materialism, and as one follows the steps in his career, one cannot but wonder which of the two forces will triumph in his work and life."

In many ways this was for him a winter of discontent. Even when the divorce proceedings were at last under way he was unable to face either the present or the future with any degree of equanimity. Restlessness plagued him and, surrounded by friends, he was often lonely. Nor did his writing bring him satisfaction, although once he would have rejoiced not only in the effortless performance of his work, but in the sums he received for it. In a moment of bitterness he wrote to Bamford, "I wish I had never opened the books at all—not only biology, but Browning, Milton, Shakespeare, and all the rest, including that charlatan-philosopher, Emerson."

One strong interest sustained him: the growing storm in Russia. When in January 1905 he was asked to speak at the regular university meeting at the University of California on the twentieth, he promptly accepted. Two days before Bloody Sunday in St Petersburg he faced an audience of students and professors who were confidently expecting the author of *The Call of the Wild* to speak on literature, with: "I received a letter the other day. It was from a man in Arizona. It began, 'Dear Comrade.' It ended, 'Yours for the Revolution.' I replied to the letter, and my letter began 'Dear Comrade.' It ended, 'Yours for the Revolution.' "

Midway he appealed directly to the students: "As I look over the universities of my land today, I see the students asleep, asleep in the face of the awful facts of poverty I have given you, asleep in the greatest revolution that has come to the world. Oh, it is sad! Not long ago revolutions began, grew, broke out in Oxford. Today Russian universities seethe with revolution. I say to you, then: in the full glory of life, here's a cause that appeals to all the romance in you. Awake! awake to its call!"

And he closed his speech with: "The capitalist class has been indicted. It has failed in its management and its management is to be taken away from it. Seven million men of the working class say that they are going to get the rest of the working class to join with them and take the management away. The revolution is here, now. Stop it who can."

To Bamford he wrote, "Certainly, my idea was not to modify, when I gave it (the Revolution speech) at the U. C., but to make it a stinging blow, right between the eyes, and shake their mental processes up a bit, even if I incurred the risk of being called a long-haired anarchist." This was precisely what he was called on many occasions during the ensuing months while he urged his passionate espousal of the Russian revolution in numerous speeches and articles, and prominently identified himself—to the delight of the Socialist party leaders who appreciated the value of this advertising—with the socialist movement.

Before the month of January was over a call was issued to the American Socialists to express their solidarity with the Russian revolution in a practical way by collecting money and sending it to the Russian leaders. Jack's name was signed to this document, along with those of Eugene V. Debs, Victor Berger, Morris Hillquit, A. M. Simons, J. A. Wayland and others. Nominated again that spring by the Socialist party for mayor of Oakland, he received nearly a thousand votes as compared with his two hundred and forty-five four years earlier.

When *The War of the Classes*, a collection of socialistic essays appeared in April 1905, the *International Socialist Review* wrote triumphantly, "Just now Jack London's fame as an author is being pushed close by his notoriety as a socialist. At least that is the way the capitalist critics put it. The trouble with London is that he is not the ordinary kind of a literary socialist. It would be easy to name a half dozen prominent writers of the last decade who have occasionally admitted that they were socialists, but their socialism was generally of such a mild inoffensive sort that it didn't hurt them much with their capitalist friends. London, however, is the genuine, old-fashioned, proletarian, class struggle socialist. His socialism is like everything else about him, virile, combative and genuine to the backbone. . . . There are enough striking illustrations and strong quotations between the covers of this little book to supply a small army of soap box orators with ammunition."

Typical of the opinion of the other camp was a review of the same book in *The Bookman*: ". . . Certainly no other American, and probably no English writer, has produced anything in the advocacy of socialism that can compare with it in forcefulness and literary merit." The following year his essay, "What Life Means to Me," met a similar determined broad-mindedness from many critics. "Whatever may be thought of Mr London's social theories," wrote one of them, "there can be but one opinion of his mastery of English style. There is nothing dead about his literary art. Its spell holds thousands who hate and fear his 'views.'"

It was during that summer of 1905 that the differences between the Left and the Right wings in the Socialist party definitely crystallized. As a result of the growing class consciousness of the workers, 1905 was marked by some of the most vicious struggles in the history of the labor movement. Among these was the Chicago Teamsters' strike in which a number were killed and hundreds were wounded. The membership of the A. F. of L. had jumped from around two hundred and seventy thousand to a little over a million and a half, and the Socialist party had trebled the twelve thousand members it had had in 1901.

The socialism of the Right wing was in reality a radical populism. Having espoused the cause of the small businessman who was being crushed by monopoly, it regarded the workers essentially as a tail end to the middle class in its fight for self-preservation. Its whole policy was oriented toward making the Socialist party as effective a vote-getting machine as possible, and it hoped in the end to bring about a peaceful transformation of capitalist society into a socialist one through a parliamentary majority.

Repelled by the Right wing's neutral attitude toward the trade-union movement and its temporizing with the Gompers officialdom, the Left wing struck out for militant industrial unionism outside of the A. F. of L., whose continued indifference toward organizing the unorganized masses and narrow craft unionism were too much for their indignant impatience. In 1904 an informal conference had been held in Chicago by six prominent Socialists and trade unionists. These men, with the subsequent co-operation of others, were responsible for launching the Industrial Workers of the World, later to be known as the Wobblies. As a result of its activity among the unorganized unskilled workers, this organization was frequently referred to by its opponents as "I Won't Work," "I Want Whisky," "International Wonder Workers," "Irresponsible Wholesale Wreckers," "Imperial Wilhelm's Workers" and similar uncomplimentary titles.

The first convention of the I.W.W. was held in Chicago in June of the following year. Clarence Smith, general secretary-treasurer of the American Labor Union, explained the reasons for initiating the I.W.W.: ". . . It therefore seemed the first duty of conscientious union men, regardless of affiliation, prejudice or personal interest, to lay the foundation upon which all the working people, many of whom are now organized, might unite upon a common ground to build a labor organization that would correspond to modern industrial conditions, and through which they might finally secure complete emancipation from wage-slavery for all wage workers."

The two main sources of the I.W.W. were Daniel De Leon's theory of industrial unionism, and the militant, uncompromising spirit of the Western Federation of Miners. As a matter of fact the American Labor Union, which, as one writer said, was merely another name for the Western Federation of Miners, formed the backbone of the I.W.W. The whole ideology of the organization was permeated by the defiance of the unskilled and revolutionary workers; its trend was toward the mass in the gutter and constituted an unmistakable challenge to the skilled aristocrat of labor.

At the very start the new organization was threatened by the divergence of opinion which existed among the predominant elements attending its first convention. On such general conceptions as the unceasing struggle between capital and labor and the necessity of overthrowing the wage system and thereby abolishing capitalism, they were essentially in agreement, but the means of achieving this goal brought out the differences among them.

Those who advocated the "identity of interest" between capital and labor and the typical "Gomperite" were conspicuously absent. Vincent St John classified the leading elements at the first convention as follows: parliamentary Socialists, two types: impossibilists (Marxian) and opportunists (reformist); anarchists; industrial unionists, and "labor union fakers." By the latter term was understood careerists eager to profit personally by the movement even though, in order to do so, they would have to attach themselves insincerely, to be sure, to some doctrinal faction. Despite the ambiguity of the classification, it somewhat defined the various tendencies.

Three outstanding leaders of the radical movement of the time, De Leon, Eugene V. Debs and "Big Bill" Haywood, were the most influential of the early leaders of the I.W.W. Debs voiced the optimism and the earnestness of purpose which was shared by many at the outset of the movement when he said, "I believe it is possible for such an organization as the Western Federation of

Miners to be brought into harmonious relations with the Socialist Trade and Labor Alliance . . . and I believe it is possible for
these elements . . . to combine here . . . and begin the work of
forming a great economic or revolutionary organization of the
working class so sorely needed in the struggle for their emancipation."

Haywood, who had already gained fame as an uncompromising fighter in the fierce struggles of the Western Federation of
Miners, and who was destined still later to become widely known
as the champion of the neglected unskilled workers and to figure
in many sensational battles between labor and capital, came out of
the West full of militant spirit. He did not believe in agreements
or contracts. "We have not got an agreement existing with any
mine manager, superintendent, or operator at the present time,"
he said. "We have got a minimum scale of wages . . . the eight-
hour day, and we did not have a legislative lobby to accomplish
it." Now he wanted to build a similar kind of organization for all
industries.

It was Haywood who aptly characterized the attitude of the
I.W.W. toward the A.F. of L.: "It has been said that this convention was to form an organization rival to the A.F. of L. This
is a mistake. We are here for the purpose of forming a *labor* organization."

The most prominent man at the convention, Daniel De Leon,
said, "During this process of pounding one another, both sides
have learned, and I hope and believe that this convention will
bring together those who will plant themselves squarely upon the
class struggle and will recognize the fact that the political expression of labor is but the shadow of the economic organization."

With the exception of Debs and a few others, the members of
the Socialist party were afraid that De Leon would make of the
I.W.W. the same shadow of the Socialist Labor party as he had
earlier made of the Socialist Trade and Labor Alliance. Most of
the leading Socialists still believed in boring from within locally,
and did not think it necessary for the economic organization to
have any political connections. But to the extent of looking upon
the craft union as a most effective instrument for continuing the
capitalist system, they were in agreement with De Leon.

The element which was later to become dominant in the
I.W.W., the direct actionist and antipolitical group, among whom
were certain anarchist tendencies, developed from the Left wing

of the Socialist party. These veered rapidly toward syndicalism as a reaction against the parliamentary opportunistic socialism of the Socialist party and the sectarianism and "purity" of the Socialist Labor party.

Before it hit its main stride just prior to the war with the influx of the agricultural workers the organization went through precarious stages and was threatened with bitter factional struggles, marked finally by the withdrawal of the Western Federation of Miners. The Socialists who remained loyal to the Socialist party left during the first few years because the I.W.W. advocated "direct action and sabotage."

The fight which resulted in 1908 in the establishment for a time of two I.W.W.s was between the De Leon faction, which was described as doctrinaire, and the direct-actionist faction of St John. The point at issue was whether or not to retain the political clause in the preamble. De Leon fought for it; St John and Trautmann were opposed. The latter won. Following this defeat the De Leonites organized the Detroit I.W.W., which did not last long. St John, who possessed great organizational skill, became the undisputed theoretical leader of the I.W.W. This remarkable man, who never attained the mass prominence of many others, and who lived as much as possible in obscurity, even as he died in San Francisco unknown to legions of his friends, will always be remembered by the affectionate nickname, "the Saint."

De Leon had striven to have the organization not only wage war on the capitalists primarily in the "economic field," "in the shop" and "on the job," by strikes and boycotts, but he wanted it to go further "under the protecting guns of a labor political party." To him the trade unions were the nuclei of the future society, and he desired to win over the labor movement for revolutionary socialism. He despaired of achieving any economic unity of the workers in the A.F. of L., but in the I.W.W. he saw such an opportunity. Economic unity was to him the basis for the political unity of the class.

In the West the Wobblies were bitterly opposed to both the Socialist party and the Socialist Labor party. To them affiliation or any kind of entanglement with either would seriously compromise the future of the movement. Without any theoretical opinions of the state, but solely as a result of their own local experiences, they repudiated political action of any sort; many times parliamentarism was mistakenly confused with this.

Led by John H. Walsh, the "Overall Brigade" made a success-ful tour from the Pacific coast to Chicago, dressed in blue over-alls, black shirts and red ties, and wearing I.W.W. buttons. They held meetings in all the important towns on their itinerary, and each meeting heard the lusty blast of "Hallelujah, I'm a bum!" De Leon, who was extremely effective in the East, could make but little headway with this overalled constituency. He was no more impressed by them than they were by him, and dismissed them as "traveling bumwards."

The I.W.W. was essentially a prewar movement, reflecting not only the political immaturity of the unskilled migratory workers, but their brutal exploitation and American revolutionary tradi-tion. Its history is a long trail of red from the blood shed by its martyrs. The names of Joe Hill, Frank Little and countless others will always stand out as those of fearless pioneers of a movement fighting, wisely or unwisely, for economic emancipation.

From the very beginning the movement knew no color line, creed or nationality. It was "one big union." George Speed typi-fied this ideology when he raised his voice in one of the early con-ventions against the chauvinism of the white workers toward the Japanese, the brown menace which was replacing the yellow peril. Fighting against terrific odds, the I.W.W. filled prisons and left its dead in many a city street and rural community in the struggle for "free speech." No territory was too tough for them. Disre-garding danger, they invaded it if exploited workers were to be found there. In dirty boxcars through fields of golden wheat, in timber camps hidden by forests, on the water fronts of cities pulsating with commercial and industrial life, the I.W.W. left its imprint of uncompromising struggle against capitalism.

In its heyday the I.W.W. was the symbol of the romantic period of the American labor movement. The World War and American participation in it, and the period immediately follow-ing, saw the beginnings of its downward course. Its disintegra-tion was the price the workers had to pay for the inadequacy of the labor political parties of the time, but it was a price that has left its compensation: solidarity and militant struggle.

Jack, although he was yet to appreciate the significance of the influence of the Right wing over the leaders and the policies of the Socialist party, nevertheless regarded the appearance of the I.W.W. as rich with promise for future developments. He admired and respected its organizers, and its militant spirit was in complete harmony with his own at that particular time.

But even as his long interest in the socialist movement was approaching its culmination, other interests were taking shape which would run counter to it and in the end prove to be more powerful. In the middle of April he had gone to Sonoma County to visit Charmian, who had returned from the East and was staying with her aunt near the little town of Glen Ellen. And there before many months had passed he made two decisions whose effects were to be far reaching: to leave the city for good and reside henceforth in the country; and to build a boat and sail it around the world.

In June he purchased one hundred and twenty-nine acres in the vicinity, the first unit of what was to become his hillside ranch of fifteen hundred acres. "Oh, take my word," he wrote joyfully to Bamford, "there is no place like the country." As this new perspective unfolded, plans crowded thick and fast, every one of them entailing expenditures. He was scarcely under way in his schemes to develop the place as a home before he was deeply in debt. It was exhausted vineyard land that he had bought, and as such presented a challenge which, temperamentally at least, he could not evade. Although he announced to all and sundry that he had no intention of becoming a farmer or even of attempting to derive any part of his income from the ranch, but merely to make his home upon it, he was soon launched on the long, expensive series of experiments which would continue to the end of his life, to prove the value of scientific farming on his own land. On one point he did not protest in vain: the ranch never contributed to his income; on the contrary, it continually absorbed an enormous portion of what became a very large income from writing.

His move from Oakland marked a distinct break with his old life and associations—a break which had existed in fact for some time. Of the friends he had made at the start of his struggle to become a "brain merchant," Bamford was the sole survivor of any consequence. In July Jack sent Bamford his resignation as regular member of the Ruskin Club, "as I have now left Oakland for good."

Bess and his daughters had been installed in a bungalow not far from the house he had bought for his mother. All of them saw him only on his rare, brief visits to Oakland, when he occupied a room set apart for him in Flora's home. Bess, hurt and bewildered by the unexpected turn of events, devoted herself to her children, while Flora slowly and reluctantly resigned herself to a drab existence on the far edge of her son's life. As she moved heavily into her sixties, she rebelled more than once at her economic dependence and the dullness of her life. When she gathered together a few piano pupils or undertook to bake bread for several regular customers, she was regarded by friends and relatives as eccentric or perversely desirous of making it appear that Jack was not properly caring for his mother. She vouchsafed no explanations, but when she was asked to cease her activities she yielded quietly.

It was during the summer that the first unit of the ranch was bought that a suggestion offered first in jest—to outdo Captain Slocum in sailing around the world in a small sailboat—took definite form. Despite the debts he had incurred Jack's financial prospects never looked brighter. Writing already completed or under way, as well as stories and books sketched and ready to be written, would, he was sure, bring in more than sufficient money to meet both his needs and his pleasures. But, unaware, he was binding himself to a servitude from which he would never be released. Had he forgotten what he had written not many years earlier about the "writer folk" whose "standard of living goes up as fast as their capacity for winning bread increases?" He genuinely disliked being in debt, therefore he determined to get clear of it as rapidly as possible. "Rushing faster than ever these days," he told Bamford at the beginning of autumn.

He had agreed to go East that winter on a lecture tour, welcoming the generous fees offered by various women's clubs, as well as the opportunity such a trip would offer to speak for the socialist cause. At the end of November he would be legally free to marry Charmian. Then, upon completion of the tour, he would hasten back to California, to the ranch, to the building of the boat, and to the writing which would pay for these luxuries, and more.

CHAPTER

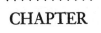

22

JACK LONDON'S first and only lecture tour progressed smoothly for only a limited time before a mounting wave of criticism engulfed him. By the time he returned to California three months after leaving he had become the target of attacks from every quarter, not excluding the Socialist party.

Depending upon the organization which sponsored his speech, he was variously billed as "Daring traveler, an original Klondiker, an experienced seaman, a prominent Socialist, the American Kipling," or, "Novelist and Socialist friend of the Under Dog." By invitation of the faculty of Bowdoin College, for instance, he spoke of his "experiences as Tramp, Klondiker and Correspondent, with reading." To radical groups he delivered his essay, "Revolution."

The first blow to his popularity as a speaker was the result of his precipitate marriage to Charmian Kittredge in Chicago toward the end of November, immediately upon receiving word from California that a final decree of divorce had been granted to Bess. It was all too apparent to the good people who belonged to various clubs and literary societies that Jack London had "abandoned his wife and babies for another woman." Women's clubs in Iowa passed resolutions rebuking him for having left his first wife, and cancellations of lecture engagements came in from all sections of the country.

In interviews Jack retaliated savagely. Then, perceiving the futility of fighting a prejudice so deeply rooted, he sank into bitter silence. If not only strangers, but certain friends as well, had been able to keep their own counsel on this matter, it is possible that what amounted eventually to a "persecution mania" of Jack's might not have had such an excellent start, and everyone concerned been better off.

Jack's soft shirts, greeted at first as "delightfully Western," soon became ominous symbols of the socialism he openly preached. "Perhaps he wears it for comfort," commented many, "but it is reasonable to suspect that London may also be partial to it as the garb of the wage worker whose cause he so vigorously champions." Others, with severe logic, questioned his socialism itself. Apparently he took this belief very seriously, but what, they asked, about the Korean servant who traveled everywhere with him? P.S. Williams reported in the *Overland Monthly:* " 'He even sat in his chair and let that heathen Jap bring him a drink!' indignantly declared one hard-boiled capitalist who had become rich by shining his own shoes and shaving himself for some three-score years." And, indeed, the spectacle of the president of the Intercollegiate Socialist Society, whom the *International Socialist Review* had described as a "genuine, old-fashioned, proletarian, class struggle socialist," traveling about the country in Pullman cars and accompanied by a Korean valet was more than a little ridiculous.

The Intercollegiate Socialist Society had come into being in September 1905. In the 1904 presidential election the Socialists had quadrupled their 1900 vote, polling four hundred thousand. This tangible indication that socialism was interesting greater and greater numbers of Americans, and the sympathy expressed on every hand the following year, even in unexpected quarters, for the revolutionary workers in Russia, inspired Upton Sinclair, George Strobell and a few others to organize a society to promote "an intelligent interest in Socialism among college men and women, graduate and undergraduate." A call was issued, signed by ten outstanding Socialists, including Jack London, and at an organizational meeting in New York on September twelfth, under the chairmanship of W. J. Ghent, Jack London was unanimously elected the first president of the Intercollegiate Socialist Society, an office he held until his resignation in May 1907.

The organization met sharp criticism from the conservative press. *Collier's Weekly,* which, a few months later, very inconsistently paid Jack London five hundred dollars for "Revolution," although it never published the essay, attacked Thomas Wentworth Higginson, known affectionately as "the grand old man of Harvard," for placing his name on the call. Higginson's reply that the society hoped to create *students of socialism*, not to produce Socialists, reflected the attitude of many moderates within the party or sympathetic to it. Some Socialists, however, among them Bamford, protested the organization of the society on tactical grounds and refused to support it.

Jack's confidence that the movement would actually "produce Socialists," indicative of his ardor for the cause at this time, placed him far to the Left of the moderates, and resulted in the only open disagreement he ever had with Bamford. "It is my firm belief," he wrote Bamford in February 1906, "that the groups of the I.S.S., in the different Universities, will be captured by the Socialists and will themselves ultimately make of the I.S.S. a Socialist organization.

"I found colleges in the East where there were only one or two Socialists, and where, therefore, a Socialist group could not be formed. On the other hand, in those same colleges I found a number of Socialistically inclined and non-Socialist students, earnest and sincere, who were eager to form an I.S.S. group. In such instances there could have been no straight Socialist group formed at all. Nothing would have been done.

"As it is, a socialistic group is formed, and I doubt not that the majority of the members will be hammered into Socialism, and a small minority hammered out of the group. In the meantime, discussion takes place, reading is done, and the word 'Socialism' becomes a less misunderstood term in such a college."

And three days later: ". . . I am, however, very sorry that we are to direct our efforts against each other rather than against the common enemy. A lot of us get together and work hard to form the I.S.S. and when we've got a lot of men interested, some of the other comrades direct their efforts to turning the men whom we have interested away from the purpose in which we have interested them. Of course, it's all immaterial, and will be just the same in a thousand years; but nevertheless it is the amusing side of it that strikes my funny-bone.

"Because you do not back up Sinclair's call, and because you don't think our tactics are the best in this very minor movement, is all very well; but I scarcely see why such act and belief should necessarily impel you to action against this little minor movement."

It took far less than a thousand years to prove not only the immateriality of the disagreement but Jack's overoptimism as well. The society developed slowly, finally achieving sixty or seventy undergraduate chapters in various colleges and about a dozen alumni groups during the great years of the Socialist party, which climaxed its vote-getting efforts in 1912 with a vote of nine hundred thousand. When the Second International went to pieces during the war the I.S.S. succumbed along with it. A handful of devoted survivors struggled to revive it until 1921 when, in order "that the society might adjust itself to the broader basis for study and discussion increasingly demanded by college students and groups interested in our work," it became the League for Industrial Democracy.

Jack London invaded even Harvard and Yale that winter with lectures under the auspices of the I.S.S. "In the great room of the Harvard Union," wrote John Ellis, "sat two thousand university men—the pick and flower of perhaps the most luxurious bourgeois society in the world." Looking at Jack on the platform, these young men liked him, his smile, the warmth of his personality, his "football physique," and, liking him, they could not believe that he meant what he said in his indictment of the capitalist order whose heirs they were. The tales of injustice and suffering he told them struck them as fantastic, and they laughed.

Striving to startle them into at least a recognition of the reality of the class struggle, he used his most vivid colors in a bold description of the scope of the international revolutionary movement and the deadly earnestness of its purpose. ". . . In the United States we are enabled to carry on this revolution peaceably," he said in essence. "In Russia it is not so. If the law does not permit peaceable destruction of society, they will resort to force themselves. They will meet violence with violence . . . In Russia there is no civilization. The government executes revolutionists . . . I am a revolutionist, yet I am a fairly sane and normal individual. I speak and think of these 'assassins' in Russia as my comrades. So do all the comrades in America, and all the seven million comrades in the world. This is shown by the fact that we do back up all the comrades in Russia. They are not disciples of Tolstoy, nor are we. We are revolutionists!" At this the

Harvard college boys decided to humor him and applauded up-roariously.

Jack had been delighted with Paul Shorey's description of the university scholastic ideal as "the passionless pursuit of passionless intelligence." The basis of his contempt for college education as he had found it was precisely its lack of passion, of vitality, of awareness of life. But this complete indifference to the fate of millions of fellow human beings which he encountered among the students in the wealthy Eastern universities shocked him.

At Yale he challenged the students even more forcefully than he had at California. Woolsey Hall was crowded. At least a hundred professors were present and more than a thousand students. In addition there were hundreds of citizens, Socialists and socialist sympathizers, and many workers who, determined that Jack should receive a hearing, were prepared for trouble.

"I went to the University," Jack told the students. "I found the University, in the main, practically wholly so, clean and noble, but I did not find the university alive. I found that the American university had this ideal, as phrased by a professor in Chicago University, namely: 'The passionless pursuit of passionless intelligence'—clean and noble, I grant you, but not alive enough . . . And the reflection of this university ideal I find—the conservatism and unconcern of the American people toward those who are suffering, who are in want. And so I became interested in an attempt to arouse in the minds of the young men of our universities an interest in the study of socialism . . . We do not desire merely to make converts . . . If collegians cannot fight for us, we want them to fight against us—of course, sincerely fight against us. But what we do not want is that which obtains today and has obtained in the past of the university, a mere deadness and unconcern and ignorance so far as socialisim is concerned. Fight for us or fight against us! Raise your voices one way or the other; be alive!"

Alexander Irvine, who practically singlehanded had arranged the Yale meeting, reported: "A woman—a lady—went out swearing. A few students tried hard to sneer, but succeeded rather indifferently . . . Jack London gripped by the intellect and held them . . . There was some applause at the beginning and some at the close, but at neither end was it intense or prolonged."

A portion of the press strove to be high-minded and adopt a

liberal tone toward Jack's socialistic speeches. An editorial in the
Yale Review took the unassailable position that people "should
hear and know about these things," at the same time deploring
the lack of "constructive suggestions or of original information"
from Jack. One newspaper felt that the speech, far from being
a catastrophe, was a good thing, for now people would awaken
to the danger and stem the tide of radicalism by—introducing
reforms! More than one editorial writer soothed outraged citizens by pointing to the fierce activity of the muckrakers in their
exposures of graft and assuring them that waves of reform would
undoubtedly soon "deprive the socialist of his excuse for preaching his doctrines."

The New York Times did a neat job of red-baiting. Praising
Jack for his fearless manner and forthright presentation, com-
mending him for his "courage and honesty," and commenting
that the best way to understand socialism was from such people,
it blandly repeated Jack's most revolutionary phrases and statements, out of context, for the benefit of its conservative readers.

Now it was the turn of the Socialist party bigwigs to be horrified. Comrade London had gone too far! Granted that he had
been misrepresented and misquoted. Granted that he had not
given the words "To hell with the Constitution!" as his own, but
had quoted those of Major General Bell of Colorado to striking
miners, not only as an example of "the spirit animating the
capitalist satraps," but "to warn the capitalists that the workers
may someday use the same term if the capitalists insist upon making reverence for the Constitution an excuse to continue labor's
oppression." Besides, had he not also quoted Eugene Debs's
"There is no good capitalist and no bad workingman," and made
a very bad impression upon people who might not be Socialists
but were at least sympathetic? Something must be done or the
party would lose support and votes!

In vain the Right wingers had sought to make it clear that all
Socialists did not take Jack London's "extreme" view of things.
Introducing Jack at a big meeting in the Grand Central Palace
in New York, J. G. Phelps Stokes had openly declared that he
and a number of others did not agree with London that "the
catastrophe which these things (the accumulation of wealth and
power in the hands of the few, and the like) threaten will necessarily come upon us."

As a party spokesman, Upton Sinclair undertook to answer the

New York *Times* editorial and show how really harmless Jack's speech had been, after all. "The blood-red banner?" Jack had meant by that a "symbol of the Brotherhood of Man, and not of war and destruction." True, Jack had·said something like, "We Socialists will wrest the power from the present rulers by war if necessary. Stop us if you can!" But Jack had not meant that at all in relation to the United States, where, as in all countries in which universal suffrage and free speech prevailed, the Socialist party was a party of constitutional agitation. Everyone knew that the Socialists resorted to force only in those countries where those rights were denied. Mr Sinclair bogged down pretty badly when he tried to contradict the *Times's* statement that all Socialists were working for the redistribution of wealth, for he seemed unable to make it clear just what the Socialists *were* working for in that connection, but he ended on a high note. To the *Times's* salute to Jack—"few Socialists have Jack London's courage"—Sinclair replied, as convincingly as possible under the circumstances, "They're all courageous!"

The little town of Derby Neck, Connecticut, precipitated a minor crisis when its public library banned Jack's books from the shelves and sent out copies of resolutions urging other libraries to take similar action. More serious was the hue and cry that followed immediately: "Boycott all magazines which contain stories by Jack London!" The *Press* in Grand Rapids, Michigan, remarked, "A number of newspapers are calling for the novelist's suppression."

Jack, hurt and baffled by the reception accorded his activity on behalf of the one thing he felt mattered most to him, not only from those who professed to admire his far less sincere literary work, but from his comrades in the movement as well, listened to the advice which poured in from all quarters and made no comment. But once back in California, in the midst of developing his ranch, building his boat and writing wholly acceptable stories and books to meet his mounting expenses, Jack acted, and began work on *The Iron Heel*.

Four years earlier in *Our Benevolent Feudalism*, W. J. Ghent had summed up the dominant economic tendencies in the United States as "an irresistible movement—now almost at its culmination —toward great combinations in specific trades; next toward coalescence of kindred industries; and thus toward the complete integration of capital." Out of these changes and their effects already being manifested upon people in all walks of life, rose his prediction of the emergence of "a renascent Feudalism, which, though it differs in many forms from that of the time of Edward I, is yet based upon the same status of lord, agent, and underling."

Jack had been tremendously impressed by Ghent's book when it first appeared. Now, disillusioned with the American socialist movement, contemptuous of the pacifism, cowardice and essential insincerity of its leaders, and with Ghent's prognosis of the integration of capital not only verified but exposed on every hand by the blazing torches of the muckrakers, he took Ghent's thesis of the emergence of a new feudalism and reared upon it the brilliant superstructure of *The Iron Heel.*

He had never considered the masses capable of helping themselves; on the contrary, he had long been convinced that the many "fool men" would always have to be led by the few, superior individuals. Until now he had been unwilling to question the abilities of the leaders of the Socialist party. Enthusiastic and confident, he had challenged: "The revolution is here, now. Stop it who can!" More than once he had declared: "Socialism wins this century!" But his experiences during the winter of 1905–06 had opened his eyes. At a time when leadership was needed more than ever before he believed that the Socialist party had no leaders worthy of the name.

A sentence from Ghent's book—"A gigantic merger of all interests, governed by a council of ten, may supplant the individual dukedoms and baronies in the different industries"—had fired his imagination. Brushing aside Ghent's ironic description of the coming feudalism as "benevolent," Jack evoked the vision of the oligarchy, which would "walk upon the faces of the working class" and crush them under the "iron heel of a despotism as relentless and terrible as any despotism that has blackened the pages of the history of man."

It was with this new perspective that he wrote *The Iron Heel,* reaffirming his faith in the ultimate achievement of socialism, but ruthlessly placing the overthrow of capitalism three long centuries ahead and, further to dramatize his points, exaggerating the weakness of the working class and the overwhelming strength of its oppressors. Nevertheless the book is in no sense of the word pessimistic. "Be alive!" Jack had told the young men of Yale. "Be alive!" he now exhorted the Socialists and class-conscious workers. "See the danger which threatens you. Wake from your dreams of ballot-box victories. Cease talking of the Brotherhood of Man, and prepare to fight for it!"

The Iron Heel was based on what Jack had absorbed from his study of Marxian economics and the many books he had read on kindred subjects, but events and incidents of the preceding few years crowded dramatically to the foreground. The 1905 Russian revolution and the organization of the I.W.W. contributed much to the militant spirit of the book, while the indignation he still felt as a result of his recent encounters with "respectable" Socialists, who feared the very word "revolution" and believed that one day capitalism would be peacefully voted out of existence, spurred him on in his determination to show them the fool's paradise they were living in.

That the Russian masses, oppressed past belief by the autocracy, had responded to the call of their leaders and actually risen in revolt gave Jack hope. If this could happen in a country like Russia surely no "iron heel" could permanently endure anywhere, even if the period of the insurrection had to continue for centuries. In the face of the savage retaliation against the defeated workers and revolutionists by the Russian government, were not the revolutionary leaders re-forming their ranks and preparing for a new revolt? Were not the stirring words of Ernest Everhard at the close of *The Iron Heel* essentially their words? "For this time lost . . . but not forever. We have learned. Tomorrow the Cause will rise again, strong with wisdom and discipline."

The one factor which tempered Jack's despair over the radical movement in America at this time was the formation of the I.W.W. Its avowed intention of organizing the unskilled workers and its militant industrial union program inspired him to believe that revolutionary sentiment was actually awakening in the American labor movement, and that the "elder statesmen in the A.F. of L.," as Ernest Untermann has put it, "would be shaken out of their complacency." Once workers were organized, they were no longer entirely helpless, Jack believed. If the I.W.W. succeeded even partially in organizing the unskilled workers along industrial union lines, what a source of power would be available during the revolutionary days to come! And, and most immediately, he asked, was not the organization of the I.W.W. a corroboration of the correctness of his own disagreement with the policies of the Socialist party?

His indictment of the party leaders for their refusal to gauge realistically the strength of the adversaries of the party and of the working class was both direct and implied in *The Iron Heel.* When organized labor had been crushed by the oligarchy with the help of the middle class, and then the middle class was liquidated in turn, Ernest Everhard pinned his faith thenceforth on revolution. "In this," wrote Jack, "he was in advance of his party. His fellow-socialists could not agree with him. They still insisted that victory could be gained through the elections . . . They were merely incredulous, that was all. Ernest could not get them seriously to fear the coming of the Oligarchy. They were stirred by him, but they were too sure of their own strength. There was no room in their theoretical social evolution for an oligarchy, therefore the Oligarchy could not be." And to drive the point home, Jack first permitted the Socialists a landslide vote in a national election in which they won fifty seats in Congress, and then demonstrated its meaninglessness when they found themselves with even less power than they had had before.

Assuming, perhaps with an excess of optimism, but probably for fictional purposes alone, that the minority demand for a general strike to be called at the first sign of mobilization for war, which had been voiced at the International Socialist Congress at Stuttgart in 1907 but rejected as impractical, had actually been adopted, Jack cunningly strengthened his case against the reformers. In *The Iron Heel* this use of labor's most powerful weapon was spectacularly successful in stopping war between the United States and Germany before a shot was fired. But such was the power of the oligarchy that the unprecedented victory of a united international working class did not deter in the slightest its monstrous growth.

The types of active revolutionists which he sketched in this book were at once a rebuke and a challenge to the smug, pacifist Socialists he detested. Except for Everhard, his hero, he did not concern himself especially with the leaders of the revolutionary forces beyond intimating that their intelligence, wisdom, courage and idealism were little short of superhuman, but his description of what he named the "fighting groups" was enthusiastic. "The bravest, and the most combative and self-sacrificing of our comrades went into the Fighting Groups," he wrote; and in a footnote: "Everhard was the father of this curious army . . . In some respects, despite his great economic and sociological contributions,

and his work as a general leader of the Revolution, his organization of the Fighting Groups must be regarded as his greatest
achievement."

According to Jack, these groups were "modeled somewhat after
the Fighting Organization of the Russian Revolution." His inspiration had been the Social Revolutionaries, a group which was
an expression of the Russian Populist movement. Due to the wide
publicity which resulted from their terrorist methods, the average
American radical was far better acquainted with this than with
other revolutionary organizations in Russia.

He had always thrilled to individual acts of bravery, especially
when a principle was involved. In *The Iron Heel* he glorified the
role of terrorists: "They gave up their lives for humanity, no
sacrifice was too great for them to accomplish, while inexorable
necessity compelled them to bloody expression in an age of blood.
The Fighting Groups constituted the one thorn in the side of the
Iron Heel that the Iron Heel could never remove."

Few of Jack London's books, even those which were consciously autobiographical, are so intensely personal as *The Iron
Heel.* Ernest Everhard was the revolutionist Jack would have liked
to be if he had not, unfortunately, also desired to be several other
kinds of men. His best knowledge of the class struggle and the
socialist movement, his best speeches and essays he gave to Everhard, as well as the achievements of other men. Everhard's book,
for instance, entitled *Working-class Philosophy,* was John Spargo's
Socialism: a Summary and Interpretation of Socialist Principles.
Everhard's love story and marriage were Jack's, and the revolutionists' Sonoma County refuge was placed on his recently
acquired ranch.

An experience which occurred shortly after his return from the
East indicates that even as early as April 1906 the book had
already taken shape in his mind: "In a dozen different quarters
. . . in the working-class ghetto, and in the factories, fires started
. . . All night these tens of thousands fled before the flames.
Many of them, the poor people from the labor ghetto, had fled all
day as well." These sentences might have been taken directly
from *The Iron Heel,* but they are to be found in "The Story of an
Eye-Witness," Jack London's story of the San Francisco quake
and fire, published in *Collier's* on May 5, 1906. Jack never forgot
the scenes he had witnessed during that day and night of terror
and destruction. They reappeared with telling effect years later

in his fantastic *The Scarlet Plague*, but his first use of them was in *The Iron Heel*. The closing scenes of the ill-fated First Revolt in Chicago were played against a sky darkened by smoke from the burning of the "great labor ghetto."

Of Jack's many experiences during his lecture tour, one which received no publicity at the time, although he referred to it often in conversations, was used in *The Iron Heel*. In the middle of December 1905 Jack had written to Bamford from New York, "Oh, I have some stories to tell you when I get back about my clashes with the masters of society!" During the early part of his stay in New York he had been invited to speak to an exclusive group of extremely wealthy men and women. Two accounts of this meeting are available, Jack's own story, which he told to members of the Socialist party in Oakland soon after his return and which was reported in the *Socialist Voice* for April 7, 1906, and one by Joshua Wanhope, contained in his article "In Memoriam," published in the New York *Call* on November 24, 1916. Both of these are basically alike, and both closely resemble the scene in *The Iron Heel* in which Ernest Everhard addressed the Philomath Club.

Jack's speech to the rich New Yorkers was clearly the first draft of the challenge flung by Everhard to the "masters of society" on the eve of the rise of the oligarchy. As Wanhope recalled the occasion, Jack climaxed his talk with a direct attack upon his audience: " 'You have been entrusted with the world; you have muddled and mismanaged it. You are incompetent, despite all your boastings. A million years ago the caveman, without tools, with small brain, and with nothing but the strength of his body, managed to feed his wife and children, so that through him the race survived. You, on the other hand, armed with all the modern means of production, multiplying the productive capacity of the caveman a million times—you incompetents and muddlers, you are unable to secure to millions even the paltry amount of bread that would sustain their physical life. You have mismanaged the world, and it shall be taken from you!'

"The 'silk-stockinged audience' murmured their perturbation, anger and impatience, but the unrelenting London went on: 'Who will take it from you? We will! And who are we? We are seven million socialist revolutionists and we are everywhere growing. And we want all you have! Look at us!' continued London, shaking his broad shoulders and stretching forth his muscular hands.

'We are strong! Consider our hands! They are strong hands, and even now they are reaching forth for all you have, and they will take it, take it by the power of their strong hands; take it from your feeble grasp. Long or short though the time may be, that time is coming. The army is on the march, and nothing can stop it, that you can stop it is ludicrous. It wants nothing less than all you have, and it will take it; you are incompetent and will have to surrender to the strong. We are the strong, and in that day we shall give you an exhibition of power such as your feeble brains never dreamed the world contained!'

"There was a loud murmur of protest and dissent and one or two respectable-looking persons choked up, and it seemed as if they were about to have apoplexy. London walked down from the rostrum through a sea of blasted, purple faces distorted with rage, but no attempt was made to detain him . . . It was not until he was well out of earshot that some of the stunned audience plucked up enough courage to remark that 'he ought to be in jail.' "

It was this reaction of the audience to Jack's scornful words which dictated the remainder of the powerful scene in *The Iron Heel* in which Everhard's challenge was accepted and flung back at him, and the issues involved forcefully and dramatically stated. " 'This, then, is our answer,' said Wickson (soon to become an oligarch). 'We have no words to waste on you. When you reach out your vaunted strong hands for our palaces and purpled ease, we will show you what strength is. In roar of shell and shrapnel and in whine of machine guns will our answer be couched. We will grind you revolutionists down under our heel, and we shall walk upon your faces. The world is ours, we are its lords, and ours it shall remain. As for the host of labor, it has been in the dirt since history began, and I read history aright. And in the dirt it shall remain so long as I and mine and those that come after us have the power. There is the word. It is the king of words— Power. Not God, not Mammon, but Power. Pour it over your tongue till it tingles with it. Power.' "

The reception accorded *The Iron Heel* did not surprise Jack. Magazines and newspapers which were in the habit of enthusiastically welcoming everything he wrote dismissed it with a few elaborately casual remarks or ignored it entirely; the socialist press reviewed and attacked it carefully. The Socialist party leaders shrewdly refused to be maneuvered into taking a stand either for or against it, but by their very silence condemned it. Taken by and large, however, the rank and file Socialists liked it, and such Left wingers as Debs, Haywood and Mary Marcy were outspoken in its praise.

The review in the *International Socialist Review* was written by John Spargo. "It is impossible to deny the literary skill which London displays in this ingenious and stirring romance," he said in closing. "He has written nothing more powerful than this book. In some senses it is an unfortunate book, and I am by no means disposed to join those of our comrades who hail it as a great addition to the literature of Socialist propaganda. The picture he gives is well calculated, it seems to me, to repel many whose addition to our forces is sorely needed; it gives a new impetus to the old and generally discarded cataclysmic theory; it tends to weaken the political Socialist movement by discrediting the ballot and to encourage the chimerical and reactionary notion of physical force, so alluring to a certain type or mind . . ."

A lengthy, unsigned review in the *Arena*, a magazine edited by a Socialist, B. O. Flower, attempted to correct the impression Jack had given of Socialists and socialism: "Considered from a literary and imaginative point of view . . . this is one of his greatest works of fiction; yet . . . it is to us the most disappointing work that has come from his pen." The *Arena* believed that precisely the opposite kind of literature was needed, literature which would "strengthen, encourage in spirit and hearten all reformers, no less than the people under the wheel . . . instill courage and moral enthusiasm and lead all friends of justice to unite fearlessly and resolutely in a step-by-step plan of progress that by peaceable means will lead to the triumph of justice." Mr London had surely "misread civilization since the dawn of modern times." The drama had been re-acted over and over again. Oppression increased, bore down cruelly, the people's cause seemed utterly without hope; "suddenly the great clock struck, suddenly the people, aroused, united and moved forward."

Even now, pointed out the *Arena*, the people were awakening. They should be cheered on, not discouraged. And they should be shown that "through uniting in a battle for direct legislation and the right to recall" and the like, their objectives can be obtained peacefully. "All talk of forcible revolution is not only foolish, but it is bound to injure the people's cause; and to picture the

plutocracy invincible and the people weak . . . is not conducive
to help the cause of social justice . . . The plutocracy is not invincible. The people can and will win, and we believe they will
win by peaceable measures."

"Of course," the anonymous commentator added kindly, "Mr
London has suffered so himself, and seen so much suffering of
others that he is unduly hopeless . . . Unfortunately his book is a
detriment rather than a help to the cause of social justice."

Thus did semiofficial socialist opinion dispose of Jack London's
greatest contribution to the socialist movement. Thenceforth no
cognizance was taken of the book by those whose policies directed
the progress of the Socialist party toward its tragic debacle during
the World War. In spite of being deprived of the official blessing,
however, it circulated widely among all whose political outlook
was more to the Left than to the Right. The Wobblies knew it
well, and the militant working-class element in the Socialist party.
Translations into various European languages soon added countless others to its following. To this day *The Iron Heel* remains a
perennial discovery made by those seeking for the first time to
learn something of the revolutionary movement.

In 1919 *The Iron Heel* was frequently referred to by both the
capitalist and radical press. An article in the New York *Times*, for
example, compared the description of street fighting in *The Iron
Heel* with what had actually taken place in Berlin during the
Spartakus Bund uprising. With the Palmer "red raids" in full
swing in the United States, the Socialist *Call* in New York was
fighting to keep its printing plant. A supporter wrote, ". . . Jack
London, in his splendid failure, *The Iron Heel*, warned Socialists
that their press might be taken away from them."

Even more significant was an article in the Butte *Daily Bulletin*,
reprinted in the New York *Post* on May 19, 1919—an article
originating in a section of the country which for long had been
a bloody battlefield in the struggle between capital and labor:
"Those who have read Jack London's *The Iron Heel* will have
no difficulty in recognizing the historical epoch through which
we are passing. The ruthless suppression of all groups opposed to
capitalism is outlined in this work. Many of the passages might,
without exaggeration, be termed prophetic.

"Many of labor's best and bravest are going to fall in the dark
days to come. Liberty for the workers is almost dead, but out of
the soil soaked with the blood of the martyrs to labor's cause, will

spring others who will carry on the fight . . . Yet the sons of labor will die as men should die, face to face with torture, called upon to give all they have to give. Heroes all, they will cry, as the martyred workers have always cried when their end was near: 'Freedom! We who are about to die, salute thee!' "

Four years later *The Iron Heel* received the accolade of Anatole France in a preface to the first edition published in French. Conditions in postwar Europe, the prostration of the socialist parties outside of Russia, and the slow, deadly concentration of the forces of reaction everywhere had not distorted or shortened France's historical perspective. ". . . For the moment, socialism in France, as well as in Italy and Spain," he wrote, "is too feeble to have anything to fear from the Iron Heel, for extreme weakness is the unique salvation of the weak. No Iron Heel will walk upon this dust of a party . . . But one day the struggle between Labor and Capital will recommence. Then will we see days like those of the revolts in San Francisco and Chicago whose unspeakable horror Jack London anticipates for us. . . .

"In 1907 they cried to Jack London, 'You are a frightful pessimist!' Sincere socialists accused him of throwing terror into the party. They were wrong. Those who possess the rare and precious gift of foresight must publish the dangers which they anticipate. I remember having heard the great Jaurès say several times: 'The strength of the classes against which we have to struggle is not sufficiently recognized among us. They are strong, and virtue is loaned them; the priests have abandoned the ethics of the church for that of the factory; and the moment classes are threatened, the whole of society will rush to protect them.' He was right, as London is right in holding up to us the prophetic mirror of our faults and our indiscretions.

"Let us not jeopardize the future; it is our own. The plutocracy will perish. In its very power the signs of its ruin may already be perceived. It will perish because every caste government is doomed to die; the wage system will perish because it is unjust. It will perish, swollen with pride and at the height of its power, just as slavery and serfdom have perished.

"Even now, if one observes it carefully, one can see that it is decrepit. This war, desired by the great commercial interests of all the countries in the world, this war which was their war, this war in which they placed hopes of new riches, has caused such widespread and deep destruction that the international oligarchy itself has been shaken and the day nears when it will collapse upon a ruined Europe.

"I cannot tell you that it will perish at one blow and without struggling. It will struggle. Its last war will perhaps be long, and of varying fortunes. Oh, ye heirs of the proletarians, ye generations of the future, children of the new days, you will struggle, and when cruel reverses make you doubt the success of your cause, you will again take courage and say with the noble Everhard: 'For this time lost, but not forever. We have learned. Tomorrow the Cause will rise again, strong with wisdom and discipline.' "

During those months in 1905 while Jack followed from a distance the fortunes of the Russian revolution, Leon Trotsky was actively participating in it. Within a few months of Jack's death, Trotsky was again an outstanding figure in a second and successful Russian revolution. Thirty years after *The Iron Heel* was written, this revolutionist read it for the first time.

"The book produced upon me," he wrote in 1937, "—I speak without exaggeration—a deep impression. Not because of its artistic qualities: the form of the novel here represents only an armor for social analysis and prognosis. The author is intentionally sparing in his use of artistic means. He is himself interested not so much in the individual fate of his heroes as in the fate of mankind. By this, however, I don't want at all to belittle the artistic value of the work, especially in its last chapters beginning with the Chicago commune. The pictures of civil war develop in powerful frescoes. Nevertheless, this is not the main feature. The book surprised me with the audacity and independence of its historical foresight.

"The world workers' movement at the end of the last and the beginning of the present century stood under the sign of reformism. The perspective of peaceful and uninterrupted world progress, of the prosperity of democracy and social reforms, seemed to be assured once and for all. The first Russian revolution, it is true, revived the radical flank of the German social-democracy and gave for a certain time dynamic force to anarcho-syndicalism in France. *The Iron Heel* bears the undoubted imprint of the year 1905. But at the time when this remarkable book appeared, the domination of counter-revolution was already consolidating itself in Russia. In the world arena the defeat of the Russian proletariat gave to reformism the possibility not only of regaining its temporarily lost positions but also of subjecting to itself completely the organized workers' movement. It is sufficient to recall that precisely in the following seven years (1907–14) the international social-democracy ripened definitely for its base and shameful role during the World War.

"Jack London not only absorbed creatively the impetus given by the first Russian revolution but also courageously thought over again in its light the fate of capitalist society as a whole. Precisely those problems which the official socialism of this time considered to be definitely buried: the growth of wealth and power at one pole, of misery and destitution at the other pole; the accumulation of social bitterness and hatred; the unalterable preparation of bloody cataclysms—all those questions Jack London felt with an intrepidity which forces one to ask himself again and again with astonishment: when was this written? really before the war?

"One must accentuate especially the role which Jack London attributes to the labor bureaucracy and to the labor aristocracy in the further fate of mankind. Thanks to their support the American plutocracy not only succeeds in defeating the workers' insurrection but also in keeping its iron dictatorship during the following three centuries. We will not dispute with the poet the delay which can but seem to us too long. However, it is not a question of Jack London's pessimism, but of his passionate effort to shake those who are lulled by routine, to force them to open their eyes and to see what is and what approaches. The artist is audaciously utilizing the methods of hyperbole. He is bringing the tendencies rooted in capitalism: of oppression, cruelty, bestiality, betrayal, to their extreme expression. He is operating with centuries in order to measure the tyrannical will of the exploiters and the treacherous role of the labor bureaucracy. But his most 'romantic' hyperboles are finally much more realistic than the bookkeeper-like calculations of the so-called 'sober politicians.'

"It is easy to imagine with what a condescending perplexity the official socialist thinking of that time met Jack London's menacing prophecies. If one took the trouble to look over the reviews of *The Iron Heel* at that time in the German *Neue Zeit* and *Vorwaerts*, in the Austrian *Kampf* and *Arbeiterzeitung*, as well as in the other Socialist publications of Europe and America, he could easily convince himself that the thirty-year-old 'romanticist' saw incomparably more clearly and farther than all the social-democratic leaders of that time taken together. But Jack London bears comparison in this domain not only with the reformists. One can say with assurance that in 1907 not one of the revolutionary Marxists, not excluding Lenin and Rosa Luxemburg, imagined so fully the ominous perspective of the alliance between finance capital and labor aristocracy. This suffices in itself to determine the specific weight of the novel.

"The chapter, 'The Roaring Abysmal Beast,' undoubtedly constitutes the focus of the book. At the time when the novel appeared this apocalyptical chapter must have seemed to be the boundary of hyperbolism. However, the consequent happenings have almost surpassed it. And the last word of class struggle has not yet been said by far! The 'Abysmal Beast' is to the extreme degree oppressed, humiliated, and degenerated people. Who would now dare to speak for this reason about the artist's pessimism? No, London is an optimist, only a penetrating and far-sighted one. 'Look into what kind of abyss the bourgeoisie will hurl you down, if you don't finish with them!' This is his thought. Today it sounds incomparably more real and sharp than thirty years ago. But still more astonishing is the genuinely prophetic vision of the methods by which the Iron Heel will sustain its domination over crushed mankind. London manifests remarkable freedom from reformistic pacifist illusions. In this picture of the future there remains not a trace of democracy and peaceful progress. Over the mass of the deprived rise the castes of labor aristocracy, of praetorian army, of an all-penetrating police, with the financial oligarchy at the top. In reading it, one does not believe his own eyes: it is precisely the picture of fascism, of its economy, of its governmental technique, its political psychology! The fact is incontestable: in 1907 Jack London already foresaw and described the fascist regime as the inevitable result of the defeat of the proletarian revolution. Whatever may be the single 'errors' of the novel—and they exist—we cannot help inclining before the powerful intuition of the revolutionary artist."

23

ALTHOUGH Jack London's life was one which fell far short of fulfillment and he lived many years of mediocrity after his promise had spent itself, no single event marked that end. One traces it rather by jagged edges, as if a sheet of paper had been clumsily torn across.

During, roughly, the years 1906 to 1910 his work, his interests and the man himself underwent great change as the more compelling of the desires and ambitions he had acknowledged years earlier inexorably established their ascendancy over the weaker. Not all at once did he permit the latter to give way and fall back. He could not believe that all things were not possible for him, nor admit that making a great deal of money and living accordingly would not affect him in fundamental ways.

Even when his one-time devotion to the socialist cause had become merely a nostalgic sentiment, alien to his life, he clung to it stubbornly, deceiving himself for some time with loud words and empty gestures. Consistently he maintained a bold front in regard to the quality of his literary output, though none knew better than he how tawdry it was and how he was misusing his talents. And to the very end, despite all provocation, he kept up what had become pure bluff, that he loved life and was finding it finer and more satisfying than he had ever dreamed it could be. " ' 'E liked it all,' " he was fond of quoting from Kipling, but as the years passed more than a hint of defiance was in his voice, for though in increasing measure he was getting some of the things he had thought he wanted, Jack was finding very little in life that he liked.

The conflict between Jack's socialist beliefs and his writing career, which resulted in contradictions that have mystified many, was never so clearly demonstrated as during the period which immediately followed the lecture tour. A tempting offer from a large Eastern magazine to investigate and write up the child-labor situation in the Southern cotton mills placed him in a quandary. His interest in socialism and the class struggle, intensified by his contempt for the leaders and policies of the Socialist party, was at its height. He was preparing to write *The Iron Heel.* At the same time he was undertaking expensive developments on his ranch and building the boat in which he intended to sail around the world. Every bit of spare time had, perforce, to be devoted to writing which would pay for these luxuries.

It was essentially a muckraking job that was expected of Jack, but he was sure that, once started upon it, he would be unable to stay within the limits of muckraking. Resentful memories of his own exploitation as a young boy in the jute mill, and his subsequent understanding of why child labor existed and continued to exist, would lead him, he knew, straightway to an indictment of the system which demanded and enforced such exploitation. The time spent on such work was the least of its drawbacks. If the magazine printed such articles as he would write, which was doubtful, might not a new cry arise of "Boycott all magazines for which Jack London writes?" And if that happened how would he be able to pay for his boat and complete his plans for the ranch?

Pleading pressure of work already contracted for, he refused the assignment. But in the days which followed he thought often and regretfully of the opportunity he had let pass. Finally, putting other work aside, he wrote "The Apostate." This story of a child worker, used up physically, mentally and emotionally by the machines at which he had toiled until nothing remained but the vestiges of a brute instinct of self-preservation, first published in the *Woman's Home Companion,* became an extremely popular pamphlet among the Socialists.

His next compromise was far less effective. Later during the same year the San Francisco *Examiner* asked him to report in his own way the Haywood, Moyer and Pettibone trial in Idaho. Jack, exasperatedly urging on the completion of his boat, refused. The article on the case he felt compelled to write was hastily done and had but limited circulation in the socialist press.

His fear lest his income be jeopardized by his radicalism was amply illustrated when he spoke at a mass meeting in Oakland in February 1907, held under the auspices of the Socialist party to commemorate the first anniversary of the Haywood-Moyer kidnaping. As he spoke of this case which nakedly revealed the viciousness of the class struggle, he forgot his ranch and his boat and the money he owed and needed. ". . . If the work of freeing Moyer and Haywood and Pettibone is to be carried to a successful conclusion," he exclaimed, "we must lift up not only our fingers but our fists!" But when an *Examiner* reporter asked him after the meeting just what he meant by "fists," he quickly backed water.

"I surely had no intention by my use of the word 'fists' to propagate a doctrine of violence," he explained. "I was trying to make a striking figure that would signify that Socialists must make their moral resistance effectual; and they must secure every legal resource within their power to fight this case when it comes up again on March fifth. Probably I might have secured a better figure, but I am not by any means an experienced public speaker, and must ask to have any ambiguity or double meaning that might be given the words excused on that score."

Five years later the same dread of shocking his readers into refusing to buy his books set the tone of the introduction he had agreed to write to *Prison Memoirs of an Anarchist*, by Alexander Berkman. He had been greatly stirred by Berkman's story, but although nothing in the book required him to take a position for or against Berkman's beliefs, Jack went to unnecessary lengths to make it clear that he had no sympathy whatsoever with anarchism. His most forceful utterance, however, was cryptic, to say the least. "The man who can't shoot straight," he wrote, "can't think straight."

According to Emma Goldman, Berkman attempted to persuade Jack to write a different sort of introduction, reminding him that although Georg Brandes was not an anarchist, he had written a sympathetic preface to a similar book—Kropotkin's *Memoirs of a Revolutionist*. But Jack, pointing out that he was writing in America and Brandes in Europe, declined to change his attitude, and his preface was not used by Berkman.

Jack could not forget the incident. Not long before his death it reappeared, distorted by bitterness, in an article which reeked of self-pity: "I was naïve enough to think that when one intellectual disagreed with another intellectual the only difference would be intellectual. I have since learned better. Alexander Berkman could not see his way to using my introduction, and got someone else to write a more sympathetic one for him. Also, socially, comradely, he has forgotten my existence ever since."

The Snark, the name borrowed by Jack from Lewis Carroll for his forty-five-foot sailing boat, cost thirty thousand dollars to build, and at least a thousand dollars a month to operate during the twenty-seven months of the trip. The voyage, which fell far short of encircling the globe, continuing only as far as Australia, cost him his health and literary reputation for some time.

From the start the undertaking seemed to have been doomed to disappointment. The boat was begun just before the 1906 earthquake and fire in San Francisco and was built during the period of fantastically high prices which followed. If Jack had been the eminently sensible and practical man he believed he was he would have purchased, for at least one third the sum he expended on the Snark, one of the numerous excellent boats for sale in any of the Pacific coast ports. Or if he insisted upon building his own boat he would have waited until prices had returned to normal. And in any case he would have employed an expert, not only on boat-building but on sailing, instead of the amateur he placed in charge of both.

But delays and frustrations merely strengthened Jack's stubborn determination to make the trip how and when he planned it. "The more difficult the feat, the greater the satisfaction at its accomplishment," he wrote confidently when the boat had barely been started. His ability to derive satisfaction from difficulties was severely tested. Wrangling with everyone even remotely concerned finally gave way, long before the boat reached Australia, to sickness, and which was worse for Jack is debatable. The nervous energy he expended from the time the keel was laid until he gave up and entered a hospital in Sidney is incalculable, and undoubtedly left permanent effects upon him.

To raise money necessary for the venture, he contracted with the *Cosmopolitan Magazine* and received a two-thousand-dollar advance for an exclusive story of the trip. Then he contracted for exclusive rights to articles on various phases of life observed on the trip to the *Woman's Home Companion*. There were no conflicts between the contracts, but with each magazine jockeying for the most advantageous advertising of the material it was to publish, a row inevitably ensued, and the contract with the *Cosmopolitan* was broken. Jack actually wrote a mere handful of mediocre articles on the subject of the voyage, later collected in *The Cruise of the Snark*.

His disillusionment with his shipbuilding superintendent and sailing master, Roscoe Eames, husband of Charmian's aunt, proceeded rapidly. But instead of discharging him Jack childishly quarreled with him. Neither knew the first thing about navigation, but both were determined to be known as the "captain." Jack wrote Eames in December 1906, "If I am not to be captain of my own boat, what the devil am I to be?—only the 'angel?' ... It is my firm and abiding intention to be myself captain of the Snark." That settled it, naturally, as far as Eames was concerned. He failed, however, to learn how to navigate, and when the Snark reached Honolulu he was relieved of his duties and sent back to San Francisco.

Meantime Jack had studied navigation, and not until he reached the Marquesas did he hire a professional captain to sail the boat. The same incredible carelessness marked his choice of a crew. They left San Francisco without an experienced able-bodied, or even an ordinary seaman aboard, except for Jack, and did not obtain one until they reached the Marquesas. Sheer luck had accompanied Jack's hiring, sight unseen, of young Martin Johnson as cook. Johnson stayed with the ship from the start of the cruise to the end, dependable and cheerful in the face of every disaster.

Not the least of Jack's annoyances connected with the Snark trip were the jibes from all quarters at his status as a Socialist in relation to the expensive and dangerous undertaking. One of the gentlest of these from a socialist source was quoted by Jack in an article: "Many of my brother Socialists objected to my making the cruise, of which the following is typical: 'The Socialist cause, and the millions of oppressed victims of capitalism, has a right and claim upon your life and services. If, however, you persist, then, when you swallow the last mouthful of salt chuck you can hold before sinking, remember that we at least protested.' "

But the *Bookman* commented: "While the Socialists are gloating over the gruesome picture of the impending struggle that Jack London painted in *The Iron Heel*, and the powers that be are fixing his status once for all in the class of undesirable citizens, the irresponsible London himself appears to be taking matters very calmly. The (accompanying photograph) does not indicate that he is spending his days in brooding over the cataclysm. On the contrary, he looks remarkably well-fed, happy and contented —for a Socialist. But there are Socialists and Socialists."

As the voyage across the Pacific continued, Jack, having placed Mrs Payne in charge of all his affairs, discovered that it was practically impossible either to direct his operations on the ranch through her or, what was infinitely more important, market his writings. Chaotic best describes the condition of his affairs when he finally returned to California.

More deeply disillusioned than he would admit by the reality of the adventure he had thought would be so fine, his health and nerves shattered by a vicious combination of specific tropical diseases and the general effects of the tropics on a white man, he was forced to go to work immediately and desperately to re-habilitate himself as a "popular" writer. Vast sums of money were needed, not only to square the debts which had accumulated and provide the wherewithal for his increasing responsibilities, but to realize the new plans he had formulated for himself. And Jack London had feared that his prominent identification with the socialist cause would be too costly!

Soon after Jack returned to the ranch in the summer of 1909 he learned of the eucalyptus "boom" which was sweeping the state. The growing scarcity of Eastern hardwoods for poles, ties, furniture and veneers and the like had inspired California lumber-men to find a substitute. Eucalyptus, several species of which had been brought to California from Australia and the adjacent islands as early as the 'fifties, seemed to answer all their demands and more. Its growth was incredibly rapid and it thrived in soils and under climatic conditions unfavorable to most other trees and plants. One "authority" wrote of eucalyptus, "It promises to be the means of making California the home of the large wood-using industries and causing this state to be even more prominent than did the discovery of gold."

Jack's ranch, which had been enlarged during his absence by the acquisition of one hundred and ten additional acres, contained much poor land. Reading the glowing brochures of the various eucalyptus stock-selling corporations which had sprung up, Jack was dazzled by the possibilities offered if he were to cover his worthless acres with these miraculous trees. Before the year was out he had planted his first fifteen thousand seedlings. The following year eight hundred acres were added to the ranch, and in 1912 four hundred more. Before Jack's enthusiasm for eucalyptus had passed he had put in nearly one hundred and fifty thousand trees and spent approximately fifty thousand dollars, on which he was sure he would make a thirty per cent profit.

To friends, relatives and the press he announced that he was sick and tired of writing and intended to do no more as soon as his eucalyptus trees began to bring in money. In January 1911 he was widely quoted as saying: ". . . I have been trying hard to get out of the writing game for many years. . . . I did it to make money, and I made it. I made up my mind some time ago that as soon as I saw my way clear to making money in another direction I would quit pen scratching for good. I think my eucalyptus trees will help me make my get-away in the near future, and it will be a relief for me to get out of the scorching focus of the public eye . . . One has to burn whole gallons of midnight oil to get ideas and lately it has been wearing on me."

His attitude toward the venture was strictly commercial. In July 1910 he had asked the American Corporation for Investors in New York how much it would pay him for writing a "good general word" for eucalyptus planting, but the best it could offer him, already so rich in acres, was the opportunity to buy a five-acre tract at half price. The next month Jack endorsed eucalyptus planting in a pamphlet issued by the same corporation. Three months later, still the businessman, he was writing to the corporation to inquire if it had come to any conclusion regarding the return due him for his endorsement. But his investment in eucalyptus was not to yield even this small profit.

Alarmed by the amount of capital invested and the increase in acreage planted with eucalyptus on the assumption that stupendous profits would result, the United States Forestry Service issued a warning bulletin. Seeking to aid eucalyptus growers, it had published after careful study all the information it could concerning the tree and its uses. "But," said the bulletin, "information presented for this purpose has at times been misused. Short passages have been quoted in such a way as to convey a misleading impression and sometimes even to falsify the original meaning. Extravagant estimates of the probable returns from planted eucalyptus have been widely circulated, and there is reason to fear that many persons have formed an altogether false idea of the merits of eucalyptus growing as a field for investment. . . ." This, and even more discouraging information, reached Jack too late; his money had been spent. Eucalyptus wood proved a failure in every respect. Thousands of the trees still stand on Jack's ranch, ragged and neglected, as worthless as the soil in which they were planted.

The "beauty ranch," Jack called the place, determined that its expense should be dwarfed by the pleasure it gave him. "I wanted to be able to go all up and down those beautiful green ridges, and always to be on my own land." Thus he liked to explain his ownership. His efforts to realize something on his investment, however, never ceased. The fact that previous owners of each of the six ranches he had united into one had lost their land through bankruptcy was a constant challenge to him. "By using my head, my judgment, and all the latest knowledge in the matter of farming," he wrote, "can I make a success where these . . . men failed? I have pledged myself, my manhood, my fortune, my books and all I possess to this undertaking." The raising of blooded livestock, among other experiments, followed the eucalyptus planting, and failed just as miserably to make money. Toward the end Jack began to speak of it sadly as the "ranch of good intentions."

His reputation as a popular and successful author was soon reestablished and his income rose accordingly. Once he had maintained that he would regard ten dollars a day from writing as an ample daily wage, but this attitude had not lasted long. "Success inevitably breeds a higher standard of living." Thus in 1910 he restated to John S. Phillips of the *American Magazine* what he had written a decade earlier. Before many years had passed he had increased his income to approximately seventy-five thousand dollars a year, by dint of astute bargaining with editors and publishers, and without the benefit of motion-picture sales. And yet, thanks to his constantly rising standard of living, his poor business judgment, as well as his consistently bad luck, he was not only always in debt but he failed signally to obtain almost everything he set his heart upon.

His most spectacular disappointment was undoubtedly the "Wolf House," the vast edifice of stone and redwood he built on the ranch to be his home. Three years went into its construction, and more than seventy thousand dollars, but shortly before it was ready for occupancy it was destroyed by fire, probably of incendiary origin, although this was never proved. Jack did not rebuild the house, nor even make plans for another. Until his death his ranch home was a simple farmhouse, to which he had added a small workroom, and an adjoining stone winery which served as living room, dining room and kitchen.

But a far deeper disappointment was his failure to realize one of his earliest and dearest ambitions—fatherhood. His two daughters were being raised by their mother in Oakland. When they were small he had not missed them especially, and his brief but frequent visits to them had sufficed. But the more than two years he was away on the Snark made a gap in his relations with the little girls that visits could bridge to a certain extent, but could not fill. Busy on the ranch after his return, he came to Oakland less frequently than before. Meantime the girls were growing up, and for them Jack London, somewhat incredibly their father, was a glamorous person who came into their lives at intervals, but whom they did not know very well.

He had hoped for a child, especially a son, from his second marriage, but the daughter Charmian bore him the year after their return to California lived but a few days. When a few years later he asked that Joan and little Bess come to live with him on the ranch for a time so that all might get acquainted with each other, the girls, pawns in a situation neither understood, were unwilling to leave Bess.

Letters largely replaced visits and outings during the last years of his life when he spent little time in California, but it was through these, and because the girls were no longer children, that father and daughters finally came to know each other. Unfortunately for all of them, however, Jack's death came before the relationship he had yearned for, and which would have grown only through day-by-day living together, had been achieved.

Failure, disappointment, frustration and bitterness—these were the dominant themes in the closing years of the life of the "most successful and highly paid author in America." Jack London's hatred of writing increased in direct proportion with the money it brought him, for the latter stimulated him to greater and greater extravagance, which in turn increased his burden of debt, and this could be paid off only by more writing—a vicious circle.

Jack's methods of obtaining material as his creative impulses

began to flag under the unceasing strain upon them came under
fire as early as 1906 when charges, not of plagiarism but of "identity of time and situation," were brought against him by the
New York *Sunday World* in connection with one of his finest
short stories, "Love of Life," which had appeared in *McClure's*
in December 1905. Four years earlier, in December 1901, the same
magazine had published "Lost in the Land of the Midnight Sun,"
by Augustus Biddle and J. K. Macdonald, "the true story of the
wanderings of Charles Bunn, who fought starvation for eight
days on the rusty rocks of the Arctic Barren Grounds." In what
the *World* called a "deadly parallel," eighteen excerpts from each
story were published side by side, proving beyond question that
Jack had merely rewritten the Biddle account, retaining not
only the main outlines of the story, the setting and the season of
the year, but innumerable details as well.

Biddle, a Canadian free-lance journalist, had met Bunn on the
latter's return from his Alaskan experience, and piece by piece
had extracted his story, frequently tearing holes in it in order to
see if he were telling the truth. "My greatest grievance against
Mr London," said Biddle, "is that he has used a score of times the
very color of my tale, utilizing certain digressions of my own
which I used to give vividness to the narrative."

Jack, airily declaring that "life is so short and people so silly
that from the beginning of my career . . . I made it a point to
deny nothing charged against me in the newspapers," conde-
scended to answer the *World's* charges at the request of the
Bookman. Biddle's story, he maintained, was a narrative of fact
describing the actual suffering of a man with a sprained ankle
in the country of the Coppermine River; it was not fiction, it was
not literature. He freely admitted having used "Lost in the Land
of the Midnight Sun" as material for "Love of Life," but he had
also used a newspaper account of a prospector who had been lost
near Nome, and an incident contained in Lieutenant Greely's
narrative of the Greely polar expedition, and to all of this he had
added his own experience of hardship, suffering and starvation, as
well as the whole fund of knowledge of similar experiences of
other men.

"I, in the course of making my living by turning journalism
into literature," he summed up defiantly, "used material from
various sources which had been collected and narrated by men
who made their living by turning the facts of life into journalism.

Along comes the space-writer of the *World* who makes his living by turning the doings of other men into sensation. . . . Well, all three of us made our living, and who's got any kick coming?"

The following year new charges of plagiarism arose: *Before Adam* had been inspired too literally by Stanley Waterloo's *The Story of Ab; The Call of the Wild* owed much to *My Dogs in the Northland*, by Dr Edgerton R. Young, showing "certain startling resemblances, marked similarities in personnel of leading dog characters, and in circumstances and situations, though far inferior to it in delineations of dog nature." Jack coolly admitted that he was indebted to both sources, claimed that he had written his thanks to Dr Young for the material used, although this was denied by some of Young's friends, and demanded to know: "What is plagiarism?"

The last serious charge of plagiarism came from Frank Harris and was directed against *The Iron Heel*. In May 1901 Harris had published an article in the *Candid Friend*, a British publication, entitled "The Bishop of London and Public Morality." In *The Iron Heel* this article reappeared almost word for word as "The Bishop's Vision." This time Jack attempted to defend himself rather than to defy his accusers, but defiance would have become him better and been more effective, for his excuse was very lame indeed.

He claimed that he had read the article in question reprinted in an American newspaper, and that he had mistaken it for a genuine speech delivered at a public meeting by the bishop of London. Inasmuch as the "speech" had been written in Harris' most ironical vein, and was essentially an attack upon the church as an instrument of capitalism, Harris could only fall back in amazement and conclude that since Jack had so easily mistaken a sensational sham speech for a real one, American gentlemen must be as naïve and as ignorant as British colonials.

In 1910 Jack decided to try another method of rendering his writing task easier: the purchase of story plots. His ability to put words together in an original and distinctive manner had become almost automatic. Long since he had mastered every trick of writing needful to convey the "Jack London" approach and style. With a supply of ready-made plots at hand, he believed he would be able to turn out stories in the best Jack London manner with a minimum of effort, and without the annoyance of being accused of plagiarism.

When a young writer named Sinclair Lewis, eager to give up
the job he had and devote full time to writing, offered to sell him
plots, Jack bought a number. The arrangement, however, failed
to bring much satisfaction to either party. Jack paid very little
for the relatively few ideas he bought, and those which he used
did not sell for as much as usual. The reasons he gave for rejecting
most of the plots which Lewis submitted indicate how indifferent
he had become toward writing: "Some of the rejected ones were
not suited to my temperament; others did not suit because I am
too lazy to dig up requisite data or atmosphere." Later in the same
letter he cautioned Lewis, ". . . and for heaven's sake remember
the ones I take, so that you won't make the mistake of writing
them up yourself sometime!"

"The Dress Suit Pugilist," which Jack bought from Lewis for
seven dollars and fifty cents, became *The Abysmal Brute*. In
1911 Jack wrote Lewis, ". . . working steadily on Smoke Bellew
tales and the Sun tales . . . You see, I haven't been using up any
short story ideas at all . . . Frankly, I don't know whether I'm
making or losing money by working up some of those other short
story ideas I got from you. Take *The Abysmal Brute*, for instance. I got $1200 for it, after it had been refused by the first-
class magazines." Asserting that if the time spent on *The Abysmal Brute* had been put into the Smoke Bellew or Sun stories,
he would have made three thousand dollars out of it, Jack more
or less terminated the arrangement with Lewis. He continued to
the end of his life, however, to buy plots as the occasion arose,
some of the best of his last stories being based on ideas he had
bought, at more generous prices than he had paid Lewis, from
George Sterling.

It was while the plagiarism charges were at their height that
Jack received a new kind of publicity, becoming the principal
target of Theodore Roosevelt's campaign against "nature-faking."
Why the President should have suddenly decided at this time to
pose, backed by his friend and admirer, John Burroughs, as a
scientific authority on wild animals is mystifying, unless it was
that he counted on the resultant publicity superimposing a picture of Roosevelt the scientist and animal lover on that of "trust-
busting" Roosevelt, cutting a pathetic figure in the midst of the
1907 panic.

Apropos of Jack's dog story, *White Fang*, Roosevelt stated
in an interview published in *Everybody's* for June 1907: "I can't

believe that Mr London knows much about the wolves, and I am certain he knows nothing about their fighting, or as a realist he would not tell this tale." Jack was indicted on two counts: he had permitted a bulldog to whip a wolf dog, and a lynx to be victim in a fight to the death with a wolf dog. When an Associated Press correspondent reached Jack in Honolulu for comment, Jack's first response was that he thanked God he was not an authority on anything. Then he pounced delightedly on the second charge. Roosevelt had unfortunately read Jack's book too hastily: it was not the lynx which had killed and eaten the wolf dog, but the reverse.

Several months later, in Papeete, Jack disposed of the first point in an article entitled "The Other Animals." "President Roosevelt does not think a bull-dog can lick a wolf-dog," he wrote. "I think a bull-dog can lick a wolf-dog. And there we are. Difference of opinion may make, and does make, horse-racing. I can understand that difference of opinion can make dog-fighting. But what gets me is how difference of opinion regarding the relative merits of a bull-dog and a wolf-dog makes me a nature-faker and President Roosevelt a vindicated and triumphant scientist." There the matter rested. New terms were coined for newspaper copy, and nature-faking was forgotten, although years later, in 1921, it knew a brief resurrection when Vilhjalmur Stefansson revived the charges against Jack London, Robert W. Service and James Oliver Curwood.

As soon as *The Iron Heel* was completed Jack had set to work on a series of articles which recounted his experiences as a hobo. Although they appeared in the *Cosmopolitan* under such a muckrake title as *My Life in the Underworld*, they bore no resemblance to the literature of exposure. Twelve years had passed since Jack had joined the "after push" of Kelly's army at the summit of the Rockies, and more since he had gone "over the hill" for the first time. Fatigued by the strain of writing *The Iron Heel*, and in the midst of the harassments which accompanied the building of the Snark, Jack escaped happily into the past, reliving his adventures as he set them down in clean, vivid prose. He was not yet thirty-one, but his youth seemed far behind him. A gentle nostalgia touched the writing of many passages: "The day was done—one day of all my days. Tomorrow would be another day, and I was young."

That Brett should have advised against publishing the articles as a book is not altogether surprising. As a publisher, he was convinced that it would not have a good sale, and that it would hurt rather than help Jack's reputation as a popular writer. Jack retorted, "It was my refusal to take cautious advice that made me," and, retitled, *The Road* was released to an indifferent public. Brett's judgment had been correct. The book did not sell well, and, with *The Iron Heel* and *Martin Eden*, brought about the estrangement between Jack and the majority of his readers which lasted until the appearance of *Burning Daylight*.

But that Jack's personal friends should have disapproved of the book somewhat startled him. Sterling and others of his recent acquaintances, blinded by the prejudices of their class, were horrified by Jack's presentation of himself not only as a bum who had knocked at back doors for handouts, but who had actually been imprisoned for vagrancy. To Sterling, Jack wrote, "I cannot get a line on why you wish I hadn't written *The Road*. It is all true. It is what I am, what I have done, and it is part of the process by which I have become. Is it a lingering taint of the bourgeois in you that makes you object? Is it because of my shamelessness? For having done things in which I saw or see no shame? Do tell me." There is no evidence, however, that Jack ever received satisfactory answers to these questions from Sterling or anyone else.

Of all Jack London's serious works, none has been more widely misapprehended than *Martin Eden*, which he began to write soon after the Snark reached Honolulu. Most readers, ignoring the tragic ending which Jack deliberately conceived and logically reached for this novel, have regarded it solely as a "success" story. It has been known as the book which inspired not only a whole generation of young writers but others in different fields who, without aid or encouragement, attained their objectives through great struggle. Some people, completely identifying the author with his main character and forgetting Martin Eden's scorn of socialism, believed his suicide to have been the result of his radical beliefs and, according to their own attitude, applauded or protested.

Jack himself was largely to blame for the mistaken impressions of his readers. In the copy of *Martin Eden* which he inscribed to Upton Sinclair he wrote, "One of my motifs, in this book, was an attack on individualism (in the person of the hero). I must have bungled, for not a single reviewer has discovered it." Few discovered it for the simple reason that while Jack rejected individualism intellectually, his sympathy remained always with the individualist. Martin Eden's struggle to rise from obscurity to fame was his own, and Jack was proud of both.

But one must seek deeper for the true cause of the confusion produced by this book. Up to a certain point Martin Eden was Jack London. They differed, according to Jack, in their attitude toward socialism. Martin Eden, the reactionary individualist, isolated from the vital force of a world-wide revolutionary movement that sought to destroy the regime which enslaved and crippled most of mankind, was doomed to disillusionment and bitterness, with suicide at the end. Jack, on the other hand, a Socialist with a warm interest in the fate of those less fortunate than himself, would escape this fate. So Jack reasoned. But it was self-deception as futile as it was tragic, for even as he wrote *Martin Eden*, Jack's isolation from the socialist movement had begun.

Brissenden, who was to Martin Eden what Strawn-Hamilton had been to Jack, said to Martin, " 'I'd like to see you a socialist before I'm gone. It will give you a sanction for your existence. It is the one thing that will save you in the time of disappointment that is coming to you. . . . You have health and much to live for, and you must be handcuffed to life somehow. As for me, you wonder why I am a socialist. I'll tell you. It is because socialism is inevitable; because the present rotten and irrational system cannot endure; because the day is past for your man on horseback. . . . Of course I don't like the crowd, but what's a poor chap to do? We can't have the man on horseback, and anything is preferable to the timid swine that now rule.' "

Jack had slipped his handcuffs. Never again, although he would talk much of socialism, would he be a participant in the socialist movement. His position during the next few years would be described today as that of a "sympathizer" on the "periphery," although considering his income, he was not a generous contributor to the cause. And as other interests demanded more and more of his time, the distance between him and the socialist movement widened until he no longer felt its pulse beat, knew aught of its victories and defeats, or remembered its principles. When Jack's "time of disappointment" came there was no longer any "sanction" for his existence.

As if he knew what the end of his life would be Jack London

wrote his own obituary in *Martin Eden,* a story not of success, but of failure. At the same time, consciously deciding his future as a writer, Jack made of *Martin Eden* his *salve atque vale* to literature. The conclusions reached by Martin Eden when he questioned the validity of his popularity were Jack's own rationalization of why he would never again exert himself artistically. "It was the bourgeoisie who bought his books," reasoned Martin Eden, "and poured its gold into his money-sack, and from what little he knew of the bourgeoisie it was not clear to him how it could possibly appreciate or comprehend what he had written. His intrinsic beauty and power meant nothing to the hundreds of thousands who were acclaiming him and buying his books. He was the fad of the hour, the adventurer who had stormed Parnassus while the gods nodded."

When *Burning Daylight* appeared, a success story with a happy ending, reviewers sighed with relief. Although one of them, remarking on Jack's "chastened" mood, said, "Five years ago he would not have been such a mollycoddle," the book took its place immediately in the ranks of the best sellers. The comment of the *Bookman's* reviewer was typical: *"Burning Daylight* has some interesting revelations to make. They show us a Jack London who no longer desires to preach his very amusing radicalism, but who is willing to come back to his power as a storyteller. Also a Jack London who has passed through the sad phase of unrest out of which Martin Eden grew—it's certainly sad to have one's emotions take such unpleasant forms—and who has attained a calmness of mind by reason of which his glowing, vivid style, with the assurance of ripened maturity, can pour itself out into a vehicle of great pleasure for the reader. In this novel Jack London does not preach anything . . . has attained the objectiveness necessary to true fiction . . . (so) has lost one of his most annoying faults and made *Burning Daylight* a better novel than he has given us for many a day. . . . It reads well as a book, and its author may be forgiven some recent failures for its sake."

Was Jack deceived? The cynical attitude toward writing which he expressed in an interview in 1911 makes one certain that he was not: "I have no unfinished stories. Invariably I complete every one I start. If it's good, I sign it and send it out. If it isn't good, I sign it and send it out." Five years later, hearing that Jack had in his possession certain stories without value for the magazines he regularly wrote for, Waldo Frank asked if he might publish them in the magazine he was then editing. Jack, regretting that such stories did not exist, replied apologetically, "I do not mind telling you that had the United States been as kindly to the short story as France has always been kindly, from the beginning of my writing career I would have written many a score of short stories quite different from the ones I have written."

Nevertheless on the rare occasions when Jack permitted himself the luxury of writing stories unlike those his readers expected of him, he was acutely conscious of the fact. Two stories almost totally unrecognizable as Jack London's, entitled "Samuel" and "The Sea Farmer," were accepted and published by the *Bookman* in 1912 and 1913. Of the first Jack said, "This yarn of mine, 'Samuel,' is one of my half-dozen best short stories that I have ever written."

He invariably answered letters from young writers eager to know the secret of successful authorship. His advice to one of these was: "Take your time; study the stuff of the other fellows who've mastered the trick—study until you can turn the same trick. Take your time; elaborate; omit; draw; develop. Paint—paint pictures and characters and emotions—but paint, paint, draw, draw. And take your time. Spend a day on a paragraph, or on ten paragraphs. Grab your motif. Master it. Make it live and spout blood and spirit and beauty and fire and glamor."

His own method of composition he described in a letter to Karl Edwin Harriman, editor of the *Red Book:* ". . . From time to time I keep catching glimpses of my hero and making sporadic notes. But I certainly shall not attempt to realize him. I've three or four stories in this fashion already up in the air, with slight notes taken on them. But I never compose a story, outline a story, until I actually set to work on it. Then I take my period of mulling and immediately follow this mulling with the actual writing. And I am unfortunately so made, that if ever I soak myself in a thing, and then let any time whatever elapse, I am done with that thing forever. I can never again realize it. When I get soaked, then I pitch in immediately to do the work."

Letters revealing his writing methods occur rarely in the files of his correspondence, but those which reveal his business methods are numerous. When, for example, the *Cosmopolitan* deleted "objectionable phrases," profanity and the like from *My Life in the Underworld,* and then paid him only for the number of

words actually printed, it received a sharply worded demand
from him that he be paid for the number of words submitted.
His manuscripts always bore his own word count, and editors
came to accept this without question. He marketed his own wares
with greater efficiency than the average agent, unhesitatingly
describing his work in glowing terms and usually receiving his
own price.

Money consciousness touched every phase of his activity. "Jack
London says his socialism costs him several thousand a year," reported the Los Angeles *Record* in January 1911. Later in the same
year he wrote to a businessman with whom he was dealing, ". . .
I have been boycotted and blacklisted by stupid capitalists on account of my socialism, and made to lose more money on account
of my socialism to the tune of hundreds of thousands of dollars.
I tell you the foregoing because this is the day of dollars. I in-
terpret my actions to you in terms of dollars. . . ."

But that socialism of Jack London's was undergoing great
change. Although he was unaware of it his status as property
owner and employer was definitely altering his point of view, and
he was often hard put to it to rationalize the inevitable contradictions which arose. While the great house was being built, for
instance, he was prone to remark piously how glad he was to be
able to offer employment to so many workers. His attitude toward these workers, however, was an employer's; "my inefficient
Italian laborers," he called them irritably.

But he could not forget socialism. The further he moved away
from the movement, the more it nagged him. Soon after his return from the Snark trip he had begun the steady drinking which
would continue to the end of his life, and while he drank he
usually discussed socialism with whomever would listen to him,
arguing, defending, defying. And every once in a while during
these years he would take a stand on various matters which revealed him apparently as a militant, uncompromising revolutionist.

Early in his association with the socialist movement he had
accepted as inevitable the eventual achievement of socialism, but,
deceived by the peaceful aspect of the development of capitalism
during this period, he believed that a long time would elapse
before it reached its peak and began to decay. "I should like to
have socialism," he had written Cloudesley Johns in 1901, "yet I
know that socialism is not the very next step; I know that capital-

ism must live its life first. That the world must be exploited to the utmost first; that first must intervene a struggle for life among the nations, severer, intenser, more widespread, than ever before, I should much more prefer to wake tomorrow in a smoothly-running socialistic state; but I know I shall not; I know that a child must go through its child's sicknesses ere it becomes a man. So always remember that I speak of the things that are; not of the things that should be."

Eight years later these beliefs and his contempt for the re-formism of the Right wing socialists in America dictated his criticism of the Australian Labour Party. As reported in the *Worker* of Brisbane in 1909 Jack accused the Labour Party of "trying to prevent capitalism from ripening, of trying to head off a logical action." "Capitalism should be permitted to ripen," he said. "A newer system can only grow out of the decay of the older. I am not an advocate for palliatives. Your labor legislation seems to me to have headed off and retarded that development which implies the growth of a revolutionary spirit in order to effect a revolutionary purpose. You can't create a 'complete change,' or establish a new social order, until the economic processes bring things to a head. Why, your phenomenal advance, as it is de-scribed—heralded throughout the world—has already almost reached the inescapable climax of collapse. You are static. That's what happens when you try to prevent a process."

During this period while capitalism seemed to have unlimited possibilities for development, Socialists, with few exceptions, failed to gauge correctly the tempo at which it was ripening and, continuing to adapt themselves to its peaceful development until such time as it became rotten-ripe, deleted the revolutionary content of their movement. The World War caught these people totally unprepared for the spectacle of capitalism involved in that struggle for existence which they had not expected to occur for many years. They were not only unready to take a revolutionary position against a capitalist war, but actually unwilling to do so. And while Socialists hastened to come to the aid of the govern-ments of their respective countries, the Second International col-lapsed.

Belief in the inevitability of socialism as a process independent of human action, and underestimation of the speed at which capitalism was moving toward a crisis was catastrophic for Jack London after he had become a rich man. The inclination to minimize the importance of the roles of both the party and the individual and so rationalize decreased activity and withdrawal in practice, if not in fact, from the socialist movement, was fatally easy, and was offset only by his understanding of the true nature of the class struggle.

Asked in 1912 if he were a direct actionist, by a Socialist who defined the term as "one who favors strikes and the like," he replied, "Yes, I am a direct actionist, as you call it. Direct action, as I understand it, is teaching us the true fighting spirit, which is going to be the greatest asset the people of the masses possess when the great struggle finally comes between them and their present masters. There is a hard time coming. We shall have a big fight, but the masses will conquer in the end, because they form the stronger and more stable body. The story of that struggle will be written in blood. The ruling classes will not let go until it is."

Under no circumstances would he abandon this conviction. On the other hand, faced with the realization that not only the leaders of the Socialist party, but the majority of its members as well, rejected his point of view, he refused to make the slightest effort to show the movement how it was betraying the workers and defeating its alleged purposes. It was all very well to imagine himself Ernest Everhard, but be him he would not.

An early attempt to solve the dilemma in which he found himself came to nothing. Eschewing political activity in the socialist movement, he would become a theorist. Together with Ernest Untermann, translator of Marx's *Das Kapital*, he planned to write a book which would be a discussion of Marxist theory. Lack of time for such an undertaking, and realization of the amount of studying he would have to do before the book could even be started, resulted in endless delays and postponements. To the end, however, he spoke fondly of the project, hoping that someday he would get around to it.

For Jack there was only one solution: retreat. And retreat he did, sad and cynical by turns, from everything and everyone who would remind him of the battle in which he would not participate. The ranch and his interest in agriculture, the ever-renewed plans for a voyage around the world which would last for years, the lengthy residences in Hawaii, the increasing indulgence in alcohol, these and others were plans for escape—escape from himself, from activity with groups of other human beings, from movements, from civilization, from life itself.

At rare intervals he was able to attain the sanctuary of intellectual and emotional remoteness from life where nothing could touch him. In such a mood he wrote: "Of what ledger-account is the tiny life of man in a vastness where stars snuff out like candles and great suns blaze for a time-tick of eternity and are gone?" But most often he stayed close to life, goaded by dissatisfactions and disappointments, striking back sometimes, but succumbing more and more to pessimism and despair while he walked daily with what he called the "Noseless One"—his comrade, Death.

In the files of a small socialist publication on the Pacific coast may be found an unforgettable picture of Jack London when he was beginning to learn how to protect his vulnerabilities with cynicism and had taken leave, for a little while, of the "Noseless One."

"I dream of beautiful horses and fine soil," he told the young radical who had asked to interview him. "I dream of the beautiful things I own up in Sonoma County. And I write for no other purpose than to add to the beauty that now belongs to me. I write a book for no other reason than to add three or four hundred acres to my magnificent estate. I write a story with no other purpose than to buy a stallion. To me, my cattle are far more interesting than my profession. My friends don't believe me when I say this, but I am absolutely sincere.

"You may wonder why I am a pessimist; I often wonder myself. Here I have the most precious thing in the world—the love of a woman; I have beautiful children; I have lots and lots of money; I have fame as a writer; I have many men working for me; I have a beautiful ranch—and still, I am a pessimist. I look at things dispassionately, scientifically, and everything appears almost hopeless; after long years of labor and development, the people are as bad off as ever. There is a mighty ruling class that intends to hold fast to its possessions. I see years and years of bloodshed. I see the master class hiring armies of murderers to keep the workers in subjection, to beat them back should they attempt to dispossess the capitalists. That's why I am a pessimist. I see things in the light of history and the laws of nature.

"I became a Socialist when I was seventeen years old. I am still a Socialist, but not of the refined, quietistic school of socialism. The Socialists, the ghetto Socialists of the East, no longer believe in the strong, firm socialism of the early days. Mention confiscation in the ghetto of New York and the leaders will throw up their hands in holy terror. I still believe that Socialists should strive to eliminate the capitalist class and wipe away the private ownership of mines, mills, factories, railroads and other social needs.

"I do not believe that Socialists should soften and yield, eventually becoming mere reformers whose greatest desire is economy in government and low taxes, and the like. They should take upon themselves the task of doing away with the robbing capitalist system, do away with the profit system and place the workers in possession of the industries."

"Are you opposed to political action?" he was asked.

"I believe there is much to be gained by entering political campaigns. The real advantage, in my opinion, is the great opportunity to educate the workers to an understanding of the wrongs of the present system and the meaning of class consciousness."

"Do you believe in sabotage and syndicalism?"

"Hopelessly so. I have believed in them for twenty years. I look upon myself as a veteran in the socialist movement. I joined it when it was disgraceful to be known as a Socialist. I believe that any means will justify the end. I believe in any method to bring about the socialist commonwealth."

"You think that a peaceful and legal change is impossible?"

"History shows that no master class is ever willing to let go without a quarrel. The capitalists own the governments, the armies and the militia. Don't you think the capitalists will use these institutions to keep themselves in power? I do."

"What do *you* intend to do, Mr London?"

"I feel that I have done my part. Socialism has cost me hundreds of thousands of dollars. When the time comes I'm going to stay right on my ranch at Glen Ellen and let the revolution go to blazes. I've done my part." After a pause, he added, "That's the way I feel now. I suppose when the time comes I'll let my emotions get the best of my intellect and I'll come down from the mountain top and join the fray."

"What a grim, pessimistic view you have, Mr London!"

"Well, I'm a pessimist. I admit it."

CHAPTER

24

IT WAS in the spring of 1911 that Jack London publicly voiced his revolutionary sentiments for the last time and wrote his last piece of propaganda. News of the outbreak of revolution in Mexico in 1910 had awakened in him an enthusiasm such as he had not felt since the 1905 revolution in Russia. Eager to publicize his support of the revolutionists, he addressed a letter in February 1911 to the "dear, brave comrades of the Mexican Revolution," which, first published in the socialist press, was reprinted in many newspapers throughout the country.

"We socialists, anarchists, hobos, chicken thieves, outlaws and undesirable citizens of the United States," he wrote, "are with you heart and soul in your effort to overthrow slavery and autocracy in Mexico. You will notice we are not respectable in these days of the reign of property. All the names you are being called, we have been called. And when graft and greed get up and begin to call names, honest men, brave men, patriotic men and martyrs can expect nothing else than to be called chicken thieves and outlaws.

"So be it. But I for one wish that there were more chicken thieves and outlaws of the sort that formed the gallant band that took Mexicali, of the sort that is heroically enduring the prison holes of Diaz, of the sort that is fighting and dying and sacrificing in Mexico today.

"I subscribe myself a chicken thief and revolutionist.

"Jack London."

338

When the newspapers solicited a direct statement from him he was quoted as saying: "I hope the people of the United States will resent this latest action of the United States government in proposing to overawe the Mexican revolutionists, but I'm afraid they will not. The action of the government is logical. It regards dollars, not democracy, and therefore it will send its troops to protect its dollars. It may be necessary to send troops into Mexico to crush the rebellion. Diaz is afraid all hell may break loose. If the United States government wants to invade Mexico, it can find plenty of legal pretexts, but it would be a burning shame. It might end the revolution, but it certainly cannot crush the revolutionary spirit in Mexico."

This revolution was the third major political upheaval in Mexico since 1810, although from that year until 1877 disturbances had been practically continuous. The first revolution had resulted in independence from Spain and brought the Mexican whites into power; the second, the Reforma, had placed in control the *mestizo*, the combination of Mexican Indian and Spaniard; the last introduced the Indian peasant as a conscious entity for the first time.

In all the revolutions were conflicting forces which prevented their full development. Aware that the breaking up of an entrenched, cruel administration invariably inflames those who have been its victims, Mexican "politicos" managed to engineer and control from the top every break with the past so that the reins of the revolution would not fall into the hands of the peon. Nevertheless the movement led in 1810 by Hidalgo and continued for a brief time by his successor, Morelos, had not only been a literal acceptance of the revolutionary slogan of "liberty, equality and fraternity," but had indelibly stamped Mexico with the influence of the ideas of the French Revolution. This influence persisted, and time after time the masses, goaded past endurance by suffering and deprivation, followed leaders who raised any semblance of that slogan.

In 1877 General Porfirio Diaz brought to an end more than a half a century of vicious struggle for power between conservatives and middle-class liberals in which the *mestizos* and Indians had been used as pawns. Proclaiming himself the "hero of peace," and assuring the people that his would be the "last revolution," he made himself the president of Mexico. Between 1880 and 1884 he arranged to have the constitution conveniently amended in order that he might be re-elected, and from 1884 until 1911 he remained in office, a president in name, a dictator in fact. Popular government became a farce. Under his rule Mexico drifted more and more toward reaction, and although prosperity came to the country it was not for the oppressed people but for the ruling class and foreign capital.

Two of Diaz' policies were especially responsible for this state of affairs. Thanks to the cupidity of the church, the Indians and *mestizos* had always been land hungry, but Diaz made matters infinitely worse. By a presidential decree in 1890 he expropriated the tillable lands of the villages, which until then had been inalienable. For the majority of the Indians only these communal lands stood between them and starvation. By 1910 barely three per cent of the rural heads of families owned any real property, and this group was composed of less than a thousand powerful landowners whose vast estates ranged up to six million acres in size. Meantime ten million Indians, practically three fifths of the population, had become serfs. At the outbreak of the revolution the condition of the masses was more desperate than it had ever been.

With the same disregard for tradition, Diaz cast aside a principle concerning mines which had been followed since colonial times. Mining laws passed in 1884, 1892 and 1909 granted landowners the right to exploit subsoil deposits without governmental approval. This right had previously been reserved first for the king and later for the nation.

The effects of these policies were glaringly evident by 1910. Of the various imperialist nations who had coveted Mexico's wealth, the United States, her every move sanctified by the Monroe Doctrine, had been the most successful, although in furthering her colonial ambitions she had found the economic penetration of Mexico more difficult than in the case of the tiny Central American republics. By 1902 Americans held well over three hundred million dollars in Mexican railways; in 1911 this figure had more than doubled. Behind the railroad builders and promoters came the American mining men. With sufficient capital for machinery and the technical skill of American engineers, tremendous sums could be realized from the abandoned or inadequately developed Mexican mines. In 1902 American mining properties in Mexico were valued at ninety-five millions; nine years later they totaled a quarter of a billion.

The same mining interests, flanked by the ubiquitous land speculators, also acquired ranching, farming and timberlands, large holdings being typical of American ownership. Practically all the petroleum wealth of Mexico had been given away by Diaz before 1910. Four great combines were in complete control of Mexican oil: Doheny, Standard Oil and Waters-Pierce allies, Royal Dutch and the Pearson interests.

The total of American investments in Mexico at the close of the Diaz regime has been estimated at a billion and a half dollars. Thus, although powerful American interests were opposed to Diaz toward the end of his career because he had begun to favor European capital, America was vitally concerned when the political machine of the aging Diaz crumpled before the accumulated hatred of the landless Mexican masses, and the mild democrat Madero made his triumphant and messianic entrance into Mexico City in the spring of 1911.

Ten years before this occurred, a young Mexican intellectual, speaking at the opening convention of the Liberal party, had denounced Diaz as one of the greatest criminals in Mexico. The convention was stirred into action by the burning words of this young leader, Ricardo Flores Magòn. From then on the party grew, despite ruthless persecution by the government. Its leaders were jailed and exiled, yet it continued to smuggle its propaganda across the American border into Mexico.

In 1906 it challenged the imposed and continued re-election of Diaz. That same year the first strike in an American mining concession broke out. The exiled leaders returned to Mexico and raised the cry of revolt. The demands of the strikers in Cananea were answered with bullets, and when they still showed resistance, armed "reinforcements" were brought from Texas, with the government's approval, to take charge until Diaz' *rurales* had "restored order." The next year textile workers in the Rio Blanco were shot down by government troops when they, too, went on strike for the first time.

Again in 1908 the Liberal party attempted to awaken the masses against the iron heel of Diaz. The response to their efforts was growing. And although on the surface Mexican life appeared calm, and the Diaz regime was regarded as most benevolent by those who were enjoying and profiting from Mexican bonds, underneath, the rumbling of revolutionary torrents was growing louder and louder.

Mexico was a land full of the capped dynamite of political, economic, social and moral grievances. Only a spark was needed to set off this dynamite with a deafening detonation. That spark came as a change of administration was being demanded by a political opposition led by Madero, as students clamored for a new deal, as labor demanded recognition, as the Yaqui, the Mayan and the peon groaned for deliverance from their slavery. And although the man who raised the standard of revolt against Diaz was entirely inadequate and incompetent, he became the rallying point for the whole opposition, which converged into a main stream of support for Madero's struggle to remove the dictator who pandered the wealth blooded and sweated out of the bodies of the unfortunate Mexican people.

The theoretical leader of the revolution and of the as yet weak proletariat was Magòn, as Emiliano Zapata was the champion of the peasants. After an intimate acquaintance with Diaz' prisons between 1901 and 1903, Magòn fled to El Paso and later to St Louis, Missouri, in order to be even less accessible to the long arm of Diaz, who never abandoned his efforts to have him done away with. During these years of exile Magòn, his brother, Enrique Flores Magòn, and Librado Rivera published their paper, *Regeneraciòn*, and in 1905 they brought out the program which was to be the inspiration for future democratic movements in Mexico.

Their demands were for an eight-hour day, enforcement of the anticlerical provisions contained in the constitution, the nonre-election of Diaz, a minimum wage law, abolition of debt peonage, state seizure of idle lands and their distribution to those who were eager to work and needed them. Madero's program, Zapata's Plan of Ayala, articles twenty-seven and one hundred and twenty-three of the 1917 constitution, as well as all labor legislation sponsored from the time of Obregón to Cardenas—these have their source in Magòn's 1905 program.

After the two attempted revolts led by the Magònistas in 1906 and 1908, the American government saw to it that Magòn made a broad acquaintance with American prisons. It was during this time that Magòn came to the conclusion that the only agency which could abolish all classes in society was the working class. Neither the American Socialist party nor the A.F. of L. impressed him favorably. But he was strongly attracted by the I.W.W., which was at that time very popular with the immature Mexican working class. It is not surprising, considering his background—Mexico with its Spanish heritage and its lack of industrial development—that he became an anarcho-communist.

Emerging from prison in 1910, he renewed his revolutionary activity, but with the Madero movement sweeping the country, his efforts were unavailing. Thenceforth all superficial political aims and evidence of lack of social vision on the part of Madero and his various successors received Magòn's sharp criticism. In a similar way, the preamble to Zapata's Plan of Ayala influenced all measures proposed for the redistribution of the land.

The Magònistas were responsible for a unique episode which took place during the early part of the revolution, when, with American Wobblies and others interested merely in adventure, they raided Lower California, seized Mexicali and set up the "Socialist Republic of Lower California." Their success was of brief duration. Magòn and Dick Ferris, president of the republic, were arrested by the United States government for violation of the neutrality laws. From then on Magòn was rarely outside of American prisons. Released from McNeil's Island in 1914, he was jailed again in 1916 when, consistently fighting for his revolutionary aims, he exhorted Carranza's soldiers to use their guns against their officers and for the emancipation of the betrayed masses.

Four years later the Obregón Congress voted him and Librado Rivera life pensions in acknowledgment of their services to Mexico. Both refused to accept them. Magòn's unquenchable spirit is best revealed through his own words: "If my sufferings and my chains serve to accomplish the unification of the proletarian organization, I bless my sufferings and I love my chains." In 1922 Magòn was returned to Mexico from Leavenworth prison, a corpse.

Shortly after the capture of Mexicali Jack London wrote "The Mexican," a short story in which his warm sympathy for the revolutionists was so perfectly balanced by a superb description of a prize fight that it was promptly accepted and published by the *Saturday Evening Post*. How close he was in spirit to the revolution, and with what detail he had followed its progress is amply revealed in this story:

"Once started, the Revolution would take care of itself. The whole Diaz machine would go down like a house of cards. The border was ready to rise. One Yankee, with a hundred I.W.W. men, waited the word to cross over the border and begin the conquest of Lower California. But he needed guns. And clear across to the Atlantic, the Junta in touch with them all and all of them needing guns, were adventurers, soldiers of fortune, bandits, disgruntled American union men, socialists, anarchists, rough-necks, Mexican exiles, peons escaped from bondage, whipped miners from the bull pens of Coeur d'Alene and Colorado who desired only the more vindictively to fight—all the flotsam and jetsam of wild spirits from the madly complicated modern world. And it was guns and ammunition, ammunition and guns—the unceasing and eternal cry."

The boy, Felipe Rivera, who had come to the Junta to "work for the Revolution," undertook to provide money for guns and ammunition. Unknown to the Junta, he had long made a meager living, and contributed small sums to the movement, by victories over local fighters in the Los Angeles prize ring. Now he pledged himself to win a fight with the coming lightweight champion, a fight in which he had insisted that "winner takes all," a fight which was, nevertheless, to be "fixed" so that he would lose.

Waiting in the ring for his opponent, "the things Rivera fought for burned in his brain. . . . He saw the white-walled, water-power factories of Rio Blanco. He saw the six thousand workers, starved and wan, and the little children, seven and eight years of age, who toiled long shifts for ten cents a day. He saw the perambulating corpses, the ghastly death's heads of men who labored in the dye-rooms. He remembered he had heard his father call the dye-rooms the 'suicide-holes,' where a year was death.

". . . The strike, or, rather, the lock-out, because the workers of Rio Blanco had helped their striking brothers of Puebla. The hunger, the expeditions in the hills for berries, the roots and herbs that all ate and that twisted and pained the stomachs of all of them. And then, the nightmare; the waste of ground before the company's store; the thousands of starving workers; General Rosalio Martinez and the soldiers of Porfirio Diaz; and the death-spitting rifles that seemed never to cease spitting, while the workers' wrongs were washed and washed again in their own blood . . ."

As Rivera went into the fight, "a vision of countless rifles blinded his eyes. Every face in the audience, far as he could see, to the high dollar-seats, was transformed into a rifle. And he saw the long Mexican border arid and sun-washed and aching, and along it he saw the ragged bands that delayed only for the guns. . . ." And when he had won: "His knees trembled under him and he was sobbing from exhaustion. Before his eyes the hated faces swayed back and forth in the giddiness of nausea. Then he remembered they were the guns. The guns were his. The Revolution could go on."

Three years passed. Jack London wrote no more of the Mexican revolution, or of any revolution. He increased his earnings, enlarged his ranch, built the Wolf House, became an employer of labor, a host to hordes of admiring guests. But in Mexico the revolutionary struggle continued.

Madero revealed not the slightest understanding of his country's problems, let alone a solution for them. His cure-all was a naïve belief that "effective suffrage" would settle everything to everyone's satisfaction. But the agricultural masses wanted land, and there arose in their midst a leader who was determined that they should get it. Emiliano Zapata waited, but not for long, for Madero to pass the land-reform measures which he had promised. Then, under Zapata's leadership, the Indians and the peons began to solve the problem in their own way by taking the land from the enormous haciendas, and plowing and planting and harvesting it, even as in 1905 the peasants had taken over the great estates in Russia.

Zapata's Plan of Ayala, issued in November 1911, although far from perfect was the most important social program which appeared during the revolution, and was in essence a demand that one third of the haciendas be given to those who had no land. Zapata's struggle to obtain land for his people continued until his death, and as he fought Madero, so he fought each succeeding government because none of them kept the promises they had made.

Meantime the influence of the United States was being keenly felt in Mexico. The Taft administration had picked De La Barra to succeed Diaz and was therefore hostile to Madero. Henry Lane Wilson, the American ambassador, did everything in his power to help Madero's enemies, and his role in the fate of Madero was unenviable. Inherited by Woodrow Wilson's administration, Ambassador Wilson aided the successful counterrevolution which placed Huerta in power in February, 1913, his saber still dripping with the blood of Madero. But Huerta soon evidenced the same policy against American and for European investments which had resulted in America's withdrawal of support from Diaz. The United States refused to recognize Huerta, and four months after Woodrow Wilson was inaugurated Ambassador Wilson's resignation was demanded.

During several succeeding years Mexico presented to the undiscerning, especially in the United States, a picture of horror and chaos as, unheralded, name after name of leaders and heroes blazed up in the revolution and vanished. All were more or less illiterate; all were fired to a greater or lesser degree by the wish to right the people's wrongs. But even when they wished to lead, to formulate constructive programs, they could not, for the revolution move forward so swiftly and erratically that they could not even keep up with it. Behind the revolution and driving it on was an outraged people whose activity boiled and seethed within the narrow confines set by a purely local perspective. They not only lacked any semblance of class consciousness; they were not even aware that they were part of a nation. The urban working class had barely begun to grow; the middle class was weak and frightened; the capitalist class was practically nonexistent save as agents of foreign capital.

The undiscerning saw nothing but violence, lawlessness, betrayal, intrigue and the criminal destruction of private property. Of the discerning, some were revolutionists, and they saw Magòn, Zapata and Pancho Villa, and their unrelenting efforts on behalf of the Mexican people. But others saw Mexico's fabulously rich oil wells, and watchfully noting events, bided their time until they might strike effectively and secure them. Mexican oil motivated the official attitudes and diplomatic maneuvers of every imperialist power which interested itself in Mexico during these years.

Huerta faced more than the disapproval of the United States. Zapata, Villa, and a lesser but luckier man, Carranza, had united at the head of those to whom the counterrevolution had meant the end of all their hopes.

Pancho Villa, born Doroteo Arango the year Diaz first took office, was the most romantic of the revolutionary figures and probably the best known both inside and outside of Mexico. Outlawed at sixteen when he had killed a local despot, he placed himself and his band at the disposal of Madero in 1910. From then until his death he fought for the revolution. They—he and the revolution—were much alike: backward, confused, brutal, heroic and fearless. He hated all the enemies of his oppressed people, the big landowners, the overseers, the priests, and foreign-born Spaniards who lorded it in a country not their own, and in time he came to hate the *gringos*.

This hate was returned in full measure, but the people loved him. Long before his death he had been charged with every crime in the calendar, but he had also become the legendary hero of countless popular ballads in Mexico. So great was his influence that for a time, during the latter half of 1914, the Wilson administration was considering supporting him as the strong man of Mexico.

Huerta, rapidly losing ground, but confident of the wisdom of his course, provoked a situation whose outcome proved contrary to his expectations. An affront to an American naval officer in Tampico, when American marines landed on forbidden military preserves, was followed by a demand from the United States that the American flag be saluted. Huerta refused to comply with this demand, believing that the threat of a foreign invasion would swing popular support to him and weaken his opponents. It was the moment for which the United States had been waiting. On April 21, 1914, America seized Vera Cruz. At once Villa, Zapata and Carranza, leading the struggle against the usurper, Huerta, roused the Mexican people to a storm of protest against America's military intervention. Helpless, Huerta resigned on July fourteenth.

Carranza, self-acclaimed leader of the revolution, immediately set out to make himself head of the state, only to meet the sharp opposition of Zapata and Villa, who refused to abandon their revolutionary aims. From July 14, 1914, until January 1915, Mexico City knew six changes of government. Then, in a desperate attempt to win popular support away from his adversaries, Carranza issued a provisional decree for the restitution of the communal lands. The move was successful. The United States, impressed by Carranza's "amenability to reason" and his increasing stabilization, recognized him as president of Mexico.

The peak of the revolution had passed. Magòn raised a cry of protest which was silenced behind the walls of an American prison. Villa and Zapata fought on for the revolution, while Mexico became known as the "land where peace breaks out once in a while." In 1919 the peasants were plunged into despair when Zapata was treacherously ambushed and assassinated; four years later Villa met the same fate. The oil wells were safe.

So closely was the American press watching the situation in Mexico during the Huerta regime that arrangements for correspondents had been made months before the Tampico incident occurred. Jack London, having agreed to represent *Collier's* for the sum of eleven hundred dollars weekly, was summoned by wire on April 16, 1914, to leave the next day for Galveston, whence he was to go by army transport to Vera Cruz.

In Galveston he waited in vain for his credential from Washington, although all the other correspondents had received theirs days before. Shortly before sailing time he learned why it had been withheld, the reason being what Jack always referred to thereafter as the "Good Soldier canard."

Two years earlier the Seattle *Times* had reported that a circular had recently been posted around the principal docks of the city bearing some such caption as "Young Man, Don't Be A Soldier, Be A Man!" and that after a quiet investigation the government suspected the Wobblies of distributing it, and Jack London of having written it.

In the *International Socialist Review* for October 1913 appeared an article entitled "The Good Soldier," by Jack London: "Young men: The lowest aim in your life is to become a soldier. The good soldier never tries to distinguish right from wrong. He never thinks; never reasons; he only obeys. If he is ordered to fire on his fellow citizens, on his friends, on his neighbors, on his relatives, he obeys without hesitation. If he is ordered to fire down a crowded street when the poor are clamoring for bread, he obeys and sees the gray hairs of age stained with red and the life tide gushing from the breasts of women, feeling neither remorse nor sympathy. If he is ordered off as a firing squad to execute a hero or benefactor, he fires without hesitation, though he knows the bullet will pierce the noblest heart that ever beat in human breast.

"A good soldier is a blind, heartless, soulless, murderous machine. He is not a man. He is not a brute, for brutes only kill in self-defense. All that is human in him, all that is divine in him, all that constitutes the man has been sworn away when he took the enlistment roll. His mind, his conscience, aye, his very soul, are in the keeping of his officer.

"No man can fall lower than a soldier—it is a depth beneath which we cannot go. Keep the boys out of the army. It is hell. "Down with the army and the navy. We don't need killing institutions. We need life-giving institutions."

Was Jack London the author of "The Good Soldier?" From April 1914 until his death he denied it emphatically, yet the rumor persisted. It is significant, moreover, that he did not ask the *International Socialist Review* to publish a denial of his authorship, and that, as his hatred of Germany grew to almost a mania between 1914 and 1916, he should finally have attributed the origin of "The Good Soldier" to Germany. Certain radicals, especially Wobblies, maintain that Jack often voiced such antiwar sentiments prior to 1912. In 1898 he had written to Ted Applegarth, "A soldier's life is a dog's life at best." H. R. Lytle, who was with him in Kelly's army, reported that as early as 1894 Jack's attitude toward soldiers was unfavorable and believed that this had been influenced by his and others' experiences with Pinkerton detectives and state militias during the march of the unemployed.

Examination of the text of "The Good Soldier" permits one to hazard a guess. With the exception of the second paragraph the style of writing bears no resemblance to Jack London's, but that paragraph is curiously reminiscent not only of the manner in which he wrote but of that in which he spoke. Might it not be possible that, talking informally as was his wont with one or more of the numerous radicals who frequently stopped on the ranch for a few days, he had expressed such an indictment of militarism, and that this was afterward written down by a listener from memory?

When it first appeared it did not bear his name, but if the guess is correct, word would certainly have been passed around that this was what Jack London had said to so-and-so last month or last year in Glen Ellen. One finds it difficult to believe that a publication such as the *International Socialist Review* would have published the article without assurance from reliable sources that the sentiments it contained were Jack London's. In any case, whether the guess is correct or not, Jack did not trouble to deny his authorship until he discovered that General Funston was withholding his war correspondent's credential because he believed that Jack had written "The Good Soldier."

Jack remained in Vera Cruz save for a short trip to Tampico until the early part of June, fretting and fuming because there was no war to report. Toward the end of his stay he fell ill with acute bacillary dysentery, and although this dictated his departure as soon as he was able to travel, he was not sorry to go. He had nothing but contempt for the Mexican revolution, and he was furiously angry that the United States, having gone so far as to seize Vera Cruz, did not proceed to take over the entire country.

Oliver Madox Hueffer, a fellow correspondent, recalled after Jack's death that Jack often spoke in Vera Cruz of his desire to write a novel dealing with the Mexican revolution, and that while he was in Tampico he had been gathering material for this project. The book was never written, but there is no doubt that if it had been it would have been difficult to recognize its author as the man who had written *The Iron Heel* and "The Mexican," and who three years earlier had concluded a letter to the "dear, brave comrades of the Mexican revolution" with: "I subscribe myself a chicken thief and revolutionist, Jack London."

The several articles he wrote for *Collier's* during his stay in Mexico reveal such a complete *volte face* in his attitude toward the Mexican revolution and America's role in it that one is almost tempted to believe that they were written under his name by an entirely different person. For the second time Jack's reactions to the inhabitants of a foreign country were those of a provincial, middle-class American. All that he had learned from Marx and Engels, his many times reiterated belief in the international revolutionary movement, the solidarity he had expressed so often with the struggle of workers against their oppressors, succumbed to the race prejudice and glorification of the Anglo-Saxon of Benjamin Kidd, and to the "big-brother" propaganda with which American imperialism masked its self-interest.

For the peon Jack had a condescending pity: centuries of oppression had bred him into a weak, docile being, "the selected burden-bearer of the centuries," ignorant, helpless and hopeless. "He has never heard of economic principles, nor a square deal. Nor has he thrilled, save vaguely, to the call of freedom—in which event freedom has meant license, and, as robber and bandit, he has treated the weak and defenseless in precisely the same way he has been accustomed to being treated. . . . He is not fighting for any principle, for any reward. It is a sad world, in which witless, humble men are just forced to fight, to kill and be killed."

But for the *mestizos*, whom he scornfully called "breeds," he had nothing but loathing and contempt: "And it is just precisely this twenty per cent half-breed class that foments all the trouble, plays childishly with the tools of giants, and makes a shambles and a chaos of the land. These 'breeds' represent neither the great working class, nor the property-owning class, nor the picked men of the United States and Europe who have given Mexico what measure of exotic civilization it possesses. These 'breeds' are the predatory class. They produce nothing. They create nothing. They aim to possess a shirt, ride on a horse, and 'shake down' the people who work and the people who develop, . . . They are what the mixed breed always is—neither fish, flesh or fowl. They are neither white men nor Indians. Like the Eurasians, they possess all the vices of their various commingled bloods and none of the virtues."

Huerta apparently struck him as the best of a bad lot: "Huerta is the flower of the Mexican Indian. Such Indians have appeared on occasion in the United States. Huerta is brave. Huerta is masterful. But even Huerta has never betrayed possession of high ideals nor wide social vision." As for the other leaders, he denied the sincerity of their aims, believed that they were nothing but adventurers, "child-minded men, incapable of government," out to rob and pillage and, what was worse, to "shake down" the gringo oil men "who had found and developed the oil-fields."

"The phrases and slogans of the Mexicans do not mean what they seem to mean," he scoffed. "Countless Americans think the present revolution is an expression of the peon's land hunger. Madero raised that cry. Zapata still raises the same cry. . . . Villa still shouts 'free land.' . . . What peon with any spunk in him, would elect to slave on a hacienda for a slave's reward when, in the ranks of Zapata, Carranza or Villa, he can travel, see the country, ride a horse, carry a rifle, get a peso or so a day, loot when fortune favors, and, if lucky, on occasion kill a fellow creature— this last a particularly delightful event to a people who delight in the bloody spectacles of the bull ring."

As he saw it, the problem was to save Mexico from herself, from "the insignificant portion of half-breeds who are causing all the trouble. They should not form the government at all. And yet they are the very ones who insist on forming it, and they cannot be eliminated by those who should form it, namely, the twelve million peons and the nearly three million peaceably inclined half-breeds."

And his solution:

". . . It is still abhorrent for a nation to step in between a handful of rulers and their millions of mismanaged and ill-treated subjects. Yet such interference is logically the duty of the United States as the big brother of the countries of the new world. . . . The big brother can police, organize and manage Mexico. The so-called leaders of Mexico cannot." And to clinch his argument, he stated: "The educated Mexicans, the wealthy Mexicans, the business and shop-keeping Mexicans, hail American intervention with delight." .

While Jack was writing these articles in Vera Cruz, many American radicals believed that he was somewhere in northern Mexico at the head of a band of revolutionists. Newspapers bore such headlines as "Jack London Leads Army of Mexican Rebels." Daily appeared new rumors: that he was wounded, that he had been captured, that he had won a smashing victory. Jack's comment, added gratuitously to denials of the rumors, that under no circumstances would he want to be leading rebels in Mexico was the first inkling the radicals had of his changed point of view. Nevertheless they were totally unprepared for the articles in *Collier's*.

Protests in the radical press throughout the United States were tinged with bitter reproach. Even the mildly liberal *Nation* remarked, "The extremely readable letters from Mexico in *Collier's* are not written by 'Yours for the Revolution Jack London' but by plain 'Jack London.' . . . That an eminent apostle of red revolution should audibly be licking his chops over millions of gold dollars wrested from its rightful owner, the Mexican peon, by the predatory ministers of international capital, is somewhat disconcerting."

The most serious attack upon Jack for the reversal of his socialist principles in regard to Mexico was published a year later in the *Appeal to Reason*. The author of the article, John Kenneth Turner, had recently returned from Tampico where, somewhat to his surprise, since he was a well-known Socialist, he had been entertained by the oil men. "They hoped to win me," he wrote, "to their cherished theory that God created Mexico not for the Mexicans, but for the American and English oil men." As a result of this experience he began to wonder what had happened to Jack London the year before in Mexico which might have accounted for the articles in *Collier's*.

"Socialist London turned out a brief for the oil man, a brief for intervention, a brief for what Mexicans call 'Yankee Imperialism,'" he summed up. And then: "What influences other than flattering good fellowship may have been exerted to bring about this remarkable result, in the particular case of Jack London, I do not know. But I know that this insidious thing is used effectively in the corruption of others, not only of well-known writers, but of naval officers, consular agents and newspaper correspondents."

This veiled charge of subsidization from a Socialist evoked furious comment from Jack and heightened his growing bitterness against the socialist movement in the United States. He seemed not only to be completely unaware of how far he had strayed from Marxism in the years since he had written *The Iron Heel*, but to have forgotten that a scant four years earlier he had warmly supported the Mexican revolution and described the possible invasion of the United States "to protect its dollars" as a "burning shame."

Turner was wrong. The flattering good fellowship of the oil men had not influenced Jack London, nor had he been subsidized by them. His was a more tragic sellout, for he had been subsidized, bought body and soul, by the kind of life he had thought he wanted, and it was destroying him.

ON THE SURFACE the last years of Jack London's life were showy and brilliant. He was the highest paid author in America. Fame such as no other writer of his time enjoyed was his. Many in other fields of endeavor whose incomes were as large or larger envied him his independence, his freedom to travel, the few hours a day his work required. Those who were struggling to realize some measure of their own dreams and ambitions were spurred on by the well-publicized saga of his success.

But no one knew better than Jack London how ephemeral were his fame and his income, and how swiftly they would slip away if once he relaxed his efforts to retain them. If only he might derive the same income from some activity other than writing! If the ranch would begin to pay dividends! If even one of his investments might prove fortunate! Then, perhaps, life might once more have savor and meaning. Perhaps, free of the compulsion to write, the creative gift he had ruthlessly commercialized until it was almost exhausted might revive, and he would write because he wanted to the books and stories which he had never been able to afford.

These hopes came to nothing. The ranch did not pay. The investments—and they were many, for his urgency to escape from writing made him an easy mark for every Rufus Wallingford who sought him—were failures. Day in and day out, as long as he lived, he would write popular fiction, and conceal from readers, editors and publishers how almost unendurable the task had become. Successful Jack London, at the peak of his career, admired and envied, was a weary, bewildered, prematurely aging man, with failing health and a dying spirit. To the end, however, he kept up a magnificent bluff.

"I'm going to do some big, good, decent work in the next five years with you," Jack told Roland Phillips of the *Cosmopolitan* in the spring of 1913, shortly after he had signed a five-year contract with that magazine for all his fiction. "Why, man, I haven't begun to write yet!"

Of the book he was then engaged in writing, he wrote Phillips, "As I go over this novel, I am almost led to believe that it is what I have been working toward all my writing life, and now I've got it in my two hands. Except for my old-time punch, which will be in it from start to finish," he boasted, (and no agent could have represented him better than he did himself) "it will not be believed that I could write it—it is so utterly fresh, so absolutely unlike anything I have ever done. . . . Oh, of course, I can do the short stories in the cold, calm confidence and surety of the trained craftsman, but here, in this novel, I am hot. It will be big stuff. It will offend no one, and it will hold suspense to the last page. And—it will be just about 100,000 words and no pruning or condensation necessary for serial publication. It will be a clean-cut gem, even in serial form—a jewel of artistry. You will not need to subtract a word. . . . Lord, Lord, man! I haven't begun to write yet!" A year later, plugging the short story he was then writing, he told Phillips, "It will be entirely different from any short story that ever was written in the world before in any language."

The autobiographical urge grew very strong in his later years, as the desire for new experiences dimmed and died and he began to feel that his youth was far behind him. "We oldsters," he used to say to astonished contemporaries still in their thirties. Often he spoke of himself as "the ancient." But while nostalgia for his vanished youth sometimes touched his reminiscences, bitterness was uppermost. There had been much in his life that he would not forgive. Harsh memories of poverty, lack of advantages, slights he had received and suffered over, wounds to his pride and his ego—these he clung to tenaciously.

"When I finally get around to writing the story of my life," he used to tell his daughters, "it's going to be a true story, and not a pretty one. People won't like it, for I'm going to write about everything that happened to me, and say what I think of the whole business." As long as his income depended upon writing, of course, he could not consider publishing such a book, but, some day, he promised himself, he would write it.

As early as 1911 he had told an English publisher that he planned to write his autobiography and publish it while he was still alive, but that he could not see his way to it for years to come. A year later, having worked out a method of using autobiographical material without harming his sales, he was writing *John Barleycorn*. The success of this book tempted him to repeat the performance. "In addition to the steady output of fiction now planned," he wrote to a magazine editor, "I have also planned two other volumes of personal reminiscences. Each of these shall be written as soon as I can get around to it. And each of them will merit a sequel. The first book is my personal reminiscences as a writer, from the very beginning of the game, when I started to educate myself, up to the present moment. Very similar in a way, although entirely different in treatment from *John Barleycorn* reminiscences. The other will constitute the nine years of preliminary farming, and my present experiments which I am carrying on here at Glen Ellen. . . . If I live to be five hundred year old, I should never be able to do the work I have already mapped out and filed away. I have plots of over one hundred novels filed away on my shelves and possibly five hundred short stories."

Early in 1914 he wrote Phillips, "Three more novels I have up in the air to be entitled (1) *The Man Who Passes* (a New York novel); (2) *The Box Without a Lid* (on all the world); (3) *Jane Barleycorn* (a companion, in fiction form, to *John Barleycorn*)." The latter was a tentative title for a book which he frequently discussed with friends at the time, and which was to be based on his experiences with women. That, for the most part, he did not consider these happy ones, and that his estimation of the women he had known was not very high, is clear from his final decision to make the book, if he wrote it at all, so brutally frank that it would have to be published under a pseudonym.

Although none of the autobiographical books were written Jack never abandoned the idea. A few weeks before his death he wrote his London agent, Mr Hughes Massie, concerning the possibility of writing a book on his experiences as an author, and among the very last notes he made on the tablet he kept on his bedside table was: "Socialist biography. *Martin Eden* and *Sea Wolf*, attacks on Nietzschean philosophy, which even the socialists missed the point of." He never ceased to wonder why his most serious books had been misunderstood. To Mary Austin he wrote the year before his death: "I have again and again written books that failed to get across. Long years ago, at the very beginning of my writing career, I attacked Nietzsche and his super-man idea. This was in *The Sea Wolf*. Lots of people read *The Sea Wolf*, no one discovered that it was an attack upon the super-man philosophy. Later on, not mentioning my shorter efforts, I wrote another novel that was an attack upon the super-man idea, namely *Martin Eden*. Nobody discovered that this was such an attack. At another time I wrote an attack on ideas brought forth by Rudyard Kipling, and entitled my attack "The Strength of the Strong." No one was in the slightest way aware of the point of my story. . . . And I do not worry about it. . . . I go ahead content to be admired for my red-blooded brutality and for a number of other nice little things like that which are not true of my work at all."

1913—Jack's thirty-seventh year—saw the appearance of four books by him, bringing the total of those he had published since 1900 to thirty-six; nearly twenty more were to be published in the next few years, none of which were outstanding. Although he stoutly defended his work against criticism as, for instance, "So many people have written me, registering nothing but disgust for *The Little Lady of the Big House*. Darn it all—I like that story," he sometimes revealed his complete lack of interest in what he wrote to those who were near him. "It looks as if I am trying to see how many books I can publish before I die," he inscribed in a book for Bess, and in another appeared the weary comment, "Just one more of the many I shall write ere I cease and be dust." A month before his death he sent a copy of *The Turtles of Tasman* to his daughters, on the flyleaf of which he had written, "Yarns, just yarns. There may be some little meat of meaning in them. Who knows? Who knows?"

"Times have changed," Jack wrote to a woman magazine writer, explaining why historical and descriptive material did not sell. "No longer do the magazines care for anything but muckraking: industrial articles, advertising articles and fiction. Fiction always, fiction first, last, and forever." Few reviewers bothered any more to criticize his work seriously, for it was obvious that Jack was no longer exerting himself, but merely giving his public what it wanted. Sometimes, however, a reviewer was stung to protest: "Jack London has recently informed a listening world that he could do more work if only he did not sleep. We are sometimes tempted to wish that Mr London would not only sleep a little longer, but not work quite so hard when he is awake; in other words, that he would stop and think a little more. Then he might become a great American story-teller (for he has the gift), and not merely a popular romancer." Of *The Valley of the Moon* the New York *World* said, ". . . the story it tells is delightfully free from the fetters of convention," adding tersely, "Its freedom, indeed, strongly suggests that of the fairy story, with an ending in perpetual prosperity and good cheer."

John Barleycorn, published in 1913, the last of his books of any significance, had proved something of a sensation. All who had fought against the liquor traffic—ministers, educators, prohibitionists, the W.C.T.U.—regarded it as a milestone in their campaign. But others were equally enthusiastic. A young man named Floyd Dell wrote in the Chicago *Post* that *John Barleycorn* was "the saga of drink, and of all the splendor, perhaps a meretricious splendor, that drink brings into a man's life." Another young man named Joyce Kilmer hailed it as an event of primary literary importance. Elbert Hubbard proclaimed it a "classic." Charles Vale said in the *Forum*, "Nothing so frank and sincere, and therefore clean and beautiful, has been written for a long time. For Jack London is not merely the author of many ridiculously successful books. He is a man, and a poet."

But André Tridon, who not long before had included Jack London in a list of young American novelists who were "fizzling out one after another," refused to regard *John Barleycorn* either as a literary achievement or as an arraignment of alcohol, but as an arraignment of the chief reason why Jack was "fizzling out." "I knew there was something the matter with London's stuff," he wrote in the *New Review*. "His vocabulary was apparently gone, his imagination seemed to be failing him, he repeated himself frightfully, his stories were becoming as safe as those of any popular novelist. Read *John Barleycorn* and you will soon enough discover what ails him. He will tell you himself, and the tragedy of it is he does not even seem to know how far gone he is."

Jack, charged Tridon, had repeated "ad nauseam" that drink was too accessible: "Miserable excuse! Ice cream is accessible even more so than whisky. Sociability demands alcohol," he continued, "and sociability is above discussion. Why? Who will deliver us

from the tyranny of the absurd word? Who will deliver us from
the sociable idiots, thieves of our time and energy, with whom
we have to compromise intellectually for fear a discussion might
delay their departure; deliver us from the gregarious feasts at
which food and talk and drink-talk are even more depressing
than the overfeeding and overdrinking they entail. . . .

"Does Jack London still enjoy those things when his knock-
ing about every country and every sea has shown him the broader
side of the world's life, or does the former roustabout enjoy going
to 'people's' houses and having 'people' at his own house? . . .
Oh, Jack! cease to abuse alcohol. It isn't alcohol that is troubling
you, it's people, the small, nice, human, uninteresting, hearty,
loyal, trashy people with whom you drink. Alcohol may have
something to do with your temporary downfall, but people have
had and are having more to do with it. For one thing your friends
should be damned. They have killed your wonderful vocabulary.
Only a solitary man can preserve a beautiful choice of words. As
soon as you express your thoughts in conversation you are compelled to relinquish all the fine shadings. . . .

"May I suggest a cure for London's ailment?" he summed up.
"To live in some large city where 'people' are so cheap a com-
modity that we don't go to their houses nor let them come too
often to our lodgings, and we enter sociability under the heading of dissipation or profit and loss. . . ."

A copy of the *New Review* containing Tridon's article came
into Jack's hands. Judging by the course he continued to pur-
sue, he paid no more attention to Tridon's diagnosis and advice
than he did a little later to that of the various medical men concerning his physical condition. The causes Tridon had assigned
for the inferior quality of Jack's work were not causes but symptoms themselves. Nevertheless he had described with fair accuracy
the lengths to which Jack's "sociability" had taken him.

Despite his travels and experiences, Jack apparently still enjoyed "those things"—going to "people's" houses and, more especially, having "people" at his own home. And under no circumstances would he leave the ranch and live in a city. For Jack London, who once had joyfully come to grips with life, hailing struggle as much for its own sake as for desired ends, was now in full
retreat from it, and "people" and the ranch were the escapes he
had chosen.

From the time he wrote *Martin Eden* all his work had been

done primarily for the ranch. As its needs grew he became even more businesslike in his relations with editors and publishers. Certainly no American writer before him so successfully manipulated the matter of advances for work not yet completed. He was among the first to see the possibility for increased returns from writing offered by motion pictures and flung himself energetically into the Author's League fight for revision of the copyright laws so that authors might have undisputed ownership of motion picture and other rights to their works.

When he realized that his investment in eucalyptus was a failure he turned his attention to stock breeding, determining finally to produce the finest strains of Shire horses, Shorthorn cattle and Duroc Jersey hogs in America. But his ambition was even larger than that: the ranch was to become a self-subsisting colony. Then, indeed, his escape would be complete from the world, whose demands from him for more than tales with which to pass the time he could shut out in no other way. And, ever an excellent rationalizer, he persuaded himself, a Socialist and still a member of the Socialist party, that "in the solution of the great economic problems of the present age" he saw "a return to the soil."

With his tremendous energy and earning power devoted to the realization of his ambitions, and with his stepsister, Eliza Shepard, as superintendent of the ranch from 1910 on, the progress he made in half a dozen years is not surprising. His reverence for science which in his youth had led him to Darwin, Spencer and others, now dictated research into the scientific manipulation of animal husbandry, breeding and farm management. He used to say that he devoted two hours a day to writing and ten to farming, which meant detailed planning, and the reading not only of books on the science of agriculture but of countless government bulletins and reports.

The first manure spreader in the vicinity, the first concrete silo in California, the application of new methods worked out in agricultural colleges throughout the country, the erection of stone barns and water troughs that would "last a thousand years," and more cottages for his laborers and their families as the number of men on his pay roll grew larger—these gave tangible evidence of his activity. Despite his use of the most up-to-date American ideas about farming, however, he was critical of them. "I have observed," he told his friend, Henry Mead Bland, "that Americans, through their leaders who make a scientific study of the soil, know a great deal of 'why' things are done, but not much of the 'how'; while in Japan, China and Korea, much is known of the 'how' but very little of the 'why.'" Among the various travel plans he considered during his last restless years was one to the Orient where on journeys through the interiors of Japan, Korea, China and India he expected to discover more of the "how" than was known in America.

The intense activity which had characterized his life since the start of his career grew more intense, as if by never relaxing, by working beyond his strength, he might be less aware of the unrest and dissatisfaction which tormented him. Writing, ranching, studying agricultural problems, caring for an incredibly large correspondence and, when this was done, entering feverishly into various sorts of recreation with his guests—with five or six hours sleep, the twenty-four hours that made a day and a night passed quickly, but never quickly enough.

He could not keep it up, of course. Gradually the hours increased which were spent with others, talking, drinking, playing cards and rougher, more boisterous games and practical jokes than those he had enjoyed in the Bungalow days. Meantime as his health began to fail his delight in exercise and sports diminished until finally his existence became almost sedentary.

In 1912 he had sailed as a passenger around the Horn in a four-masted bark; three years later he went to sea again, but this time on a passenger steamer bound for Hawaii. Here he fell victim to the charm which life in these islands offered to a famous well-to-do man like himself. The middle class which he had wooed since his high-school days, and whose respect and admiration he had won for his writings, now sought him out and welcomed him in good fellowship for himself. He entertained and was entertained, enraptured by the rituals and customs which dated from the tribal ceremonies of aboriginal times and which had been adopted, colonial-fashion, by the American residents in Hawaii, and joyfully surprised by what he considered the simplicity and openheartedness of these people of wealth and leisure.

An acquaintance in Honolulu was impressed by his gaiety at this time. "His remarks, his observations, his stories," she wrote, "were as light and as frothy as the spray that dashed over the coral reef and broke on the shore at our feet. . . . It is difficult to tell just when Mr London did the quantity of writing which came from his pen. He was so much in evidence in Honolulu and elsewhere in the islands that it seemed hardly possible to associate him with the prolific writer he was known to be." To Joan he wrote during his second visit, the year of his death, "I grow more and more in love with Hawaii, and I am certain, somewhere in the future (not too remote) that I shall elect to make Hawaii my home."

Hawaii, then, was to be the ultimate refuge. Even the ranch was to be abandoned for an easier existence which would demand so little of him. In those pleasant islands where only a minimum of physical and mental exertion was necessary he would catch but faint echoes of that war of the classes which once had stirred him so profoundly and which, at close range, still moved him more than he would admit. Hawaii also had a labor problem, of course. Workers on the great plantations were mercilessly exploited, but they were not "whites," but "browns," "yellows" and "breeds," and Jack had long since ceased to be concerned about what he regarded as "inferior" races.

When his last collection of short stories, *On the Makaloa Mat*, was published nearly three years after his death, a reviewer for the New York *Sun* poignantly summarized the end of what had promised to be such a brilliant literary career: "His last phase was Hawaii. It is a little odd to think of him, after all his waywardness of living—marching with Coxey's tatterdemalion army . . . tramping everywhere with tramps and knowing the Road at its most stony-hearted, answering the Call of the Wild with a whoop that startled many others into whooping, cruising around the world in a way all his own, having literary adventures with John Barleycorn—after that reaching his last and to him most enjoyable phase when basking in the warmth of Honolulu, disporting himself in the surf at Waikiki with garlands around his neck."

The Star Rover, which was completed shortly before he went to Mexico in 1914, was Jack's last attempt at a serious work. Into this extraordinary and little-known book he flung with a prodigal hand riches which he had hoarded for years, and compressed into brilliant episodes notes originally intended for full-length books. Of all his later work, only portions of this novel and a few short stories reveal the fulfillment of the artistic promise so evident in his early writings. After *The Star Rover* he made no further effort to write well. A fortunate combination of mood and material might result in a few excellent pages or a finely wrought short story, but for the most part he deliberately employed the skill

he had once striven so hard to acquire merely to shorten the time
needed to produce his daily thousand words.

That his skill in writing propaganda had not diminished was
evidenced in *Michael, Brother of Jerry*, his last dog story. As
vigorously as he had once championed the cause of exploited
workers, he advocated in this book an end to training animals for
the vaudeville stage. Immediately after its publication in November
1917, Jack London clubs, as suggested in the preface to the
book, began to be formed in the United States. The same people
who were enthusiastically buying Liberty bonds and war-saving
stamps and economizing on sugar and flour in order to finance
America's participation in the World War, were also rising
sanctimoniously from their seats in theaters whenever animal acts
were exhibited, and stalking out in silent protest against the
cruelty practiced on the animals during training. Animal lovers
in various European countries followed suit. By 1924 the Jack
London clubs throughout the world had a reported membership
of four hundred thousand, and in the United States at least animal acts had practically disappeared.

With the outbreak of the World War in Europe, the great majority of the Social Democratic parties joined their governments
to help prosecute the war. The largest and the most influential of
these was the German, and its collaboration with the general staff
won applause even from the Junkers. That the European socialist
leaders were disloyal to their convictions and obligations is evident
when one recalls the stand they had taken at Basle in 1912.

At this special International Socialist Congress a resolution was
passed which registered the high-water mark reached by the international socialist movement in its revolutionary development. It
was the result of years of theoretical formulation and political
agitation of socialist thought on the question of war. And as if it
had been intended to answer the later arguments of the leaders of
the international socialist movement when they sought frantically
to establish their prowar stand as rational and consistent with their
former antiwar utterances, the resolution stated that a war of "the
great nations of Europe . . . cannot be justified by even the
slightest pretext of being in the interest of the people!"

Each of the respective socialist groups who became collabora-
tors of their belligerent governments tried to justify their position
by accusing the enemy of being the greatest threat to civilization,

and each tried to show that their side was the progressive side. Reaching back into the past, and using Marx as their authority, they drew analogies with previous wars, and pictured the countries they were serving as champions of democracy and leaders of the oppressed. The particular side the Socialists were fighting on became the "holy" side. In much the same way it has become the fashion today among certain radicals to divide the great powers into "democratic" and "fascist" nations, and then to try to show that in a war between a "democratic" nation, such as England, and a "fascist" nation such as Germany, it is the duty of the masses to support the roaring lion who has suddenly been transformed into a peaceful jackal. This formula does not exclude, however, the overnight transformation of Germany into a "democratic" nation, if pacts become the criterion.

But, swimming against the torrential streams of social patriotism and war mania which infected the socialist ranks, were a handful of revolutionaries in the various socialist parties who continued to express and develop the revolutionary Marxist position on war that had been adopted at the Basle Congress. This political tendency received its clearest expression from the then obscure Russian revolutionist, Lenin, who at first had only his comrade and wife, Krupskaya, and his collaborator, Zinoviev, to listen to him. Infuriated with the high priests of socialism for what he charged were acts of betrayers, he thundered that the key to a correct attitude toward the war was to recognize it as an imperialist war.

With typical energy, indefatigable effort and sharpness of tone and ideas, he rescued Marx from deletions and distortions. To those who tried to rationalize their postwar position by comparing the World War with those of the end of the eighteenth and the whole of the nineteenth centuries, he replied by analyzing both categories of wars in great detail. The earlier wars, he pointed out, were "national" wars which had accompanied and aided in the formation of "national" states. They signified the tearing down of feudalism and represented the struggle of the new bourgeois society against the old order.

According to Lenin, the establishment of national states had been essential in the development of capitalism. The nation's struggle for self-determination, for independence, for popular representation, for cultural freedom, was, at that stage of the growth of capitalism, necessary for the expansion of the productive forces. Such were the wars beginning with the period of the French Revolution and continuing down to the Italian and Prussian wars. Even when led by a Bismarck, their role in securing the full growth of capitalism and of drawing all of the nations into capitalist society remained unchanged.

But this war, Lenin cried, was an imperialist war. Having reached its fullest development, capitalism was making the turn downward and, growing more and more antisocial as it decayed, it had to rely to an ever increasing extent upon violence and repression. The European countries had reached a relatively equal stage of capitalist development. In each, capitalism had yielded as much as it could give, and now, cramped in these national shells, it was compelled, in order to continue to exist, to redivide the world market by force, and fight for what free land remained on the globe.

It was just as impossible, he asserted, to pass from capitalism to socialism without breaking through national boundaries, as it had been to pass from feudalism to capitalism without establishing those national boundaries. And all revolutionary Socialists must regard the wars of the present epoch, except those of the oppressed people, such as the Chinese against Japanese imperialism or of the Hindus against British imperialism, as imperialist wars which must be transformed into civil wars.

Attacking the "fatherland" idea invoked by the patriotic Socialists when they called upon the workers to respond to the call to the colors, Lenin referred to the *Communist Manifesto*, in which Marx had explained that this was an historical category which corresponded to certain stages in capitalist development. Once it had been capable of some good; now it was entirely superfluous. "The proletariat cannot love what it does not possess," said Lenin. "The proletariat has no fatherland."

And the answer of the proletariat to imperialist wars must be the same as that given by the masses in Paris in 1871 after the Franco-Prussian War, and in Russia in 1905 after the Russo-Japanese War. To advocate this and to lead the struggle was the role of all Marxian Socialists, and, charged Lenin, the leaders of the Second International who were not doing this were betraying the masses.

Other voices besides Lenin's could be heard giving similar counsel: war did not obliterate class lines but continued the class cleavage under military conditions, aggravating them and adding to the misery of the masses; war was not to be regarded as a sin, which was a futile position; war, as the continuation of the class struggle increased a thousandfold, must be fought as relentlessly and as firmly as the capitalists were carrying on the slaughter. This element was only a handful, and their voices did not carry far, but they agreed that the main enemy was the capitalist class at home, and that to end war it would be necessary for the workers to overthrow it and win political power.

Outstanding among these clear-sighted ones were Rosa Luxemburg and Liebknecht in Germany, Trotsky in Paris, and Martov, Kier Hardie in England and Eugene Debs in America, and to a greater or lesser extent they conducted themselves in line with Lenin's position. They agreed that unless the World War was followed by successful revolutions there would be other wars, and that the concept of the World War as the "last war" was not only a stupid myth but a dangerous one. Civilization was at stake, they cried, and only by raising the banner of civil war would it be possible to achieve victory for socialism as against the threatening abyss of a reaction that would be worse than anything yet experienced under capitalism.

As early as 1915 the disintegrating effects of the European war on the American Socialist party were plainly to be seen. As the war had taken the European socialist leaders by surprise—and by this time many of these had moved Rightward from a patriotic position to an open imperialist stand—so were similar shiftings to be seen in America.

Not nearly so strong as its sister parties in Europe, nor as important, and enjoying no comparable electoral possibilities, the American party had a better opportunity to take an antiwar position. The late entry of the United States into the war, and the great number of foreign born in the Socialist party ranks, of which a substantial part, if not a majority, were Jews, Germans and Russians, likewise contributed to the party's stand against war. When America joined with the Allies, the pro-German and the anti-Czar sentiment of these elements played more than a minor role.

In the European parties the division of opinion regarding the war had found the radical intellectuals clawing at each other as representatives of their particular governments, and the interests of the working class forgotten. The same thing happened in America. With the precedent of supporting the war already established in Europe by the revered pontiffs of the Socialist International, the arguments in America were about the same in tone, if less pretentious theoretically. That the chance of gaining or losing by one's stand on the war was not an unappreciable factor was evidenced in a number of cases. Unlike the workers, intellectuals sometimes have more than one way out.

Thus many of the American socialist leaders manifested great horror at Germany's contempt for treaties and solemn covenants, while others shook their fists in defense of the Kaiser as against the oppressors of Jews, Hindus, Chinese and other downtrodden people. Some even echoed Victor Berger's cry, "You know I have always hated the Kaiser, but when I see the world taking arms against him I feel that I must seize a rifle and take my place in the ranks and fight for him!" In the emotional confusion produced by the line-up of forces abroad, international sentiments, abhorrence of capitalist wars, and belief in the solidarity of the working class of all countries wavered and fell back.

It was not long before pro-Ally and pro-German sentiment began to be voiced by various leaders in the party, but despite their propaganda the great majority of the rank-and-file members clung to an antiwar position. In the fall of 1915 the National Executive Committee of the party submitted a referendum to the membership on a proposal to expel from membership any socialist official who should vote money for naval or military purposes. When the results were announced in December the pro-Ally group was outraged. The size of the vote indicated that many had refrained from registering an opinion. Nevertheless over eleven thousand had endorsed the proposal as against the less than eight hundred who were opposed.

Immediately the pro-Ally members began to leave the party, denouncing as pro-German all who disagreed with their sentiments, but wholesale secession of this group did not take place until after the St Louis Convention in April 1917. On the eve of its collapse the American Socialist party, in a majority resolution on the war, reiterated its basic principles. "The only struggle which would justify the workers in taking up arms," read the resolution in part, "is the great struggle of the working class of the world to free itself from economic exploitation and political oppression. As against the false doctrine of national patriotism, we uphold the ideal of international working class solidarity. In support of capitalism we will not willingly give a single life or a single dollar; in support of the struggle of the workers for freedom we pledge our all."

But the party did not prove as militant in action as it had been in words. The noble Debs, supported by a tiny, organized Left-wing minority, groped for a revolutionary Marxist antiwar position. While the lone socialist congressman, Meyer London, debated the war bills which he would or would not support, Debs spent his time in prison with the same courage he had demonstrated on the outside in his fight against capitalist wars. In the end the struggle against war on the part of the American Socialist party was dissolved in the pacifist People's Council, which might be characterized as a Left "League Against War and Fascism" of its day, before the latter dropped "against war and fascism" from its title.

Jack London's position in the controversy was easily predictable after his open advocacy of American intervention in Mexico, as revealed in the 1914 articles in *Collier's*, with their indication of the final triumph in his mind of Benjamin Kidd's prejudices over the principles of Marx and Engels. In October 1915 he wrote to Hughes Massie in London: " . . . I would rather be a dead man under German supremacy than a live man under German supremacy. If the unthinkable should happen, and England be shoved into the last ditch, I shall, as a matter of course, go into that same last ditch. . . ."

For a long time his only contact with the socialist movement had been through reading the articles of the intellectual Socialists and the parlor pinks. *The Iron Heel* had roused their bitter condemnation of his brand of socialism, but that was nearly a decade back. Now Jack found himself in perfect harmony with their attitude toward the war. News of the results of the 1915 referendum vote astounded and enraged him. The exodus of the pro-Allies from the party had scarcely begun before he joined it.

In March 1916 he presented his resignation in a letter which epitomized the strength and the weakness, the contradictory ideas and the confused thinking which had characterized his career as a Socialist from the beginning.

"Dear Comrades," [he addressed them for the last time] "I am resigning from the Socialist Party, because of its lack of fire and fight, and its loss of emphasis on the class struggle.

"I was originally a member of the old revolutionary, up-on-its-hind-legs, fighting Socialist Labor Party. Since then, and to the present time, I have been a fighting member of the Socialist Party. My fighting record in the Cause is not, even at this late date, already entirely forgotten. Trained in the class struggle, as taught and practiced by the Socialist Labor Party, my own highest judgment concurring, I believed that the working class, by fighting, by never fusing, by never making terms with the enemy, could emancipate itself. Since the whole trend of Socialism in the United States during recent years has been one of peaceableness and compromise, I find that my mind refuses further sanction of my remaining a party member. Hence my resignation. . . .

"My final word is that liberty, freedom and independence are royal things that cannot be presented to, nor thrust upon, races or classes. If races and classes cannot rise up and by their strength of brain and brawn, wrest from the world liberty, freedom, and independence, they never in time can come to these royal possessions . . . and if such royal things are kindly presented to them by superior individuals, on silver platters, they will know not what to do with them, will fail to make use of them, and will be what they have always been in the past . . . inferior races and inferior classes.

"Yours for the Revolution,
"JACK LONDON."

This curious document was widely debated for some time, but Jack made its meaning impossible of misinterpretation, not only by the repeated statement, "I resigned from the Socialist Party because they would not fight," but by his numerous public utterances on the subject of the war:

"I am with the Allies life and death, Germany today is a paranoiac. She has the mad person's idea of her own ego, and the delusion of persecution. She thinks all nations are against her. She possesses also the religious mania. She thinks that God is on her side. These are the very commonest forms of insanity, and never before in history has a whole nation gone insane."

"I believe the World War so far as concerns, not individuals but the entire race of man, is good.

"The World War has compelled man to return from the cheap and easy lies of illusion to the brass tacks and iron facts of reality.

"The World War has redeemed from the fat and gross materialism of generations of peace, and caught mankind up in a blaze of the spirit.

"The World War has been a pentecostal cleansing of the spirit of man."

And finally: "I believe intensely in the pro-Ally side of the war. I believe that the foundation of civilization rests on the pledge, the agreement, and the contract. I believe that the present war is being fought out to determine whether or not men in the future may continue in a civilized way to depend upon the word, the pledge, the agreement and the contract."

Surely no prophet of those days was at once so emphatic and so wrong! When his choice of the presidential candidates was solicited shortly before the election in November 1916 he stated: "I have no choice for President. Wilson has not enamored me with past performances. Hughes has not enamored me with the promise of future performances. There is nothing to hope from either of them, except that they will brilliantly guide the United States down her fat, helpless, lonely, unhonorable, profit-seeking way to the shambles to which her shameless unpreparedness is leading her. The day is all too near when any first power or any two one-horse powers can stick her up and bleed her bankrupt. We stand for nothing except fat. We are become the fat man of the nations, whom no nation loves. My choice for President is Theodore Roosevelt, whom nobody in this fat land will vote for because he exalts honor and manhood over the cowardice and peace-lovingness of the worshipers of fat."

The following April the United States entered the war on the side of the Allies. By that time Jack London had been dead nearly five months. Undoubtedly he would have rejoiced when war was finally declared. And one can feel regretfully certain that he would have disputed one of the paragraphs in the majority resolution on the war adopted at the St Louis Convention: "When Belgium was invaded the government enjoined upon the people of this country the duty of remaining neutral, thus clearly demonstrating that the 'dictates of humanity,' and the fate of small nations and of democratic institutions, were matters that did not concern it. But when our enormous war traffic is seriously threatened our government calls upon us to rally to the 'defense of democracy and civilization.' "

With increasing momentum Jack was moving toward death. It is impossible to deny that he was unaware of this, but he made no effort to turn aside. Although his health had never fully recovered from the shattering effects of the tropics, he was not seriously ill until the summer of 1914 in Mexico. A year earlier he had rapidly recovered from an operation for appendicitis, but his physician, Dr William S. Porter, warned him then that continued indifference toward his bodily well-being would have serious consequences, for his long indulgence in alcohol was at last beginning to take its toll. He good-humoredly agreed with Porter, listened to his advice as to the regime he should follow, and did nothing about it.

By 1915 many symptoms of uremia were being manifested, nervous tension, irritability, insistence upon his judgment and opinions being always accepted as correct and final, argumentativeness, as well as physical discomfort in the way of cramping of muscles and rheumatism, which on occasions became so painful as to require the use of a prescription containing monobromated camphor, hyoscyamine and opium. Other physicians now told him that he must follow a careful diet and take more exercise. He did neither.

He had always been fond of swimming, and until 1916 he indulged in this sport with fair regularity, in Hawaii or in the lake on the ranch. Detesting walking in any of its forms, tennis and golf failed to interest him, but he frequently rode horseback when he was on the ranch, until the last months of his life. But it was not enough. The lithe, well-knit, graceful body had vanished beneath an unhealthy corpulence. He was only of medium height, and now he was weighing nearly two hundred pounds. As for diet, he boasted loudly of his "cast-iron stomach" and ate as he pleased. Unfortunately, raw fish and raw meat and twelve-minute duck did not constitute a helpful diet for one suffering from uremia.

His irritability increased, and friends of long standing, even so sympathetic a friend as George Sterling, were soon unable to endure the spectacle of Jack, once so warmly hospitable and kindly, as domineering, ungracious and rude. Aware as he must always have been of the inevitable end of his course of least resistance, he was unable to see, or perhaps unwilling to admit, that it was the unpleasant effect of his malady that was driving his friends away. He began to feel sorry for himself, to lament the perfidy of friends and relatives and, at the same time, to become even more furiously angry and abusive with anyone who did not agree with him. "It's a pretty picayune world," he would say bitterly.

Over and over again his condition was brought to his attention, and each time more desperate measures were prescribed to save him, and each time, save for a period of six weeks, when his death was less than six weeks away, he refused to take the advice urged upon him. When his digestive apparatus failed the last year he adjusted himself to it rather than to try to correct it, eating little until the crises had passed, then returning to the foods whose consumption, he knew, spelled his doom. And for the first time in his life he made the acquaintance of insomnia.

In the summer of 1916 he underwent the agony that results from a calculus. This was followed in September by an attack of rheumatism so severe and so painful that he kept to his bed for more than a week. The warning was unmistakable, and for the moment he drew back. Although he gave up the last pretense of taking exercise, from then until the duck season opened in the middle of October, he rigidly followed the diet that would delay his next bout with the pain which had become almost unendurable.

"I would rather be ashes than dust!" Jack often announced during those last years, and when asked to explain what he meant he would gladly enlarge on the theme: "I would rather that my spark should burn out in a brilliant blaze than it should be stifled by dry-rot. I would rather be a superb meteor, every atom of me in magnificent glow, than a sleepy and permanent planet. The proper function of man is to live, not to exist. I shall not waste my days in trying to prolong them. I shall use my time."

On other occasions, caught up by enthusiasm for a new plan or project, he would exclaim. "I want to live a hundred years!" To his daughters, one evening near the end, he said suddenly, "You are almost young ladies now. Life is not easy for young people. So you must think of me as a rock on which you can build, on which you can depend, always. Wherever you are, whatever happens, you can count on me."

One afternoon he talked with a magazine editor who was visiting him in Glen Ellen, listlessly outlining his writing plans and his ambitions for the ranch. "If you keep up that clip," the editor remarked, "John Barleycorn won't hurt you much." Jack was silent for a moment, then, "There's always the Noseless One close by," he answered cryptically.

Never before was Jack, always an essentially lonely person, so alone as during the last part of his life. The friends of his youth were far behind him, and he had made no new ones of like caliber. There was no one to guess and answer his need, rekindle the eagerness for life which once had burned so brightly, help him to discover new and worthier goals to replace those so long since attained that they had ceased to interest him, and he could not accomplish this alone.

Tormented by his illness, he withdrew more and more into himself, turning at last in distaste from the anodynes—people and alcohol—which he had employed to dull his deep unhappiness. Part of a sentence, heavily underscored by him in Dr Beatrice Hinkle's introduction to Jung's *Psychology of the Unconscious*, which he was reading at this time, gives one an insight into what may have passed through his mind during sleepless nights and on other occasions when he sat alone and in silence: ". . . the character and intelligence which makes it possible for him to submit himself to a facing of his naked soul, and to the pain and suffering which this often entails."

He was striving desperately to discover where he had gone wrong, why success had meant failure in that it had not brought him happiness and content, what, if anything, he could find to persuade himself to stop short of the brink to which he had now come so close. He was not yet forty-one years old, but it was too late. He was too tired and too ill to save himself, to think back over his life honestly and dispassionately, or to recognize past errors.

When he reviewed his youthful struggles he knew only pride of attainment and tearful resentment that it had all turned out so badly for him; when he looked at the long row of books he had written he recalled sadly that the better critics had derided most of them, and forgot how many he had written carelessly, pandering to cheap tastes solely to make money; when he rode over the ranch, noting how his dream of aiding the human race by breeding better livestock was taking visible form, he did not think of the strength and talent which had been despoiled for its sake, nor remember that once he had clearly seen and voiced the need to join the greater and more immediate struggle which would free mankind from the darkness and oppression of a class society.

He caught at straws. He would leave California forever and make his home in Hawaii. He would stay on the ranch, continue his operations, build a general store, a school for the workers' children, a post office. Soon the place would be self-subsisting, like a feudal manor of older, simpler days. His workers would live there and die there, their children would be born there. And with the world shut out, he would grow to peaceful old age, a patriarch among his people.

In another mood he would decide to travel. He would learn the "how" of oriental agriculture on long, leisurely journeys through the Asiatic countries. Or, what was more immediately important, he would mend his broken financial fences in Europe. The war was playing havoc with his royalties from the belligerent countries. A trip to the neutral Scandinavian countries might result in advantageous publishing arrangements.

It was this that he finally fixed upon, postponing decision on other plans to a later date. If death had not intervened it is likely that he would have been not far from Russia when the February revolution occurred in 1917. One regretfully rejects the temptation to speculate on what effect this might have had upon him, whether his vision might have cleared, and his old loyalties revived as he witnessed the stirring events of 1917, or whether, rejoicing at the February revolution, he might have refused, as did so many, to accept that of October.

Passively, almost as if he were a spectator who stood neither to win nor lose, he entered the last weeks of the contest between the life that was in him and death. The outcome he knew, but it would be no victory for the Noseless One. In a symposium on euthanasia published in the *Medical Review of Reviews*, he had written, "Man possesses but one freedom, namely, the anticipating of the day of his death. . . . I believe in the individual's right to cease to live." And when that day would come he neither knew nor cared.

He was ready to leave for New York in October, but a lawsuit over water rights brought against him by his neighbors dragged on into November. Since the middle of October when he had abandoned his careful diet to consume daily two large underdone wild ducks, his physical condition had been growing steadily worse, but pain, his enemy, held back. On November fourteenth the case came to a gratifying conclusion for him. A week later, unexpectedly, and at night, the enemy struck.

The lawsuit had taken all his energy. Ill and exhausted, he had lingered on at the ranch to rest before starting on his journey. Now it was Tuesday; he would leave at the end of the week. He retired early with the boxes of reading matter it was his habit to read in bed. There were a few personal letters to write; then he hoped he would be able to read himself to sleep in a short time. One of those letters was to Joan, and when he wrote it and placed it for the Japanese boy to pick up in the morning and place in the mail sack, he had not changed his plans.

"Next Sunday," [he wrote] "will you and Bess have lunch with me at Saddle Rock, and, if weather is good, go for a sail with me on Lake Merritt?
"If weather is not good, we can go to a matinee of some sort.
"Let me know at once.
"I leave ranch next Friday.
"I leave Calif. Wednesday following.
                                                        "DADDY."

What occurred that night, when the pain came, how long he wrestled with it before he sought relief, or whether he intended that relief to be temporary or permanent—these matters can only be surmised. No one saw him from early evening until he was found, unconscious, the next morning. Some of the workmen told George Sterling that they thought they had heard him walkind around outside during the night, yet they could not be sure.

But two small vials which once had contained "morphine sulphate with atropine sulphate" gave mute evidence of what was probably his last act that night. He had taken a lethal dose, but who could say whether it had been with suicidal intention, or merely an overdose miscalculated in the midst of his agony? One of the attending physicians, Dr Thomson, believes the former to be true, Dr Porter, the latter. Sufficient doubt existed among the four physicians who attended him to permit the cause of his death to be stated as "uremia following renal colic."

All day they worked to save him, and as long as he was completely unconscious, they met with fair promise of success. Physical reaction to their treatment was soon manifested. But as soon as consciousness began to stir dimly in him it seemed, to some who watched, as if he summoned the last of his strength of will to resist all efforts to reawaken in him the urge to live.

At no time did he show the slightest evidence of co-operation. In a desperate attempt to rouse him, workmen shouted to him over and over again that the recently completed dam, which had been the cause of the water rights suit, had burst, but to no avail. Those at his bedside thought that once he smiled, and each saw something different in the expression that twisted his mouth for a moment and was gone—recognition, farewell, triumph, perhaps, that he was making his escape despite them.

Hope waned as the November afternoon drew to an end. At a little before eight in the evening he died. "I leave ranch next Friday," he had written to Joan. On that day his body was taken to Oakland for cremation, and two days later his ashes were buried beneath a red-brown boulder on a hill slope not far from the ruins of the Wolf House.

News of Jack London's death was published throughout the world, and for the last time his name blazed on the front pages of American newspapers. For weeks articles about him appeared in various periodicals. Five months later the United States entered the World War. Jack London's opinions could no longer be solicited, but his name was still good copy. Thus many newspapermen made and published the discovery that among the young soldiers and sailors in the British and American forces Jack London was the favorite author.

Meantime, especially on the Pacific coast, his name began to acquire notoriety of an entirely different sort when a small group of Left-wing Socialists, rebelling against the conservatism of the Socialist party and calling themselves by an outlandish name as yet unfamiliar to most Americans—Bolsheviks—christened their meeting place at 1256 Market Street in San Francisco the Jack London Memorial Hall. Throughout the war they did their best to publicize the answer given in October 1917 by the Russian masses to the imperialist war in Europe. And throughout the war the hall was the scene of frequent "red raids." One indignant prosecuting attorney described the Jack London Institute as "the nerve center of radicalism on the Pacific coast."

The war years moved swiftly into the postwar years, and little by little Jack London's fame among middle-class readers in America diminished. The generation which had been brought up on him remained loyal, but the younger people were growing up in a world that did not resemble Jack London's. They read *The Call of the Wild* in school and usually forgot who had written it, although on November 23, 1916, news of his death had been announced in public schools throughout the country; or, emerging into their 'teens, they dismissed *The Sea Wolf* and *Burning Daylight* as juvenilia and turned to what they called "modern" writers.

Jack London's death coincided with the end of a brief era which had bridged the nineteenth and twentieth centuries, and in large measure he had been the voice of that era. Five years later the overwhelming majority of his books and stories were dated. To dwellers in an urban civilization, the frontier has little meaning, and sailing ships are never to be seen except in motion pictures; scientific agriculture is generally accepted, although self-subsisting farms are still a sore point with many disillusioned farmers; and when daily the newspapers announce new scientific marvels and one lives on intimate terms with inventions scarcely dreamed of in Jack London's youth, his nineteenth-century reverence for science seems to many a little absurd.

And yet Jack London had been one of the three young pioneers who at the turn of the century had blazed the literary trails into modern American literature. Although a few predecessors had shown the way, Stephen Crane, Frank Norris and Jack London had vigorously insisted upon introducing themes, characters and styles of writing previously unheard of in American literature, but already large and vital in American life. All three died young, but Jack London lived longer in the twentieth century. All were timely, catching unerringly the drumbeats of the new day, which was to develop swiftly into a day of struggle, but Jack London was a Socialist, and with conscious social perspective he had inquired into history for pattern or lack of pattern. Before he fell victim to the competitive spirit and commercialism of the times he had described, more boldly and with more fundamental insight than Frank Norris, the real protagonists in that struggle and its causes, and had foreseen its end.

Many of Jack London's popular stories, which had received so much acclaim and brought him such rich returns, are practically forgotten now, and their author has become a legendary figure of the vanished prewar period. Of the fifty-odd volumes he left, the dozen or so which remain in favor have a devoted following. But, aside from *The Call of the Wild*, his reputation rests most securely today on the handful of books he wrote on social themes which contain conclusions as valid today as they were thirty years ago, and of greater importance since the changes which are taking place in the world are visible now to even the most obstinate. These books have a significant international following.

It is not surprising, therefore, that as his fame diminished in America during the prosperous postwar years, it should have increased in Europe where the end of the war had brought neither peace nor security. The dominant theme in all of his writings was struggle—the struggle of the individual to survive in a hostile environment or to be successful against great odds, and the bloody struggle of the workers against the capitalist class. Middle class and working class alike in Europe responded to this theme, the former finding temporary escape from unpleasant realities in tales of unfamiliar frontiers and success stories, the latter new courage from *The Iron Heel* and the socialist essays.

European critics wrote articles and essays on the best-known American writer of the twentieth century, and beautifully bound sets of his translated works stood on the shelves of many private libraries. But a dispatch from Rome to the New York *Times*, dated October 9, 1929, gives a wider and more significant view of his popularity: "The Italian Government has forbidden the sale in Italy of cheap popular editions of some of the works of Jack London, Tolstoy and other 'revolutionary' writers. The contention of the Italian Government is that these books, bought in bulk abroad by anti-Fascist interests, were being sold in Italy at absurdly cheap prices as part of a campaign for the overthrow of the Fascist regime. The decree affects only Jack London's 'revolutionary' works and not all of his books. Similarly it affects only the ultra-popular low-priced editions of his books and not the ordinary editions which find their way into libraries or the hands of the cultured classes." Similar action took place in Germany four years later when Hitler came into power.

Two days before Lenin died in January 1924 his wife, Krupskaya, read to him Jack London's "Love of Life." "It was a very fine story," she wrote in her *Memories of Lenin*. "In a wilderness of ice, where no human being had set foot, a sick man, dying of hunger, is making for the harbor of a big river. His strength is giving out, he cannot walk but keeps slipping, and beside him there slides a wolf—also dying of hunger. There is a fight between them: the man wins. Half-clad, half-demented, he reaches his goal. That tale greatly pleased Ilyich. Next day he asked me to read him more Jack London. But London's strong pieces of work

are mixed with extraordinarily weak ones. The next tale happened
to be quite another type—saturated with bourgeois morals. . . .
Ilyich smiled and dismissed it with a wave of the hand. That was
the last time I read to him. . . ."

Because of this mixture of strength and weakness, literary
critics in general, whether European, British or American, have
had a difficult time estimating Jack London's literary worth and
assigning him his place in the ranks of American authors. C. Hartley Grattan posed their dilemma very well when he described
Jack London's works as balanced precariously on the fence that
separates literature from popular stuff. "The least critical bias will
push it one way of the other," he wrote. "Yet there is great writing in London, and he will remain to puzzle the historians of
American literature for years to come."

Most historians of literature have, unfortunately, one trait in
common: failing to appreciate the intricate process of the interactions between an author and his environment—and the extent
of the author's awareness or lack of awareness of this—they seek
to judge his literary merit with a purely arbitrary yardstick
whose markings are the results of predilections and prejudices
formed, in turn, by the interactions between themselves and their
own environments, and often lacking in historical perspective.
Any attempt to judge Jack London's work without appreciating
the environmental forces which shaped his life and his work is
certain to produce unsatisfactory results for, probably more than
any other writer of his generation, he was profoundly and consciously affected by his times. It has proved as impossible to fit
him into the usual formal literary categories as it has been to
ignore him. By some he has been called the last of the frontier
writers, by others the first of the "proletarian" school; he evades
both classifications.

The great mass of criticism of Jack London's work consists
either of complimentary generalities, grudging admissions of an
artistic talent which failed, nevertheless, to realize itself, or terse
summaries of the good and the bad, which are essentially con-
fessions that Jack London still remains a puzzle to literary historians. A very few critics have tried to analyze and explain his
contradictions; none have wholly succeeded.

Thomas Moult wrote in the London *Bookman* of Jack London's "compelling artistic impulse": "It is a mistake to underestimate this artistic impulse of Jack London. When we have sifted

the husks that came of the hasty writing to which he became regrettably prone in his later period, there remains the grain of a positive literary quality. . . . Behind it all thrilled a personality which was the embodiment of high noons in a decade of literary twilights. . . ."; and Stephen Graham in the *English Review:* ". . . He was a voice out of the depths, out of the unknown life of the people. . . . He wanted his brothers and sisters to have more life. . . . He was a man with a bugle, an awakener, an annunciator, a wall-shatterer, a herald of dawn, a man standing on a slag-heap, sword in hand and pointing with his sword."

Typical of American professorial comments are the following:

From *The Cambridge History of Literature,* by Frederick Lewis Pattee: "Force he undoubtedly had and freshness of material, but, lacking poise and moral background and beauty of style, he must be passed as an ephemeral sensation as regards all but a handful of his stories."

From *The American Spirit in Literature,* by Bliss Perry: "His books are very uneven, but he wrote many a hard-muscled, clean-cut page."

From *A History of American Letters,* by Walter Fuller Taylor: "At his best . . . he is of value for his immense, driving energy, for his intelligent concern over social evils, for his ability to convey the thrill of clean-limbed action, and for his poetic response to the beauties of primitive landscape."

Waldo Frank believes that Jack London, being a self-conscious, socially conscious man, could have found himself only in a sort of immediate expression that clinched the problems of his day. "Like his country," Frank sums up, "London was corporeally mature, innerly a child. He mastered the outward circumstance of life, and then played with toys. The world was his by physical and intellectual possession: but he preferred to live in a nursery and blamed his excess drinking on the fact that no Nurse was there to keep the liquor from his lips."

The attempt to understand the puzzle by psychological means is probably best exemplified by Ludwig Lewisohn: ". . . Perhaps his ablest full-length novel is *The Sea Wolf,* which can be used briefly to explain both Jack London and his popularity. The average, ignorant reader, shorn by civilization of the full expression of his primitive instincts, both sexual and aggressive, identifies himself with sadistic joy with the pseudo-Nietzschean captain and through this identification satisfies his lust for ferocity and raw force. Nor is that all. The satanic captain's cruelty is directed against a boy belonging to the most sheltered section of capitalistic society. Thus there enters the further motive of satisfied envy, parading sincerely as a desire for leveling justice, and there enters, in the case of many readers, a satisfaction (through the relations of the cruel captain and the delicate lad) of unconscious homo-erotic wishes. No wonder that Jack London is popular and continues so."

Lewis Mumford has written that in his first phase, Jack London was a "picturesque pirate, gaily embracing the slattern, adventure"; in his second, "a sleek and consciously virtuous missionary, for whom adventure is a 'white man's' diet that must be swallowed at any hazard. In short, London turned out to be a red-blooded prig. . . . One cannot help thinking that the strenuous activities of London's successful years were a continual running away from himself. What was the self from which he ran away? It was the self of an artist, a minor artist, to be sure, but a real one, an artist who might rank with Gissing or Reade."

One day, no doubt, some literary historian will produce an adequate evaluation of Jack London's writings and assign to him the probably minor position in American literature to which the small amount of genuinely artistic work he left entitles him. But before that day, and after it, he will remain significant to all who respond to his challenge: "Be alive! Be positive! Take sides!" and to all who are striving to realize the social ideals whose enunciation was Jack London's most sincere and greatest achievement.

INDEX

Abysmal Brute, The, 327
American Federation of Labor, the, 61, 78, 118, 119, 124, 160, 161, 162, 290, 292, 305
American Labor Union, the, 124, 290–91
American Railway Union, the, 121, 137
American Railway Union Strike, the, 63, 84, 85, 121
Applegarth, Mabel, 97, 99, 100–01, 102, 103, 104, 133, 167–68, 169, 172, 174, 175, 176, 178, 194, 195, 216, 222
Applegarth, Mrs, 99–100, 103, 140
Applegarth, Ted, 97–8, 104, 127, 137, 166, 167, 169, 174, 176, 194, 216, 349
Atherton, Frank, 31–5, 38, 44, 67, 98, 231
Australian Labour Party, the, 334

Bamford, Frederick Irons, 95–6, 215–16, 219, 240, 257, 289, 295, 296, 299
Before Adam, 326
Bellamy, Edward, 113–14
Berger, Victor, 120–21, 162, 163, 206, 367
Berkman, Alexander, 318–19
Bernstein, Eduard, 121, 162
Bland, Henry Mead, 29, 360
Bolshevik Party, the, 115–16
Bolsheviks, the, 119, 277
Booth, Tom, 180, 181, 257
Brotherhood of the Co-operative Commonwealth, the, 121
Browne, Carl, 21, 60–2, 86

Bryan Democracy, 109–13
Burning Daylight, 147, 329, 331, 377

Cahan, Abe, 117, 119, 121, 122, 162, 206
Call of the Wild, The, 12, 147, 252–55, 261, 287, 288, 326, 376, 377
Chaney, William Henry, 2, 5, 6–12, 13, 134–35
Children of the Frost, The, 228, 231, 251
Chinese Question, the, 19, 20, 21, 122
Coxey, Jacob, 60, 61, 63, 71, 81, 85, 86
Coxey's Army, 60–2, 71–2
Cruise of the Dazzler, The, 241
Cruise of the Snark, The, 320

Daughter of the Snows, A, 226, 229
Debs, Eugene, 63, 118, 121, 137, 161, 162, 291, 292, 302, 310, 366, 368
De Leon, Daniel, 2, 113–20, 122, 123, 162, 183, 206, 264, 291, 292, 293, 294
Dell, Floyd, 358
Depression of 1873, the, 18

Ferris, Dick, 343
Fish Patrol, the, 40, 44, 46–7
Fiske, Minnie Maddern, 102
France, Anatole, 312–13
Frank, Waldo, 332, 380

Game, The, 287
George, Henry, 21, 22, 113, 114–15

Ghent, W. J., 122, 242, 244, 249, 255, 298, 303–04
God of His Fathers, The, 228, 254
Goldman, Emma, 318
Gompers, Samuel, 61, 119, 161, 163, 290
Graham, Stephen, 380
Grattan, C. Hartley, 379
Greenback Labor Party, the, 17, 21
Greenback Movement, the, 17–18, 60

Hagerty, Father, 162
Hardie, Kier, 366
Harriman, Job, 122, 161, 162, 187, 206
Harris, Frank, 326
Haywood, Moyer, Pettibone Trial, the, 317–18
Haywood, William, 162, 291, 292, 310
Heinhold, Johnny, 44, 69, 103
Hill, Joe, 294
Hillquit, Morris, 117, 119, 121, 122, 162, 163, 187, 206
Hubbard, Elbert, 358

Intercollegiate Socialist Society, the, 298–300
International Workingmen's Association, 2
Iron Heel, The, 83, 171, 181, 242, 247, 249, 255, 264, 280, 303, 304–15, 317, 320, 326, 328, 329, 350, 353, 368, 378
Irvine, Alexander, 301
I.W.W., the, 124, 183, 290–94, 305, 311, 342–43

Kamenev, Leon, 276
Kautsky, Karl, 119
Kearney, Dennis, 6, 19–22, 60, 61, 122–23
Kelly, Charles T., 62, 63, 75, 76, 80, 81, 86
Kelly's Army, 62–3, 71–81, 329, 349
Kempton-Wace Letters, The, 223–24, 229, 241
Kidd, Benjamin, 210–12, 285, 350, 368
Kilmer, Joyce, 358
Kittredge, Charmian, 258, 260–61, 263, 286, 295, 296, 297, 324
Knights of Labor, the, 119, 160
Krupskaya, N. K., 364, 378–79

League for Industrial Democracy, the, 300
Lenin, Nikolai, 116, 117, 119, 120, 184, 272, 276, 278–79, 315, 364–65, 378–79
Lewis, Austin, 180, 181, 184–85, 187–91, 206, 208, 215, 257
Lewis, Sinclair, 327
Lewisohn, Ludwig, 380
Liebknecht, Karl, 366
Little, Frank, 294
Little Lady of the Big House, The, 357
London, John, 13–14, 23–5, 27–9, 31–2, 36, 44, 65, 72, 92, 104, 129, 134, 135, 140, 150
Luxemburg, Rosa, 315, 366
Lytle, H. R., 73–4, 77, 80, 349

Maddern, Bess, 97, 98, 99, 100–03, 104, 130, 133, 166, 167, 176, 195–96, 216, 224, 225, 227, 229, 233, 234, 240, 241, 251–52, 255–56, 261, 262–63, 286, 295–96, 297, 324, 357
Magòn, Enrique Flores, 342
Magòn, Ricardo Flores, 341, 342, 343, 346, 347
Magonistas, the, 188, 342, 343
Marcy, Mary, 310
Martin Eden, 171, 172, 178, 179, 186, 253, 329–31, 356, 357, 359
Martov, Julius, 366
Marx's First International, 2, 20
Mensheviks, the, 277
Mexican Revolution, the, 338–43, 345–48
Michael, Brother of Jerry, 363
Miliukov, Professor Paul, 277
Moult, Thomas, 379
Muckrakers, the, 241–47
Mumford, Lewis, 381

National Labor Party, the, 60
National Labor Union, the, 160
Nationalist Movement, the, 114

On the Makaloa Mat, 362
Oyster Industry, the, 39–40
Oyster Pirates, the, 39–46

Panic of 1893, the, 54–9
Pattee, Frederick Lewis, 255, 380
People of the Abyss, The, 240, 241, 242, 247–50, 252
People's Party, the, 60, 121
Perry, Bliss, 380
Pick Handle Brigade, the, 19
Plekhanov, G., 277
Populism, 63, 109–13, 120–21
Populist Party, the, 17, 60
Prentiss, Jennie, 13, 23, 40, 43, 227, 256

Revolution, 209
Rivera, Librado, 342, 343
Road, The, 84, 183, 329
Roulston, Jane, 180–81, 257
Russian Revolution of 1905, the, 264–80, 338
Russo-Japanese War, the, 266–71

Scarlet Plague, The, 308
Schwind, Max, 126, 129
Sea Wolf, The, 253, 261, 281, 286, 287, 288, 356–57, 377, 380
Second International, the, 118–19, 300, 334
Shepard, Eliza, 23, 128, 360
Silver Movement, the, 17–18
Sinclair, Upton, 120, 298, 299, 302–03, 329
Single Tax Movement, the, 114–15
Slocum, Mrs Amanda, 5, 11, 12
Social Democratic Party of America, the, 121–22, 161, 228
Socialist Labor Party, the, 21, 86, 113, 115–20, 122–23, 125–26, 128–29, 133, 135, 161–62, 179, 180, 181, 183, 188, 189, 191, 204, 207, 208, 215, 228, 292, 293, 368–69
Socialist Party, the, 118, 122, 150, 161–62, 163, 164, 264, 290, 293, 300, 304, 305, 311, 335, 368–69
Socialist Trade and Labor Alliance, the, 118, 292
Son of the Wolf, The, 220, 224, 226, 228
Spargo, John, 307, 310
Speed, George, 76–7, 80–1, 86, 181–83, 186, 187, 188, 294

Stalin, Joseph, 276
Star Rover, The, 282, 362
Stedman, Seymour, 121
Sterling, George, 258–60, 262, 327, 329, 371, 375
St John, Vincent, 291, 293
Strawn-Hamilton, Frank, 88, 126, 127, 181, 183–87, 188, 209, 219, 257, 330
Strunsky, Anna, 180–81, 216–19, 223, 229, 232–33, 235, 240, 251, 252, 257

Tales of the Fish Patrol, 44
Taylor, Walter Fuller, 380
Third International, the, 120
Trautmann, 162, 293
Tridon, André, 358–59
Trotsky, Leon, 266, 276, 278–79, 313–15, 366
Turner, John Kenneth, 352–53
Turtles of Tasman, The, 357

Untermann, Ernest, 209, 305, 335

Vale, Charles, 358
Valley of the Moon, The, 358
Villa, Pancho, 346–48, 351

War of the Classes, The, 209, 289
Weaver, General, 60, 79
Wellman, Flora, 2–6, 10–14, 22–5, 27–32, 36–8, 44–5, 65–7, 72, 82, 92, 104, 129, 134, 135, 140, 150, 166, 168, 181, 185, 193, 195, 204, 212, 224, 225, 227, 296
Western Federation of Miners, the, 124, 291, 292
Western Labor Union, the, 124
Whitaker, Herman, 126, 127, 130, 136, 180, 181, 225, 227, 257
White Fang, 327
Workingmen's Party of California, the, 20, 21
Workingmen's Party of the United States, the, 20, 21, 113
World War, the, 363–68

Zapata, Emiliano, 342, 343, 345, 346, 347–48, 351
Zinoviev, G. E., 276, 364